Multimedia in the Classroom

Palmer W. Agnew
Binghamton University
(State University of New York)
and New School
(New York City)

Anne S. Kellerman
Binghamton University
(State University of New York)
and New School
(New York City)

Jeanine M. Meyer
Pace University
(New York City, Westchester)

ALLYN AND BACON
Boston London Toronto Sydney Tokyo Singapore

Vice President, Education: Nancy Forsyth
Editorial Assistant: Kate Wagstaffe
Production Administrator: Catherine Martin
Cover Design: Suzanne Harbison
Manufacturing Buyer: Aloka Rathnam
Marketing Manager: Kathy Hunter
Reviewers: Joseph L. Minkin, A. James Albert, Monroe Judkovics
Electronic Production: MediaLink Associates, Inc.
Text Design and Composition: Palmer Agnew, Anne Kellerman, Jeanine Meyer

Limits of Liability and Disclaimer or Warranty

We have used our best efforts in preparing this book for you. We will not be liable in any event for incidental or consequential damages in connection with, or arising out of, the furnishing, performance, or use of this book. The information provided is distributed as is. Readers attempting to adapt these techniques to their own environments do so at their own risk. For safe operations of apparatus you should read and heed cautions that appear in your user's manuals.

Trademarks, Copyrights, or Registered Materials

This book mentions computer hardware, software, magazines, and companies that have either trademarked, registered, or copyrighted their names. Most computer hardware and software and many of these companies' names have trademarks or registered trademarks. Because this book mentions numerous product names and company names, the individual trademarks have not been listed. All terms that we know are trademarks or other service marks are capitalized. We cannot attest to the complete accuracy of this information.

Some of the artwork in this book is from Lotus SmartPics for Windows © 1991 Lotus Development Corporation. Lotus and SmartPics are registered trademarks of Lotus Development Corporation. Lotus SmartPics are the basis for Figures 2-2, 2-3, 7-7, 7-8, 8-1, and 15-10. In addition, we use the following Lotus SmartPics as chapter logos for Chapters 7 through 12.

Dedication

Parents and inspirations of the authors:

Anne Wright Agnew and Ralph Palmer Agnew

and

Esther Weber Minkin and Joseph Louis Minkin

Table of Contents

PREFACE   IX

PART A - FUNDAMENTALS   1

PART B - PROGRESSION OF PROJECTS 175

We thank the following people whose digitized images appear in the book

Names	Figures
Aviva Sari Meyer	8-3
Joseph and Esther Minkin	11-4
Ralph and Anne Agnew	11-5
Deborah and Bernardo Torres	12-7
Coralia Rebecca Torres	13-2
Daniel Zvi Meyer	15-6
David Louis Kellerman	A-2

Preface

Multimedia in the Classroom explores concepts, processes, and tools that will help you use multimedia to achieve specific educational outcomes in kindergarten through twelfth grade education. The book is for preservice teachers, in-service teachers, educational technologists, administrators, supervisory or support people, and even parents. Although we intend the book primarily as a textbook for upper class students or graduate students, we include sufficient detail to make the book suitable for use as a self-study book for life-long learners, as a handbook for practicing professionals, and as a guide for decision-makers and planners.

Many educators feel intuitively that multimedia can increase motivation and can promote authentic learning in classrooms. In *Multimedia in the Classroom*, we move beyond intuitive feelings to methods that work reliably. The book progresses systematically from basic ideas, which will help you get started using multimedia, to more advanced considerations, which will help you use multimedia even more effectively with more students. The basic ideas tell how you can get started and make significant progress with a relatively small investment, by knowing what available hardware and software your students can use immediately, what to buy first, and what you can defer. The advanced considerations address the common problem of not knowing what to do with a technological innovation after you exhaust a list of suggested activities.

In *Multimedia in the Classroom*, we discuss many ways in which you can use multimedia, including having your students work with existing multimedia titles. We strongly emphasize using multimedia by helping your students research a topic, gain knowledge, organize what they learn, and represent their knowledge as they actively create a multimedia project. We describe how you can challenge students at all skill levels. Creating multimedia projects can help your students to achieve goals that include:

- developing higher-order thinking skills and interpersonal skills.
- learning content by engaging multidisciplinary subjects.
- developing technical competence and media literacy that will empower the students throughout their lives.

We fully explore how to set such suitable pedagogical objectives and then how to select or invent projects that will help your students meet your objectives.

We discuss six concrete multimedia projects in detail. These projects form a progression that introduces text, graphics, images, audio, and video. You can create these projects yourself, in order to learn successively more demanding aspects of multimedia. In your K-12 environment, you can help your students create these and other projects, in order to meet specific academic goals. We stress using projects in real-life situations that make the activities meaningful for students.

We discuss how you can adapt each project to suit a wide variety of computers and circumstances, including scaling the project up or down to fit the facilities or students. You can benefit from studying *Multimedia in the Classroom* without using any computer equipment and without actually creating any projects. However, hands-on activities make learning significantly more interesting, effective, and meaningful, both in higher education and in K-12 schools.

We assume that you have some experience using either Apple Macintosh or Intel-based personal computers. We made our discussions sufficiently general that you can apply what you learn to whatever hardware and software you and your students have available.

Multimedia in the Classroom has the following organization and highlights.

Part A - Fundamentals

- Chapter 1, Using Multimedia for Effective Education, defines multimedia, discusses the role of multimedia and multimedia projects in K-12 classrooms, and presents a structure for the goals that you can help your students achieve by creating multimedia projects.

- Chapter 2, Multimedia Hardware, discusses general computers and particular additional equipment that your students will need for particular media. Our historical approach prepares you to use effectively several generations of existing computers, as well as generations of more advanced computers that your school may obtain.

- Chapter 3, Multimedia Software Tools, discusses authoring systems and additional tools that students use when creating projects.

- Chapter 4, Roles of Existing Multimedia Content, discusses many sorts of available multimedia content and titles. It suggests ways that you and your students can use such multimedia consistently with copyrights and ethics.

- Chapter 5, Organizing Information, illustrates several important hypermedia organizations that students can employ to master subject material. Trees, tables, and networks are examples of useful organizations.

- Chapter 6, Process and Projects, discusses a general four-step process for coaching and facilitating students who are creating multimedia projects. It also introduces the progression of six projects.

Part B - Progression of Projects

- In Chapter 7, Current Events, the class creates a news archive with which students can interact and discover meaningful relationships among events.

- In Chapter 8, Critics' Circle, each group of students creates an interactive presentation in which critics voice opposing points of view on a topic.

- In Chapter 9, Trailers, each group of students selects and narrates clips from a movie, to produce a trailer or preview that would motivate a selected audience to see the movie.

- In Chapter 10, Science Quiz, the class constructs a quiz in which students challenge one another to match graphs of position and velocity against videos of corresponding motions.

- In Chapter 11, Memoirs, the class interviews adults on the subject of how historical events have affected the adults' lives, assembles audio and video records of the interviews, and summarizes the results.

- In Chapter 12, Research Magazine, the class uses a computer network such as Internet to work with other classes and prepare a multimedia magazine.

Part C - Advanced Topics

- Chapter 13, Advanced Techniques, suggests ways to improve the creation process and the projects by using each individual medium more effectively.

- Chapter 14, Production Company, discusses organizing a class into an amateur production company to create more ambitious projects.

- Chapter 15, Variations, provides ideas for many ways to modify any project including the six in Part B to fit your environment and objectives.

- Chapter 16, The Idea Book, describes using multimedia to record your ideas for the classroom, primarily as a productivity aid.

- Chapter 17, Assessment, covers the all-important issue of reflecting on projects in order to achieve continual improvement and assign grades. Assessment makes multimedia part of the main stream of education, rather than just an occasional entertaining diversion.

- Chapter 18, Moving Forward and Providing for the Future, ends the book with a look into the future. We suggest ways in which you can help students learn by expanding your school's use of student projects over several years.

We consistently connect theory to practice. Each chapter contains four sections that provide necessary background, underlying theory, practical applications of the theory to your classroom, and a summary.

We want to thank our families, friends, teachers, students, and many colleagues around the world who have helped us refine, develop, and test our ideas. We want to thank our editors and our reviewers.We especially want to thank Mike Braun, Dr. Cathy Collins Block, Dr. Sandra Flank, Dr. Florence Mann, Dr. Miriam Masullo, Lucie Fjeldstad, and Dr. Frank Moore. These people were especially instrumental in making it possible for us to refine our ideas and to test them out in very rigorous environments. They also gave us excellent inspiration and counsel along the way.

Palmer Wright Agnew   *Anne Sheila Kellerman*   *Jeanine Minkin Meyer*

Part A - Fundamentals

- What is multimedia?

- What kind of equipment do I need?

- How do I get this picture into that computer?

- I learned on an IBM PC in college and now I have an Apple. Do I have to start from scratch?

- How can I learn to use multimedia software?

- How can hypertext help my students learn academic content?

- Won't all of this be outdated in a few months?

Chapter 1

Using Multimedia for Effective Education

In this chapter, we explore:

- the nature of multimedia and of student-created multimedia projects.

- why multimedia projects are important to you, as an educator.

- the five useful media, namely text, graphics, images, audio, and video.

- six representative multimedia projects, which we discuss in more detail in Chapters 7 through 12.

This chapter's Background section defines multimedia and introduces important aspects of multimedia projects. The Theory section discusses why you can expect students to learn more effectively and efficiently by creating multimedia projects. The Practice section suggests concrete activities for becoming familiar with multimedia. Finally, the Summary section recapitulates the chapter's key terminology, which we use throughout the book.

Background

This book discusses how you can help students create multimedia projects in order to learn academic subjects and other life-long skills. Creating a multimedia project gives students the exciting opportunity to use several media to express information. The five useful media are text, graphics, images, audio, and video. Creating multimedia gives students the important additional opportunity to organize these media and to see and hear media instantly on request. Organizing and interacting with media helps students achieve goals that you select. The primary purpose of creating a multimedia project is to help the creators achieve academic goals. Although other people may use the completed project for education or enjoyment, that is a bonus.

Students create a multimedia project by creating media and then creating links among the media. In case you are unfamiliar with links, here is an overview. Students create a link to take them instantly from one part of the project to another selected part, both while they are creating the project and after they have finished the project. Links make creating a multimedia project more educational than piling notebooks, sketch pads, photographs, audiocassette tapes, and videocassette tapes into a shoe box. Links are possible because students store all media on a computer's disks (also called hard drives or fixed disks). A disk, unlike a shoe box, gives students instant access to any desired contents. With instant access, students can organize the information that they create for the project by linking together related pieces of information.

Here is how links work. Students create a computer screen that expresses a particular piece of information. They may decide to create some or all of text, graphics, images, and video to show on the screen. They may also create audio that will play while the screen is visible. Students create other such screens that employ appropriate media to express other pieces of information. Then the students organize the information by creating one or more buttons on each screen. A typical button links the screen on which the button appears to another screen. Selecting such a button, usually by pointing at the button and clicking the mouse, tells the computer to erase the current screen and show the other screen. Another sort of button links to additional information that the students decided to make available for the current screen. Selecting such a button may tell the computer to start playing audio or video or may tell the computer to pop up new text or some other medium on the current screen.

Links thus make a multimedia project interactive. A computer usually requires less than a second to get requested information from its disk to its screen or to its speakers. As a result, whether creating a project or using the completed project, students interact with the project's information about as rapidly as if they were interacting with a highly responsive person. In fact, to qualify as true multimedia, a project must not only use several of the five media but must also use links to be interactive.

This Background section continues by discussing the role of multimedia projects in education, the role of computers in multimedia projects, and the evolution of multimedia.

Multimedia Projects

This book describes how present and future educators in elementary schools, middle schools, and high schools can help their students learn by helping the students create multimedia projects. Six chapters near the center of the book describe six sample projects that employ increasingly sophisticated media and techniques. We recommend that you, the reader of this book, play the role of a K-12 student and create some or all of these sample projects. By doing so, you will learn how to create multimedia projects. More importantly, you will learn how to integrate multimedia projects into your classroom curricula in order to help your students achieve selected academic goals. Some achievable goals include improving higher-order thinking skills, enhancing interpersonal group skills, learning content by constructing and organizing representations of knowledge, and incidentally learning how to make effective use of media and computers.

Of course, student-created multimedia projects, which are the primary subject of this book, are not the only way to use media such as audio and video in classrooms. Students can achieve some academic goals by listening to and watching audiovisual curriculum materials in which a professional has carefully selected information, has represented that information by appropriate media, and has organized those media into a particular sequence for delivery on a television set. Teachers can obtain such audiovisual curriculum materials on television networks, videotapes, CD-ROM discs, and laser discs. Teachers can also create the materials themselves. Chapter 4 discusses ways in which teachers and students can make effective use of existing materials.

This book is dedicated to the proposition that students can learn more effectively and efficiently by becoming actively involved in selecting, representing, and organizing knowledge than by passively observing existing materials. We recommend that students themselves decide what pieces of information to include in a project; represent the pieces of information by preparing appropriate text, graphics, images, audio, and video; and link the pieces of information together into a meaningful organization. This chapter's Theory section presents our rationale for recommending this active pedagogical approach. Articles in the References section present other aspects of the theory behind the recommendation. *101 Success Stories of Information Technology in Higher Education* and *Assessments of Multimedia Technology in Education: Bibliography* make particularly strong cases.

Creating a multimedia project can give students the opportunity to learn significantly more than they could learn by creating a report that contains text and images or even by creating a videotape that contains all five media. In either a report or a videotape, creators must organize information linearly, that is, in a single sequence from beginning to end. In a multimedia project, however, creators use links to arrange information in more meaningful organizations.

For example, in the Current Events project, which is the subject of Chapter 7, students write paragraphs that describe events, collect pictures of the events, and draw timelines and maps to show how the events relate to one another. That is, students employ text, images, and graphics. The students also create two sets of links. The students create one set of links that join the events in chronological order, just as the students might paste successive clips in a scrapbook, to emphasize the events' sequential nature. The students create buttons along a timeline, one button for each month. They then create a link from each button to the first event that occurred in the corresponding month, and so on. The students also create a second set of links that join events that occurred in the same city, to show how occurring in a common location can relate events to one another. The students place these buttons on a map. They link the button for a particular city to an event that occurred in that city. The resulting project is thus a nonlinear organization, as opposed to one that merely lists the events in one particular linear order.

Students could decide to create several other sets of links, as well. One set could join all the events that relate to a given subject, whenever and wherever those events occurred. More advanced students could draw a concept map of events' social, political, and economic contexts and create links from each concept to corresponding events. Other sets of links could connect causes to effects, generalizations to specific examples, general discussions to more detailed explanations, one example of a concept to other examples of the same concept, or an opinion to contrary opinions.

Other projects add the remaining two media. Chapter 8 describes Critics' Circle, in which students use audio to record their spoken opinions. Chapter 10 describes Science Quiz, in which students use video of themselves walking at various speeds in front of a distance-measuring probe.

All media involve links. Links that join different pieces of text are called hypertext links. The combination of links and text is called hypertext. Similarly, links that join other media, in addition to text, are called hypermedia links. The combination is called hypermedia.

Real events or other pieces of information relate to one another in many important ways. Creating a linear report or videotape would force students to select one relation, such as time, and organize material according to that single relation. Creating a multimedia project on a computer allows students to use links to visualize more relations and organize information in more meaningful ways. Creating the Current Events project gives students unique opportunities to think about and understand the ways in which events actually relate to one another, such as time and location. Creating other multimedia projects helps students to learn and practice a wide variety of methods for using hypermedia links to organize information. Chapter 5 summarizes and analyzes several useful organizations. Organizing information is often crucial for mastering content.

The Role of Computers in Multimedia

Creating media and links by using a computer allows students to create multimedia projects in which links come alive. By using a multimedia authoring system program, students can create media, buttons, and links quickly and easily. Students or other users can then select any button and quickly see and hear the corresponding part of the project. In the Current Events example, students create buttons such as the buttons that correspond to months along a timeline. A user can select any desired buttons to see events in any desired order. A user can select the button for a particular month and quickly see the corresponding event's description and picture. After reading about the event and looking at the picture, the user can select one of several buttons to determine what part of the project the user will see next. Selecting one button tells the computer to show the screen for the next sequential event. Selecting another button tells the computer to show the timeline screen again. Selecting yet another button tells the computer to show the map on which students placed buttons corresponding to cities in which events occurred.

Students who create a project thus organize a body of information by deciding what information they want to place on each screen, deciding what buttons they will create on each screen, and deciding what links to create for the buttons. Each link tells the computer to do a particular action when a user selects the corresponding button. Some buttons link to new screens; other buttons link to new information that appears on the current screen. For example, selecting a special type of button called a hot word can tell the computer to pop up a small window on the existing screen that gives the word's dictionary definition, or shows a picture of what the word denotes, or pronounces the word.

Whereas some applications use computers merely to facilitate activities that students could perform in other ways, multimedia uses computers to help students perform activities that were previously impossible. A word processor makes a typewriter that can change and reformat pages, and a spreadsheet makes a sheet of squared paper that recalculates numbers, so either just makes a function that was already possible go faster and easier. However, the links that are a key part of multimedia projects allow users to interact with information in completely new ways.

Typical Multimedia

A multimedia project, in general, consists of a collection of computer screens containing some or all of text, graphics, images, audio, and video, along with buttons that the user can select with a mouse. A typical screen, Figure 1-1, follows.

Selecting some buttons will take the user to different screens, as shown in Figure 1-2. Selecting other buttons may change the current screen, such as by popping up a definition or by starting a short audio or video clip.

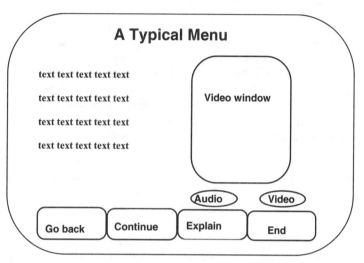

Figure 1-1: An example of a multimedia screen with four
button controls across the bottom

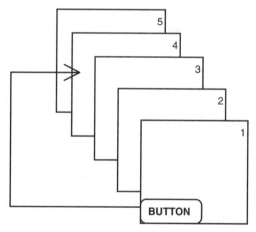

Figure 1-2: Selecting BUTTON on screen
1 to show screen 4

The student creator, using a software authoring system, specifies in the vocabulary of
the authoring system that when a user selects the button he or she is taken to screen 4.
For a typical authoring system, this might mean a student creator writing something like
the statement "LINK 4" or selecting a LINK statement out of a menu and then
writing "4."

Evolution of Multimedia

Whereas media are almost as old as the human race, multimedia is barely a generation old. Throughout human history, dedicated and talented specialists have recorded their ideas and feelings in media that ranged from Lascaux cave art and cuneiform writing, to printed prayer wheels and bibles, to the latest books and television programs. The essence of multimedia, however, is interactivity rather than just multiple media. For the first time in our generation, enormous improvements in the function, speed, and price of personal computers and other digital electronics are making it possible for students to learn by creating and interacting with multiple media.

Multimedia has evolved from simple beginnings a generation ago. At first, multimedia meant a class seeing and hearing a presentation that required an audio tape player and either a film-strip projector or a slide projector. A beep on the tape, interspersed with narration and background music, told the operator when to advance to the next picture. Later, multimedia came to mean a larger audience seeing and hearing a more complex presentation that required several audio tape players, slide projectors, and movie projectors, all under the control of a special purpose computer. Today, multimedia has come to mean an individual or a small group using a personal computer to interact with information that is represented in several media, by repeatedly selecting what to see and hear next. Students can create such multimedia projects by using a computer and a multimedia authoring system. Students can even use the most recent versions of some word processing programs, such as Microsoft Word for Windows, to create documents that include all five media and, to some extent, hypermedia links.

The evolution of multimedia has thus made it possible for students to become actively involved in creating their own projects, rather than remaining passive observers of presentations that professionals created. As the following Theory section discusses, increasing students' active involvement holds real promise for improving education's effectiveness. Although others may find completed projects highly attractive and educational, it is the creators themselves who derive the greatest benefit from multimedia projects.

The next section discusses the educational advantages of creating multimedia projects and takes a closer look at the five media. It then provides a thumbnail sketch of each of the six projects that this book suggests, emphasizing how each project encourages students to express information in appropriate media.

Theory

Creating multimedia projects has a unique combination of properties that conform to important modern methods for improving educational outcomes.

- It enables students to represent information using several different media.

- It enables students to employ hypermedia links to organize information in many meaningful ways.
- It involves a sufficiently wide variety of activities and skills that all members of a group can work on effectively over an extended interval.

We take as given that students learn better

- if they construct knowledge actively rather than merely receiving information passively;
- if they learn to work in groups as well as to work alone; and
- if they learn by using multiple sensory modalities in addition to using the most important modality, namely writing and reading text.

Student-created multimedia projects are beneficial, in addition, because they often involve substantial work, open-ended assignments, theme-based activities, and knowledge and experiences that the students draw from a wide variety of sources. The projects tend to be interdisciplinary activities that involve teamwork and profound application of concepts. Creating such a project is a way for students to achieve high self-esteem, to increase their ability to function as self-directed learners, to learn to think effectively, and to practice problem-solving and decision-making (Rowe, 1994). It requires and rewards good planning and execution skills. It requires new skills and is an opportunity to build life-long skills.

Some comments from K-12 students in relation to their experiences with creating multimedia projects are "I passed biology finally in summer school and had a great time!", "Imagine me doing extra credit!", and "Can I sign up for this class twice?"

Media

Representing information by first understanding what is required by the assignment and then collecting and developing appropriate information using appropriate media effectively is central to creating multimedia projects. Although there is no universally recognized terminology, we shall refer to the media by the following five names.

Text	-	letters, numbers, and special symbols
Graphics	-	lines, circles, boxes, and other shapes filled with shades of gray or colors
Images	-	still pictures with shades of gray or colors
Audio	-	voices, natural sounds, music, and sound effects
Video	-	pictures that appear one after another sufficiently rapidly to give the illusion of continuous motion, without jerking or flickering

We use these five names consistently throughout the book. The name of each medium covers a variety of similar forms. For example, students can create images by using computer software called a paint program. Students can also capture images by scanning photographs or magazine pages. For another example, video includes animation, which students create by producing many images and playing the images sufficiently rapidly to give the illusion of motion. Computer programs are available to help students create animations by filling in images between a starting image and an ending image. Students can also capture video from the output of a video camera or video cassette recorder. We describe hardware and software that are involved in these methods in Chapters 2 and 3, respectively. Chapters 13 and 14 provide more concrete suggestions.

Using consistent names for the five media helps keep multimedia comprehensible. However, you will need to recognize several synonyms for these names. The medium that we call graphics is also known as vector graphics. The medium that we call images is also known as pictures, bit maps, or raster graphics. What we call video, of course, is also known as movies, moving pictures, or motion pictures. As if these synonyms were not sufficiently confusing, the part of a computer that connects to the computer's display screen may be called the display adapter, the graphics adapter, or the video adapter, all referring to the same hardware.

Expressing information by using several of the five media allows a student to learn material more completely, and remember it longer, than the student could do by expressing the information in only one medium. Perceiving a subject with both the sensory modalities of hearing and seeing, and seeing not only text but also graphics or images, involves more of the brain than does using any single medium. Moreover, using more media increases the likelihood that a student will connect a classroom experience to an experience in the wider outside world. Both factors aid absorption and retention.

Different students learn best by using different media. By recognizing and understanding different learning styles such as spatial, verbal, kinesthetic, or musical, a teacher can bring different students' capabilities to full potential. However, teachers must avoid using such differences as a form of labeling of students. If a teacher discovers that a particular student learns significantly more easily by using images rather than text, the teacher may decide whether to emphasize that student's use of text or images.

The medium on which education relies most heavily, text, is not always the most effective medium for all sorts of information or for all students. An often quoted remark is that we gather information approximately 10 percent from words themselves, 40 percent from the way words are said, and 50 percent from what we see. In general, we remember more of what we experience than of what we see, more of what we see than of what we hear, and more of what we hear than of what we read.

With only a few hours of well-coached practice, students can use multimedia computers to create media for use in their projects. Learning to create professional quality images, audio, and video takes years of instruction, decades of practice, and probably a strong native predilection. Nevertheless, students need not leave these media to professionals. After all, it takes years to learn to create professional quality text, yet writing is one of students' most important activities. The thrill and surprise of hearing and seeing themselves and their school mates on a computer helps students ignore the fact that their first images, audio, and video may be below the standards of television advertisements and programs that they hear and see every day.

Another reason why students learn better by using more media is that different types of information are most comprehensible when expressed or illustrated in different media. The next section gives several examples of making good use of particular media.

Media and Projects

The six projects that Chapters 7 through 12 describe play several roles in this book. The projects illustrate how students can achieve a wide variety of different goals by creating different projects. The projects introduce media that require successively more demanding techniques, hardware, and software. Finally, the projects illustrate using different media to represent different sorts of information. We next present a brief introduction to the projects, the media and equipment that they employ, and the information that the media represent.

Three media, text, graphics, and images, can suffice for creating the Current Events project, which Chapter 7 describes. Many schools have sufficient hardware to allow students to create Current Events without adding any special multimedia hardware to the students' computers. A school might need to add multimedia software such as an authoring system to the students' computers. The school may also need to obtain one method for digitizing images, such as a computer with a scanner, which many classes can share. We discuss in Chapters 2 and 3 the special multimedia hardware and software that these and other projects require.

In Current Events, as in other projects, text is generally the most effective medium for expressing concrete facts such as who was involved and what transpired. Learning to use hypertext links to organize textual information is one of the most challenging and valuable aspects of multimedia projects. Graphics, such as a timeline and a map, are ideal for diagrams that show how events relate to one another, such as temporally and spatially. Images add impact to many events. In selected cases, such as a photograph of a person, an image can be worth more than a thousand words of description.

The Critics' Circle project, which Chapter 8 describes, adds the medium of audio. Students speak into a microphone and the computer converts their voices to digital form. The computer stores digital audio as a sequence of ones and zeros on the computer's disk, just as the computer stores spreadsheet files or word processing files. To create this project, each group of students needs access to a computer that can record and play back audio, as well as show images, graphics, and text. Many schools have already obtained such multimedia computers either by buying fully equipped computers or by upgrading existing computers to handle audio.

Critics' Circle uses digital audio to record and play back the actual voices of several student critics who give their opinions on a selected subject. Audio conveys the critics' emotions better than text could do. The project also uses images of the critics' faces. Images emphasize that these are real people whose opinions deserve consideration, even if others disagree with the opinions. Because the critics are the students who create the project, the students can enjoy hearing and seeing themselves on the computer. In addition to using the other media, the students prepare a dispassionate and reasoned summary of the critics' opinions in the medium that is most appropriate for that purpose, namely text. Hypermedia links allow students or other users of the project to see and hear critics' opinions in any order and to read and think about the summary whenever they desire.

The remaining four projects introduce successively more demanding uses of the video medium. Chapter 9 describes the Trailers project, in which students use computers not only to record and play digital audio but also to control a laser disc (or CD-ROM player). Except for the laser disc player and the television monitor that the player drives, Trailers requires no more hardware than does Critics' Circle. This project uses analog video. The video signal goes directly from the laser disc player to a television monitor, without being converted to digital form and without passing through the computer.

To create a trailer, students use a movie that is available on a laser disc (or a CD-ROM). The students select a hypothetical audience, such as travel buffs, to whom they want to make the movie appeal. The students select short portions of the video, called clips, by clicking a mouse button when they see the desired start point and clicking again when they see the desired stop point. They need not use the selected clips in the order in which the clips appear on the disc. The computer can execute the student-specified link from the end of one clip to the beginning of another clip in less than a second. Next, students prepare and record the narration, called a voice-over, that will play while each clip is playing. Students do their best to use the media of video and audio to persuade the selected audience to go see the movie. Students will find that professionally created video on laser disc, together with their own voices, can be very persuasive indeed. This can help the students to realize the extent to which they themselves can be persuaded by the same media in the hands of others.

In Science Quiz, as described in Chapter 10, students need access to a video camera and a computer that can digitize video and then record the digital video on the computer's disk. Many students can share one such camera and one such computer. This is true because each student need spend only a few minutes digitizing video. Students can spend most of their time creating Science Quiz using a computer that has no special multimedia hardware at all. This is true because any reasonably fast computer can play digital video. As we discuss in Chapter 2, using a faster computer or adding special digital video playback hardware does produce higher quality video.

Science Quiz uses digital video to show details of motion. One student operates a video camera while another follows instructions such as to walk forward slowly, then stand still, and finally back up rapidly. Equipped with digital video files that contain clips showing several different motions, and other files representing subjects' positions as graphical representations of position plotted against time, the creators assemble a quiz. The quiz challenges users to link back and forth among the clips and graphs until the users can recognize which clip goes with each graph. Although the video must be clear, this project can succeed even if the video is not particularly aesthetic. Moreover, the video need not be synchronized with audio.

Chapter 11 describes the Memoirs project in which students interview adults and create and organize digital video, digital audio, and associated textual information. While creating this project, many students can share one computer that is capable of recording digital video along with synchronized digital audio. Students spend most of their time creating the project using less expensive computers that can record and play digital audio and can play digital video.

In Memoirs, the adults reminisce about public events that have most strongly affected their lives, such as wars or the civil rights movement. Students use video cameras to record the interviews. Audio and video media capture intonations and body language, which are vital for understanding how the adults felt about the events. Students then convert the audio and video to digital form and store the digital media on a computer's disk. A computer can link to any requested part of any interview essentially instantaneously. Students also collect facts about the events discussed from sources such as CD-ROM encyclopedias. Students prepare and include in the project data on the frequency with which interviewees discussed events. Students or others who use the completed project can invoke parts of all of the project that relate to a particular event, in order to compare ways in which one event affected different adults. Alternatively, users can ask to see, read, and hear one adult's interview or hear parts of different interviews in any selected order.

Juxtaposing and comparing different adults' reactions to events can be remarkably illuminating. This most important aspect of Memoirs would be impossible to achieve without digital video and digital audio. Storing interviews on VCR tapes would allow users to see interviews in only one sequence, rather than seeing parts of interviews quickly in any desired sequence. Storing the interviews on a laser disc or CD-ROM would provide rapid access to desired parts. However, laser discs are economically viable only for storing thousands of copies of the same audio and video. Writing CD-ROMs is costly but will soon become more affordable.

The sixth project, Research Magazine, which Chapter 12 describes, introduces transmission of media from one computer to another computer that may be located across the country or around the world. The media flow over wide area networks (WANs) that connect students' computers. For this project, students need access to a computer that has communications software and a connection to some networking delivery service such as Internet, Prodigy, America Online, or one of the special academic networks that many states provide. The students use the delivery service to send multimedia that they create.

Research Magazine introduces no new media. However, using a network require students to use media differently. Multimedia projects that contain images, digital audio, and especially digital video tend to be large, whereas WANs tend to be slow and expensive and therefore not a good way to deliver large multimedia projects. In the next century, fiber optic cables may make long-distance communication of high quality digital video commonly available and affordable. In the 1990s, however, networks remain a scarce resource. This project challenges students to select media that will make optimal use of the available network.

Selecting Projects

This book's six projects are not the only ones that you could use to learn about successive media or to introduce the media to your present or future students. It is not even necessary to learn about all five media or to learn the media in the order that we selected. Because the main purpose of student-created multimedia projects is not to learn multimedia techniques, but to master subject matter and achieve other academic goals, readers should think about how variations of this book's projects, and completely different projects, will better help their students to reach the desired outcomes as part of the school's curriculum and operational environment. Chapter 15 describes several variations of each of the six projects. Teachers and students can devise far more variations, as well as entirely new projects, to achieve desired goals. The key to defining or selecting a project is knowing the desired goals.

Goals

Learning to use media effectively to represent different sorts of information and learning to appreciate how others use media are genuinely useful in their own right. However, the main reason for teachers to challenge students to create multimedia projects is to help students learn subject material and to develop their ability to analyze and draw conclusions about the subject material.

Creating multimedia projects can help students achieve a wide variety of goals. Each of Chapters 7 through 12 discusses the specific goals that the corresponding project can help students meet. Those chapters illustrate not only how to determine what goals a given project can help students meet but also how to select and create projects for the purpose of achieving given goals.

Table 1-1 introduces four categories into which we divide such goals. Table 1-1 also presents some examples of goals taken from this book's projects.

Table 1-1: Sample goals for a multimedia project

Higher-order thinking skills
- Applying complex concepts
- Understanding and designing navigation and tours through information
- Presenting information appropriately and effectively
- Selecting media and using them effectively
- Using media to exhibit sense of the times, drama, and impact

Group and interpersonal skills
- Working successfully in a group
- Improving interpersonal relationships
- Planning useful interim milestones
- Working with members of other groups in the class
- Interacting with people outside the classroom

Content or discipline
- Learning significant facts and concepts in a given discipline
- Learning interdisciplinary topics
- Understanding and using vocabulary, symbolism, and interpretation

Technical skills
- Learning project planning and execution skills
- Using an authoring system's tools
- Using hypermedia links to organize information
- Using, text, graphics, images, audio, and video more effectively

Motivation

The fact that a multimedia project is likely to be viewed and appreciated by a larger audience than a single teacher motivates students to create an excellent project. The authors' experience with student-created multimedia projects, from kindergarten through graduate school and from New York, New York, to Sitka, Alaska, is that creators and others vigorously admire completed projects. This strongly positive reaction motivates students to improve their use of media as they create multimedia projects for academic purposes.

Creating multimedia projects motivates students to work in a quality manner harder and longer than in many other activities because the resulting projects are more attractive and more interesting than most. Simply spending more time and effort on a task can result in additional learning. We have heard teachers say that the major advantage of creating multimedia projects is that it brings into the classroom students who would otherwise be absent, so any other advantages are gravy.

Pitfalls and Bypasses

Students may find graphics, images, audio, and video enormously appealing in comparison to text, perhaps because the other media are more novel than text. Nevertheless, reading and writing text will remain critically important. Teachers should require students to create text as part of any multimedia project. Introducing hypertext is one way to give text its own novelty.

Multimedia projects enhance rather than replace linear writing assignments. Computer monitor screens are not optimized for reading large volumes of linear text. If a student simply types in text on one screen after another, a teacher must decide whether to suggest that the student change to a word processor for entry and a printer for output or suggest that the student change to a more effective use of multimedia.

It is important to maintain high standards for research, including encouraging students to use original sources and multiple sources. Teachers must dissuade students from thinking that, because a CD-ROM can contain as much text as several hundred books, one CD-ROM must therefore represent all the possible points of view about a subject. Similarly, because of their tendency to feel that seeing is believing, students may feel that finding one picture or video clip that represents one side of an issue must resolve all controversies. One advantage of having students create images and video clips themselves is that students can learn to recognize that these media need not tell the whole story.

Metalevel, metacognitive, and higher-order thinking skills can be taught. However, like teaching specific subject content material, teaching these requires explicit attention and frequent reconfirmation.

One of the challenges of multimedia is preventing students from majoring in the minors, that is, from specializing in one medium to the exclusion of achieving the desired goals. However, there is a corresponding opportunity. Teachers can use students' willingness to spend far more than the required time on task to enhance the students' general learning. Chapter 17 addresses the issue of assessment by focusing on the more general topic of continual reflection, that is, on assessment by the students, the class, teachers, and the larger community. Effective assessment is essential in order to raise working on multimedia projects above the status of occasional entertaining diversions. Assessment requires continual conscious effort to avoid mistaking aesthetics or even glitz for deep understanding and mastery of subject matter. In almost all cases, an attractive result is not itself the desired end. However, the chance to produce a project that others will appreciate is a strong lever with which to motivate students to excel.

Relation to Writing as Process

Chapter 6 presents a process that teachers and students can use together to guide their respective parts of creating a multimedia project. This process includes relevant aspects of writing as process, in which students brainstorm, consider their audience, prewrite, write, edit while assisted by feedback from others, rewrite and refine, and publish. The process for multimedia creation emphasizes using milestones to assure that students perform all steps, despite a natural tendency to concentrate on one especially appealing or difficult step.

Organizing Information

Organizing information by using hypermedia links allows students to explore several different ways in which pieces of information relate to one another. Learning to organize information is vital, whether for one's self or for an audience. An important life-preparation skill is being able to articulate the right question to get the right information in a sea of information that may or may not be hypertext. One way to obtain this skill is to organize information for others to use. Hypermedia links among different pieces of information vividly represent the wide variety of relationships that can exist among the pieces. Students find these links most useful if they themselves discover the relations and create the links.

Learning Multimedia Skills

One reason for learning about multimedia is that creating hypermedia links and expressing information in multiple media are worth learning in their own right. Such skills will serve students well throughout their adult personal lives and working lives. Many of today's students will spend significant portions of their adult lives preparing informal or even formal multimedia for their customers, clients, friends, patients, employees, employers, and communities. Just as computers have made desktop publishing easy and economical, so that almost anyone can produce attractive newsletters and bulletins, multimedia will allow almost anyone to include audio and video in their day-to-day communications. Creating multimedia projects helps prepare students to use media effectively when communicating with individuals, with moderate size groups, and even with mass audiences. Like desktop publishing, multimedia yields the best results when a person who knows a subject expresses the subject, rather than having to call in a professional printer or a media expert. Also like desktop publishing, creating multimedia reaps huge dividends from even a few hours of learning what to do and what not to do.

Authentic Learning

Creating a multimedia project is an authentic reason for employing a group of students and produces an authentic result. The creation process often contains enough different tasks to justify assigning tasks to different students, either on the basis of interest and experience or simply in rotation. Different students can perform some of these tasks in parallel. However, in many cases, some students cannot begin particular tasks until after other students have completed their tasks. Thus, creating multimedia projects gives students the opportunity to learn and practice the skills involved in working jointly toward a common end. In this case, the end is a completed project that the creators themselves and other users will find highly attractive and may even find useful. To this extent, the result is significantly more authentic than, for example, a written report that no one other than the teacher who assigned it is likely to read. The result may have an authentic use such as informing, persuading, or teaching others.

Brands of Computers and Software

We made most of this book sufficiently generic that you can apply what you learn to any computers and software that you have available. We occasionally give specific examples that relate to Apple Macintosh computers or to Intel-based personal computers and to these computers' respective operating systems. In the category of Intel-based computers, we include IBM PCs, clone computers that use Intel 80x86 chips, Pentium chips, and clones of those chips. In the category of Apple Macintosh computers, we include Apple's various models such as the Quadra, Performa, and the PowerPC, along with any clones. Specific examples will help you understand what is going on. If you are familiar with a particular brand of hardware or operating system, examples that relate to another brand will help broaden your knowledge because computer hardware and software exhibit important underlying similarities across brands and across generations. You can adopt the next section's practical suggestions with the assurance that you will be able to apply what you discover to many environments.

Practice

Creating multimedia projects is an experience. A most practical way to approach this experience is to observe cases where multimedia already exists and consider other cases that might use multimedia in the near future.

Observe Existing Multimedia

Visit a local school or college that is already using multimedia. Ask what they are doing with the technology and what results they are achieving. Ask how the teachers and students learn to use multimedia, what equipment they have, and what additional equipment they would like to get. On a college campus, talk to people in the school of education, computer center, and library. If a local elementary school, high school, or college has no multimedia, visit or telephone to ask if they plan to use multimedia in the future.

Visit a college or municipal library. Access information on a CD-ROM encyclopedia. Search the on-line catalog for articles on both education and multimedia.

Visit a computer store or office supply store. Collect literature on some multimedia computers. Ask a salesperson to show you a multimedia computer running some multimedia, such as a game and an encyclopedia. Ask the sales person to describe their best features. Ask if the demonstrated multimedia computer is suitable for creating multimedia, as well as for playing commercial multimedia. For example, ask if it includes a microphone for recording audio, or merely includes speakers for playing back audio. Ask the sales person to recommend what else you would need to buy to create your own multimedia. If the sales person uses a lot of unfamiliar jargon, don't worry about it. You can visit the store again after you have read Chapters 2, 3, and 4.

Visit a video-game room in a mall and try some of the games. Observe who is present, particularly the age and sex of the users. See how different users participate. Are they actors in the games? Are they observers? Do they play other roles? Do users act first and then think or do they think first and then act? Observe what the games are like, how the games use different media to achieve desired results, and the games' degrees of interactivity and educational value.

Visit a mall, supermarket, airport, or public building that contains a kiosk, that is, a computer in a piece of furniture or a display case. A kiosk often contains a touch-sensitive screen. Note which media the kiosk shows on its screen and how it interacts with users. See what functions the kiosk allows users to perform, such as getting information or placing orders. Consider how the kiosk differs from video games, what the kiosk used to grab your attention, how many choices each new screen presents to the user, how the user interacts with the screen, and how the kiosk disguises the fact that it is really a computer.

If possible, log on to an information service such as Prodigy or Internet or have someone show you how to do this. Prodigy is a multimedia system that relies on hypertext, graphics, some images, and a small amount of audio. Locate forums that include discussions on multimedia or on use of educational technology.

Visit a photography store or department in a mall or supermarket and ask for a demonstration of Kodak Photo CD. Many multimedia computers can read the discs that these stores produce from your negatives or slides. This is a very convenient way to convert your students' slides or negatives into a form that a computer can store and process.

Visit a Radio Shack store and ask for a demonstration of the Miracle Piano Teaching System. Consider how this product uses both a multimedia computer screen and a keyboard to interact with a user.

Observe Potential Multimedia

Carefully observe information that is not multimedia. Consider how adding more media or adding interactivity could make this information more useful or more attractive.

Read a newspaper. Identify places where you might want to access more information about particular subjects. Identify places in the newspaper where you might want to see video or hear audio.

Think about some document, such as your resume or autobiography, that you might traditionally create in text by using a word processor. How and where would you like to add graphics, audio, or video to such a document? Would you reorganize the text if you could offer readers hypertext that would take readers to different sections rapidly? Would you use less text if the document were for display on a computer screen rather than for printing on paper?

Recall some specific media that made you happy, sad, or afraid.

Watch several television shows. Note that television programs are not multimedia. Although they use all of the media, the programs are not interactive. That is, a viewer has no control over what she or he sees, beyond turning the television set off or changing to another channel. Consider the extent to which a program in which people who are not video professionals have sent in interesting or funny video clips is more interactive than other programs, as is a radio talk show. Consider whether you might enjoy interacting with a program by selecting one of several different endings or by deciding when to replace live action by an instant replay of past actions. Invent other ways to convert television from passive viewing into active participation.

Watch a televised news program. Identify places where you might want to get more details on the current story rather than going on to the next story.

Consider what you like about the television programs' style and use of media and what makes them effective. Note that what an adult likes may or may not be what children of different ages like. Note some techniques to think about using in multimedia creations. Consider what the words compelling, engaging, and entertaining really mean. How do these words apply to some uses of different media and not to other uses? Find some examples where creators used different media to tell about the same thing in different ways. Find unique characteristics of each medium such as video to show things that change, still images to show more detail, and text to give sports scores. List some skills with different media that programs' creators require. Consider which of these skills are accessible to children.

Watch some television commercials. Note that a commercial tends to tell a story, as does a program, even though a commercial lasts less than one hundredth as long as a program. Consider whether a commercial must use media differently from a program in order to be effective and compelling. Consider what you remember about commercials. Do you think that children remember what you do?

Other Practice

Take a field trip to a bookstore, find the multimedia book section, and browse through the books. Consider whether the books' level of detail and explanation are suitable for accomplishing your objectives.

Go to a newsstand and pick up some of the latest magazines that talk about multimedia and CD-ROM multimedia titles. Consider subscribing to the ones you like best.

Investigate what multimedia support is available from a local school or college and how you can get some of it.

Request some multimedia software and hardware catalogs by calling mail-order houses' 800 numbers. The references include some such numbers. Other numbers appear in appropriate magazines.

Talk to friends and colleagues. Some may be using multimedia and even multimedia projects already.

Take an Equipment and Skills Inventory

Take a survey of the class (either in college or K-12 school) to determine how many students have the following equipment or have corresponding skills and experience.

- Video camera or camcorder
- Still camera
- Digital still camera
- Audio cassette recorder
- Video cassette recorder (VCR)
- Laser disc player
- Music system with compact disc-digital audio (CD-DA or just CD) player
- Computer with a word processor
- Multimedia computer with audio card and CD-ROM drive
- Artists' equipment, such as for oil or watercolor painting

- A box of photographs or slides (an associated experience is sorting them and deciding which to put into an album)

Share your experiences with each other.

Summary

We wrote this book to describe how you can help students create multimedia projects using multimedia computers. To make sure that terminology is clear, we summarize with definitions of some words that we use throughout the book.

We are the authors. You are the readers. Students are children in K-12, that is, kindergarten, elementary school, and high school.

Projects are interactive combinations of some or all of the media, namely text, graphics, images, audio, and video. Students create projects by researching information, planning how to represent the information in appropriate media, using hypermedia links to connect different pieces of information, and reflecting on the result. Although people other than the creators may use and enjoy a completed project, a project primarily benefits the students who create the project.

Multimedia computers store the media and links that students create. By selecting a button on a computer's screen, a user invokes a hypermedia link. That is, the computer jumps from one piece of information to another desired piece very rapidly.

> **We use some side-bars, formatted like this paragraph, to present information that you may or may not find interesting, useful, or entertaining. You may choose to read such side-bars at any time as you read the text, or even to skip them.**

References

101 Success Stories of Information Technology in Higher Education. New York: McGraw-Hill Primis, ISBN: 0-390-59763-5,1992. This document is the result of a challenge by Joe Wyatt, the chancellor of Vanderbilt University, at the 1989 EDUCOM conference to identify 100 exemplary cases that demonstrated the impact of information technologies on higher education.

Assessments of Multimedia Technology in Education: Bibliography. (Information Resource Guides Series #IRG-11), Institute for Academic Technology (IAT). Compiled by Carolyn Kotlas, MSLS, University of North Carolina. This document includes government, private industry, and K-12. Contact the publications editor, Jonathan Pishney, at Jon_Pishney@unc.edu or (919) 405-1942 for more information on how to get this valuable list.

Brooks, Jacqueline and Brooks, Martin. *In Search of Understanding-The Case for Constructivist Classrooms*. Alexandria, Virginia: ASCD, 1993.

Brown, Laurene Krasny. *Taking advantage of MEDIA-A manual for parents and teachers*. Boston: Routledge & Kegan Paul plc, ISBN 0-7102-0402-7, USA, 1986.

Dewey, John. *Experience and Education*. New York: Collier Books, 1938.

Goodlad, J. *A Place Called School*. New York: Mc-Graw-Hill, 1984.

Harel, I., and Papert, S. *Constructionism: Research reports and essays*. Norwood, NJ:Ablex, 1985-1990.

Hodges, Mathew E. and Sasnett, Russell M. *Multimedia Computing: Case Studies from MIT Project Athena*. ISBN: 0-201-52029-X, New York, NY: Addison-Wesley Pub. Co., 1993. This is a view of how educators are actually using multimedia technology.

Nix, Don and Spiro, Rand, editors. *Cognition, Education and Multimedia: Exploring Ideas in High Technology*. Hillsdale, New Jersey: Lawrence Erlbaum Associates, 1990.

Pea, R. D. "Learning Through Multimedia." *IEEE Computer Graph. Applications*. Volume 11, no. 4, p. 56-66, July, 1991.

Rowe, Superintendent Lawrence A. "New York's Goals" Johnson City, NY: *Binghamton Press*, 1/16/94.

Shneiderman, Ben. "Engagement and Construction: Educational Strategies for the Post-TV Era." *Journal of Computing in Higher Education*. Volume 4, no. 2, p. 106-116, Spring, 1993.

Sizer, Theodore R. *Horace's School: Resigning the American High School*. New York: Houghton Mifflin, 1992.

A sampling of catalogs: TigerSoftware has several catalogs for both Macintosh and PC equipment, software, and titles. A contact number is (800) 238-4437. EDUCORP is a source for educational titles and digitized media suitable for including in your own projects. A contact number is (800) 843-9497. Magazines on newsstands can provide more 800 numbers for other sources of catalogs.

Chapter 2

Multimedia Hardware

In this chapter we explore:

- types of computer hardware that you and your students may find in school.

- the suitability of different generations of computers for creating different multimedia projects.

- special multimedia hardware that your students may use not only to store each of the five media in a computer but also to get the media out of a computer.

- alternative types of special multimedia hardware that you might select.

- how to match projects' hardware requirements to computers that you have available or can obtain.

This chapter's Background section discusses four generations of computers that your students may use to create multimedia projects. The Theory section discusses the special hardware that allows your students to use each of the five media. Then the Practice section suggests approaches that you can use to determine what your students require and what is available. Throughout the chapter, we use words and concepts that will help you and your students communicate with other people.

Background

This chapter introduces what you need to understand about hardware, that is, about computers and about the additional hardware that multimedia requires. What you need to understand depends on how deeply you will be involved with hardware. At one extreme, you might expect an educational technologist to select late model multimedia computers, prepare these computers for your students' use, and solve whatever problems arise. In this case, you might proceed directly to the next chapter and learn about software. At the other extreme, you might expect to be the educational technologist on whom others rely. In that case, you might spend more time on this chapter than on any other chapter in the book. Then you would go on to learn far more about particular hardware products. In between these extremes, you are likely to be involved in making good use of several different kinds of existing computers and adding special multimedia hardware gradually as you can find the money and the time. In that case, you might want to read this chapter, remember some of the vocabulary and underlying concepts, and go on to practice the material in later chapters. You could then return to this chapter when you have questions about hardware.

Having questions will make this chapter's answers more interesting. For example, consider selecting parameters to produce digital audio that has acceptable quality with a minimum file size. Information that allows you to make this selection is really dull until your students are out of space on their disks or are dissatisfied with the quality of their audio. Then, the information suddenly becomes interesting. In the meantime, please be aware that affordable hardware limits what your students can do with multimedia. Hardware not only limits how good a medium sounds or looks but also limits how much of each medium your students can create and store. In many cases, you will want to understand enough about hardware to set up equipment so that your students will not run into hardware's limitations.

You and your students are likely to be faced with a large variety of significantly different computers that are more or less suitable for creating multimedia projects. This Background section continues with a discussion of how the present situation came about and how the varieties of available computers are likely to change in the near future. The subsequent Theory section describes the unique hardware that each medium requires. It includes a brief history of each medium and a table that will help you see how different hardware performs the same functions for different media. Finally, the Practice section suggests how you can match your school's available hardware against particular projects' required hardware and how you can overcome the inevitable mismatches.

You will find that asking a computer guru is by far the most useful way to get information about computer hardware. However, in order to ask meaningful questions and to understand the answers, you must speak some of the language and understand some basic concepts. In this chapter, we do not supply all the answers that you will need. However, we introduce words and concepts that will allow you to communicate with computer gurus. The most important computer networks are networks of people who help each other use computers.

Students who neither select hardware nor set up hardware can create multimedia projects without knowing this chapter's contents. However, as students progress toward adult roles, they too will want to understand details that underlie computers' capabilities, in order to make their own intelligent decisions. You can decide to what extent and at what time you want to guide your students toward finding their own answers to questions about hardware. For example, they might ask why there are so many different kinds of computers around their school and ask which ones are suitable for creating multimedia projects. Here are some answers.

Today's plethora of significantly different computers is one of the consequences of rapid technological development and enormous price reductions. Because progress is likely to make a computer technically and economically obsolete long before the computer's parts wear out, a school is likely to have many different generations of computers in service at any one time.

In less than one human generation, personal computers have progressed through at least three generations of increasingly economical products that are capable of handling increasingly demanding media. In each generation, low cost base models handled some media and relatively expensive options allowed users to upgrade the base models to handle additional media. In general, successive generations of computers became able to handle media in the same order in which we introduced the media in Chapter 1, namely text, graphics, images, audio, and video.

Early 1980s Generation

Many personal computers in the early 1980s could handle only text. User input was limited to typing text on keyboards and user output was limited to text display screens and text printers. The only way users could make lines and boxes was by entering peculiar text characters that included single and double lines and box corners.

Fortunately, it was possible to upgrade many computers in this and later generations. Some upgrades take the form of optional adapter cards. Adapter cards contain additional electronic circuitry and plug into large sockets on a computer's main circuit board, which contains most of the computer's circuitry. Other upgrades are optional boxes, such as displays and printers.

Users could upgrade the early 1980s generation of computers so that software could identify, address, and change every point on a screen or on a printed page. These options allowed users to draw respectable graphics that included such figures as diagonal lines and circles. However, because typical screens could display only two colors (black and green) or four colors, these computers could not display good colorful images.

Late 1980s Generation

The late 1980s saw many computers that could address more points on their screens and could also display 16 different colors at a time. Such computers could not only display text and graphics but could also display an acceptable image of a subject that was carefully selected to have only a limited range of colors. These computers' displays are called VGA.

Optional display adapter cards allowed users to upgrade this generation of computers to Super-VGA (S-VGA), which could show 256 different colors at a time. Displaying 256 unique colors suffices for displaying quite good images, even when a subject has a wide range of colors. This generation of computers is common in the mid-1990s and allows students to create some meaningful and colorful multimedia projects.

Other optional adapter cards for the late 1980s generation of computers allowed users to add digital audio capability to a base computer. Digital audio capability means that the computer can record and play back sounds. For example, a student can speak into a microphone. A digital audio adapter converts the microphone's output signal to the form that the computer can write onto a disk. (This component is sometimes called a hard disk or hard drive, to emphasize that it is not floppy, or is called a fixed disk, to emphasize that you can not remove the disk from the computer.) The computer writes audio as an ordinary file, just like a file that contains a word processing document. Later, the computer can read the audio file from the disk. The adapter converts the file's information back to a signal that is suitable for playing through a speaker.

The microphone's output and the speaker's input are analog signals, whereas signals that a computer can store on its disks are digital. Converting analog audio to digital form and writing the digital form on a computer's disk makes it possible for students to create projects that can instantly start playing any desired audio selection. Unlike a tape recorder, a disk can find the beginning of any selection in a small fraction of a second. Thus, digital audio is what allows interactive multimedia projects to include audio as well as text, images, and graphics.

Students can use a computer that can display at least 256 colors, and can record and play digital audio, to create most multimedia projects. In fact, such computers are often called "multimedia computers, " especially if the computers have the additional ability to read Compact Disc-Read Only Memory (CD-ROM) discs. CD-ROM disks look exactly like the CD discs that replaced phonograph records. A computer can read a CD-ROM if the computer has a CD-ROM drive. (Relative to the spelling, round flat things that were not originally intended for use with computers are spelled with a "c," unlike the "k" in computer disks.) Students will find that CD-ROMs are an excellent source of professionally created media. However, for optimal learning, students should create and digitize their own original media, in addition to combining media into completed original projects. Having a CD-ROM drive is neither necessary nor sufficient for creating multimedia projects.

For creating and digitizing original media, students need access to a computer that is equipped with some additional hardware. This hardware is available as options for the late 1980s generation of computers. With additional hardware, for example, students can scan photographs into the computer to create images. Fortunately, several classes can share one computer that contains this additional hardware, so a less expensive setup suffices for most of the time that students spend creating or using a project.

Mid-1990s Generation

In the mid-1990s, many base model computers can display at least 256 colors and also have digital audio capability, either built into the computers' main circuit boards or packaged on adapter cards that come as standard parts of the base computers. These computers are also likely to come with CD-ROM drives. These affordable multimedia computers make student-created multimedia projects feasible for the first time in the mid-1990s. As the ability to create more sophisticated media has moved from high-priced adapter cards to reasonably priced base models, this ability has decreased significantly in price. Many school districts can now afford enough multimedia computers that each small group of students can have access to one such computer for long enough to create a project. Many homes now have such computers, as well. These multimedia computers allow users to create text, graphics, images, and audio.

The mid-1990s generation is also suitable for upgrading to handle digital video. A school that has dozens of such computers might choose to add a digital video capture adapter to only one or two computers. Students can use a computer that has been upgraded with this adapter to convert moving pictures to computer files. That is, the computer can accept an analog video signal from a video camera or from a video cassette recorder (VCR), can convert the signal to digital form, and can store the resulting digital form on the computer's disk. As we note in this chapter's Theory section, digital video files can be absolutely enormous, even after applying sophisticated compression techniques that reduce the files' sizes.

Several classes can share one computer that has a digital video capture adapter because, fortunately, students can use normal multimedia computers without any upgrades to play back digital video. As the name implies, a computer needs a digital video capture adapter card in order to capture digital video, but a computer does not need such a card in order to play back digital video. Many students can use a single computer that has a digital video capture adapter to prepare video files and then transfer those files to the many normal computers that the students use for actually creating projects. A local area network makes transferring files easiest, but sneakernet works fine, too. With sneakernet, students (typically wearing sneakers) carry diskettes containing files from computer to computer.

Analog video capability, which is an alternative to using digital video, can involve attaching a laser disc player, also known as a video disc player, to a computer. A project running on the computer controls the player by sending signals over a cable that connects the computer's serial port to a corresponding port on the player. (A serial port may be the same port to which you connect a modem.) These signals can tell the player to go rapidly to a specified place on the disc, start playing, and play video and audio until reaching another specified place on the disc. The player produces analog video and analog audio, which drive a television monitor and amplified speaker, respectively. Audio and video from a laser disc player do not actually pass through the computer and are not converted from analog to digital form. Thus, a laser disc player provides perhaps the only significant example of interactive analog audio and analog video.

A great deal of high-quality analog video, including movies and educational titles, is available on laser discs. Laser discs are popular because they produce high-quality video, because they allow rapid access to any desired video segment, and because schools have been accumulating them for almost two decades. We discuss how to select laser discs in Chapter 14.

Analog video has both drawbacks and advantages, in comparison to digital video, that could determine which form your students employ. Analog video's primary drawback is that using a laser disc player limits students to using professionally prepared media. Very few students can afford to create their own laser discs. The secondary drawback is that, to create or use a project that includes laser discs, each group of students needs access to a computer that has an attached laser disc player and a television monitor. Laser discs have advantages over digital video that may be important in some situations. Laser discs produce video that actually has higher quality than does broadcast television, whereas most digital video available in the mid-1990s produces smaller, slower, and less colorful video than does broadcast television. Moreover, a considerable number of schools already have laser disc players but do not have computers with digital video capability.

Figure 2-1 shows a mid-1990s generation multimedia computer. The right column and the television monitor on top are expansion items that need not appear on the computers that all groups of students use most of the time. Dotted boxes represent pieces of hardware that are actually invisible inside the computer. Thick arrows indicate connections among pieces.

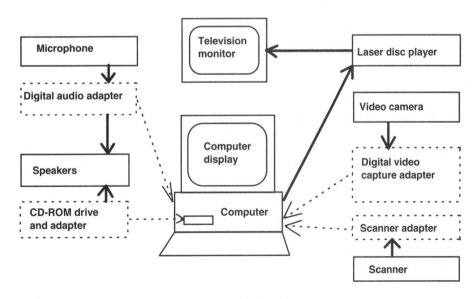

Figure 2-1: A fully expanded mid-1990s computer

The Next Generation

As you would expect, today's generation of multimedia computers is just one step along the history of personal computers, rather than the end of the road. Of the five media, digital video has the most room for improvement. Playing back digital video on a slow base model computer limits the user to showing video in a small window, that is, playing video in only a small fraction of the computer's screen. A slow computer also limits the user to showing only a few pictures per second. To avoid any jerking, a computer must show 30 complete pictures (called frames) each second. This rate of 30 frames per second is called full-motion video. Television sets and analog video show full-motion video.

It is reasonable to foresee that the next generation of computers will have faster processors, faster disks, and perhaps special video playback hardware. Such computers will come closer to allowing users to show full-motion digital video on a base model computer's entire display screen. Digital video will also benefit from future computers' ability to increase the number of colors that can appear on the screen from 256 to about 16 million. Sixteen million colors is called true-color, because it can reproduce as many colors as a television screen can reproduce or as a human eye can distinguish. Providing more colors will also improve future computers' ability to show natural images. Next generation computers will also have sufficiently large disks to store many high-resolution images and to store long segments of digital audio and digital video. Such computers will gradually become common, thereby encouraging today's students to use full-motion, full-screen, true-color digital video routinely in their adult personal and occupational communications.

Theory

This section discusses the hardware that your students need in order to handle each of the five media. If it seems that this section contains a lot of unrelated vocabulary and concepts, this is simply because each of the five media has its own unique characteristics. You need some information to help your students use a microphone and a digital audio adapter card to put audio into a computer. You need different information to help the students use a video camera and digital video capture adapter card to put digital video into a computer.

After covering each medium separately, we present a table that shows how different pieces of hardware perform all the functions on all the media, so that you can make cross-comparisons and cement your knowledge. The subsequent chapter discusses how multimedia authoring software helps a creator combine several media into a single multimedia project without worrying about the underlying hardware's individual peculiarities.

Each medium requires hardware for converting the medium's unique external analog form to a computer's internal digital form. Each medium also requires hardware for converting the digital form back to the medium's unique analog form, so that people can see or hear the medium. For each medium, we concentrate on multimedia hardware that is economically available in the mid-1990s, but we mention hardware to which students can look forward in subsequent generations.

Why Convert Media to Digital Form?

Why should you and your school go to the trouble and expense of providing computers that allow students to convert analog information to digital form and then convert the media back to analog form for display? The technical reason is that the digital forms of all media are identical, being simply long strings of zeroes and ones. What this means to your students is that the same disks can store all the media, the same circuits can process all the media, and the same networks can transmit all the media. Details follow.

- A computer can store all media in digital form on the same disk. At any one time, a given disk may contain many files, each of which contains one or more of the five media. Moreover, students can erase a part of a disk that stored a text report yesterday, use the same part to store a digital video clip today, then erase that and store a digital audio clip in the same part tomorrow. Contrast this situation with the requirement for an audio cassette recorder to store analog audio and a separate VCR to store analog video, each medium on its own unique type of tape cassette.

- A disk can move from one file to another in less than 20 thousandths of a second, whereas a tape may require up to several minutes to wind from the end of one clip to the beginning of another clip. A disk's fast access allows the interactive access to media that characterizes multimedia projects. Note that being digital is not necessary for fast access, because a laser disc is analog and has fast access, like any disc or disk. Moreover, being digital is not sufficient for fast access, because digital audio tape is digital but has slow access, like any tape.

- Digital copies are perfect. In the digital world, a copy of a copy of a copy is indistinguishable from the original, whereas a fourth generation VCR tape is visibly degraded. The reason why digital copies are perfect is that, when copying digital information, hardware need only determine whether each symbol represents a zero or a one. When copying analog information, hardware must attempt to reproduce the exact value of a continuously varying electrical or magnetic signal and always makes small errors.

- Digital processing is far more flexible than analog processing and takes advantage of today's continual improvements in the function, performance, and price of digital electronics. A personal computer's processor chip can handle routine functions for all media, rather than requiring separate electronics for each medium.

- A digital network connecting computers can transmit all media. The anticipated national information infrastructure (NII) or information superhighway may well consist of a single set of connections. Contrast that prospect with today's requirement for a telephone network to carry analog audio and a completely different cable network to carry analog television. Future digital networks will use the best features of today's telephone and cable networks and also the best features of today's computer networks.

Digital forms of different media require different amounts of storage space on a disk and require different data rates on a computer's connections or over a network. The following discussions of the five media give rules of thumb for estimating how much space each medium will occupy on a disk. You will find such estimates useful either for obtaining hardware that will handle what students create, or for scaling what students create to fit the hardware that is available. The last part of this section summarizes sizes of all the media.

Text

Using computers is the latest of a long series of important innovations in creating, storing, distributing, and reading letters and numbers. Cuneiform writing, pressing the end of a triangular reed into a sheet of damp clay, improved on making a clay model of a goat or other item paid as taxes. Brushing ink on a papyrus scroll produced a document that people could more easily carry long distances but required readers to roll carefully to get from one part of the scroll to another. Writing by hand on cut sheets of papyrus or vellum allowed readers to flip rapidly past pages that they did not need to see. Printing with movable type made many copies of the same document available to many readers. Ball point pens facilitated casual writing. Computers extend each of the earlier steps by making it still easier to create text documents, store documents on disks, find what you want to read by following hypertext links from one part of a document to another, and transmit documents long distances quickly over networks.

For easy and rapid reading, particularly in groups, we recommend that students create text screens that have no more than 40 to 60 characters per line and have no more than 7 to 10 lines per screen. One of the more difficult challenges in helping students create multimedia projects is weaning them away from entering screen after screen of dense text, which the students expect others to read linearly, one screen after another. A large amount of linear text does not make a good multimedia project. For multimedia projects, students need encouragement to break the mold of linear text. In addition to appropriate amounts of text, students should use hypertext and other media.

Computers make hypertext possible, because you can use a computer to link to whatever you want to see next on the screen almost instantly. Computers also make hypertext necessary, because you are not as comfortable reading a large amount of text on a computer screen as on a sheet of paper. The reason has to do with a hardware concept called screen resolution. Screen resolution is one of the three main decisions you must make when you obtain a computer display.

Selecting a Display for Text and Other Media

Most computer display screens can show 2000 text characters, including blanks and punctuation marks. This is about the same number of characters as a printed page can contain. However, we recommend that students use larger characters in their projects and limit each text screen to at most 600 characters. When students use only part of a screen to show text, they should show correspondingly fewer characters.

Why should your students avoid cramming 2000 characters onto each screen? The reason is that a computer's display screen shows much coarser text than you are accustomed to reading on paper. Computer hardware shows text on a display screen by converting each letter into dots called picture elements (pixels). For example, a letter "L" may be a vertical column of pixels and a shorter horizontal row of pixels. A printed page, too, shows text as dots. However, a typical printed page uses about 20 times as many dots to show each letter as does a computer screen. That is why printed text appears smoother, and is easier to read, than a computer display.

When you select a computer display for your school to purchase, you need to decide what screen resolution you want. That is, you must select how many pixels you want the display to show. This section mentions that you also need to select a display size and a dot pitch. However, an important and perhaps surprising point is that even the best computer display that you can select has far less resolution than does a typical printed page.

We next discuss resolutions that you can select. Here we emphasize text. In subsequent sections, we apply the same concepts and terminology to images and to digital video. Chapter 14 explains that in order to create projects that will look good on television, you need to take into account the fact that television screens have significantly lower resolution than do computer screens.

A typical mid-1990s computer display screen can show 640 pixels across each horizontal row, from left to right, and can show 480 rows of pixels vertically, from top to bottom. Computer literature calls this resolution 640 by 480 or 640 x 480. Such displays also go by the name video graphics array (VGA). To compare this screen's resolution to a printed page's resolution, we need to convert the number of pixels to a number of pixels per inch, which is simply another way of measuring resolution.

For example, consider a computer display screen that measures about 11 inches horizontally and 8 1/4 inches vertically. Dividing 640 pixels by 11 inches (or dividing 480 pixels by 8.25 inches) shows that this typical computer screen has a resolution of 58 pixels per inch. Table 2-1 places this resolution in context.

Table 2-1: Some typical resolutions

Display	Resolution, in pixels / inch
Computer display	58
Laser-printed page	300
Photocopied page	300
Printed book page	1200

In our example, we used what computer catalogs call a 15-inch display. Such a display's physical tube has a diagonal measurement of 15 inches. However, if you measure the screen, you will find that only about 13 1/2 inches of the tube's diagonal is actually capable of showing pixels. If you can afford a 17-inch display, you will find that more students can read the display more comfortably.

You may also be able to afford a computer display adapter and display screen that provide a higher resolution than 640 x 480 pixels. Some computers produce 1280 pixels horizontally and 960 pixels vertically, or 1280 x 960 pixels. On a 15-inch display, this doubles the traditional resolution to about 118 pixels per inch. However, there is no plan to increase today's typical resolution by a factor of five, to match the resolution of a copier or laser printer, let alone to increase typical resolution by a factor of 20, to match the resolution of a book printer. Thus, in our use of computers we must live with limited screen resolution for the foreseeable future.

Your remaining selection is a display's dot pitch. A color display may consist of a myriad of tiny red, green, and blue dots, which you can see with a good magnifying glass. If you measured the distance between the centers of any two neighboring red dots, you would get about 0.28 mm. This is the display's dot pitch. Converting this number from millimeters to inches and taking the reciprocal shows that 0.28 mm between dots corresponds to 91 red dots per inch (and the same for each of green and blue). Such a display could show a resolution as large as 91 pixels per inch. Although it is a computer's display adapter that actually determines the screen resolution, a smaller dot pitch does give a smoother appearance at any resolution.

By selecting the highest resolution, the largest display size, and the smallest dot pitch that your school can afford, you will make it easiest for your students to read text on the screen. You will also improve graphics, images, and video. However, you still will want to encourage your students to use relatively few text characters on each screen.

Providing Disk Space for Text

Text involves computers' disk space as well as screen resolution. Should you worry that your students may write enough text to overflow their computer's disk space? Suppose your students are typing away furiously and they have 30 million Bytes (30 MB) of disk space free. (Note that we capitalize the word "Byte" to remind you to capitalize its abbreviation "B.") How soon will disk space force them to stop typing? Would they have enough space to store an entire book? Would you believe that they could store 50 books?

Each page of the Fawcett Crest paperback edition of Peter Benchley's book *Jaws* contains about 2160 text characters. The book's 278 pages thus contain about 600,480 characters. A computer can store each character in one Byte. (One Byte consists of eight bits. Each bit can have either of the two values 1 or 0. A Byte has 256 possible values. To get 256, multiple two by itself eight times.) The American Standard Code for Information Interchange (ASCII) arbitrarily assigns each text character to one of the 256 possible values of a Byte's eight bits. For example, ASCII assigns capital "A" to the bits 01000001. Thus, there is no problem storing even the large amount of text in *Jaws* on a computer. A typical computer could store the book's 600,480 Bytes on half of one floppy disk. Your students could write 50 such books before overflowing their available 30 MB.

Of the five media, text demands by far the least storage space. As we have just seen, publishers could distribute a couple of paperback books on one diskette. However, publishers can put a truly amazing amount of text on one CD-ROM disc.

One CD-ROM disc can hold about five hundred fifty million text characters (550 MB). One disc can thus hold about one thousand books the size of *Jaws*. Anybody would prefer to carry home one 4.75-inch-diameter disc that weighs less than an ounce instead of a thousand new paperbacks that weigh about 300 pounds. Anybody would prefer to pay the manufacturing cost of the disc, which is about 50 cents, instead of the printing costs of the thousand books. However, only an omnivorous reader who is preparing for a slow cruise around the world might be willing to pay for the information content, including the authors' royalties, of a thousand new books. What sorts of books could be on a CD-ROM that contains hundreds of books, yet costs only about $30.00? The answer is old books that are no longer under copyright protection.

Sending Text Over Networks

Suppose that your students have entered some text and want to send the text to students in another city. Could they send the text using an ordinary telephone line and modem (modulator demodulator) connected to their computer? Yes, your students could send the text as fast as the other students could read the text.

One of the authors likes to read a page of *Jaws* in about 50 seconds. This is a data rate of 43 Bytes per second or 345 bits per second. (These important units of capacity or data rate are usually distinguished by writing 43 Bps or 345 bps, respectively. Because "bit" and "Byte" start with the same letter, it is necessary to capitalize "Byte" in order to tell the abbreviations apart.) Even with the slowest of today's networks, which run at 300 bps, one computer can send text to another computer at about a person's normal reading rate. With a faster network, running at 9600 bps, one computer could send the entire book to another computer in about eight minutes. This transmission time or data rate is less than the time it would take to check the book out of a library and is negligible in comparison to the time required to read the book.

Some forms of text do require special handling on networks. Formatted text files, for example, such as the forms produced by word processor programs and some hypertext programs, include special symbols, control characters, or binary numbers in addition to ASCII characters. Most times you do not know that these are part of the file. Networks that expect only ASCII characters garble such text beyond redemption, unless you specify that the file must be treated as a binary file rather than as text. Making this specification is usually easy to do if you remember to do it.

Text thus poses few problems for disk space or network capacity. Other media, particularly audio and video, pose more severe problems. As we shall see, the same 30 MB might hold as little as three minutes of digital video.

Graphics

As was the case for text, using computers was by no means the first innovation in creating and reproducing graphics, which are line drawings. From lines scratched on Lascaux cave walls 17,000 years ago, to copper engravings reproduced on a massive scale a century ago, artists have improved their abilities to depict the world in straight and curved strokes and to allow more people to view their artistry. Computers have made a particularly large increase in the ease with which people who are not artists can create graphics. Perhaps a computer's greatest improvement over previous methods is the ease with which a creator can add something, dislike the result, and erase what she added without destroying what was already there. Another major improvement is the ease with which anyone can make lines that are straight and circles that are round.

The hardware that graphics require is now familiar to most computer users. For input, a computer needs a mouse or some other pointing device such as a digitizing tablet or touch screen. For output, the computer needs display hardware that can change the brightness or color of individual pixels on the display screen. Beyond these requirements, the magic in graphics is mainly in the software, such as a draw program. A draw program may interpret a user's succession of quick mouse movements as specifying that the next object will be a circle, selecting where the circle starts, and dragging the circle out to the desired size.

Graphics make relatively modest demands on a computer's storage and processing and on a network's data rate. A computer stores a graphic circle by storing just a few numbers, such as one number that identifies the object as a circle, two numbers for the coordinates of the circle's center, and one number each for the circle's radius, thickness, and color. If each of these numbers is two Bytes long, then the circle occupies only 12 B on a computer's disk. A complex graphic with 2000 such objects may therefore occupy about 24,000 Bytes (24 KB). Using information from the previous section, we see that a graphic occupies about ten times as much storage as does a page of text. As we shall see in the next section, an image often occupies ten to one hundred times as much space as a graphic. This is because a computer must store an image of a circle by storing separately the color and intensity of each of the many pixels that are on the circle's circumference.

A more sophisticated form of graphics stores a three-dimensional object by storing three coordinates for each of many points that outline the surface of a physical object such as the space shuttle. Short straight lines that join these points amount to a wire frame model of the physical object. Determining the object's appearance from a given direction, including erasing parts of the surface that would be hidden behind other parts and realistically shading the visible parts, requires hardware to evaluate an awesome number of trigonometric functions. This type of three-dimensional (3D) graphics is moving slowly from expensive engineering workstations that contain special processing and display hardware to high-end personal computers that contain powerful main processor chips. Students can look forward to rotating 3D graphic models to create animations using future generations of normal personal computers.

Images

Computers provide new ways for students to create an image, that is, a single still picture with no movement. Traditional methods of creating an image include oil painting, in which an artist places different pigments on different parts of a canvas, and photography, in which different amounts of colored dyes go on different parts of a piece of film or paper. A computer stores an image in digital form by storing a color and brightness for each pixel. For example, an image that has a resolution of 640 x 480 pixels consists of several numbers that specify the color and brightness of each of 307,200 different pixels.

Depending on how students create images, they may require no additional special multimedia hardware or they may require any of several different kinds of special hardware. With no more hardware than they require to create graphics with a draw program, students can create an image with a paint program. Students use a mouse and a paint program to paint colors and intensities of pixels directly onto a computer's screen, as if they were applying oil paints. A paint program interprets a student's mouse movements as selecting a particular tool, such as a paintbrush of a given width and color, and moving the tool across the screen to deposit the color.

Alternatively, with special input hardware, students can capture natural images of physical objects such as buildings, photographs, paintings, or the students' own faces, instead of taking photographs. Images may be in color, in shades of gray, or in stark black and white. Students may also obtain images in the form of clip art on diskettes, on CD-ROM discs, or over networks from other computers.

As we noted in our discussion of generations of personal computers, displaying natural images places a requirement on a computer's hardware that extends far beyond the requirements for displaying text and graphics. Displaying an image requires a greater color depth, that is, requires the computer to display a greater number of different colors at one time. Whereas four colors usually suffice for displaying text and 16 colors often suffice for displaying graphics, displaying natural images requires at least 256 colors. Using only 16 colors to display an image usually produces an unpleasant posterized effect in which, for example, a subject's forehead is made up of only three large bands of uniform color. In fact, displaying images benefits significantly from having as many as 16 million colors.

Choosing Image Capture Hardware

Image is the first medium for which creation, rather than just display, may require special multimedia hardware. You are almost certain to need to decide among several attractive alternative methods with which your students can capture images. Students can capture a photograph as a digital image by using a scanner attached to a special adapter card in a computer. They can also capture an image from a single frame of video by connecting a video camera, VCR, or digital camera to another special adapter card in a computer. Finally, they can take film to a photo finisher, get back a Kodak Photo CD, and read files from this disc. Students can use any of these methods to convert real-world analog images into digital files on a computer's disk. Thus, you are likely to choose one or more of scanners, video cameras, digital cameras, or Photo CD for capturing natural images of physical objects. We next discuss how you can make this choice.

A scanner captures flat originals such as photographs, magazine pages, book pages, hand drawings, and small paintings. A flat-bed scanner looks like a small photocopier that has a glass plate on which to place a flat original. However, instead of producing a paper copy of the original, a scanner sends an electronic analog version of the original over a cable into a special hardware adapter card in a computer. The adapter card converts the analog signal to digital form and sends the digital form to the computer's disk. A hand-held scanner performs the same function as a flat-bed scanner, at lower cost. However, a hand scanner covers only about half the width of a printed page and requires the user to drag the scanner smoothly across the original.

A video camera or digital camera captures images of three-dimensional originals such as people, buildings or landscapes. As this chapter's Analog Video section discusses, a video camera produces an analog video signal. A digital video capture adapter card can convert the analog video signal to digital form, producing a stream of images that give the illusion of smooth motion. An important additional use of a video camera and video capture adapter card is to convert a selected portion of an analog video signal into one single digital image. Figure 2-2 shows a typical setup.

A digital camera is simply a video camera that can produce one image at a time rather than a rapid succession of images. The digital camera may be packaged together with a type of video capture adapter, sometimes called a frame grabber, that is capable of digitizing only a single still image rather than a continuous stream of video. Such a digital camera produces a digital signal that can connect to a standard port on any computer, which therefore need not contain a video capture adapter. Should you obtain

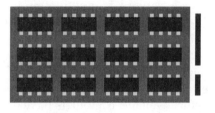

Object   **Video camera**   **Digital video capture adapter**

Figure 2-2: Capturing video

a digital camera, if your school already owns a video camera? Probably not, because the digital camera is likely to cost more than a video capture adapter card would cost.

Buying a video capture adapter would allow you to use your existing video camera for the same function as a digital camera provides, and for the function of producing digital video as well. However, students may find a digital camera somewhat more convenient to use than a video camera and a video adapter.

Should you obtain a scanner, if your school already has either a video camera and video adapter or a digital camera? Using a video camera or digital camera to produce still images is very flexible because the same hardware can digitize flat originals as well as three-dimensional originals. However, resolution appears again here. A video camera or digital camera usually produces images that have significantly lower resolutions than images that a scanner produces. A video camera and video capture adapter, or a reasonably priced digital camera, produce an image that has a resolution of at most 640 x 480 pixels, more often about 320 x 240 pixels. A digital camera that produces images with a high resolution of 3060 x 2036 pixels may a bit out of your school's price range at about $28,000.

For high-resolution images, a scanner is thus very attractive. A typical scanner can subdivide an original's information into at least 300 pixels per inch. Multiplied by a flat-bed scanner's typical dimensions of 8.5 x 11 inches, this gives an image resolution of 2550 x 3300 pixels. Multiplied by a hand-held scanner's typical area of 4.5 x 3.4 inches, the same 300 pixels per inch gives an image resolution of 1350 x 1020 pixels. Thus, the resolution of a flat-bed scanner or a hand-held scanner can far exceed the resolution of a video camera or an affordable digital camera. A scanner also exceeds the resolution of a computer's display screen. A scanner is useful for many special situations, such as:

- creating and storing a large image and then allowing a user to zoom in to display a small part of the image at a computer screen's full resolution,
- capturing and processing a high-resolution image and finally reducing the resolution to a computer display screen's resolution, and

- creating a high-resolution image for display on a high-end workstation, which would be more typical of a doctor reading an X ray than of a student creating a multimedia project.

Why not always capture images at very high resolution, just in case someone wants to apply sophisticated processing or wants to display the image on a high-end workstation? Image is the first medium that requires you and your students to consider whether available computers have enough disk capacity to store all of the medium that the students would like to create.

Providing Disk Space for Images

A scanned image that includes 2550 x 3300 pixels and uses 3 Bytes for each pixel to specify one of 16 million colors occupies about 25 MB, or 25 million Bytes. This could very well be about all the storage space that students can count on having available for an entire project. Even a single full-screen image that fills a 640 x 480 screen and uses 3 Bytes for each pixel occupies 921,600 B, which is almost 1 MB. Fortunately, a typical medium-resolution image that has 320 x 240 pixels and uses one Byte for each pixel to specify one of 256 colors occupies only 76,800 Bytes. Students can store 325 such images in 25 MB of disk space, 18 such images on one diskette, and about 7500 such images on one CD-ROM.

But don't students just read other people's clip art from CD-ROMs? Students can't write images on their own CD-ROM disc, can they? Kodak's Photo CD technology gives students the opportunity to do just that! One Photo CD disc can contain about 100 high-resolution photographic images that occupy about 5.5 MB each. The disc stores far more information about each image than a computer screen can show at one time, partly to allow a user to zoom in to magnify a small part of an image.

To use Kodak Photo CD, students take pictures with an ordinary film camera, using either print film or slide film. A photo finisher that is equipped to make Photo CD discs then develops the film, digitizes the images, and gives the students back a disc for less than about $1.00 per image. Not all CD-ROM drives can read Photo CDs, so check the specifications before you buy a drive. If you want to take a disc back for the photo finisher to write images from successive rolls of film on the same disc, you will need a drive that supports multiple sessions, so check that specification, too.

We discuss drives that allow students to write their own CD-ROMs in this chapter's section on the future of digital video. Such drives allow students to think about saving large numbers of high-resolution images, or enormous numbers of medium resolution images, that they capture or scan.

Audio

Recording audio has a much shorter history than does recording the three media we discussed in the preceding sections. In 1877, Edison invented a phonograph in which sound's changing air pressure moved a diaphragm that caused a stylus to create a more or less deep helical groove in a cylinder made of tin foil. Running the stylus along the groove again moved the diaphragm and reproduced some of the original sound. By 1894, Berliner was using acid to etch a spiral groove in a zinc disc, with a diaphragm superimposing waves on the spiral. Casting plastic replicas of the zinc disk allowed wide distribution of commercial Gramophone recordings. Listeners could place the playback needle on different grooves to access different audio segments.

During World War II, German officials recorded propaganda speeches as varying magnetizations of oxide coatings on plastic tapes. Officials could thus copy and distribute the tapes instead of repeating their speeches for different time zones. In 1946 and 1947, Bing Crosby solved the same time zone problem by recording the first prime-time network radio shows on wax discs and magnetic tapes. Reel-to-reel tapes progressed eventually to economical and convenient audio cassette tapes that allowed individuals to record their own material, as well as allowing mass distribution, but did not allow rapid access to different audio segments. Compact discs (CDs, formally named compact disc-digital audio or CD-DAs) replaced successors of Gramophone records by digital discs that manufacturers could turn out cheaply by the thousands, and on which listeners could select individual audio segments rapidly, but which individuals could not create for themselves in small quantities.

Digital audio on disks is the first recording technique that has the advantages of all the earlier techniques. Digital audio also has a final additional advantage, which appears last in the following list of advantages. Together, these advantages make audio feasible in multimedia projects.

- Individuals can record their own audio and edit the result.
- Manufacturers can produce large numbers of copies cheaply.
- Listeners can access different segments rapidly.
- Listeners can erase unwanted audio and record new audio.
- Listeners can store the other four media on the same disk.

Using Audio Capture and Playback Hardware

A digital audio adapter card, or the corresponding circuitry built into a computer's main circuit board, performs both capture and playback. Capture involves converting an analog signal, such as the output of a microphone, to a digital form, and then recording that digital form on the computer's disk. Playback means converting the digital form back to an analog form that can drive a speaker.

A digital audio adapter is flexible. It can do a good job of capturing any sort of audio, including music and voice. At some point when your students begin to capture audio, the computer is likely to ask them how many samples per second they want, how many bits per sample they want, and whether they want stereo or mono. When they turn and ask you, will you know the answers? The right answers depend on whether the students want to capture high-quality music and do not care how much disk space the file occupies, or whether they want to capture a lot of speech but are worried about overflowing their disk.

Depending on how you answer the questions that the capture process will ask, the sound that comes back out of the speaker may be a good replica or a bad replica of the sound that went into the microphone. Correspondingly, the digital form of a given number of seconds of audio may consume a large or small amount of space on a disk. In order to achieve good results without consuming excessively large amounts of disk space, you must be able to select answers that balance an acceptable size of a given number of minutes of digital audio against a desired audio quality level. You can do this easily if you understand something about capturing digital audio.

Hardware captures audio by using a sampling method such as pulse code modulation (PCM), which works as follows. Sound is a continuously varying air pressure. A microphone converts the air pressure to a continuously varying electrical signal called voltage. (If your car has a volt meter, the needle reads about 14 volts most of the time, but it varies when you start the car or turn on the head lights.) The microphone's varying voltage is analogous to the varying air pressure, which explains the name "analog." Capture may consist of sampling the varying voltage 8000 times per second. The adapter card's circuitry measures what the voltage is that many times, each and every second. At each sample time, the hardware records the value of the voltage at that instant, by recording a number in digital form. The adapter card needs you to tell it not only how many times you want it to sample the voltage each second, but also how many bits of information you want it to save for each measured voltage, such as 8 bits. The resulting succession of numbers is the digital form of the sound that the microphone heard. The adapter card's hardware sends those numbers to the computer's disk. So, what answers do you give your students?

On the one hand, your students might want to produce excellent quality music-grade digital audio. In this case, your answers might match the sampling standard that the common CD-DAs use. This standard specifies sampling the microphone's analog audio voltage 44,100 times per second (44.1 KHz) and saving 16 bits, or two Bytes, of data per sample. This multiplies out to 88,200 Bps.

Music on a CD almost always has two stereo channels. One channel goes to a speaker that is on the right side of the listener and the other channel goes to a speaker that is on the left side of the listener. Adding the data rates of the two individual channels gives a total of 176,400 Bps. In other units that may be more meaningful, this data rate is about 10 MB per minute or 600 MB per hour. An hour of music-grade digital audio thus fills a CD-DA disc, whereas eight seconds of such audio fills a diskette. This explains why music comes on CDs rather than on diskettes.

On the other hand, your students might want to produce adequate quality for voice, and produce as small an audio file as possible. In this case, your answers might match the sampling standard that long-distance telephone networks use. This standard specifies sampling the monaural analog audio signal 8000 times per second and saving 8 bits, or one Byte, of information about each sample. This works out to 8000 Bps or just under one half MB per minute. A diskette can hold approximately 180 seconds, or three minutes, of this voice-grade audio. To save disk space, it is important to suggest that your students specify mono, rather than stereo, when they digitize voice.

As these two examples show, you can give answers that fit any required quality of digital audio. For example, if students have 30 MB of disk space available for a project, they might want to allocate 10 MB for one minute of high-quality music, another 10 MB for 20 minutes of voice, and the rest of the space for text, graphics, and images.

In the future, your students can look forward to computers that have larger disk storage capacity, so that they can store more minutes of digital audio. Future computers may also have hardware that can compress digital audio to fit the same number of minutes of audio into a smaller space.

How CD-DA Became CD-ROM

Distributing music as digital audio on compact discs led directly to distributing text and other media on CD-ROM discs. In fact, the people who designed the CD-ROM standard decided to use almost exactly the same recording method as CD-DA discs use. A normal speed CD-ROM drive plays at a data rate of 150 KBps. (For technical reasons, this is somewhat less than the CD-DA rate of 176,400 KBps that we noted in the previous section.) We shall see that this rate of 150 KBps is extremely important for distributing digital video on CD-ROMs.

Some CD-ROM drives run at data rates that are two, three, or four times the base rate of 150 KBps. Such drives are termed double-speed, triple-speed and quad-speed drives, respectively. A full CD-ROM disc holds about 550 MB of data. This capacity is independent of the data rate; a faster drive can simply play selected parts of the 550 MB in less time.

Different CD-ROM drives not only have different data rates; more expensive drives can also move more quickly from one part of a disc to another part. Computer catalogs specify this by giving a number called access time. More expensive drives have shorter access times.

Analog Video

Recording many pictures and displaying them sufficiently rapidly to give the illusion of continuous motion has a history that is longer than the history of recording and playing audio. Research into the underlying phenomenon, persistence of vision, began in 1824. Each major innovation then emerged from decades of development as what appeared to be a memorable overnight success.

Photographic film was the initial analog video technology. In 1877, Eadweard Muybridge met Leland Stanford's challenge to determine whether a galloping horse ever had all four hooves off the ground at once, by triggering many cameras in succession. In

1895, Edison installed, on Broadway, peep shows that displayed 15 seconds of action such as his assistant's sneeze. The next year, Edison and others projected almost one minute of film. In 1903, a director in the Edison company told a story, *The Great Train Robbery*, in eight minutes. In 1912, *Quo Vadis?* ran for two hours. In 1927, the synchronized sound of Al Jolson in *The Jazz Singer* made silent films obsolete. The next year, Walt Disney's *Steamboat Willie* synchronized sound with animation. In 1939, *Gone With the Wind* made color a major box office draw.

After a century of development, electronic technology finally joined film in the world of analog video. In 1936, the British Broadcasting Corporation inaugurated partly mechanical television broadcasting. In 1940, the National Television Standards Committee (NTSC) defined a black and white electronic broadcast standard. NTSC then extended that standard in 1954 to include color that was compatible with the tens of millions of black and white sets then in use. North America and Japan still use this compatible color standard.

All television broadcasts were live until 1956 saw the first program recorded on videotape. In 1978, two competing types of laser discs became parts of a single universally adopted standard. During the early 1980s, home VCRs became sufficiently inexpensive and common that rental movies could begin to supplement but not decrease movie theater attendance. During the late 1980s, consumer video cameras merged with video cassette recorders and the resulting camcorders improved sufficiently in price, size, and weight to completely replace film-based home movies.

Now it is possible to use a computer's display screen to show analog video. Your students can either use the entire screen to show analog video, or they can show the video on just a small part of the computer screen. In the latter case, the part of the screen that students use to show video is called the video window. This function requires special hardware that is called a "video-in-a-window" adapter. It is important to distinguish this video-in-a-window adapter from the digital video capture adapter that we mentioned in this chapter's section on mid-1990s computers and that we discuss further in the section on Digital Video.

A video-in-a-window adapter simply converts all or part of a student's computer screen into a television screen. That television screen can show analog video that comes from a laser disc player, from a video camera, or from a VCR. The VCR, in turn, may play a tape or may tune an educational channel from an antenna or from a cable. The adapter itself may be a card inside the student's computer or may be a small box near the computer.

A video-in-a-window adapter can be very useful for a project in which students display analog video. The Trailers project, which Chapter 9 describes, uses analog video of a movie that comes from a laser disc player. For Trailers and other projects that involve analog video students may use an actual television monitor, as the top half of Figure 2-3 shows. Alternatively, students may use a video-in-a-window adapter and show the video on the computer screen, as the figure's bottom half shows.

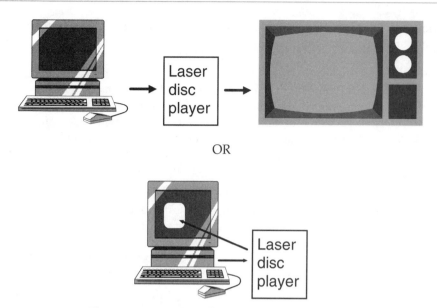

Figure 2-3: Two ways to display analog video

Digital Video

As we noted in the history of analog video, Edison showed tiny and brief moving pictures in 1895 and projected as much as a minute of film the next year. The history of digital video is now beginning almost exactly a century later than the history of analog video. In the mid-1990s, one minute of small screen video occupies about 9 MB on a disk, which is about as much space as many users want to devote to digital video. Within the next few years, much longer segments of full-screen video will become commonplace. Cries of "Bytes! Camera! Action!" will ring out over the land.

Digital video is highly desirable for student-created multimedia projects because only digital video enables students to create their own video and also access different video segments rapidly on a disk. (To recap, whereas students can create their own analog video tapes, tapes take as long as several minutes to reach a desired segment, and whereas laser discs can reach a given segment rapidly, students can not economically create their own laser discs.) Digital video is highly desirable outside the classroom, as well. Consider two examples. High definition television (HDTV) will be digital and is planned to replace analog television broadcasting throughout the world. Precursors of the national information infrastructure (NII) such as Internet are starting to transmit digital video along with other media in digital form.

Most digital video starts out in the form of analog video, because analog video comes from all video cameras, VCRs, laser disc players, and television stations. Knowing something about analog video makes it easier to create good digital video. We discuss this further in Chapter 13 on Advanced Techniques.

Capturing and playing back digital video pose significant challenges for mid-1990s computer hardware. Capturing digital video that has the same quality as a VCR tape requires specialized hardware, which costs several thousand dollars. Moreover, playing back such digital video also requires specialized hardware, which costs several hundred dollars. Fortunately, students can capture digital video that has lower but adequate quality by using a computer that contains a digital video capture adapter that costs only a few hundred dollars. Many groups of students can share this single computer. Even more fortunately, computers require no special hardware at all to play back this lower-quality digital video. Thus, groups of students can employ normal multimedia computers most of the time, even while they are creating projects that include digital video.

We next discuss these two approaches to digital video under the names hardware decompression and software decompression. One of the methods you are most likely to hear associated with hardware decompression is motion pictures expert group (MPEG). Some of the most common names for software decompression methods are joint photographic experts group (JPEG), Indeo, Cinepak, and Video 1.

Like many other topics that relate to multimedia projects, the difference between expensive hardware decompression video and affordable software decompression video is a quantitative topic. The quantity involved here is the data rate, that is, the number of Bytes per second that students produce when they convert analog video to digital video and save the captured digital form on a computer's disk. Resolution is as important here as for text and for images.

Hardware Decompression Approach

VCR-quality digital video has the same quality as the analog video that you get when you play a VCR tape on a television set. To capture VCR-quality digital video, you must capture a data rate of approximately 6.6 MBps. You can derive that capture data rate by multiplying the following numbers.

320	pixels per horizontal row from left to right across the frame
240	rows of pixels from top to bottom of the frame
3	Bytes of information about the brightness and color of each pixel
30	frames per second

The first two numbers give full-screen video resolution, even though a typical computer display screen has a resolution 640 pixels per line by 480 lines per frame. This is because VCR-quality television has about half the resolution of a computer screen. A full computer screen can show all of the detail that a video signal contains by expanding each of the video's pixels into a square that is two pixels wide and two pixels high.

The third number gives true-color, because 3 Bytes can contain any number between zero and about 16 million. This is about as many different colors as a television signal can transmit and as many different colors as a typical person's visual system can distinguish. The fourth number gives full-motion video, that is, no jerking, even when a subject moves rapidly across the screen. (The product of these numbers is actually 6,912,000. Computer convention says that 1 KB = 1024 B and 1 MB = 1,048,576 B. Thus if you divide 6,912,000 by 1,048,576 you get the answer as 6.5918 MBps and round it off to 6.6 MBps.)

This calculation shows that, in order to capture full-screen, true-color, full-motion digital video, which looks about the same as what students would see by playing a VCR tape, students would need access to a computer capable of handling 6.6 MBps. This means that the computer would be able to transfer data at 6.6 MBps from a digital video capture card, across the computer's main system bus, and onto the computer's disk. Later, to play back the same high-quality digital video, the computer would need to read data from its disk at 6.6 MBps and transfer this data across its bus to its display adapter.

The data rate of 6.6 MBps is too large for any but the most powerful personal computers to write on their disks or to read back from their disks. Most computers that are installed in schools in the mid-1990s handle data rates that range from 150 KBps to 1.5 MBps. A CD-ROM plays back digital video at 150 KBps or at two, three, or four times that rate. Thus, today's computers are not suitable for recording or playing back uncompressed full-screen, true-color, full-motion digital video.

A second reason for not using digital video that has a data rate of 6.6 MBps is that it would rapidly fill up any reasonable amount of available disk space. For example, two hours of such digital video would occupy almost 50,000 MB of disk space. This is more like the capacity of a million-dollar mainframe than the capacity of a personal computer.

For capturing VCR-quality digital video, the best solution is sophisticated digital video compression and decompression such as MPEG. An adapter card that implements the MPEG compression standard captures approximately 6.6 MBps from the incoming analog video. The adapter card then compresses the information by a factor of 45 without destroying the video's quality. The card sends the resulting data rate of 150 KBps across the computer's bus to the disk. Later, the disk reads the same data rate back for display. Designers selected this data rate to match single-speed CD-ROM drives so that CD-ROM drives, too, could play back VCR-quality digital video.

To capture VCR-quality digital video, a computer thus needs an MPEG compression card that costs several thousand dollars. More significantly, every computer that plays back such video from a disk or from a CD-ROM needs a corresponding MPEG decompression card that costs several hundred dollars. The cost of equipping many playback computers with special decompression hardware is the major problem with this approach. This approach to digital video is called the hardware decompression approach, in order to remind you of the approach's major problem.

In the mid-1990s, hardware decompression is reasonably common in industrial training installations, but its high cost makes it unusual in schools. By the late 1990s, the prices of both the compression and decompression cards will have dropped by at least a factor of ten, so many students will gain access to digital video that has VCR quality.

Software Decompression Approach

In the mid-1990s, most schools are well served by a digital video solution that uses less costly adapter cards for capture and needs no special hardware at all for playback. This is called the software decompression approach to digital video, because a personal computer's main processor executes software to decompress the digital video.

Examples of suitable capture adapter cards are Intel's Smart Video Recorder for Intel-based personal computers and Digital Film, Video Spigot, and Spigot Power AV for Macintosh computers.

In the software decompression approach, what is it that allows the capture adapter card to be less expensive, and what is it that makes the special decompression card completely unnecessary? The answer is not the data rate, because both the hardware decompression and software decompression approaches often use the same magic single-speed CD-ROM data rate of 150 KBps. What changes is the compression factor and thus the quality of video. A large compression factor, such as MPEG's factor of 45, requires sophisticated and expensive hardware for both compression and decompression. The software decompression approach gets by with a smaller compression factor such as five, by settling for lower-quality video.

The quantity of Bytes per second that students typically produce when they use the software decompression approach is approximately 750 KBps. You can derive this data rate by multiplying the following numbers.

160	pixels per horizontal row from left to right across the frame
120	rows of pixels from top to bottom of the frame
2	Bytes of information about the brightness and color of each pixel
20	frames per second

The first two numbers give one-quarter-screen resolution, meaning that the resulting video occupies only half the computer screen's width and half its height. The next number gives high color but not quite true-color. The last number may show some jerking and flickering but does show motion clearly.

This capture data rate of 750 KBps requires a compression factor of only five, in order to reach the magic 150 KBps data rate. Compressing by a factor of only five is what makes possible a relatively low-cost video capture card, which converts analog video to digital video and then compresses the digital form down to 150 KBps before sending the data to the computer's disk.

We would like to be able to say that typical mid-1990s personal computers have processors that can perform decompression by the same factor of five, using available software. In fact, only above-average computers can do such decompression. Slow computers may limit playback speed to as little as one frame per second, even with this quarter-screen high color video. Thus, in many cases, the reduced cost comes with significantly reduced quality of the resulting digital video. Fortunately, the software decompression approach meets or exceeds the requirements for essentially any student-created multimedia projects.

Note that the above numbers for MPEG and for Intel Smart Video Recorder are merely examples selected to convey a feeling for the orders of magnitude for the data rates involved. Both types of hardware are sufficiently flexible to create many different data rates and correspondingly different video qualities. Many comparable products exist that produce a wide range of possible results. In particular, professional multimedia creators often achieve high quality by paying service bureaus to compress video on massively parallel supercomputers. This approach can achieve compression ratios significantly greater than 45 and can achieve quality significantly better than that of a VCR. In general, it is possible to vary each of horizontal and vertical resolution, color depth, frame rate, and compression ratio, in order to achieve a desired combination of digital video quality and cost.

The Future of Digital Video

One reason why people would prefer to buy inexpensive compression hardware, and buy no decompression hardware at all, is that a battle among competing digital video standards is raging in the mid-1990s. Few people want to buy expensive hardware that a subsequently selected standard may render obsolete. It is useful to consider the history of VCRs. VCRs could not become really popular until either JVC's video home system (VHS) or Sony's Betamax had emerged as a clear winner. Only when consumers knew that there would be lots of tapes of one type, and when producers knew that there would be lots of machines of one type, did the market for both tapes and machines take off. (The favored type happened to be VHS, but Betamax would have done just as well.) A similar situation now applies to digital video. Consumers do not want to invest in a particular expensive digital video adapter, until they can be sure that other people will produce lots of multimedia content that uses that adapter's compression or decompression algorithm. Companies do not want to invest in developing either adapters or content, until they know which type consumers will buy.

In the mid-1990s, although a reasonable fraction of all computers have drives that play CD-ROMs, few schools can create their own CD-ROM discs. In the unlikely event that students wants a few thousand discs that all contain the same video and other media, a school can pay a vendor about thousand dollars to make a master disc of the material. After making such a master, the vendor can stamp out CD-ROMs for a few dollars per disc. In the more likely event that students want just one copy of a disc, a school can pay a vendor roughly $40 to produce a compact disc-recordable (CD-R) disc, which is also called a CD write once read mostly (CD-WORM) disc. A CD-R disc employs a different technology from true CD-ROMs. However, you can play back both types of discs on the same drives. In the future, more schools will purchase drives that write CD-Rs, as the cost of such drives drops below the cost of a typical computer. CD-Rs will give students an excellent way to carry their own portfolios, as well as encyclopedias and other multimedia content.

Media and Functions Table

So far, this chapter has discussed the hardware that applies to each medium in isolation. It is very useful to divide the functions that all this hardware performs into the simple categories of input, storage, and output and then note that each of the media needs all three categories of function. Table 2-2 helps keep separate the different pieces of hardware that perform these functions for the different media.

Table 2-2 includes most of the pieces of hardware that we have discussed in this chapter. In Chapters 7 through 12, which describe projects, we discuss similar tables that show hardware that the individual projects require. Not everything that the table shows is hardware. In the few cases where software performs a function without support from special multimedia hardware, the table includes the software's generic name in parentheses. As we shall see in the next chapter, of course, additional software is required to make all these functions work together.

Because it is possible to perform some of the functions in more than one way, the table shows alternatives separated by semicolons. A given setup might include only one of each set of alternatives. For example, if students use a computer that includes a video in a window adapter to perform the function of output for the medium of analog video, they would probably not also use a television monitor.

This table includes some types of hardware that we have not previously mentioned. One example is the musical instrument digital interface (MIDI, pronounced "middy"). This is an interface between properly equipped digital audio adapter cards and suitable keyboard instruments. MIDI allows a student to play music on a keyboard, hear what she is playing, and simultaneously record the music as a file on the computer's disk. Later, she can play the file back as music. Recall that a digital audio file contains numbers that represent successive voltage samples of an analog audio signal. A MIDI file is distinctly different. A MIDI file contains numbers that represent times of successive key presses and key releases, as well as other information such as what stops the student changed while playing the keyboard instrument. On the one hand, a MIDI file that contains a given piece of music is orders of magnitude smaller than a digital video file that contains the same music. On the other hand, MIDI is limited to music and sound effects. Unlike MIDI, normal digital audio allows students to record their own voices and record other arbitrary sounds.

Table 2-2: Media and functions

Media Functions	Text	Graphics	Images	Audio	Analog video	Digital video
Input	Keyboard; (Word-processor; Spread-sheet)	Mouse; (Draw program)	Scanner; Video camera or digital camera & Frame grabber; (Paint pro-gram)	Micro-phone & Digital audio adapter; MIDI key-board	Video camera	Video camera or VCR attached to a digital video capture adapter
Storage	Disk	Disk	Disk; CD-ROM	Disk; CD-ROM	VCR tape; Laser disc	Disk; CD-ROM
Output	Screen; Printer	Screen; Printer; Plotter	Screen; Printer	Digital audio adapter, Speaker; MIDI key-board	Television monitor; Screen & Video-in-a-window adapter	Screen & decom-pression software or hard-ware

How Big Are the Media?

In the preceding sections, we have discussed not only how your students can create and play back each medium but also how much space you need to provide on the computers that students use to store each medium. For convenient reference, Table 2-3 summarizes some of those sizes. It is clear that, as you read down the table, meaningful quantities of the media require significantly more storage space.

Table 2-3: Typical sizes of media

Medium	Amount	Bytes
Text	One printed book page	2,160
Graphics	One complex graphic	24,000
Image	One medium-resolution image	76,800
Audio	One minute of voice-quality audio	480,000
Digital video	One minute of compressed medium-resolution	9,000,000

Practice

The practical use of multimedia hardware may begin by determining several projects' requirements and obtaining hardware that meets those requirements. Alternatively, the practical use may begin by determining what hardware is available and selecting projects that make good use of that hardware. Either beginning leads to an iteration, as more demanding projects become desirable and as more hardware becomes available. We discuss first some of the practicalities of determining requirements, then discuss how to determine what is available, and finally explore some ways to become familiar with hardware. As we go along, we suggest some activities that may help clarify the discussion.

Determining Requirements

Chapters 7 through 12 tell what special multimedia hardware the respective multimedia projects require, usually in the form of devices that surround the base computer and adapters that plug into the base computer. However, requirements for the base computer itself depend less on the specific project than on the software.

As we shall see in the next chapter, the most useful multimedia software products are authoring systems. Typical authoring systems for Intel-based computers are Asymetrix Multimedia ToolBook and LinkWay Live! Typical authoring systems for Macintosh computers are HyperCard and HyperStudio. In general, any authoring system is suitable for any project. However, different authoring systems may have very different hardware and software requirements. For example, Multimedia ToolBook requires a computer that will run Microsoft Windows, whereas LinkWay Live! requires only a less powerful computer capable of running DOS.

Representative requirements of particular revision levels of three typical authoring systems follow. You should treat these lists as examples only. In particular, successive versions of the same product tend to require faster computers, more memory, and lots more disk space. You might make a practice of reading and comparing requirements lists that manufacturers print on boxes that contain software products. It is important to realize that such lists give the products' absolute minimum hardware requirements, in order to encourage potential purchasers. Very often, a product will work significantly better with a faster processor or more disk space than the list specifies.

IBM LinkWay Live! Version 1.02 requires at least the following:

- IBM Personal System/1 or IBM Personal System/2
- 80286 microprocessor
- 2 MB of RAM
- 20 MB disk and extra for video or other digitized media as required
- IBM Personal System/2 monitor

- IBM mouse (or compatible mouse)
- Appropriate multimedia devices (depending on what media you want to create or play back)

Asymetrix Multimedia ToolBook Version 3.0 requires at least the following:.

- Personal computer with 80386 processor and mouse
- 6 MB of RAM, preferably 8 MB
- 15 to 20 MB of free disk space and extra for video or other digitized media as required
- VGA, S-VGA, or other Windows-compatible display adapter and display screen (monitor)
- Appropriate multimedia devices (depending on what media you want to create or play back)

HyperStudio 2.0 requires at least the following to run on a Macintosh computer:

- Apple Macintosh computer and mouse
- 4 MB of RAM with System 7, 1 MB of RAM with System 6
- 7 or 8 MB free disk space and extra for video or other digitized media as required
- Macintosh-compatible color display screen (monitor)
- Appropriate multimedia devices (depending on what media you want to create or play back)

Like an authoring system, each piece of commercial multimedia content has its own hardware requirements. Some commercial titles specify unique requirements; others use a form of industry standard such as the multimedia personal computer standards MPC or MPC2, which Figure 2-4 shows.

For example, "From Alice to Ocean - Alone Across the Outback" comes on a single CD-ROM that contains two versions with very different hardware requirements. One version runs on a Macintosh that at least meets the following requirements:

- Macintosh LC
- 4 MB of RAM
- System software version 6.0.7 (version 7.0 recommended)
- QuickTime
- 13-inch color display screen (monitor)
- Apple CD-ROM drive or equivalent

The other version runs on a Intel-based personal computer that has at least the following capabilities:

- 80386 microprocessor running at 33 MHz
- 4 MB of RAM, 8 MB recommended
- MS-DOS version 3.1 or later and Windows versions 3.1 or later
- S-VGA display adapter card with 640 x 480 x 256 colors
- Microsoft Windows-compatible digital audio card (or use sound available at the CD-ROM drive's analog audio output connection)
- Speakers or headphone
- Windows-supported mouse or other pointing device
- CD-ROM drive with maximum access time of 300 milliseconds and minimum data transfer rate of 150 KBps

Many pieces of multimedia content specify that they will run on any computer that carries the MPC2 logo. Such a computer meets or exceeds the standard that Figure 2-4 shows.

- A 486 SX computer running at 25 MHz
- 8 MB main memory (RAM) configured as extended memory
- 160 MB disk (hard drive) capacity and 1.44 MB 3.5 inch diskette drive
- 101-key IBM keyboard
- Serial interface (9-pin or 25-pin), programmable up to 9600 bps, selectable without interrupts
- Parallel interface (25-pin)
- Display adapter and display screen with either 640 x 480 pixel resolution and 65,536 colors or 800 x 600 pixel resolution and 16 colors
- CD-ROM drive with 300 KBps sustained transfer rate and an average seek time of 400 milliseconds, CD-ROM XA ready and with multisession capability
- Mouse (2 button)
- Analog joystick port (IBM-compatible)
- MIDI port
- MPC compatible audio card with 16-bit digital sound, 8-note synthesizer with stereo channels, MIDI playback, and 20.05 KHz sampling rate (44.1 KHz recommended)
- Amplified speakers

Figure 2-4: MPC2 requirements

The bad news is that the above list of MPC2 requirements is longer and more complicated than the list of requirements for most multimedia authoring systems or titles. The good news is that if students have access to an MPC2 computer and see that a piece of software or a title specifies that it will work with an MPC2 computer, then they need not concern themselves with the list.

The trouble maker in any list of hardware requirements is the phrase "at least." This phrase implies that readers can compare different capabilities. In some cases this is a simple matter of arithmetic, such as noting that a 486 processor is better than a 386 and 8 MB of memory is better than 4 MB. In other cases, words give a hint. It is reasonably clear that a Super-VGA (S-VGA) display adapter is better than a VGA adapter. However, there is no way to tell from the words that a VESA display adapter is about as good as an S-VGA adapter or that a Pentium is better than a 486.

The MPC3 specification differs from the above MPC2 specification in two important ways. As Figure 2-5 shows, MPC3 not only specifies a larger capacity or speed for several entries, it also specifies a minimum requirement for playing back digital video.

- A Pentium or equivalent computer running at 75 MHz
- 8 MB main memory (RAM) configured as extended memory
- 540 MB disk capacity
- CD-ROM drive with 600 KBps sustained transfer rate and an average seek time of 250 milliseconds
- MPC compatible audio card with 16-bit digital sound, MIDI playback, and wave-table synthesis
- Video playback using MPEG1 hardware or software at 30 frames per second, 352 by 240 pixel resolution, and 15 bits per pixel

---

Figure 2-5: MPC3 requirements

Pick a piece of multimedia content that is available to run on both Intel and Macintosh platforms. Find out the details of the hardware requirements for your selected piece of multimedia. Here are some suggestions of content that are available on both Macintosh and Intel-based computers.

- "Microsoft's Encarta '95" is a multimedia, general-purpose encyclopedia.
- "Microsoft Art Gallery" is an encyclopedia of over 2000 masterpieces.
- "Microsoft Creative Writer" is both a writing program and desktop publishing program. It contains tools and ideas with which students age 8 and up can create projects that include writing, images, and audio.

Obtaining such a list of hardware requirements is half of what is necessary to decide whether a given authoring system or multimedia title will run on available hardware. The other half is determining the capabilities of a given hardware setup, as the next section describes.

Determining What Is Available

Hopefully, you will have some computers available that have multimedia capabilities of one form or another. For this activity, determine what is available, prepare diagrams and labels focusing on what is relevant for multimedia, and finally update the media and functions table, Table 2-2, with specific information.

It is not always easy to determine the capabilities of a given computer. One natural approach is to see what input and output jacks the computer provides. For example, suppose that a computer has a jack labeled Video In. You could visualize plugging a cable between a VCR's Video Out jack and the computer's Video In jack and conclude that the computer can either capture digital video or else play analog video in a window on the screen. This promising approach has three little drawbacks.

- There may be no label near the jack. Many computers' jacks that have different functions look identical. The jack may even be a video output jack that you can connect to a television monitor to display analog video.

- Even if the jack is labeled Video In, you need to know what type of adapter card holds the jack, in order to tell whether the jack enables you to capture digital video or play analog video in a window. If the jack has no label, you need to know the type of card in order to find a manual and look up the jack's identity.

- The adapter card itself may not be labeled. Even if you take the computer apart, pull out the card, and look at it under a magnifying glass, you my not be able to tell what function it performs or even what manual to look for.

Because of these drawbacks, by far the best way to identify what a computer can do may be to ask somebody who knows exactly what is in the computer. Ask a previous user, a sales clerk, or a computer guru who recognizes every adapter card by sight. Then label every adapter card and every jack by writing names or functions on transparent tape, adhesive tape, or masking tape. It is also useful to label the diskette drives and CD-ROM drives in the same way. It is important to keep such labels up to date when hardware or software changes, as an aid to changing the computer's configuration or replacing a wire that comes off.

As part of the same activity, it is useful to draw and post a diagram of the computer's configuration along with the configuration of any attached apparatus such as television sets or VCRs. Figure 2-1 has a suitable form for such a diagram. Your diagram of an actual setup could label each connection to tell what sort of signal the connection carries. For practice, you could label the thick arrows that represent external connections. You could identify three analog audio signals, two analog video signals, and one digital control signal. The remaining thick arrow, from the scanner to its unique adapter, is more closely related to analog video than to any other sort of signal but it need not adhere to any video standard. Power connections may be labeled on the computer, but usually need not appear on a diagram. In general, many important connections outside the computer are analog, even though most of the connections to the bus and processor inside the computer are digital. It is important to distinguish a diagram that shows all possible connections from a diagram that shows the particular connections for one project. For example, Figure 2-1 shows both the digital audio card's output and the CD-ROM drive's output connected to the speakers. However, a diagram for a particular setup would show only one or the other of these two possible connections.

Although such a diagram shows a computer's components, a media and functions table such as Table 2-2 is useful for emphasizing the components' purposes. Instead of using generic function names, as in Table 2-2, your table could show names and locations of actual products. In case your school has only one computer that is attached to a scanner, for example, a media and functions table could give the number of the room that contains that computer.

Summary

Your students require particular hardware to convert each of the five media from analog form to digital form. Once they have a medium in digital form, they can create projects that copy it, manipulate it, and display it in ways that were impossible in the original analog form. Displaying each medium, too, requires particular hardware to convert the digital form back to analog form. Considering separately the hardware that each medium employs helps keep complexity within acceptable levels. Categorizing each function as input, storage, or output also helps keep different pieces of hardware straight.

In most cases, you and your students can start creating good projects without knowing many details about multimedia hardware. You will need to understand some details to help your students to find appropriate computers, to use each medium more effectively, to solve problems as they arise, and to decide what hardware to obtain and what projects to create in the future. In a typical school, the most important details are the ones that will help your students to make the best possible use of the wide variety of available computers that span several generations of hardware. This book provides a wide variety of suggestions for using multimedia hardware and software to create outstanding projects.

References

Benchley, Peter. *Jaws*. New York, New York: Fawcett Crest, 1974.

Multimedia Marketing Council, 1730 M Street NW, Suite 707, Washington, DC 20036-4510, telephone (203) 331-0494. This council has information about MPC.

Chapter 3

Multimedia Software Tools

In this chapter, we explore:

- the most important types of multimedia software tools that your students can use to create multimedia projects.

- some specific examples of tools that will help you become familiar with such software.

- general information that will help you understand and adapt to whatever multimedia software environments are available in your school.

- terminology that will make it easier for you and your students to ask questions and understand answers.

In the Background section, we introduce software layer charts to provide a context for authoring systems and individual multimedia software tools. We discuss when and how you might select software to fill the layers, and we give examples of software layers for two types of computers. In the Theory section, we discuss software tools' characteristics, similarities, and differences. In the Practice section, we suggest activities that will help you use the theory to select software, to learn to use software, and, in general, to help your students learn to use software to create multimedia projects.

Background

Multimedia software tools are computer programs that students and others use to create multimedia projects. These tools can not only help your students express their ideas using some or all of text, images, graphics, audio, and video, but also help your students link these media together into a well-organized, coherent, and complete project. You and your students will almost certainly start by using an authoring system. An authoring system is a single software product combining several tools that work together smoothly and perform many useful functions easily. Some of the many authoring systems are Asymetrix Multimedia ToolBook, IBM LinkWay Live!, Macromedia's Director, HyperStudio, and HyperCard. There are many individual multimedia software tools that you can use to extend the functions of various authoring systems.

Multimedia software is improving rapidly. Schools will continue to use a wide range of different software. For these two reasons, you can not expect to learn about one set of multimedia software and apply that static knowledge throughout your career. Instead, we suggest that you learn to use whatever multimedia software you have available, cement what you learned by creating as many projects as possible, and use this chapter's material to see where your learning fits within the wider spectrum of software that you subsequently select and use in classrooms.

Software Layers

Selecting software to perform particular functions is a key to computer literacy. Selecting multimedia software is like ordering a five-course restaurant meal where you select an appetizer, a salad, a soup, a main course, and a dessert. You would not have a full meal if you left out the soup. You would not have a full meal if you ordered only five salads. Each course corresponds to one software layer in Figure 3-1.

There is an excellent reason for showing software layers as blocks stacked one on top of another, in a particular order, and all stacked on top of the hardware layer. Just as the hardware layer supports all the software layers, each software layer supports the layers above it. Just as the software uses the hardware, each software layer uses the layers below it. Someone must select appropriate software for each layer. It might be you.

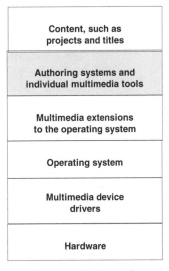

Figure 3-1: Generic software layer chart

This chapter concentrates on helping you select what to put in the shaded layer of Figure 3-1, which contains authoring systems and individual multimedia tools. This layer supports the top layer, in which you put multimedia content. As we discuss in the next chapter, multimedia content includes the projects that your students create, commercial multimedia titles and clips, and templates, which are a special sort of projects. The authoring systems and multimedia tools layer, in turn, uses the layer that contains multimedia extensions to the operating system, which uses the layer that contains the operating system, which uses multimedia device drivers, which control hardware.

Eventually, you and your students will want to select an authoring system and additional multimedia tools. However, creating multimedia projects is a lot more educational and a lot more fun than selecting multimedia software. How soon you must start selecting software, and which layers you must select, depends strongly on what you have available in your school. Some typical cases follow.

- If your school is already involved in multimedia, you are likely to find a fully configured multimedia system that contains software in all layers, including some sample projects in the top layer. If this is the case, you need not worry about selecting software until you have taken the available authoring system's tutorial and then created some small projects of your own. That experience, together with what you learn in this chapter, will enable you to decide whether you want to continue using the same authoring system or want to select different or additional software.

- If you are the first person in your school who has become involved in multimedia, you are nevertheless likely to find that your school has a recent generation multimedia computer, as we discussed in Chapter 2. Such a computer already contains all the software layers up to and including multimedia extensions to the operating system. In this case, we recommend that you select an authoring system that runs on the best available computer, and proceed to take that authoring system's tutorial, as in the preceding case.

- If your school's available computers do not include any recent multimedia computers, we strongly recommend that you obtain a multimedia computer. You will probably need to add an authoring system. Then you can continue as in the preceding case.

- If you cannot find or obtain a multimedia computer, you can upgrade the best available computer by adding multimedia hardware and software. You will need to add at least a digital audio adapter and a CD-ROM drive, and you may also need to replace the existing display adapter with one that supports more colors. You will need to select an operating system, add the appropriate multimedia extensions, and select the device drivers that tell the operating system how to control the particular multimedia hardware that you added. We do not recommend that you try selecting and installing these lowest software layers, for the first time, starting one week before the beginning of a term!

- If you cannot manage any of the above cases, for goodness sake get an authoring system that will run on some available computer. Then try creating a few simple projects that include graphics, clip-art images, and hypertext links. If experience is any guide, you will find the results so compelling that you will never rest until you are up to your ears in multimedia computers with which you can capture your own images, audio, and video.

Although the layer chart will help you avoid selecting a soup for the salad course, you must take the layer chart with a grain of salt. Looking at the chart, you would think that you could slip out a computer's existing authoring system, slip in any other authoring system, and be sure that the computer would still work. This is not true. Different authoring systems require different amounts of memory and other resources. Even more significantly of course, as we noted in Chapter 2, there are two incompatible types of hardware: Apple's Macintosh and the family of Intel-based computers. In general, before selecting a software product to go in any layer, you must check that the product runs on the type of hardware that you have available and is compatible with lower software layers. For example, on Intel-based computers, you must check whether a product requires a specific version of Microsoft Windows, rather than merely DOS, in the operating system layer. A few multimedia titles are sufficiently intelligent to adapt to the type of computer on which they find themselves running. A few multimedia authoring system products exist in multiple forms. In general, you must check whether each software product that you are considering will work on your computer. The next section gives some relevant examples and illustrates why software exists in layers.

Examples of Multimedia Software Layers

Figure 3-2 and Figure 3-3 are layer charts that show examples of software that you may select for the two major types of computers. Many excellent possibilities exist in addition to the ones that these figures illustrate.

QuickTime is a fundamental multimedia extension to the Macintosh operating system. QuickTime supports playing and synchronizing media that you select with an authoring system or with other multimedia tools. Almost all current Macintosh multimedia software tools and content work with QuickTime. You can even create QuickTime video on a Macintosh and then use QuickTime for Windows to play the video on an Intel-based computer.

The device drivers tell the operating system how to control specific hardware adapters for recording audio and video. If the device drivers layer did not exist, then your computer's operating system would have to contain separate code for controlling every existing type of adapter. Whenever a hardware vendor announced a new type of adapter with different controls,

Content
HyperCard, HyperStudio, Macromedia Director, Premiere, Photoshop
QuickTime
System 7   MacOS
Device Drivers for MacRecorder and VideoSpigot
Apple Macintosh hardware

Content
Asymetrix Multimedia Toolbook, Linkway Live!
Microsoft Multimedia Extensions for Windows (MCI, AVI), Video for Windows
Microsoft Windows
Device Drivers for SoundBlaster and Intel Smart Video Recorder
Hardware

Figure 3-2: Examples of Macintosh software layers

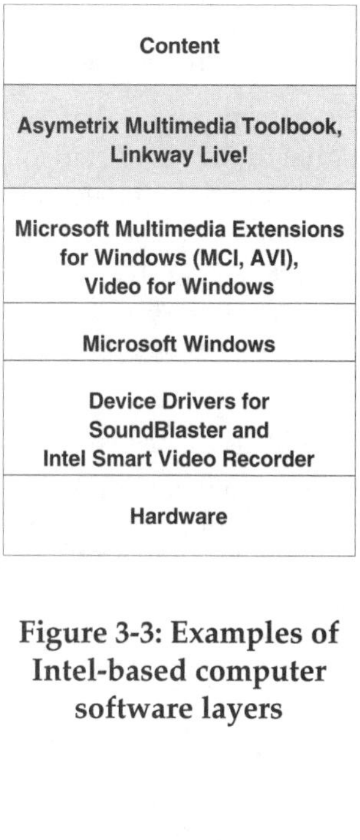

Figure 3-3: Examples of Intel-based computer software layers

the software vendor would have to release a new version of the operating system that contained code for controlling the new adapter. This would require you to reinstall the entire operating system.

Because the device drivers layer does exist, the operating system can use exactly the same code to control all device drivers, and the device drivers contain the unique code that controls particular devices. Figure 3-1's horizontal line separating the operating system layer from the device drivers layer represents the standardized interface that the operating system uses to control all devices. This illustrates what is important to you in a software layer chart. Each horizontal line represents a more or less standard interface that allows you more or less flexibility in selecting what to put in the layers above and below the interface.

When you buy a hardware adapter, you usually receive the necessary device driver software on an accompanying diskette, along with instructions on how to install both the hardware and the software. The diskette may also contain some sample multimedia content that uses the hardware adapter and its device driver.

There are several multimedia tools that you can use to capture or create graphics, images, and audio on Macintosh computers. If desired, you can then convert these captured and digitized Macintosh files to a format that you can use with multimedia tools on an Intel-based computer. We do not particularly recommend doing this, because dealing with several types of computers always adds complexity. However, it is not at all uncommon for people to create some of their media on one type of computer and then use it on another.

It is worth noting that you would need to obtain different device drivers for the same digital audio and video adapters if you replaced Microsoft Windows by another operating system, such as DOS or OS/2. When you buy an adapter for an Intel-based computer, you may get several diskettes with several different sets of device drivers for different operating systems. When you buy a new version of an operating system, you often get new device drivers for common hardware adapters. You also get suggestions that you contact the vendors of less common adapters to get corresponding device drivers.

Note also that Microsoft shipped the multimedia extensions for Windows separately from version 3 because relatively few customers wanted the extensions, but the company started shipping most extensions as part of version 3.1 as the functions became more popular. This illustrates the fact that a particular software product may contain software that goes in two or more different layers. This need not affect how you install the software, but it does help you understand the software.

Authoring Systems

In the remainder of this Background section, we discuss properties that typical authoring systems have in common and some software tools that you may need in addition to your authoring system. Then the Theory section discusses the many properties that distinguish different authoring systems and multimedia tools from one another. It is those differences that you will need to consider when you select software tools.

The only effective way to learn about multimedia authoring systems and other tools is to learn to use one authoring system and then learn the similarities and differences of other authoring systems and of specialized multimedia tools. You may find that it does not even pay to read the rest of this chapter until after you have spent an hour working through some authoring system's tutorial.

It is remarkably difficult to visualize using any authoring system until you have used one, and remarkably easy to do so thereafter. It may take five minutes to read words that tell how to use an authoring system to perform a function, even though you can actually perform the function with a few mouse clicks in five seconds. Your mind will never remember the words you read, but your fingers will never forget the clicks. Explaining that you create a button by selecting a particular sequence of buttons may sound hopelessly confusing, but confusion evaporates the first time you actually use an authoring system to perform the function.

A typical authoring system extends the concept of a draw program, with which you create graphics. Using a draw program, you may select a tool shaped like a box in order to place a box on the computer screen. You may select other tools to make circles, lines, and text as you build up·a complete graphic. At any time, you can select a box or any other object on the screen and move it, change its shape, or fill it with a different color. Because you can change the box as a whole, rather than merely changing its individual pixels, the box acts as a complete object. Creating and editing graphic objects is a good start toward an authoring system.

Using an authoring system, you can select tools to make not only box, circle, line, and text objects but also media objects and button objects. Some of the important objects that you can make with an authoring system are as follows.

- An image media object that shows any picture, such as an image that you painted with a paint program or an image that you scanned or captured from a single frame of video.

- A text pop-up button that makes text appear when a user selects the button. One excellent use of a pop-up button is text that provides further explanation, which only some users will require. A user may scroll a large amount of text up or down in a small pop-up box. An authoring system usually allows you to either type the text directly into the pop-up box or import the text from a word processor. You may also be able to copy text from another piece of multimedia content and paste the text into a project, or drag selected text and drop it into a project.

- An audio button object, perhaps shaped like an ear or a speaker, that plays a digital recording of your voice, or of any other sound that you specify, when a user selects the button.

- A laser disc control button that tells a laser disc player to find a specified frame, start playing video and audio, and stop when it reaches another specified frame.
- A button that a user selects to see video that you captured from analog video or created with an animation program.
- Several buttons that link from the present screen to other screens.

All but the last sort of button help you to make each individual screen meaningful, interesting, and dynamic. You use the last sort of button to provide ways for a user to navigate through the many screens that make up your multimedia project. Some buttons may be invisible, so that even when the user selects a plain area of the screen, a response takes place. Other buttons have particular appearances, such as rectangles that seem to depress when a user selects them. You use the authoring system to make buttons, determine what buttons look like, and determine what happens when a user selects a button.

Authoring systems provide many useful facilities that help creators to form a complete and coherent project. Authoring systems allow you to introduce background objects that will be constant from one screen to another, as well as foreground objects that change with each new screen, superimposed on the same background. Setting up a background avoids the repetitive work of placing common objects on several different screens. Perhaps more important, using a background assures consistency across several screens. For example, you may place on the background a button that returns a user back to your project's first screen. Seeing exactly the same RETURN button on each screen helps prevent users from ever feeling lost in hypermedia.

Authoring systems tend to be particularly adept at synchronizing different media, even in cases where a creator used individual tools to create the different media. Synchronization is a key part of assembling several media to form a coherent screen or project. For example, suppose your students interviewed several people, digitized audio of the interviews, and captured images of the people's faces. An authoring system provides a method for your students to synchronize showing a given face on the computer screen with playing the corresponding interview. As we note in this chapter's section on Icons and Scripts, the specific method depends on the authoring system.

One of the most attractive features of an authoring system is that when you create an image object, a button, or any other object, you can change from being a creator to being a user and see the object's results immediately. For example, create a text pop-up button, select the button, and the text pops up. Create a laser disc control button, select the button, and enjoy the video clip. Using an authoring system provides one of life's few examples of continual instant gratification. This is one of the many reasons why creating a multimedia project is significantly more interesting and educational for the creator than using the project is for a user.

Additional Multimedia Software Tools

Most authoring systems emphasize assembling several media to create complete projects. However, you may need to augment your authoring system so that your students can perform particular functions on particular media. You may need to obtain additional software tools to perform such functions as removing a coughing fit from a digital audio recording, increasing the brightness of an image, creating an animation, capturing and compressing some video, or erasing the mustache from a scanned image of the school principal.

In general, you use an authoring system to fill some of the boxes in a media and functions table, and you require additional software tools to fill other boxes. Table 3-1 shows some typical types of programs that perform several important functions on each of the media.

You will note that many of the table's boxes contain important and familiar programs. Some examples follow.

- You use a word processor to perform the functions of originating and editing the medium of text. Thus "word processor" appears in the first and last rows of the table's first column.

- You use a draw program to originate and edit graphics.

- A paint program covers at least the function of originating images.

- Some but not all paint programs also allow you to edit and enhance an image by changing brightness and contrast, applying fascinating special effects, and rearranging parts of the image.

- An animation program helps you originate one sort of digital video. Such a program creates a sequence of images that contain small successive changes, so that playing the images rapidly gives the illusion of motion.

- Completely separate software tools help you create another sort of digital video by digitizing an analog video signal that comes from a video camera or VCR.

- Related software helps you capture an image by scanning a photograph or converting a computer screen to a file.

- Still other software allows you to control a laser disc player or a CD-ROM player, or digitize an analog audio signal.

Although it is useful to think about each example in such a list, there are expository and pedagogical reasons for you and your students to use a media and functions table to organize this information. As exposition, the table's seven functions and five media are easier to comprehend than would be an unorganized list of 35 examples. You can read a column in the table to see what sorts of software you would need in order to add a medium, such as video, to your repertoire. You can read a row to see what performing a given function, such as capture, requires for different media.

Table 3-1: Media and functions for software

Media Functions	Text	Graphics	Images	Audio	Video
Originate	Word-processor	Draw program	Paint program	Synthesizer program	Animation program
Capture from analog to digital	Optical character recognition; Speech-to-text	-	Scanner control; Screen capture	Audio capture software	Video capture software
Control playback device	Text-to-speech	-	-	CD-ROM drive	Laser disc player; CD-ROM
Import or convert file types	TXT, ASCII, word-processor files	-	Many tools	Several tools	Several tools, e.g., Cinepak to Indeo
Compress; decompress	Several tools	-	Many tools	Special tools	Cinepak; Indeo; MPEG; JPEG
Library management	-	-	Slide box to show clips	Describe audio clips	Sample scenes
Edit, enhance, or reorder	Word-processor	Draw program	Paint program	Special effects, e.g., echo	Video editor

Pedagogically, the table makes important distinctions clear, such as the distinctions between originating a medium directly on a computer, capturing the medium from somewhere in the outside analog world, or importing the medium as an individual computer file. These distinctions would be only moderately interesting if they applied to only one medium. The way they apply to all media makes them important.

Another pedagogical advantage of such a table is that it invites you and your students to think about filling in unfamiliar boxes. For example, consider what it means to capture text from the outside world. Although this function would be easy to overlook in an unorganized list, it turns out that two well-known types of software tools fit in the box for capturing text. If your students want to use several pages of printed words in a project, they should consider scanning in the pages and then using an optical character recognition (OCR) program to convert the resulting images into digital text. They could, of course, use the images of the text. However, using actual text will almost certainly make the result easier to read and will certainly make it easier for the students to change the font or edit the information. Ultimately, your students may have the opportunity to capture text from spoken words by using speech-to-text software, as well as from printed words using OCR software. Your students' use of such tables need not be limited to classrooms. Noting empty boxes in a media and functions table once helped two of the authors to assure that we were creating a complete multimedia strategy for a major corporation.

Two disadvantages of learning and teaching such a table deserve mention. First, the sizes of the table's boxes give no hint of the importance of what the boxes contain, whereas a list of examples could have longer entries for more important items. For example, synthesizing sound, by creating a waveform from scratch, is far less common than digitizing an analog sound wave. Second, the table looks misleadingly complete. In fact, as you work with multimedia software, you may find several more functions that deserve rows.

Why does a typical authoring system leave some boxes in the media and functions table empty? Because potential purchasers do not need software that performs all functions on all media and do not want to pay for or install unnecessary software. We next discuss typical cases where you may want to augment your authoring system with additional multimedia software tools that fill additional entries in your media and functions table. We discuss paint programs, programs for originating animations, and programs for capturing video.

Originating and Editing Images

Although LinkWay Live! includes a paint program, Multimedia ToolBook does not. The reason illustrates these two authoring systems' different philosophies. On the one hand, LinkWay Live! runs directly on DOS. This allows LinkWay Live! to run on a computer that has significantly less memory than is required to run Microsoft Windows. This minimizes the costs of the hardware and operating system software that you need to run LinkWay Live! On the other hand, Multimedia ToolBook runs on Windows. This gives the advantages of Windows' powerful and familiar user interface and also facilitates using ToolBook in conjunction with other Windows programs. In particular, ToolBook did not need to include a paint program because Microsoft Windows Paintbrush is a paint program accessory that comes with every copy of Windows. Because LinkWay Live! authors may not have access to Microsoft Windows Paintbrush, the LinkWay Live! authoring system includes a tool called LwPaint.

Neither LwPaint nor Microsoft Windows Paintbrush provides sophisticated functions for touching up an image that you captured from a photograph or adding special effects to an image that you painted. Rainbow Paint, PC Paintbrush, Paint Shop Pro, and Adobe PhotoShop are some of many paint programs that provide such functions.

Originating Animations

You originate an animation either by painting one image at a time or by letting a computer program help you paint successive images. In this context, each image is called a frame. To show reasonably smooth motion, you need to show at least 15 frames for each second that the animation will play. You need to show 30 frames per second for really smooth animation. Thus, unless you can afford a room full of artists, you need a software tool to help paint the frames. Such a tool may be part of an authoring system or may be an additional tool.

Most authoring systems include a simple recorder tool that you can use to originate the successive frames that make up an animation. For example, you can use a paint program to make an image of an aquarium containing water and fronds of seaweed. You use the paint program to make an image of a fish, which retains its identity as a separate object. You place the fishy object near the left side of the aquarium, facing to the right. You invoke the authoring system's recorder tool. The tool prepares to record whatever steps you take next, so that the tool can repeat the same steps later. Your next steps are to drag the fish about one fifteenth of the way across the aquarium, pause, drag the fish the same amount again, pause, and so on until the fish is near the right side of the aquarium. Then you tell the recorder tool to stop recording and try out what you created. With any luck, the authoring system will show a reasonably smooth swim.

Animation programs that you can add to your authoring system provide more sophisticated tools for originating animations. Many creators use Autodesk's animation programs named Animator, Animator Pro, Animator Studio, and 3-D Studio. These programs produce FLI or FLC files, which many authoring systems accept. Animator is part of an economical package called Multimedia Explorer. Multimedia Explorer runs on DOS and includes a program with which you can play animations on Windows. Animator and the more sophisticated Animator Pro are two-dimensional animations tools. 3D-Studio has tools that help you draw realistic three-dimensional objects and then rotate or move these objects to create animations.

Although entertainment people invented animations for cartoons, students can make good use of animation to:

- explain processes in a wide variety of subjects,
- create attention grabbers,
- clarify complex concepts, and
- create video of something that does not exist or at which it is impossible to point a video camera.

For example, Figure 3-4 shows two frames from an animation that uses a cutaway view of the earth to explain and clarify the carbon cycle process. This process strongly affects earth's climate. Between the left and right frames, more carbon dioxide in the atmosphere has reflected more heat back to the earth and has partially melted a glacier. With some patience, students can easily originate such an animation using paint and recorder tools.

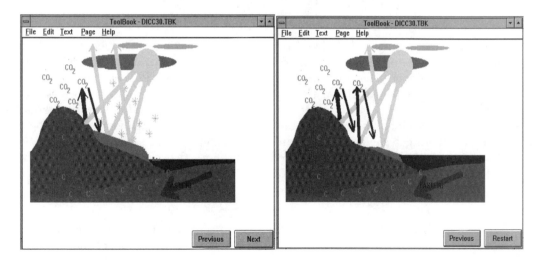

Figure 3-4: Two animation frames

A morphing tool is another sort of animation tool. For example, a morphing tool allows you to create a video that seems to show the face of a person change gradually into the face of a cat. You start with an image of the person and an image of the cat. You identify corresponding points on the two images, such as the inside corners of the respective faces' left eyes. Then you tell the program to paint intermediate frames that represent the gradual change. Another example is to morph a large glacier into a small glacier without painting all the intermediate frames.

Figure 3-5 shows a screen that you might see when using Microsoft Windows to play media. Media Player is a standard accessory that comes with Windows. It offers to play a half-dozen different options. The first option, Autodesk, plays animations from that company's animation programs. The second option, Video for Windows, applies to the other sort of video, which we discuss next.

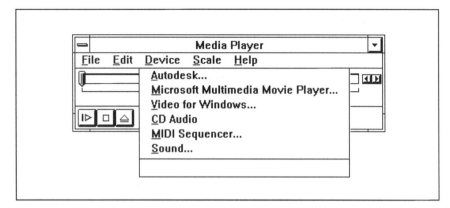

Figure 3-5: A Media Player screen

Capturing and Editing Video

Capturing and editing digital video are examples of functions for which you can expect to require separate software tools, in addition to tools that your authoring system includes. Developers of an authoring system could not possibly keep up with the flood of increasingly powerful digital video programs. Even if they could do so, you would not want to pay the price of an authoring system that supported dozens of alternative types of digital video, especially if you did not want to use such video at all. The best that an authoring system developer can do is to accept a wide selection of the file types that existing digital video programs produce and hope that new digital video programs will either produce these file types or will include programs that convert the files that they do produce into these file types.

Figure 3-6 shows a typical screen that you would see while using Video for Windows, which is a product that runs under Microsoft Windows. This product contains tools that you can use to capture and edit video. To produce this figure, we selected the VidCap icon. The VidCap tool captures analog video, producing a digital video file. As soon as you start capturing video, the window shows what you are capturing. Video for Windows contains other tools, as well. For example, selecting the VidEdit icon would bring up the video editing tool's corresponding screen.

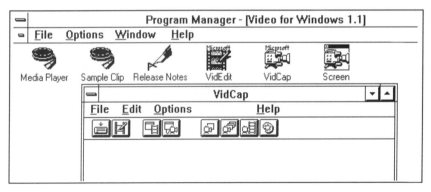

Figure 3-6: Video Capture tool's screen

Figure 3-7 shows another typical Video for Windows screen. It offers you a half-dozen different algorithms for compressing the video that you are about to capture. Using the vertical scroll bar shows still more algorithms. It is important to select an algorithm that produces a file type that your authoring system can use.

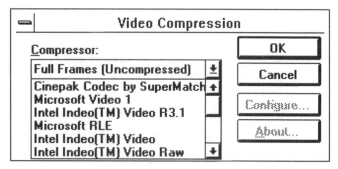

Figure 3-7: Choice of video compression techniques

Relating Authoring Systems to Additional Tools

In extreme cases, you may find that your authoring system almost disappears under a heap of separate programs that perform particular functions on particular media. Many professional producers of commercial multimedia content chose this approach, because they have already invested thousands of dollars in outstanding and expensive individual tools and because they have already invested years of effort in becoming expert at using those particular tools. Professionals may use their separate tools for creating and manipulating the desired media and then use a programming language such as C or C++ to tie the media together into a complete creation. This approach may produce the fastest running and most compact multimedia content. This approach may even produce greatest ease of use, after years of practice. However, this approach most surely does not optimize ease of learning. Thus, an academic environment tends to rely heavily on an authoring system.

When you find that you must supplement your authoring system's tools with additional individual tools, you must be certain that the authoring system and the additional tools either handle the same media formats or come with tools to convert back and forth between incompatible formats. Fortunately, most authoring systems routinely support many different formats for digitized media, particularly for images and video. In general, you will want to use tools that are part of an authoring system as much as possible, and use individual tools only when necessary. This is the easiest way to ensure that your tools have similar user interfaces and produce compatible file formats.

In the following Theory section, we discuss differences that may help you decide which authoring system and additional multimedia tools you will select to fill the corresponding layer in your software layer chart.

Theory

Any authoring system helps you create several different media and assemble separate media into a coherent piece of multimedia content. Despite having that in common, different authoring systems can:

- use completely different vocabularies, even for identical concepts,
- appear remarkably different on a computer screen,
- perform similar functions in completely different ways,
- concentrate on performing only particular functions on particular media,
- emphasize different sorts of multimedia content,
- emphasize either ease of learning or ease of use, at the expense of the other,
- have very different prices, and
- require enormously different amounts of hardware such as disk space and memory.

This section discusses a wide variety of differences among different multimedia software products, mainly authoring systems, but also including additional tools where relevant. You probably do not need to understand each difference in full detail. However, to ensure that your students will meet your objectives by creating multimedia projects, you do need to understand which differences are important in your environment.

Price and Intended Creators

Authoring system prices can range from zero, for freeware, to several thousand dollars, for professional versions. Most schools use authoring systems that cost between $100 and $300. We have visited many schools across the country and have seen schools using a wide range of authoring systems. We found instances where students were making effective use of authoring systems that we had assumed were far too expensive and complex for K-12 use. The schools obtained these authoring systems through donations, grant funding, participating in pilot projects or joint partnerships, or significant educational discounts. Several teachers said that it would be a serious error to think that using such systems was too complex for their students. One forcefully pointed out that even preschoolers know how to use home VCRs and multimedia computers, and that students in early grades have little difficulty writing programs as long as nobody tells them that programming is difficult.

One suggestion is to be innovative in getting the best authoring system you can find. Nevertheless, we suggest that the closer you stick to mainstream multimedia facilities such as QuickTime-based products for Macintosh computers and Video for Windows-based products for Intel-based computers, the more likely you are to help your students achieve long-lived skills.

Moreover, you probably realize that when a supplier places a high price on a piece of software, this does not necessarily mean that the supplier invested a lot of money in high-quality product that is easy to learn and has lots of different functions. The high price might mean only that the supplier feels that the product is too specialized to sell more than a few copies and wants to recover its investment from the price of those few copies.

A relatively new class of software, designed and priced for student use and even for home use, helps children combine (and to a lesser extent create) audio, images, and video. Examples of such authoring systems are Broderbund's Kid Pix and Knowledge Adventure's Magic Theatre. Each costs well under $50.

Economy is by no means the only attribute that makes some authoring systems particularly suitable for use by student creators. Magic Theatre comes in a red and white striped box that appears to have air-popped popcorn spilling over the top. The box also has a window showing the included free microphone that enables children to narrate their own animated videos. Including a microphone recognizes the fact that more home computers are set up for students to play back commercial multimedia titles than are set up for students to create multimedia projects.

Both Magic Theatre and Kid Pix include appropriately illustrated and clearly written manuals. The manuals and the products themselves use a happy combination of words that very young children will like, such as "boom" and "magic," along with words that children will need for other products, such as "save as" and "undo." Better yet, Magic Theatre backs up its claim that children as young as three years can use the product by providing a help facility that requires no reading. The product's audio help facility uses voice to explain any icon to which a child points and clicks the right mouse button. Kid Pix has a small-kids mode that turns off menu items that would allow a young creator to perform advanced functions, such as using an editing box. In a school environment, an on-line help facility is far more useful than a manual, less because students would need to read the manual, than because students would need to find the manual.

For situations where neither help facilities nor manuals suffice, you will need a support group. For this reason, you might try to select an authoring system and related tools that nearby educators and students are already using. Fortunately, an on-line forum brings nearby everybody in the world who shares your interests. Finding a forum on your software product increases the chance that somebody nearby will know how to solve a problem that you run into. Similarly, such a forum gives you more people you can help.

You are likely to have the pleasure of dealing with multimedia that some of your students create at home. You may want to play back their projects in class. You may also want to help your students use images or audio that they created at home, as part of class projects. This is yet another reason for you to become familiar with as many types of authoring systems and programs that convert media back and forth among the formats that different software products use.

One of the authors' correspondents writes as follows. "Students in my high school use Kid Pix all the time to create their multimedia presentations. Our foreign language department likes to use this program because students can easily record their voices and incorporate sound into the program. What our computer lab does is create a worksheet which all teachers using Kid Pix should use when asking their students to create presentations. This includes asking them to make a story board for their project and determine what will go on each screen, what resources they will use for the pictures and who will do the scanning. We have found that this method works well. Hope this helps!" Anna Maria DeMasi Lankes, Portfolio Coordinator, East Syracuse-Minoa High School.

Intended Uses

Particular authoring systems provide enhanced support for creating particular sorts of multimedia content. If you can find a product intended for exactly what you want your students to do, you will find that the product takes care of details and allows your students to concentrate on organization, subject matter, or other academic goals that you select. Of course, introducing special software for a one-time activity may not be a good investment of either your school's money or your students' learning time. In many cases, you might be better advised to use a general-purpose product.

Quest is particularly suitable for creating multimedia training materials. Quest makes it especially easy for creators to present a user with a question and then present the user with responses that are appropriate to the user's answer. Quest automatically creates a student-tracking database that accumulates statistics about what topics each user has completed, what the user's grade was, and how much difficulty the user seemed to have in getting through the material.

Other authoring systems provide optimized support for creating long canned presentations that a user watches without much interaction. Examples of authoring systems optimized for creating presentations are Asymetrix Compel for Intel-based computers and Macromedia's Action! for both Macintoshes and Intel-based computers.

Vocabulary, Metaphor, and Appearance

Although authoring systems have a great deal in common, they hide their similarities under remarkably different vocabularies. This is because each authoring system uses a particular metaphor for its screens. HyperCard uses the metaphor of a stack of index cards, so it calls a screen a card. Multimedia ToolBook uses the metaphor of a book, and IBM's LinkWay Live! uses the metaphor of a folder, so either of these authoring systems calls its screen a page. Macromedia's Director uses the metaphor of a stage scene. Thus, different authoring systems end up using completely different words even when they refer to identical concepts. The next three figures are images of screens that you may see when using the Asymetrix Multimedia ToolBook, LinkWay Live!, and HyperCard authoring systems, respectively.

Figure 3-8 shows a Multimedia ToolBook screen after a creator has made a text field, made a button, and pulled down the menu that will allow the creator to save the result as a book.

Figure 3-9 shows the first screen that you see after you start the LinkWay Live! program. This screen is the first page of a folder named "Main" that comes with the product. You can select the button labeled "Tools" to go from this page to a folder named "Tools" and access the tools that LinkWay Live! provides. You can use the right side of this page to select and open a folder, to continue working on a project.

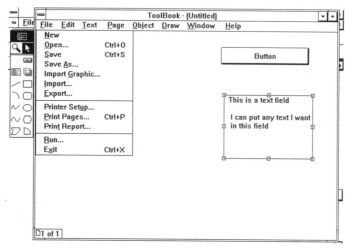

Figure 3-8: Asymetrix Multimedia ToolBook screen

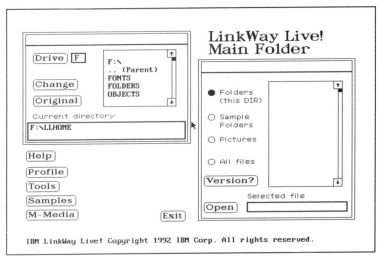

Figure 3-9: LinkWay Live!'s first screen

Figure 3-10 shows the first screen that you see when you start the HyperCard program. It is surrounded by some of the familiar paraphernalia on the Macintosh desktop. A creator uses HyperCard to create screens that represent index cards, to link the cards together, and to organize the cards into a stack.

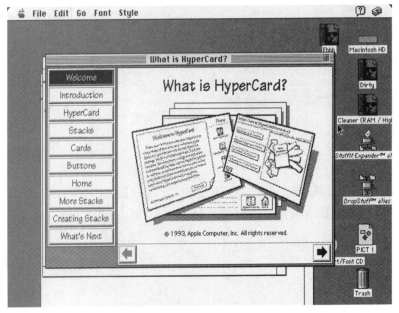

Figure 3-10: HyperCard's first screen

Different Platforms

The authoring systems and individual multimedia software tools that you select will depend strongly on what platforms you have available. That is, your choice will depend on what types of hardware you use and on what operating systems those computers run. No known authoring system runs on all computers with DOS, Microsoft Windows, OS/2, System 7 MacOS, Commodore Amiga OS, and UNIX operating systems.

Macromedia's Director is as universal as any authoring system of which we are aware. It comes in two versions, one for Intel-based computers and one for Macintosh. If you expect your students to employ both types of computers for related projects, you might want to consider having the students use the same authoring system on both types, to facilitate interchange of knowledge and ideas. While it helps to use an authoring system that has versions on both hardware platforms, it is still not true that content produced with one on one platform will run completely unchanged on the other.

In general, authoring systems that run on different types of computers differ in concept, as well as in implementation, to an extent that prevents you from easily porting multimedia content from one type of computer to another. Although you may be able to convert a digital audio file or an image file from a particular Intel-based computer's format to a Macintosh's format, or vice versa, changing a complete multimedia project from one type of computer to another may require that you totally redesign the project. It really pays to pick one type and stick with it. If you plan to create content for other people, it is even more important to know what type of computer they have available and create content that the people will be able to play.

Resource Requirements

Different authoring systems and other software tools may require significantly different amounts of expensive hardware resources. Most obviously, some require more disk space and main store or random access memory (RAM) than others. Those that perform digital video decompression on a computer's main processor, rather than on a special hardware adapter card, require an exceptionally fast main processor.

We have already noted that, although many computers installed in the early 1990s have display adapters and display screens that are capable of showing only 16 different colors at 640 x 480 resolution, you need at least 256 colors to show acceptable images or video of the real world. Some authoring systems such as LinkWay Live! accommodate this fact by using a 640 x 480 mode with 16 colors for reasonably high-resolution graphics and by allowing users to drop into a lower resolution mode, such as 320 x 200, to get 256 colors for natural images. Designers of other tools assumed that anyone who wants natural images has obtained a display adapter and display screen that can provide 256 or more colors at 640 x 480 or higher resolution. Packages that contain the latter sort of tools often say that the tools require S-VGA display adapters.

When selecting among different authoring systems and special tools, you may be able to choose between one that requires minimal hardware resources and one that requires more expensive or more special hardware. Settling for minimal resources reduces your own costs and also allows more people to use the projects that you create. Requiring more resources probably allows you to create more appealing and more useful projects.

Incidental Authoring Systems

You can expect to see traditional computer programs incorporate more and more of the functions of multimedia authoring systems. In the mid-1990s, several major word processors, database programs, and spreadsheet programs accommodate graphics and images. Some such programs are beginning to allow users to include audio and video.

For example, Microsoft's Word for Windows and Word for Macintosh allow you to insert a digital video object into a document, send the document to someone else, and have the recipient play back your video as well as read your text. This assumes that you and the recipient have appropriate multimedia operating system extensions and tools. The recipient can get by with a run-time environment that costs less than the software that you need to create the multimedia document.

Without being the least bit obtrusive about it, Word also provides some simple hypertext capabilities. If you double click the mouse while pointing to a page number in a document's table of contents, Word will show you that page. You can also edit a bookmark into any point in a document and later invoke a link that takes you to the point that you marked. As your students start selecting professional-quality programs, they will expect vendors to feature and improve links and multimedia objects.

Ease of Learning or Ease of Use

Some authoring systems emphasize ease of learning for first-time multimedia creators, whereas other products emphasize ease of use for experienced creators. Ease of learning and ease of use are more different than they may sound. A program that is easy to learn is ideal if you intend to use it for only a few weeks for fairly simple projects, because you want to spend your time using it rather than learning how to use it. A program that is easy to use day in and day out for quickly completing many large projects may require you to spend a great deal of time learning shortcut ways of doing things before you can get started doing anything at all.

Older and more experienced students will need to invest less time in learning such shortcuts, so they may find advanced products easy to learn and also easy to use. Everyone will find badly conceived or clumsily executed products both hard to learn and hard to use.

You have several opportunities to select between emphasizing ease of use or ease of learning. You can guide your decision by considering the extent to which you want your students to spend time up front, learning how to create many projects quickly, as opposed to starting right in using techniques that are more akin to brute force. The extent to which different authoring systems require creators to use scripts rather than manipulating icons may influence your choice. The next sections discuss this point further.

Icons or Scripts

In general, you are likely to find that an authoring system that emphasizes manipulating icons or pull-down menus is particularly easy to learn. Icons are small symbolic pictures or representations, often found in association with point-and-click, drag-and-drop, direct-manipulation, graphical user interfaces. Menu items are words that you click on, instead of clicking on icons.

One respected school of thought maintains that authoring systems that emphasize icons and menu items are also particularly easy to use. For example, Macromedia's Authorware Professional uses icons for playing video (by selecting an icon that looks like a television monitor), inserting video (by selecting two frames of film footage), erasing the screen (by selecting a little eraser), or inserting an animation (by selecting an arrow indicating moving materials). The system shows you, at each step, only icons that you might reasonably select at that step.

A second respected school of thought maintains that you are likely to find that an authoring system that emphasizes typing scripts is particularly easy to use. A script is a program that a creator writes in a particular authoring system's unique programming language. As you become expert in writing scripts, your fingers learn what statements to type in order to perform each function. The idea is that your conscious and creative mind can concentrate on deciding what functions to perform and the part of your mind that wiggles your fingers can handle the details. (The pun is intentional and meaningful.) Work goes quickly because your fingers never leave the keyboard. Some members of this school of thought maintain that no collection of icons can provide as much flexibility as a programming language can provide. They conclude that no authoring system can completely eliminate the need for creators to write an occasional script. Still other members of this school advise using a scripting language to take advantage of previous programming experience.

Some authoring systems combine the best of both schools by allowing you to learn by using icons and then gradually work faster by changing over to typed commands as you become more expert. In one approach, authoring systems provide ways for you to perform all necessary functions by using a mouse to select icons, but also provide keyboard shortcuts for functions that you do over and over, which do not require you to move your hands off the keyboard. This approach is familiar from major word processing programs. In another approach, authoring systems provide icons that allow you to perform all usual functions, but also ensure that even when you use icons you are actually creating hidden scripts. When you need to perform an unusual function, for which there is no icon, you simply use whatever icon comes closest. You reveal the icon's script and then edit that script to perform the unusual function.

The choice between authoring systems in which you manipulate icons and authoring systems in which you write scripts is both a matter of taste and a subject of heated debate between opposing schools of thought. For example, suppose that you want to include a particular sequence of animation files in your multimedia content. If you use Multimedia ToolBook, you will use a keyboard to write a script that lists the names of these files. If you use Authorware Professional, you will use a mouse to drag icons that represent the files into the desired sequence along an icon that represents a timeline. Public contests at conferences have not determined which is easier to learn (at least for people who attend multimedia conferences) or which is easier to use after experts learn to use it. There is some agreement, however, that if you want to synchronize a sequence of animations with a sequence of overlapping audio clips, then creating two parallel timelines with icons is somewhat easier than writing a script with interleaved start times and stop times.

Different Kinds of Scripts

Different authoring systems not only rely on scripting to different extents, they also use different sorts of scripting languages. For example, the Script language, which comes as a part of LinkWay Live!, looks a great deal like a traditional programming language, such as beginners' all-purpose symbolic instruction code, BASIC. In any such language, statements execute in the order that you write them, except when you specify explicit conditional branches, loops, or subroutines. You can include among your statements a conditional branch that goes to different parts of your program depending on whether the user has clicked on a red or a blue button. You can write statements that cause a group of five statements to loop for a specified number of times, such as to play five beeps, or loop until a specified condition becomes true. You can create a set of statements and then give the resulting subroutine a name. If you want to use these statements several times in different parts of your project, you need not retype the statements. Instead, you can just call the subroutine. If you have used a conventional programming language, LinkWay Live!'s Script language will look familiar to you. Otherwise, be assured that you and your students will catch on quickly. You and your students need not learn everything there is to know about programming, in order to create excellent multimedia projects.

As an opposite example, OpenScript, which comes as a part of Multimedia ToolBook, uses the concept of message handlers. For example, a user can initiate a message by pointing to an object and clicking the mouse. ToolBook sends that message to the corresponding object. The object needs a script that tells that particular object how to handle that particular message. This message handler script might tell the object to put text on the screen saying "OK, Chief!" and then send two messages to two other objects. Those second and third objects' message handlers would then perform other actions that the creator decided to have happen when a user clicks on the first object. In a conventional programming language, a programmer would need to make an arbitrary decision about which of the second and third objects' scripts should run first. In

ToolBook, the authoring system takes care of details such as deciding exactly when different scripts run.

Handling messages is one of the most important concepts that distinguish object-oriented programming systems (OOPS) from traditional programming languages. Despite the somewhat accident-prone acronym, OOPS constitute one of the most important ongoing revolutions in computing. Many of your students will benefit later from ToolBook's easy introduction to this concept. For example, a creator can simply click a few times to make a link button that will take a user to a different page. ToolBook writes a corresponding message handler script but does not necessarily display the script. Later, the creator can look at that script, see how it works, and see how to change it to perform other functions. In fact, you could help your students to create several projects without ever seeing a script. Then you could demonstrate how to look at the scripts and use the scripts as a rich source of examples that are easy to modify.

Figure 3-11 shows a typical script in Asymetrix Multimedia ToolBook. When a user releases the mouse button, the user initiates the message called "ButtonUp." The script tells ToolBook to handle this message by showing the user the page identified by the name flower.

```
to handle ButtonUp
go to page flower
end ButtonUp
```

Figure 3-11: A Multimedia ToolBook script example

If a creator needs a script to show a user a page named rose, the creator can use a few mouse clicks to copy this script and paste the script into a new object, and then use the keyboard to change flower to rose. After a few days of using the mouse in this way, a creator may find that it faster to use the keyboard to enter such simple scripts from scratch. This is an example of a natural change from mouse clicks that are easy to learn to keyboard clicks that are easier to use. If a creator prefers to stick with the mouse clicks, that is fine, too. In any case, after the second or third project, your students are likely to want to perform more exotic functions and will become highly adept at finding out how to do those functions.

Apple's HyperCard, which appeared earlier than ToolBook, uses a similar object-oriented script language called HyperTalk. Figure 3-12 shows a HyperTalk script.

```
on MouseUp
go to card id 5130
end MouseUp
```

Figure 3-12: A HyperTalk script example

The difference between the last two figures' sample scripts for HyperCard and Multimedia ToolBook is small. Remember that HyperCard creates metaphorical cards in a stack whereas ToolBook creates metaphorical pages in a book. In other examples, the two scripting languages differ more extensively.

HyperCard supports AppleScript as well as HyperTalk. AppleScript helps you launch and control applications as well as interchange data between HyperCard and other Macintosh applications.

In LinkWay Live!, you perform many functions by using a mouse to select menu items. Figure 3-13 is an example of using menu items to create a button that a user will be able to select in order to go to page 25 in a LinkWay Live! folder named "Corey."

1. Click on the menu item "Object" and then the pull-down menu item "New."
2. Select "Button" to tell LinkWay Live! to place a box on the screen.
3. Move and size the box to put the button where you want it.
4. Click on the selection "Link." The button name window appears.
5. Close the button name window.
6. Select a specific button icon appearance from the choices presented.
7. Fill in the prompts for folder Corey and page 25.

Figure 3-13: A LinkWay Live! procedure example

You have the option to perform the same function by using a script. Figure 3-14 shows the screen you see if you change step 4 in the above procedure. Instead of clicking "Link," we clicked "Button" and a script window appeared. We entered the one-line script shown. After you use the on-line help to see how to write the script, this method is about as fast as responding to prompts. For more complex functions, using a script may be the only way that works.

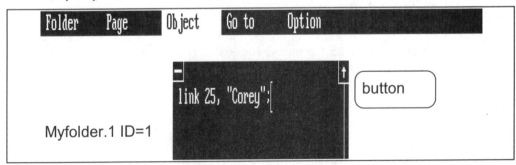

Figure 3-14: A LinkWay Live! script example

There is no reason to fear the concept of scripts. Most authoring systems that emphasize scripts provide icons or pull-down menus for performing routine functions. Scripts are forgiving programming languages that provide instantaneous verification of success or help in diagnosing failure. Your students can learn only what they need to know for any one project. They can learn more techniques gradually by observing, copying and modifying, and experimenting.

Using Programming Languages

Many authoring systems actually allow you to drop out into a general purpose programming language such as C, or into the operating system command language, to perform functions that the developers did not foresee or did not consider sufficiently important to support with shortcuts in the authoring system. For example, LinkWay Live! makes it particularly easy to exit to DOS, run a batch program, and return to running your content. Multimedia ToolBook has particularly good hooks for including C programs in a project, either to extend the authoring system's functions or to replace an existing function by specialized code that runs faster. Teachers find that junior and senior students who are studying computer programming delight in using these new skills in projects, even when the results do not quite justify the effort expended.

Software for Playing Back Content

Helping students create their own multimedia projects is a newer idea than is playing back educational multimedia titles. As a result, you may encounter a computer that has enough multimedia software to play back existing multimedia titles but does not have enough to enable your students to create projects. Similarly, you may find a computer setup that has a digital audio adapter and speakers, but has no microphone. When your students distribute their projects for other people to play, they may not want to assume that the other people have the necessary software. To solve this problem, most authoring systems provide a way for a creator to include what is called a run-time environment along with a creation. Others can use such a run-time environment to play a project, but not to change the project or create their own projects. Thus, you must not assume that a computer that suffices for playing projects also suffices for creating projects.

You may or may not need to concern yourself with multimedia software in order to play other peoples' multimedia content. When you purchase commercial multimedia titles, such as a multimedia encyclopedia, you usually receive whatever special software is necessary to play it. The content's package will tell what general software such as particular versions of DOS, Microsoft Windows, QuickTime, or System 7 that you must supply along with the necessary hardware. When you get multimedia content from another individual, you may or may not get the special software that is necessary to play that content. Some people will expect you to play their content by running a complete version of the same authoring system that they used to create the content. Other creators may provide you with a run-time version of their authoring system that allows you to play their content without having the entire authoring system. Many authoring systems include instructions on how to create a run-time version to accompany your multimedia projects. You may be able to use the complete authoring system to see inside the content, learn how it works, modify it, or even, with the creator's permission, use pieces of it in your own creations. You can not do those functions if all you have is a run-time version of the authoring system.

Practice

The practical part of multimedia software consists of learning to use at least one authoring system, at least well enough to create a simple project, and also learning where your authoring system fits into the spectrum of other multimedia software tools. Although you may not need to know all the details about how your hardware works, especially if someone else set up your computer, you really need to know how to use your software. Moreover, whereas reading about hardware may tell you all you need to know at the outset, the only way to learn about multimedia software is to actually use the software. This applies to you as well as to your students. Just as you would not be comfortable teaching driving if you have never driven a car, you cannot be comfortable teaching multimedia until you yourself have made some multimedia.

Different people, whether in K-12, college, or elsewhere, learn to use a software tool in different ways. Some people like to begin with intensive instruction during which they learn everything they will ever need to know about the tool before they begin creating a project. Other people prefer to start right in creating a project and learn how to perform each function when they find that they need to know it. We suggest that you avoid either extreme by alternating formal instruction, such as using an authoring system's included tutorial, with experimentation, such as creating small throwaway projects.

Making a Media and Functions Table

Table 3-2 is an example of a media and functions table for LinkWay Live!

Table 3-2: Media and functions for LinkWay Live!

Media Functions	Text	Graphics	Images	Audio	Video
Originate	LwEdit	Draw program	LwPaint		
Capture from analog to digital	(No Optical character recognition; no speech to text)	-	LwCaptur for screens; VidCap for analog video	Audio Control Panel	LwMovie; or MMCap, depending on your hardware
Control playback device	(No text to speech)	-	-	CD-ROM by way of DOS	Laser disc or CD player
Import file types	TXT and all ASCII files	-	PCX, GIF, TIFF, AVC, & Storyboard	WAV	FLI & ANM animation; (not AVI)

As you learn an authoring system and some related special tools, you may find it helpful to fill out a media and functions table for that authoring system. As you find out how to perform each function on each medium, you can fill in the corresponding table entry.

For example, the table shows that to put in an image, you invoke the paint program that comes with LinkWay Live! called LwPaint. To help you find LwPaint until your fingers learn the clicks, you might want to make your table's entry more explicit. You could note that, to invoke LwPaint, you can go to the "Main" screen, select "Tools," and finally select "LwPaint."

Figure 3-15 shows the first screen of LinkWay Live!'s Tools folder. You can find over a dozen of the table's entries on this screen. For example, you convert image and animation files to LinkWay Live! by selecting the buttons in the right half of the screen. The button named "GIF2LW" converts a file that uses the GIF format to LinkWay Live!'s format.

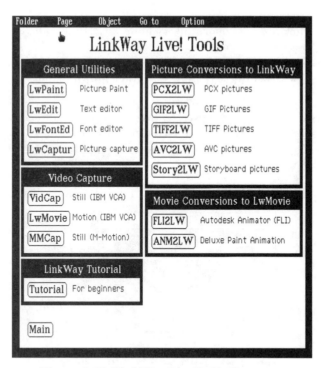

Figure 3-15: LinkWay Live!'s Tools screen

Figure 3-16 shows the screen you use to capture audio. You record your voice by clicking the button that shows a picture of sound waves impinging on a microphone and then talking into your real microphone. You can copy the control buttons, with or without the surrounding text, into a project and the buttons will still work. When you use LinkWay Live! to capture audio, you create WAV files. Many other authoring systems and individual tools can import WAV files.

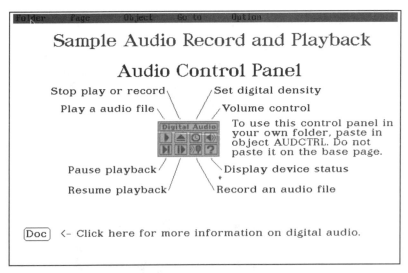

Figure 3-16: LinkWay Live!'s Audio Control Panel

Figure 3-17 shows the corresponding screen that you can use to record digital audio for use in Multimedia ToolBook. The Sound Recorder accessory comes as a part of Microsoft Windows. As a result, Multimedia ToolBook need not supply its own utility.

Figure 3-17: Microsoft Windows Sound

Recorder

If you were making a media and functions table for Multimedia ToolBook, you would put "Sound Recorder" in the box for capturing audio. If you wanted your table to include directions for finding Sound Recorder, you would write in "Program Manager," "Accessories," and "Sound Recorder." Again, to record you click on the microphone icon.

The last row in Table 3-2 shows the file formats that LinkWay Live! is capable of importing. If you created the corresponding table for an authoring system that runs on a Macintosh, your last row would note that the Macintosh deals with file formats such as the following:.

- TIFF (Tagged Image File Format) for scanned images
- JPEG (Joint Photographic Experts Group) included with QuickTime for compressing images
- PICT for images
- GIF (Graphics Interchange Format) for images
- AIFF (Audio Interchange File Format) for sound

If someone says that they have a graphics GIF file of the perfect building in Vienna that you need to illustrate your multimedia title, your tables would assure you that this is a common format for both Macintosh and Intel-based computers. However, the next question is whether your chosen authoring system can import or otherwise handle this format. All is not lost if the answer is no. It may be possible for you to use yet another tool to convert from GIF to one that your authoring system can handle.

HyperStudio 2.0 is another authoring system for the Macintosh. It includes tools for painting, animating, recording and playing back digital audio, playing CD-DA discs, CD-ROM discs, displaying Photo CD images, and playing laser discs. It also supports QuickTake digital still cameras and QuickTime video.

Making a Software Layer Chart

You may want to make a software layer chart similar to Figure 3-2 or Figure 3-3 for each computer that you use. In addition to listing specific product names, you can list major products' version numbers. This information becomes important when things go wrong. When you call a software vendor's help desk to find out why your system does not work, some of the first questions you will need to answer will concern version numbers. In many cases, you will find that your answer almost ends the conversation, as the help desk operator tells you that your problem may be that you are running with back level software and instructs you to get an update and call again if that does not fix the problem.

Learning and Teaching Multimedia Software

Learning multimedia software is a continuing process. We suggest some practices that you can use to make this process more fruitful. We divide the suggestions according to whether we suggest that you and your students do them all the time, do them when getting started, or do them when creating the projects that this book discusses. Then we continue with other steps that you may find useful.

Practices You Can Make into Habits

Take advantage of opportunities to view and demonstrate multimedia content. This includes content created by colleagues, students, friends, and professional creators. See if you can determine what authoring system each creator used. As you become familiar with more authoring systems, you will become more and more adept at recognizing authoring systems' signatures. Ask yourself which features you like and which you dislike. Consider what techniques you think you and your students would like to use. What techniques are effective in achieving goals that you think are important? Look for projects that would help students to achieve meaningful goals more efficiently and effectively.

Study other people's content from the inside. When you find that the creator of a piece of multimedia content used an authoring system that you have available, see if you can bring the content up as if it were your own project. Every authoring system provides facilities for editing individual parts of a project. You can use these same facilities to examine how each part works, unless the project's creator has set a password to prevent you from doing so. You will find that learning from others by looking at good examples is one of the most pleasant and effective ways to acquire advanced techniques. However, just as you would not want others to copy parts of your creations without giving you credit, do not use parts of other people's creations without obtaining their permission and citing them as your sources.

Explore some of the references that this book suggests. Get different viewpoints. Nobody has all the answers, or even all the questions.

Practices You Can Act on Soon

Select an authoring system to use. In either a K-12 school or a university, you can hope that multimedia support people or instructors have selected and set up hardware and software to help you get started. If so, your selection is easy. You use what is available, at the start, to avoid getting bogged down in details. If nobody has selected software for you to use, but hardware is available, then you would be well advised to select an authoring system that runs on that specific hardware setup, with its existing amount of memory, disk space, specific multimedia facilities, and software. Because it is relatively easy to learn other authoring systems after you already know one, try to start using one that is already set up. You may find later that you need one with greater capabilities or greater ease of use. Authoring systems that we have been using as sources of examples appear to be suitable selections as we write this. Many others may be at least as suitable by the time you read this.

Take your selected authoring system's tutorial. Asymetrix Multimedia ToolBook, LinkWay Live!, HyperCard, and many other authoring systems contain on-line tutorials that walk you through examples of using their most frequently used functions. You may need a little help initially finding a computer, finding the authoring system, and starting the authoring system's tutorial. You will probably find each individual function is easy to master, although the number of functions makes them somewhat hard to keep straight. Filling in a media and functions table as you go along may help. Do not feel that you must complete the tutorial in one sitting. Many people find that these tutorials become tedious after a while. After working with the tutorial for a half hour, you may find that you are very anxious to get started on a project of your own. Your students will feel the same way after a few minutes.

Take a break from the tutorial. Use what you have learned to create part of a simple project such as a very casual autobiography. Make a few screens with text, try the paint program, add some buttons, and copy and paste some clip art. Don't worry about saving your work. This eliminates the pressure of worrying about making a mistake that will destroy what you have already done. You can start your students off with an autobiography assignment and teach them just what they need to know to complete that assignment. If they get stuck, you can show them how to use the tutorial and other Help that is part of most authoring systems. Some authoring systems include sufficiently extensive Help facilities that you may never need to refer to a manual. You can access this Help at any point in the creation process. One of the most useful operations you can teach your students is how to become self-sufficient by using the Help system.

Practices You Can Apply Throughout This Book

Read about projects. Each of this book's chapters that discusses a project begins with a short description of its multimedia content as well as its educational objectives. You may find that new multimedia hardware and software make it remarkably easy for you and your students to complete these projects, including functions that you assumed only professionals could perform. Think about other contexts in which you can have your students benefit from applying these functions.

Complete as many as possible of the projects in this book. Actually completing a project will give you a larger library of techniques that you can instantly apply and help your students apply in other contexts. Learning how to use an authoring system to manipulate one of the media carries over to manipulating other media. The only situation that is better than examining other people's projects to see how they created their projects is having a library of your own projects from which you can extract pieces to use in future projects. You can also encourage your students to have their own library of projects that they can reuse for your class, for other classes, at home, and even later in their lives.

Comparison Table for Multimedia Software

Just as a table showing media and functions helps you keep track of the capabilities of one authoring system and some separate tools, you can make a different sort of table to help you compare several different authoring systems. Table 3-3 shows a typical example. Parentheses designate software tools that you may need, because an authoring system provides no tool for a particular function.

Table 3-3: An authoring system comparison

Authoring system Capability	Multimedia ToolBook	LinkWay Live!	HyperCard	Microsoft Word for Windows or for Macintosh
Metaphor is	Book	Folder	Stack	Document
Screen shows	Page	Page	Card	Page, part of page, or outline
Activate hypertext with	Hotword	Trigger in Reference Button	Hotword	Go To Button
Activate hypermedia with	Button	Button	Button	Picture icon
Put repeated items on	Background	Base Page	Background	Header or Footer
Enter text in	Field	Field	List	Document
Create image using	(Microsoft Paintbrush for Windows)	LwPaint	Mac Paint	(Microsoft Paintbrush or MacPaint)
Create graphics using	Main screen	Main screen	Main screen	Microsoft Draw
Create video using	(Intel Smart Video Recorder and Video for Windows)	LwMovie	QuickTime	(Intel Smart Video Recorder and Video for Windows or QuickTime)

Teaching Multimedia Software Tools

We suggest the following approaches, which apply to your own learning but apply particularly to teaching K-12 students.

- Teach tools that offer fundamental, generic skills.
- Teach skills that students can transfer to using other tools.

- Use templates. Teaching and learning by example are especially effective in early projects. We discuss templates in Chapter 4.

- Make cookbooks, (keyclick by keyclick directions) available, at least for emergency use.

- Teach some tools in depth; this makes it much easier for students to learn to use other tools.

- Help students learn how to evaluate tools and install tools. These are valuable life-long skills.

- Teach empowering vocabulary to help students to ask questions in such a way as to get useful answers, and to help students understand the answers.

- Train a few students in a specialty. Then give them the learning experience of training other students. There are plenty of specialties to go around.

- Consider classes and workshops that separate technical skills from academic content, especially if you find that students are learning the same technical skills redundantly in several classes. But do not assume that this is the best approach!

Some examples of techniques that teachers across the country have told us they use to teach their students how to use multimedia software tools to create multimedia projects are as follows.

Q: How young can children be when they learn to use multimedia tools? Are there special tips and techniques to use with very young children?

A: Children as young as age three can participate in creating multimedia projects. Of course, in comparison to older children, they may require more step-by-step help, and they may be more likely to combine existing media rather than creating new media.

Q: How do you teach K-12 students multimedia?

A: We have two special classes that teach only multimedia skills. We have an elementary class and an advanced class. Children enter the elementary class knowing nothing about multimedia and knowing very little about computers. By the time they complete the elementary class, they have skills that can be used in several classes. (Rhode Island)

A: We start using the language of multimedia several weeks before we actually expect the children to see multimedia computers or to learn multimedia skills. We talk about linking, selecting, navigating, and dividing large amounts of information into chunks. We talk about fields that contain text. We also talk about scenes, narration, and telling interesting stories. Students become familiar with the vocabulary of multimedia before they touch a mouse. (New York City)

A: We teach the children a few simple skills at a time, just what they need in order to complete the next few steps. We help them to acquire additional skills as necessary. After several months, we find that children come to us demanding to be taught more advanced techniques. We even teach scripting the same way. (North Carolina)

A: We teach multimedia in the context of a specific assignment over a two-week period. We find that, because of the high turnover of students in our school, we cannot assume that anyone knows multimedia from one semester to the next. (California)

Sheila Wagonner divided her sixth grade class into five groups, one group for each of her five computers. She asked each group to create a one-page multimedia project consisting of a title, three fields containing bullets, and three pop-up buttons next to each field for additional information about the bullets. She specified that the students were to put into each field one of the three most important points about whether the United States should have sent troops into Haiti in 1994. Her students had prior experience with the computers but no experience with multimedia, hypertext, or this authoring system. Ms. Wagonner spent 10 minutes showing her students how to enter the authoring system, how to create text in fields, and how to create pop-up buttons. In less than an hour, she had five multimedia projects that her students compared excitedly.

Making Do with Less

You and your students do not need any special multimedia hardware to get started using an authoring system. Simply having a computer that runs an authoring system and learning how to do hypertext make a worthwhile start. You need not spend weeks learning the intricacies of most authoring systems before starting to use them to achieve attractive and educationally meaningful results.

Summary

This chapter provides several aids to help you and your students understand multimedia software. The layer charts place authoring systems and specialized multimedia tools in a useful context of software products that fill higher and lower layers. The media and functions tables give you a way to visualize a seemingly endless list of different products by noting that each product performs one or more particular functions on one or more particular media. The Theory section discusses about a dozen characteristics that you may need to consider when you select multimedia software. The Practice section suggests specific techniques you can use to learn this subject yourself and can use to help your students learn the subject.

References

- Hands on manuals for learning about specific authoring systems:

Bull, Kinzie. *Media-Based Presentations with HyperCard*. STATE Teacher Education Server, University of Virginia, 1992.

Hall, Tom. *Utilizing ToolBook to Develop Multimedia Presentations*. Greenville, NC: TCC Publishing, 1994.

Hall, Tom. *Utilizing Multimedia ToolBook 3.0*. Philadelphia, PA: Boyd and Fraser Publishing, 1995.

Yoder, Bull, and Harris. *LinkWay for Educators, An Introduction*. International Society for Technology in Education (ISTE), 1991.

- Contact information for some vendors of major authoring tools:

Apple Computer, Inc., Infinite Loop Road, Cupertino, CA 95014, (408) 996-1010.

Asymetrix Corporation, 110 110th Avenue NE, Suite 700, Bellevue, WA 98004, (206) 462-0501.

IBM Corporation, (800) 426-2968. The Multimedia Information Center's phone number is (800) IBM-9402.

Macromedia, 600 Townsend Street, San Francisco, CA 94103, (415) 252-2000.

Microsoft Corporation, One Microsoft Way, Redmond, WA 98052-6399, (206) 882-8080.

Roger Wagner Publishing, Inc. (a source for HyperStudio), (800) 421-6526.

Chapter 4

Roles of Existing Multimedia Content

In this chapter, we explore:

- some important categories of existing multimedia content, including content that both professionals and nonprofessionals create.

- ways you can use existing multimedia content to help your students achieve desired goals by creating multimedia projects.

- basic information about copyrights and ethics, which you and your students must consider whenever using other creators' work.

The Theory section categorizes existing multimedia content, discusses sources and uses, presents a wide array of examples, and discusses issues that affect your students' use of other creators' content. The Practice section suggests activities for evaluating content and teaching about copyrights and ethics.

Background

Previous chapters mentioned that it is important to select multimedia content (also called titles) that will run on the hardware and software that you have available. This chapter discusses the more subtle matter of selecting particular multimedia content that will help your students achieve desired academic objectives. Recall that content fits in the top layer of Chapter 3's layer charts. Content includes students' multimedia projects and professional authors' commercial multimedia .

You and your students can order multimedia content from catalogs and magazines, exchange content with other teachers and students, and check content out of local libraries. At any one time, creators are now producing thousands of multimedia titles to distribute on CD-ROMs. Some inexpensive magazines come with CD-ROMs that also sample content.

After you have purchased a few discs from catalogs, every week's mail will bring catalogs that describe and illustrate new titles. Titles range from preschool fairy tales annotated with audio and video, to games and other sorts of EduTainment, to medical information and encyclopedias. Catalogs also offer CD-ROMs that contain collections of clips in various media, such as digitized photographs of beaches around the world, digitized music from the 1940s, and video clips of war footage. Vendors are distributing more and more disc catalogs in the form of CD-ROM discs. Such CD-ROM catalogs contain actual samples of the offered multimedia titles and clip libraries.

Is it possible to make any sense of this flood of multimedia? Is any of this content, especially the low-cost or free samplers, of any value in an educational context? Are such titles of any use in the context of students' creating their own projects? Each answer is a resounding Yes! Students can use existing multimedia as sources of:

- ideas and techniques for using multimedia effectively in their own projects,
- clip images and other clip media, for actual inclusion in their projects,
- subject area information, such as historical timelines that they can include in their projects, and
- reference materials to be used much as they use library books, film libraries, and even television programs.

Theory

Categories of Multimedia Content

While no recognized official categorization of multimedia content exists, we find it useful to divide content along the three dimensions that Figure 4-1 illustrates. A particular piece of multimedia has a type, a purpose, and a primary subject, just as a particular point on the earth has a latitude, a longitude, and an altitude. The types of multimedia content form the first dimension. Several of these types require explanation. A part of some complete content is anything that you select from an existing multimedia title. The part may include one or more media and may also include interactivity, such as hypertext links. For example, a part could be the portion of a chemistry tutorial that teaches about combustion.

A template is an existing multimedia title that the creator has made available for you to modify, so that you can change the material in the template to create your own project. If you find that a creator has refrained from using a password to lock you out, and if you have the same authoring system or other tools that the creator used, you have found a template.

A closed title is one that you can observe and learn from, but that you cannot modify in any way. As we discuss later, however, students may be able to grab screens from a closed title and use the screen images in their projects. As we also discuss later, it is important to give credit to such sources and to be sure that you are not violating the creator's copyright.

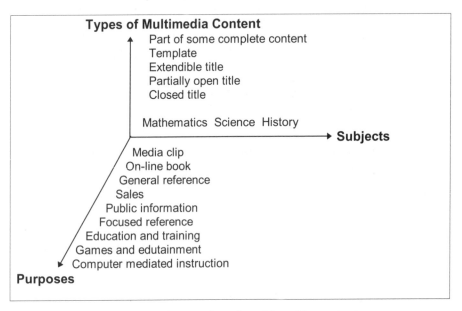

Figure 4-1: Categories of multimedia content

An extendible title contains a built-in provision for a user to add material, but not to change or delete material that is already present. In general, multimedia is most useful when it is most interactive, that is, when the user shares most control with the creator. A normal television program is not interactive, because a viewer's only choices are to watch the program, change the channel, or turn off the television set. Most multimedia projects allow users to navigate and thus select one or more paths through the project's information. A project is still more interactive if the user can add to the project, at least adding emphasis or commentary, and preferably adding actual content. Adding content is an especially valuable learning experience for students, because they will spend so much of their working and personal lives adding value to collaborative activities for which they share credit. This is the rationale behind extendible titles. For example, a chemistry teacher in California structures each semester's class around an extendible title into which each student adds information about a particular element.

The purposes of multimedia content form a second dimension. We refer here to the creator's purpose, which may be different from the way you decide to use the content. We discussed clips above. The other purposes are reasonably self-explanatory. We mention them as areas in which you might want to search for useful content. For example, some multimedia titles have as their primary purpose being either a general reference on many subjects or a focused reference on a narrow range of subjects. Some such references contain large amounts of useful text, graphics, audio, image, and video.

The third dimension is the subject that a multimedia title's creator had in mind when creating the title. Figure 4-1 shows only three of many possible subjects along this dimension. You might use a piece of content that a creator intended to be about one subject as part of a project about a completely different subject or as part of an interdisciplinary project about several related subjects.

As an example of one point in Figure 4-1's three-dimensional space, consider *Illuminated Books and Manuscripts*. You can obtain this title from IBM EduQuest at (800) 426-4338. The title's intended purpose is to be a focused reference. Its subject is history. Its type is an extendible title. Those are its three dimensions. The title is a collection of about 100 literary and historical writings. It includes opinions and commentary concerning five of the writings, in the form of multimedia. It calls each set of opinions and commentary an illumination, in the sense of a picture that a mediaeval scribe wove around the first letter of a paragraph in an illuminated manuscript. The title's many laser discs, diskettes, and CD-ROMs contain not only the writings and five illuminations but also a special multimedia authoring system. Students can use the authoring system to extend the title by creating their own illuminations of the remaining 95 writings or of any other literature.

A second example is a partially open title, on the subject of mathematics, intended for educational use. This title is *Patterns in Mathematics*. A high school student named Morgan McGuire created the title while working at IBM's T. J. Watson Research Center at Yorktown Heights, New York, in the summer of 1993. This title encourages users to modify patterns by modifying a QBASIC program that Morgan wrote and included in the title. Students who have access to his title can learn interesting mathematics by modifying the partially open title in the way that he intended. Because Morgan did not protect his title with a password, students who have access to the title, and also have access to the authoring system that he used, are free to explore the method that he devised for users to modify his QBASIC program. Such students could use his project, under appropriate circumstances, as a template. This use turns his title into a different type of multimedia content.

Sources of Multimedia Content

There is an important fourth dimension that we did not show in Figure 4-1. This dimension is multimedia content's distribution method. You and your students can obtain multimedia content on CD-ROM discs, diskettes, and laser discs from catalogs, book stores, software companies, specialized multimedia companies, publishing companies, broadcast companies, conferences, and educational archives. You can encourage your students to contribute their work to such archives, as well as accessing other students' and teachers' contributions. This chapter's References section includes a sample of catalogs and archives.

You and your students may also find a great deal of multimedia available for downloading from on-line services such as Prodigy, America Online, Internet, and CompuServe. More and more educational archives are going on-line. On-line content is often compressed, may or may not be free, may or may not be in a form that your software tools can use, and may take a long time to download. Increasing available bandwidth increases the amounts of media that it is reasonable to send over these long-distance networks.

Q: Do we distinguish using existing commercial multimedia content from using existing student created multimedia projects?

A: No, not really. Professional creators produce commercial multimedia for use by academic or general audiences. They often charge hundreds or even thousands of dollars per copy. Many nonprofessionals, including students, produce very useful and compelling multimedia content for their own use. They may give copies away free or charge a nominal reproduction and distribution cost. This chapter's references and examples include both sorts of content.

Copyright laws protect all multimedia content, whether professionals or nonprofessionals created the content. Copyright owners have the right to control who may copy their work, how many times, and for what purposes. If you use the work of others, either professionals or nonprofessionals, you must respect the copyright owner's rights. Moreover, you should give credit where it is due, as a matter of ethics and scholarship. Please understand that we mean these points to apply whenever we suggest copying others' work, even if we do not mention it each time.

Ways Students Can Use Multimedia

Students can use multimedia content in several different ways. Several of these ways deserve serious consideration, as follows.

Students can use any type of multimedia title as an example of approaches and techniques that they might use in their own projects. You can demonstrate portions of several titles during class discussions. Students can observe how other creators organized information, selected particular media to express ideas, split information among different screens, and arranged the information on each screen. Students can browse through a title, thinking about its content and techniques, and using a computer or a pad to take notes. Just as students show strong preference for particular clothes, television shows, books, or foods, students must be selective about adopting other creators' ideas and techniques. Students must realize that another creator may have made a bad selection or may have made a selection that is good for the creator's purposes but is bad for the students' purposes. Students need to develop critical judgment about multimedia content, not just for a particular project but as a life-long skill.

Students can also employ many types of exiting multimedia as sources of media clips for use in their projects, if they respect copyright owners' rights and include citations that give appropriate credit. However, using different types of content requires your students to use different techniques and different amounts of effort. When a creator intends for students to use content as clips, the creator often puts each clip in a separate file and includes instructions on how students can find and use appropriate files. Many authoring systems provide long lists of format conversion tools, called filters, that help students use image clips that come in different formats. Some audio and video format conversion filters exist as well. Nevertheless, not all clip libraries work with all authoring systems.

Students must expend more effort to use a piece of content which the creator did not particularly intend to be used as a source of clips. In such titles, even if the creator does not go out of her way to make things difficult for the students, the creator does not make parts particularly easy to find or easy to clip.

To use an image from such a title, students may be able to use the operating system's copy and paste facility. That is, students may be able to copy an image from the title and paste the image into their project. If copy and paste fails, then students need to use a screen capture tool. As we discuss in Chapter 10, a screen capture tool is a program that makes a file from whatever image is on the computer screen at an instant that the students select. Students import the resulting file into their project.

Students can capture other media, as well as images, from titles. Students can capture a screen that contains a title's text or graphics. However, the result will be an image of the letters and lines, rather than being actual text or graphics that students could edit easily. Students can capture audio by using a second computer to redigitize the sound as the first computer plays the sound. To get acceptable quality, avoid running the audio through a speaker and a microphone. Instead, connect a cable from the first computer's audio output jack to the second computer's audio input jack. Similarly, students can even capture video by using a scan converter to change the computer screen's moving pictures to analog video and using a second computer to redigitize that video. Refer to Chapter 2 for details of hardware involved in the last two types of capture.

A creator may develop a title, particularly a focused reference, using some unique authoring system, and may include parts of that authoring system in the title for students to use. Students find it easy to employ media from such a title, as long as the students use the included authoring system. Otherwise, students need to fall back on the capture techniques that we just discussed.

Your students will find that templates are an especially useful type of multimedia content. As we noted, a template is a multimedia project that happens to satisfy two criteria. First, the project's creators used the same authoring system and tools that your students have available. Second, the creators refrained from setting a password. A password would prevent your students from digging around inside the project and would thus limit the students to capturing media. In Chapter 3, we noted that students can use such a template to develop their own projects by changing each part of the template, such as a button, to replace the original content by their own content. Students can also use a template as an especially convenient source of media that are already in the required formats. Students can use authoring system facilities simply to copy a button, an image, an audio object, or any other object, and then paste the object into their own project.

You can encourage your students to establish their own personal library of templates and clips. They should maintain their library on a computer's disk if possible, or on a pile of diskettes if necessary. Eventually, they will write such a library on a recordable CD-ROM disc. They may also contribute content to local, state, or national multimedia archives by using an on-line service.

Examples of Multimedia Titles

Students can find media to use in their projects in many different multimedia titles. The following examples provide a general idea of typical titles that are available in the mid-1990s. Thousands of titles are available, and the number is growing rapidly, so we can provide only a sampling. Many titles have versions that run on either Intel-based or Macintosh personal computers. We encourage you to add your own favorites to this list.

General References and Databases

- *TIME Almanac of the 20th Century*, Compact Publishing, Inc., (202) 244-4770, contains over 20,000 articles, some complete texts of articles from the magazine, many links to photographs and video clips, along with statistics and other content that never appeared in print.

- *Microsoft Encarta '95*, from Microsoft, (800) 583-0040, is a version of Funk and Wagnall's 29-volume encyclopedia, greatly augmented with multimedia. It includes several useful tools that help students research specific topics. It provides a cut and paste facility.

- *The New Grolier Multimedia Encyclopedia*, by Grolier Electronic Publishing, Inc., (800) 285-4534, contains the full text of the *Academic American Encyclopedia*. It provides tools for the student, including Boolean searches (searches which accept AND, OR, and NOT as search terms), hypertext links, bookmarks, and cut and paste.

- *Compton's Interactive Encyclopedia for Windows*, from Compton's NewMedia, Inc., (619) 929-2599, covers many different subjects. It has over 15,000 pictures, 8,700,000 words, 45 animations, and 60 minutes of audio.

Focused References

- *Microsoft Cinemania '95*, from Microsoft, (800) 583-0040, contains information on over 20,000 movies. It includes reviews, promotional stills, dialog recordings, and video clips. In addition to its content, it provides a good example of various search criteria that students can use for their own databases.

- *Mammals: A Multimedia Encyclopedia*, from National Geographic Society, (800) 368-2728, is a special purpose encyclopedia that describes interesting animals using text, images, partial-screen video, and audio. It also includes a related game and a narrated tutorial.

- *U.S. Presidents*, from Compton's NewMedia, Inc., (619) 929-2500, is a focused database about the presidents, first ladies, and vice presidents.

- *Columbus: Encounter, Discovery & Beyond*, from IBM EduQuest (800) 426-4338, is an immense multimedia database of hypertext-linked information about Columbus in particular and the age of discovery in general, including political, economic, and social events, opinions as well as facts, Boolean searches, and timelines.

- *The Honeybee*, from The MultiMeanings Co., (803) 738-0880, is a resource tool about the life of the honeybee, for students in first through fifth grades. It covers a wide variety of disciplines from math and science to language arts and social studies. It has an on-line note-taker and a cut and paste feature.

- *History Disquiz*, from Voyager, Inc., is a CAV laser disc containing 45 minutes of archival newsreel footage. It is available through Educational Resources, (800) 624-2926.

Computer Mediated Instruction

- *Comprehensive Chemistry CD-ROM*, from Falcon Software, Inc., (603) 764-5788, contains four computer-assisted instruction programs that cover both inorganic and organic chemistry in 160 lessons. It provides video of the results of many high school chemistry experiments that can augment or replace corresponding laboratory experiences. Each of the programs is sufficiently interactive to keep students engaged and to allow them to progress at their own pace.

- *Math and More 1 and 2*, from IBM EduQuest, (800) 426-4338, provides about 12 weeks of a complete mathematics curriculum for first and second grade mathematics. Its subjects include studies of repeating patterns, using maps, and analyzing data. Its materials include both on-line and off-line activities.

- *HyperGlot Software Co. Foreign-Language Stacks*, from HyperGlot Software Co., (800) 726-5087, provides extensive multimedia instruction in several foreign languages.

- *Triple Play Plus!*, *Spanish*, from Syracuse Language Systems, comes with a microphone for your students so that the computer can listen to pronunciation and suggest improvements.

Simulated Environments

- *Hurricane Hugo*, from Turner Educational Services, Inc. and Floyd Design, (800) 344-6219, simulates living through a hurricane, to a fortunately limited extent, with animations and video, as well as presenting information about the storm's effect on Charleston, South Carolina. It is delivered on laser disc and a diskette. It provides an unusually good example of organizing information, as we discuss in the next chapter.
- *Tacoma Bridge*, from RPI University's Comprehensive Unified Physics Learning Environment (contact Dr. Jack Wilson at RPI in Troy, New York) provides a numerical model that simulates the famous collapse of Galloping Gertie. Students can interact with the model to make measurements and try out results of different conditions. This is thus a partially open title.
- *The Decisions, Decisions Collection*, manufactured by Tom Snyder Productions, and distributed through the ENHANCE catalog, (800) 777-ENHANCE, simulates issues about which students can practice thinking critically. Some issues are substance abuse, foreign policy, prejudice, and the environment. This title illustrates setting up decisions and simulating environments.

Sales Information

We encourage you and your students to explore how retail merchants use multimedia to convey information and influence buying decisions. Which techniques are useful to adopt in student projects? Which techniques turn people off and why? We have selected some illustrative examples, although not all may be in your community. These multimedia titles usually run in kiosks, which are ordinary multimedia computers packaged in tamper-resistant cases, usually with touch screens replacing keyboards and mice. They are designed for use in public places such as malls and airports.

- Mannington provides a kiosk that allows a user to chose floor covering materials and patterns interactively and use a personalized simulation of his or her home environment to select other information about floor coverings.
- Buick and Ford advertise in magazines that they will mail a diskette to a potential customer on request. Such a diskette contains a title that shows and describes current vehicles. A user can see each model in each of its available colors. Some diskettes include additional titles such as some sort of interactive game and an animation that explains how a four-stroke-cycle engine works. The latter could inspire your students to create a similar animation. These diskettes require no special multimedia hardware.

- Coca-Cola and Shell Canada have produced multimedia titles that play in public kiosks. Users can interact with information about the companies' products.
- Some Blockbuster video rental stores include multimedia movie stations that help customers select movies.

Transaction Stations

We encourage you to have your students explore other kiosks that allow users to complete transactions. Students will find that such kiosks are excellent sources of ideas about multimedia techniques, especially for achieving ease of learning and ease of use.

- The Tulare County, Florida, Welfare Department provides kiosks in widely distributed and easily available locations. Clients interact with the kiosks' multimedia content to get information about the services for which they are eligible and to apply for desired services.
- The Oregon Motor Vehicle Bureau set up kiosks that use multimedia to help people apply for drivers licenses and registrations without waiting to talk to bureau personnel.
- Walt Disney World provides information kiosks in which users can get information and make reservations. Some of these kiosks include video conferences with remote reservation agents.
- Delphi Photo provides kiosks that help customers specify how they want the company to process their films.

Magazines and Books

Many useful student projects involve using multimedia to create a story, augment an existing story, or publish a magazine. Demonstrating professionally created titles such as the following could provide valuable ideas for such projects.

- *Just Grandma and Me*, from Broderbund Software, Inc., (800) 521-6263, is one of several Broderbund living books for very young children. The books contain talking characters, animations, sound effects, music, and many buttons for children to select, including invisible buttons. Responses make children feel they are part of the story.
- *Nautilus CD*, from Metatec Corporation, (800) 637-3472, is a multimedia magazine for people interested in multimedia. It is published monthly and includes many samples suitable for demonstrating to students.
- *Newsweek Interactive*, from The Software Toolworks, (800) 234-3088, is an interactive version of the eponymous magazine.

Multimedia Composition and Analysis

Titles in this category use multimedia for analysis and annotation. Seeing such titles could inspire your students to go forth and do likewise.

- *From Alice to Ocean*, from Claris Clear Choice, (800) 325-2747, uses images and audio to analyze and expand on the eponymous book. The same CD-ROM works for both Windows and Macintosh.

- *Illuminated Books and Manuscripts*, described above, fits in this category, as well, because it analyzes compositions. It also includes tools with which students can do likewise.

- *MS Musical Instruments for Macintosh or Windows*, from Microsoft, (800) 583-0040, are multimedia explorations of musical instruments.

EduTainment

Increasing numbers of multimedia titles provide education in entertaining formats or, conversely, attempt to be more entertaining by including some educational content. One such title allows a user to simulate performing daring rescues by quickly using mathematical reasoning. Other titles allow users to win games by using critical reading skills to recognize and gather relevant facts. Some video games fit this category.

- *Number Munchers*, *Troggle Trouble*, and *Tesselmania* are three titles from MECC distributed by the ENHANCE catalog, (800) 777- ENHANCE.

Augmentations of Existing Applications

- Some versions of "Lotus 1-2-3," from Lotus Development Corporation, (800) 343-5414, allow a user to annotate a spreadsheet by recording an oral comment about a cell's number or formula. An icon showing a picture of an ear alerts another user to ask to hear the audio.

- Lotus' *Freelance Graphics, Release 2 for Windows*, from Lotus Development Corporation, (800) 343-5414, provides an animated tutorial that demonstrates how to use the program to create presentations. A user can create more interesting and effective presentations by including audio and animation.

- *Microsoft Word* for Macintosh and Windows allow users to import pictures, audio, and even video into text documents.

Games

- *The 7ᵗʰ Guest: Inside Henry Stauf's Mansion* is manufactured by Virgin Games and available through many mail-order CD-ROM catalogs.

- *Myst*, from Broderbund Software, Inc., (800) 521-6263, is a compelling adventure and mystery game without violence. The user plays the role of the main character.

CD-ROM Catalogs and Samplers

Each of the following discs includes samples of a variety of types of multimedia content and software tools. Moreover, your students could benefit from noting how the disc organizes these samples.

- *CD-ROM Today, the Disc!* comes with a monthly magazine with the natural title of "CD-ROM Today," which costs less than $10 per issue.
- *SuperStore!, Take It For A Spin TestDrive* from (800) 788-8055 has product previews that include Waterford Institute's *Rusty & Rosy Read with Me*, Jasmine *Multimedia Video Clips*, and *EarthBASE for Windows*.
- *CompuServe CD*, available from (800) CDROM89, allows students to learn about on-line services without being logged on. It contains samples of information from many CompuServe forums. Students may log on to find additional information.
- *K-12 Preview CD-ROM (Mac)* is available from Educational Resources, (800) 624-2926.
- *Educorp Windows CD Sampler* is available from (800) 843-9497.
- *Apple CD-ROM Titles Sampler* is available from (800) 571-8111.

Student-Created Projects

Students have created many substantive and attractive multimedia projects in several of the above categories. Such projects include kiosks that contribute to community services; school cafeteria menus, safety information, and newspapers; and presentations for school administrators to use at conferences. Students created the first two of the following examples using LinkWay Live! on Intel-based computers. Students created the third on a Macintosh using Apple Media Tool.

- *Tissues*, by students at Marion High School in Marion, Indiana, describes skin tissue samples with images and audio. Contact the LinkWay Archive in the References.
- *Peace Art* is by students at Enloe High School in Raleigh, North Carolina. Contact the LinkWay Archive in the References.
- *Visionary Stampede Magazine* is by students attending nine San Francisco Bay Area high schools. Contact Opportune Press Inc., in Mill Valley, California, at (415) 381-3463.

Clip Media

- *Maps! Maps! Maps!*, from Bruce Jones Design Inc., available through Enhance Catalog, (800) 777-ENHANCE, provides many sorts of maps for the DOS and Macintosh environments.

- *QC School Clip Art*, from Quality Computers, available through Enhance Catalog, (800) 777-ENHANCE, provides several collections that range from animals and flags to sports and music.

- *The Music Bakery, A CD-ROM Music Library*, from The Music Bakery, (800) 229-0313, provides various styles of clip music. Note license agreements that specify circumstances in which you may use music that you purchase.

- *Royalty-Free Digital Clips for Multimedia Presentations*, from Ask Me Multimedia Center, available from Tiger Software (800) 238-4437, includes several media clips, even some AVI morph clips and clips designed to be used as backgrounds.

- *SmartPics for Windows-Release 1.0* available from Lotus Development Corporation, (800) 343-544, provides many clips that are easy to use and nicely categorized.

Copyrights and Ethics

Whenever students use other people's work, they must be aware of important legal and ethical issues. Legally, students must make sure that their use is consistent with the rights of whoever owns the work's copyright. Ethically, and as a matter of good scholarship, students must give credit for others' work.

These considerations apply when students either copy a work or repurpose a work. Repurposing means using the work for some purpose that the work's creator did not intend. For example, the Trailers project, which we describe in Chapter 9, involves using a computer to play clips from a laser disc or CD-ROM without actually copying the clips into the computer. If your students select clips that make users want to see or rent the movie, and if the owner of the movie's copyright happens to see the project, the owner is quite likely to agree that your students made a fair use of the disc. However, if your project makes a lot of potential customers want to avoid seeing the movie at all costs, the copyright owner might decide to use the copyright laws to make your life miserable.

Consider an analogy from a time that even the authors are not quite old enough to remember. As people progressed from hunting and gathering to farming, they needed to convince strangers that hand-raised animals in pens and hand-cultivated plants in fields were not free for the hunting and gathering. Now, as we progress from an industrial society to an information society, people who make their livings by raising and cultivating information need to convince strangers that information is not free for the taking. We must all respect copyright laws, which are today's fields and pens.

Neither legalities nor ethics are unique to copying and using multimedia. Exactly the same issues apply to copying and using printed information. However, just as photocopiers made it easier to copy information that is in printed form, multimedia makes it much easier to copy all media that are in digital form. In fact, it is remarkably easy to produce either perfect copies or altered copies that are absolutely indistinguishable from digital originals. In forensic terms, multimedia increases everyone's opportunity and ability to pass off the work of others as their own work. However, making copying easier does not make copying any more legal or any more ethical.

One of the most interesting guest speakers in the authors' classes is an intellectual property attorney. We are sure that such a lawyer's stories and advice would be as entertaining and memorable in grade school as in grad school. The authors and our students learned that we could use more works than we thought, in some cases, and use less in other cases.

Copyrights

We suggest that an effective moment to introduce the subject of copyrights is just after your students have invested a large amount of time and effort in creating a multimedia project of which others might want to own copies. You could ask your students how they would react if they saw an advertisement in which Mr. X was offering their project for sale as his own work. The good news is that some student is almost sure to say, "There ought to be a law!" and give you an opportunity to reply, "There is a law, called copyright!" The bad news is that your students are almost sure to follow up with the question "What does the law say?" Unfortunately, although copyright laws apply to everybody, the laws are not really clear to anybody. Although we are not authorized to give legal advice or opinions, we hope that the following discussion will help you answer your students' question.

In brief, using someone else's work is clearly legal in some circumstances; some use clearly violates the copyright owner's rights, unless and until you obtain the owner's permission; and some use is sufficiently nebulous that you should probably avoid it unless you involve someone who is licensed to offer legal advice.

Copyright law protects works that are expressions of ideas in all forms, including print, videotape, and multimedia. Whoever owns the copyright on a work has control over who may use the work or make a copy of the work and how the person who made a copy may use the copy. The current law says that ownership of copyright belongs to the person who created the work, unless that person transfers the copyright to another person or to a company. A copyright is effective for the life of an individual author plus 50 years. The copyright on a work that employees of a company created lasts 75 years from the creation date. Congress set these details for the United States in 1978 and can change the details occasionally. Other countries have their own different copyright laws.

Under current law, every work receives automatic copyright protection the instant an author creates it, whether or not the author puts a copyright notice on the work. Lack of a copyright notice is thus no indication that anyone may use the work freely. As creators, there is nothing that your students need to do in order to obtain copyrights to their own work. Nevertheless, it is good practice to insert into each work a copyright notice similar to one of these.

© 1995 Jane Doe

© 1997 Mr. Hildebrand's fourth grade social studies class.

Even when you buy multimedia content on a CD-ROM, such as a title or a clip art library, you must be aware that what you bought was only the right to make particular use of this one copy of the content. An accompanying license agreement often spells out what rights you purchased. Clips that the license allows you to use as part of a work that you sell for profit may cost much more than clips that limit you to personal or educational use.

Owning a legitimate copy of a work is very different from owning a copyright for the work. For example, you may own a copy of the videotape of a hit movie. You may watch the movie in your home and may show it to your friends. However, you may not make and sell copies of the movie, you may not give other people the right to make copies, and you may not charge admission to a showing of the movie, without getting permission from the owner of the movie's copyright. In general, you would expect to pay a high price for such permission. Similarly, you may not repurpose the movie into a multimedia project, and sell the project or charge admission to a showing of the project, without getting permission and probably paying for this permission.

Fortunately, the concept of fair use allows many important types of copying, particularly in nonprofit academic environments. Copyright legislation defines fair use to allow making copies for use in criticism and comment (such as book reviews), news reporting, teaching, scholarship, or research. In many cases, teachers can make copies for use in classrooms, if the teachers do not make profit from selling the material, do not copy too much material, and do not use the material for too long. For example, copying one page of a long article, and using the copy in class for one day, is almost surely a fair use. Copying an entire book, and teaching from the copy for three years, almost surely violates the rights of the owner of the book's copyright, because making and using the copy substitutes for buying and using the book. In between clear examples of fair use and unfair use are gray areas for which you should get the advice of legal counsel.

Another concept, public domain, allows still more copying. A work is in public domain if nobody owns or enforces the work's copyright. That is, either the author died more than 50 years ago or the author agreed to allow anyone to copy the work without making any royalty payments. A work that is in public domain may nevertheless have strings attached, such as permission to copy it without making royalty payments only if the copy is for personal use and not for resale. A work that is publicly available is not necessarily in public domain. It does not matter if all your friends are absolutely sure that the author is eager for you to copy the work. Unless you know where there is a piece of paper on which the copyright owner wrote that you can do what you want to do with the copy, you run some risk that the copyright owner will try to sue you for making and using a copy. Your friends are unlikely to help pay your legal bills, let alone help pay a judgment against you. Sometime it is very difficult to determine who actually owns a work's copyright. The work's creator might have sold the copyright and there might now be multiple owners. Only the copyright owner can put a work in the public domain.

If your students consider copyright law to be an esoteric realm that never affects them, you can use the following price list to show them that copyrights touch their lives every day. Copyrights affect the prices they pay for information. (These particular prices are only rough approximations and are subject to change.)

$16   *Library of the Future* from World Library
$100 *Encarta Encyclopedia* from Microsoft
$995 *Encyclopaedia Britannica*

Each of the listed products is a single CD-ROM disc. A manufacturer can produce any one of the discs, along with copying information onto the disc, for a cost of two or three dollars. A bookstore or a catalog outlet can sell the disc for a cost of a few more dollars. A price of $16 thus contains a good profit on manufacturing and sales. Why does the first disc cost $16 whereas the other two discs cost much more? On the one hand, the first disc contains 450 great, old, public domain books by long-dead authors. Thus, the first disc's $16 price pays for pressing plastic, shipping, stocking, and profit, but not one cent goes to copyright owners. On the other hand, most of the second and third discs' prices pay for information. Then why is information so much more expensive on the third disc than on the second? Leaving aside the question of which disc's information involved more effort, the third disc is intended for a smaller audience. The third disc has a far higher price because it must yield its copyright owners approximately the same payment from a far smaller sales volume. The messages for your students are that most information is not free and that the price of information depends on how many people help pay the cost of producing the information.

What would happen if there were no copyright laws? Anyone would be allowed to copy the Encyclopedia or the Encyclopaedia and make a good profit selling each copy for $16. However, with no copyright laws, copyright owners could not make a living by charging for their information. As a result, few authors would bother to produce an Encyclopedia, an Encyclopaedia, or any other significant new work, for anyone to copy. In fact, without copyright laws, about all there would be to read would be old books, new government pamphlets, and of course this book, which we are writing for the fun of it.

This brings us back to where we started. You might ask your students to consider how they would feel if they were trying to make a living in any creative field and if Mr. X were free to copy and sell any work that they produced.

Ethics

Whenever your students copy or paraphrase a significant part of someone else's work, rather than creating their own work, they should put in a citation that gives credit to the source. This is the ethical thing to do, no matter whether the source is a professional creator, a friend, or a colleague, and no matter whether the work is a video clip, a paragraph from a book, or any other medium.

An effective moment to bring up this ethical point is when one student has quoted a second student without giving the second student credit for having done the related work. At this moment, you can stand back and let the second student explain the problem.

Another effective moment to bring up ethics is when one student's project has quoted a fact, without attributing the fact to its source, and a second student has challenged the fact's correctness. You can show that the first student was relying on the source to get the fact straight. Failing to give the second student enough information to check the source brought the question down on the first student's head. Again, the only reason why this discussion relates particularly to multimedia is that multimedia makes copying so easy.

Requesting Permission to Use Content

You may find yourself in the position of requesting permission to use a copyright owner's work. You should request written permission to copy parts of a work into your multimedia project, if you intend to present the project in public. You must be willing to accept "No!" as an answer. Copyright owners may require you to pay for permission to present their works in public, especially if you intend to charge money to people who attend such a presentation.

The body of a letter requesting permission to make a copy of a copyrighted work might be similar to Figure 4-2. We strongly suggest having your school's legal counsel review a letter before you mail it. When you are on the receiving end of such a letter, you probably will want to give the requested permission. Figure 4-3 is an example of an actual dialogue between one of the authors and a multimedia archive caretaker.

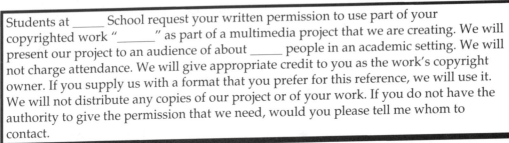

Students at _____ School request your written permission to use part of your copyrighted work "_____" as part of a multimedia project that we are creating. We will present our project to an audience of about _____ people in an academic setting. We will not charge attendance. We will give appropriate credit to you as the work's copyright owner. If you supply us with a format that you prefer for this reference, we will use it. We will not distribute any copies of our project or of your work. If you do not have the authority to give the permission that we need, would you please tell me whom to contact.

Figure 4-2: Sample form for getting permission to use copyrighted work

Bernardo, I have two questions for you.

1) Can I get a copy of the archive without contributing something now or by sending you an IOU for some content to be delivered by the end of the year? I will send the required number of diskettes.

2) What kind of releases do you recommend having the students who created the content sign in order to have their work appear in your archive and how do people handle this? I have student stacks and folders, but I have not asked any of these students' permission, so I am reluctant to send anything.

Palmer,

1) is no problem. I am providing Archive copies to anyone who complies with my guidelines for submitting a request.

2) This is a good question. From my end, it is not a problem, as I am free to presume this has been taken care of between the teacher and the student. I don't think there are many problems, as long as the stacks and folders are not being used for economic benefit; however, if I were the teacher, I would write a letter to the parents indicating my intentions, and I would ask that they send me a signed note giving their permission on behalf of the student.

My daughter's local coordinator used one of her folders at several national conferences without her permission. We only found out about it coincidentally after the fact, and it sort of left a bad taste. We would gladly have provided permission if asked, but I think it was the fact that we weren't even notified that disturbed us.

Figure 4-3: Sample dialog between a requester and an owner

Practice

Evaluating Existing Multimedia Content

You will need to evaluate multimedia content, not only to decide what to buy for use in and out of school, but also to learn to tell good content from bad or useless content. Your students will need to make the same judgments. This section suggests several ways to practice making evaluations.

Some useful evaluation criteria follow. Not all these criteria may be relevant to your particular situation. You can add or delete criteria, and then reorder the resulting list according to how important each point is to you, as you use the subsequent suggestions for practice.

- Does the content meet the objectives of your intended use in an effective and efficient way?

- What hardware and software do you require to run this content? Do you have them readily available? If you need an expensive system to run the content, can you find a less fancy alternative?

- Can you install the content to run in a LAN environment if necessary?

- What is the depth of the content's subject matter? Is there real substance or is it mostly flash and sizzle? Of course, your objective may occasionally be to pique the interest of reluctant learners by using flash and sizzle.

- Does the content present subject matter in an interesting, lively, and compelling way?

- Is the content at an appropriate age level for your intended audience?

- What is the quality of the content's interaction? Although we do not suggest a game orientation, we suggest that you lean toward making your students active rather than passive users.

- What are the content's navigation options?

- Can users personalize the content or add more content?

- Does the content include options for bookmarks, notepads for student notes, clipping information, and making automatic citations?

- Does the content's license agreement allow you and your students to make copies, repurpose the copies, or do whatever else you need to do?

- Is the content easy to install?

- Is the content easy to learn, the first time?

- Is the content easy to use, after learning how to use it?

- If the content is hard to install, learn, or use, does it nevertheless meet your objectives so well that you are willing to invest the required time and effort?

- Is the content's price a good value for what it delivers, or would you be better off finding a cheaper alternative to meet your objectives?

- Assuming the content meets your immediate objectives, does it appear to be useful for future projects or classes, or is it a one-time shot?

- Even if the content does not meet your immediate objectives, is it worth getting or keeping in mind for later use?

- Does your evaluation of the content agree with reviews in magazines?

Personal Collection

Consider getting on some of the major multimedia content providers' catalog mailing lists. See the References section of this chapter and the previous list of titles for some telephone numbers and addresses. Review information that these catalogs provide about the titles, including intended purpose, target audience, license provisions, and hardware and software requirements. As budget and available equipment allow, procure some of the sampler CD-ROMs and try them out. Which would you use as demos of ideas and techniques for your class? Which would be good sources of reference materials for your students?

Techniques from Others

Select two or three multimedia titles such as those in our list of examples. Concentrate first on those that you can obtain most easily. Identify the creators' intent and intended audience. Analyze critically the ways in which the creators used media to achieve their goals. Be sure that you can explain the function, benefits, and limitations of different media. Relate what you learn to each title's purpose and to its creator's goals and intended audience. Think about how different audiences might interpret different media. What techniques are particularly effective? Summarize these techniques for yourself and for your students.

If at all possible, use what you learned from an authoring system's tutorial to explore a title whose creator used that authoring system. Be sure to find a title in which the creator did not use a password to lock you out. In general, you will need to tell the authoring system that you are a creator rather than a user. You may also need to turn on a menu line, a status line, and other parts of the screen that creators turn off to reduce clutter for users. As we noted in Chapter 3, different authoring systems use different names for essentially identical concepts and require you to use different procedures to perform essentially identical functions.

Here is how to use an authoring system to explore an existing title and see what the creator has put into the title. Select a particular part of the title such as a button or an audio object. Tell the authoring system that you want to edit or change the selection. In almost all cases, the authoring system will respond by showing you exactly what the creator already put into what you selected. Then you may or may not decide to actually make any changes. In case you do want to try out some changes, always make a copy of the title and work with the copy rather than with the original. Using the authoring system to experiment with changing the title is the ultimate form of interacting with the title. You and your students can learn a lot that way.

As you find particularly illustrative titles that you can explore and that you have permission to use, start keeping a personal library to use with your students. Keep in mind any appealing media clips that you find while exploring existing multimedia content. Suggest that students make clips to include in their own projects, if doing so is legal and ethical. Cutting and pasting are a standard part of some titles such as *Microsoft's Encarta* that are not primarily clip libraries.

Table 4-1 is a small sample of examples that you could use to study specific techniques with your students. One of the best ways to coach your class is to show such examples of existing multimedia content and then hold a discussion of techniques. Both observations and transfer of knowledge will be best when the examples are timely and interesting.

Table 4-1: Suggested examples to explore for specific techniques

Technique	Multimedia Examples
Structure of a multimedia composition and analysis	Microsoft's *Multimedia Beethoven, The Ninth Symphony*
Timeline and retrieval methods	CNN's *Time Capsule*
Annotating documents including attaching multimedia critiques	IBM's *Illuminated Books and Manuscripts*
Look and feel of multimedia quizzes for elementary and high school students, respectively	IBM's *Math and More* and *Comprehensive Chemistry CD*
End user interfaces for E-mail and other on-line information	Prodigy, America Online, Internet, CompuServe
Compelling story telling along with use of multimedia	*From Alice to Ocean*
Kinds of interactivity	*The 7th Guest: Inside Henry Stauf's Mansion* and *Just Grandma and Me*
Special effects using video, graphics, and text	NFL football game on television
Interactivity with no keyboard and secure public operation	A kiosk in a museum, mall, or airport

As two other suitable examples, you could study the retrieval techniques that Microsoft's *Cinemania* movie database and Microsoft's *Encarta* general information database use and consider questions such as the following.

- What sorts of retrieval does this title provide?
- What other ways would you like to have available for selecting movies or general reference materials?
- What other features help a user use these titles?
- What rights do you have to repurpose portions of either title? Do you suppose Microsoft's *Encarta* is giving you a hint, when it offers to help you clip out selected text for use in your own works, and automatically includes a nicely formatted reference to itself as the source?

Some Copyright Cases to Discuss

You may want to discuss copyrights and ethics with your students, starting with a situation that puts them in the role of creators, and then generalizing from considering their own rights to considering the rights of others. Some suitable discussion cases follow.

- Suppose your students spend a year creating a project about global warming. Is someone infringing your students' copyright if he copies the project and sells it for a profit, without referencing your students, without getting their permission, and without even agreeing to give them a share of his profits?

- Are you infringing a television station's copyright if you videotape the local news broadcast of one of your student's playing the tuba in the high school band and then digitize it for your class to use in a multimedia kiosk for the school lobby ?

- Are you infringing if you use video capture of this videotape to get an image of the student's playing the tuba, have a local shop put the picture on T-shirts, and sell the T-shirts at a school fund raiser?

- Your principal brings you a professional photographer's photograph of the principal talking with members of the town board. He happened to sneeze at the wrong moment, so the picture looks as if he were scowling at the local dignitaries. He wants to use the picture in a presentation. He knows that he approved your purchase of a multimedia tool that allows your students to edit digitized images. He asks if your students can replace his scowl by a smile from another picture. Assuming that your students can meet his request, should they do so?

Summary

Just as learning to write involves reading and analyzing literature, learning to create multimedia projects involves studying other creators' multimedia. Just as all scholarship includes copying others' work and citing references, so creating multimedia involves using media clips and giving due credit. Just as you consider categories and types of books, rather than selecting at random from a library, you need to consider what sorts of multimedia content will best help your students to meet your objectives. Do the best you can until you can sign up for Comparative Multimedia 101.

What's that? Is there a hand in the back of the room? Yes, thanks for reminding us. You should indeed consider using professionally created educational multimedia titles for their intended purposes, as well as using them as sources of ideas and clips for student-created multimedia projects.

References

- Magazines that list many products and evaluate products:

The World of Macintosh Multimedia. Published quarterly. Produced by Redgate Communications Corporation, 660 Beachland Blvd., Vero Beach, FL 32963, (800) 333-8760.

Multimedia Today. Published quarterly. Edited by IBM, 4111 Northside Parkway, Internal Zip H4P-21, Atlanta, GA 30327, FAX (404) 238-4298, (800) 779-2062.

* Catalogs of products:

CD ROM Buyer's Guide. Tiger Software Catalog, (800) 238-4437, FAX (305) 529-2990.

EduCorp Multimedia Catalog, EduCorp, (800) 843-9497 or Internet:service@educorp.com

Enhance Bringing Teachers & Technology Together. (800) 777-3642.

Egghead Software. (800) EGGHEAD.

Creative Computers MacMall, (800) 222-2808.

Educational Resources Multimedia Edition Catalog. (800) 624-2926.

Sunburst, Multimedia Materials for Education, (800) 321-7511, America Online:Sunburst4.

* Archives:

LinkWay Archive maintains a free archive of LinkWay titles (called folders) on many different topics. Students created many of these. Contact:

Mark W. Whitman
InterDesign Group, Inc.,
6515 Indian Meadow Drive
West Lafayette, In. 47906
Internet:whitman@cedar.cic.net; Prodigy: RCVN75A; Voice: (317) 463-9130

Under the auspices of the Society for Technology and Teacher Education (STATE), the University of Virginia and the University of Houston have collaborated on an Internet server. The server contains discussion groups as well as TEACH-IT modules which are self-instruction hypermedia modules on various subjects. Use the server at state.virginia.edu or contact:

Bernard Robin, STATE Server Curator
Dept. of Curriculum & Instruction
University of Houston
Houston, TX 77204-5872
Voice: (713) 743 4952; Internet: brobin@uh.edu

* On line services:

America Online. (800) 827-6364.
PRODIGY Interactive Personal Service. (800)-PRODIGY.
CompuServe Information Service. (800) 848-8990.

Chapter 5

Organizing Information

In this chapter, we explore:

- the benefits of helping students learn to organize information by learning to create appropriate hypermedia links among pieces of information.

- organizations that are especially useful for particular collections of information.

- some collections of information that you and your students can use to practice selecting appropriate organizations.

This chapter's Theory section discusses 10 collections of information, such as information about Shakespeare and his plays, along with corresponding examples of suitable organizations for discussion and consideration. Then the Practice section suggests 14 exercises. Each exercise is an opportunity to try selecting an organization that is appropriate for a particular subject and a particular purpose. You can discuss these examples and try out these exercises yourself. You can also share the examples and exercises with your students, to help the students learn to organize information.

Background

In simplest terms, students create a multimedia project by researching a subject, selecting the pieces of information that they want to include in the project, representing each piece of information by creating one or more media, deciding how to organize those pieces of information, and implementing the selected organization by creating hypermedia links among the pieces. Chapter 1 noted that successful hypermedia requires partitioning a subject so that each piece of information can be related in multiple, meaningful ways and using appropriate media for each piece of information. Chapters 2 and 3 discussed the hardware and software aspects of creating different media and creating hypermedia links that express relationships among pieces of information. This chapter is about helping students learn to organize information.

As part of the process of preparing any project, you decide whether to have your students select an organization for the project's information content. On one hand, you may decide to suggest a particular organization. Each of Chapters 7 through 10 describes a concrete project and specifies a suitable organization that fits the project's information. On the other hand, you may decide to make selecting an organization be an important part of the work that your students do while creating the project. Each of Chapters 11 and 12 suggests an open-ended project for which students select the organization that they think will be most effective. Your decision depends on whether meeting the goals that you want students to achieve by creating a particular project requires the students to select an organization and not just be aware that one exists.

Meeting the goals of some projects requires students to concentrate on individual pieces of information, rather than on how different pieces of information relate to one another. For such projects, you select an organization and describe the organization to the class. To keep students even more closely focused on the information content, you may elect to give the class an actual sample project that uses the organization you selected. You then suggest that the students simply replace the sample project's information by the students' own new information. Such a sample project is thus a template for the selected organization. The students have to find and then decide how to break up their information to fit the provided organization.

Meeting the goals of other projects requires students to focus their attention on determining how different pieces of information relate to one another. For such projects, you ask your students to spend significant effort selecting an organization suitable for the subject. Selecting an organization would be straightforward if there were only a few possible organizations or if there existed a simple taxonomy of possible organizations. However, we all know that selecting an organization for an essay or for a book requires significant effort and creativity. Similarly, organizing a multimedia project is a nontrivial skill that students learn best by observing good organizations and by trying out organizations for themselves to see what works and what does not work.

Importance of Organizing Information

Organizing information by relating pieces of information to one another is an essential part of constructing knowledge. Organizing information can be the students' major learning experience from creating some multimedia projects. Selecting an organization helps students to understand meanings of, and relationships among, different pieces of information. Creating projects helps students to use information, to answer questions, and to explain situations. Students learn to fit new pieces of information and new ways of thinking about information into their existing knowledge frameworks.

Students who create a project not only learn the project's subject matter but also develop life-long learning techniques. Organizing the project's information allows them to practice articulating good questions, pursuing answers to these questions by wading into oceans of information, analyzing and synthesizing answers, and then placing the answers into a logical organization.

Learning to use hypermedia links to organize information will be important to students throughout their working and personal lives. Research on how students learn indicates that it is important for students to understand how to organize information themselves, both to learn subject matter and to understand how others organize information. The latter has always been important and will become more important as more people have access to more information in the form of hypermedia, both from on-line networks and from CD-ROM discs.

As students become familiar with a body of information and practice partitioning information into pieces, they find that the pieces relate to one another in many different ways. Selecting an organization is a matter of deciding which one or more relationships lead to meaningful organizations.

Authentic Projects

In order to achieve particular goals, it is often desirable for a multimedia project to have real or imagined users. Such a project requires students to think about how to organize information in a way that is suitable for members of a given audience. The creators can provide ways for a user to add new links or even new pieces of information to the project for other users to see and hear. One of the most desirable links that a user might want to add is a bookmark, that is, a mark that a user places on a given screen to facilitate the user's later return to that screen.

A project's creators should think about how to help users avoid getting lost in hyperspace. Creators should consider whether a user will understand the project's organization, that is, whether a user will know how to invoke links to move through the completed project without help from the creators. The creators could help users by providing a welcoming screen that explains how to use the mouse to select a button and move to the second screen. The creators might use either text or audio to present that explanation.

In general, if a user moves down through more than four levels of menus, the user loses track of the selections he has already made, suffers cognitive overload, and feels lost. Creators never need to use more than four levels of menus. For example, if each level presents five choices, then four levels suffice for presenting the user with a total of $5 \times 5 \times 5 \times 5 = 625$ choices.

Creators can provide several methods that help a user know where she is within the organization. Some of these methods involve providing a map of the information, leaving footprints or bread crumbs to remind a user that she has already seen a particular screen, checking off options the user has already selected, supplying a checklist on demand, providing landmarks, providing the ability to zoom in or out on paths, and providing the ability to mark a notebook. Providing a user with the opportunity to reverse any link she selected is particularly helpful.

Creators can help users feel familiar with a project by providing a common set of buttons that appear on nearly all screens, such as buttons that take a user to the next screen, previous screen, first screen, and exit screen. Another technique is to divide a project into several sections and give all of the screens within one section not only the same background color but also buttons that have the same distinctive shape.

Students need to remember that a computer allows a user to interact closely with the completed multimedia project. By implementing a suitable organization, creators can make a user feel that the information that the user sees and hears is very personal and that the project is very responsive.

Some assignments require the creators to make a presentation using the completed multimedia project. That is, some of the project's users may be the creators themselves. Creating linked hypermedia rather than merely a linear (sequential) presentation allows a presenter to vary the presentation at will, based on observing what interests the audience. Hypermedia links also help the presenter to answer questions by quickly accessing relevant audiovisual aids. One effective way to demonstrate a multimedia project is to show the audience how the project works, and then allow members of the audience to tell the presenter what links to activate. This is one of many differences between a multimedia project and an electronic easel audiovisual presentation aid.

Typical authentic assignments include creating a project that will run on a computer in a public location, such as a school corridor or lobby. In this situation, the creators will not be around to encourage people to use the project. When creating such a project, students should therefore include a grabber. A grabber shows attractive images or video, and plays attractive audio, until a user notices the project and selects some button. Thereafter, of course, the project responds to the user. However, whenever several minutes have gone by with no user input, the project should automatically return to the grabber.

Helping Students Organize Information

The first key to helping students create a well-organized multimedia project is for a teacher to articulate a well-thought-out assignment. Having a concrete purpose in mind is vital in order for students to determine that some organizations meet the purpose better than others. Six of many suitable types of assignments that you might select are as follows.

- Phrase the assignment in the form of a question to be answered.
- State a specific issue and require students to represent all sides.
- Provide a list of terms and ask students to define them and relate them to one another in appropriate ways.
- Challenge students to illuminate a text passage by using hot words that play audio or show images to explain the author's symbolism or to elucidate obscure vocabulary.
- Suggest that students set up a one-screen form that fits a particular spectrum of information and then fill in a few dozen of the screens with specific examples.

- Ask the students to explain a given concept by making good use of several media in addition to text. The students' thought processes may include a sort of triage to decide what information to emphasize, what information to give a subordinate position, and what information to leave out altogether.

The second key to motivating good organization is for a teacher to demonstrate excellent examples of projects that others have created. The most inspiring and challenging examples are ambitious projects that previous groups of students have created. Some commercial titles, which adult professionals with large budgets have prepared, may or may not be effective models. Students may tend to ignore such examples. The teacher can lead a discussion of how well the examples organized their information, made the essential points in a clear, crisp way, and fulfilled the intent of the assignment. From such a discussion, students learn techniques that effectively convey information relevant to the assignment.

The third key to helping students organize information is to encourage the students to unleash their creativity by finding new metaphors for information. Metaphors stimulate visualizations. Students may decide that the information will appear to be a book, a map, a library building, a town, or a picture of an object with hot areas that users can select in order to see and hear more information. For example, for an assignment to use multimedia to present information about the largest cities in a state, the metaphor could be a state map with the cities' locations as hot buttons. More creatively, the metaphor could be a photo album page containing pictures of the cities' best known landmarks. More formally, the metaphor could be an alphabetized list of the cities' names. What might be a good metaphor for a multimedia project that contrasts opinions in favor of and against a particular position? Students might select large plus and minus signs, an image of two Janus faces, or a screen that is half white and half green.

The fourth key to good organizations is helping students execute an effective process, such as the following.

- Understand the assignment.
- Brainstorm and do research.
- Select pieces of information to include in the project.
- Discuss several overall organizations.
- Select an organization.
- Decide on a metaphor for visualizing the body of information.
- Decide on one or more media to represent each piece of information.
- Prepare scripts and story boards as required.
- Fill in the organization with the media.
- Provide links among the pieces of information.
- Test the result with typical members of the project's intended audience.

Learning to use hypermedia links to organize information and applying those skills are nontrivial activities. Students do not automatically develop skills that are required for organizing information. Even after students have learned the skills, they may find the skills difficult to apply. With guidance and the inspiration of seeing some good examples, students can produce multimedia projects that indicate astonishing maturity of understanding of relevant information. As early as kindergarten and first grade, students can actively engage in organizing information and using their organization to draw conclusions about the information. Links can be as diverse as the media that the links organize.

Types of Links

Consider the "Current Events" project that Chapter 1 mentioned and that Chapter 7 describes in detail. In this project, a screen such as in Figure 5-1 could include three buttons that take a user quickly from a paragraph that describes an event to one of three other screens. One screen could tell what event happened next, after the original screen's event. The second screen is a picture of someone who was involved in the event. The third is an oral statement of the event's historical context. When a user moves the mouse so that the mouse pointer is on one of these three buttons and clicks the mouse, the user instructs the computer to traverse the corresponding link. For example, selecting the "Next event" button shows the user the screen that tells what happened next. A "Return" button takes the user back to the first page or to the main screen of the project. The main screen also has controls to allow the user to go forward and backward in a sequence of screens or to quit, that is, to leave the project altogether. In some hardware setups, such as in a public kiosk from which a mouse tends to run away, a touch-screen replaces the mouse. A user touches a button directly with his finger on the screen to activate the corresponding link.

Some screens include buttons as parts of text. When a button looks like some specially marked text, such as text that is underlined or is a different color from the rest of a paragraph, then the button is called a hot word. In different projects, selecting a hot word may pop up a box that contains a dictionary definition of the word, may play audio that tells the user how to pronounce the word, may show a picture of whatever the word denotes, may give the word's opposite, may display the word in another language, or may show the user a completely different screen that relates to the word in any desired fashion. Some authoring systems implement hot words as transparent buttons. A user finds a transparent button by moving the mouse pointer over the corresponding part of the screen and seeing the mouse pointer change shape. Another use of a transparent button is to create a button that does not obscure a picture, yet allows a user to cause a response by selecting any part of the picture. A project's creator can include a link that produces a result that depends not only on what button a user just selected but also what buttons a user has previously selected. For example, if a user has previously indicated that he likes basketball, and now selects a button that invokes a tour of New York City, then the creator may cause the tour button to invoke a link that shows a basketball game.

It is possible to begin creating a project by entering pieces of multimedia information with no inherent organization, that is, with no links. Students may subsequently impose one or more organizations on the information, after the fact. Contrast this to linear text or to a videotape where the contents are stored in one physical order, which is the only order in which users can access the material conveniently and rapidly. Linear text or videotape correspond to a river of information along which users can merely elect to paddle at different speeds. Multimedia corresponds to islands in a sea of information in which users can tour and navigate at will. Touring and navigating have different purposes, as we see next.

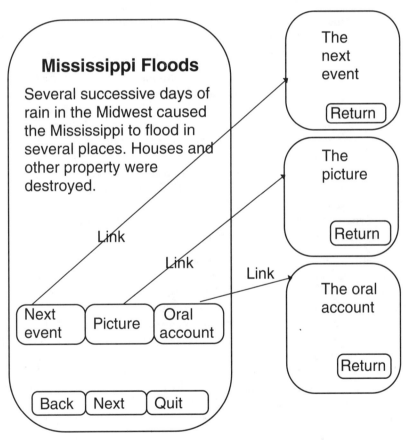

Figure 5-1: Choosing different buttons to link to different information

Touring and Navigating

A project's creators may or may not want users to see and hear the project's information in one particular order. That is, in a given sea of information, creators may want a user to follow a particular tour, visiting particular islands in a particular order. Alternatively, creators may want a user to navigate freely, to reach quickly whatever island is most interesting to the user. For example, touring is appropriate for a tutorial, whereas navigating is appropriate for an encyclopedia. The students who create a project decide whether touring or navigating is optimal for that project's users and provide corresponding links among the project's pieces of information.

On the one hand, a tutorial builds a subject by constructing a foundation of unique terminology and fundamental concepts, then piles on more complex topics. A carefully reasoned argument has one particular order in which its creator thinks a user will find the discussions and examples most convincing. The creator of a mystery story builds interest by gradually revealing some facts while withholding other facts. Such uses cry out for a tour, which the creators control at the time they organize the project's information. Creators build a tour by linking each part of a project to the part that the creators want a user to see and hear next, thus creating a linear organization.

On the other hand, information in an encyclopedia, glossary, or dictionary has no natural order. It is not true that a user will find that one piece of information makes most sense after reading the preceding piece. For example, reading an item about sculpture contributes little to understanding the next item about scum. Rather, a person who is using reference material wants to find a particular piece of information as quickly as possible. Such uses demand navigation, which each user controls by invoking the different sorts of links that the project's creators provided. As a user takes responsibility for deciding when to see each piece of information, so the user takes responsibility for asking for supplementary explanations of unfamiliar terms and concepts. Because a user may reach a particular piece of information without having read any tutorial material, the project's creators must provide links to such supplementary explanations.

On the third hand, there is an intermediate case, in between the case where the creators link information into a linear tour and the case where the creators provide links that allow flexible navigation. In this intermediate case, creators want a user to visit each of several islands of information, but are willing to allow the user to select the order of the visits. This case may irritate a user who cares about the order even less than do the creators. Hence, the creator can assure that the project offers to select an order for the user. Moreover, the creators can arrange for the project to keep track of which islands a particular user has already visited, to make it easy for the user to select a new island, even if the user has lost track of where he has already been. One good way for students to handle the intermediate case is to suggest that a user begin with a tour, but provide links that allow a user to drop out of the tour at any point and begin navigating at will.

The most important point about touring and navigating is that neither type of organization is inherent in a particular subject. Students decide whether to provide one, the other, or both by thinking about their project's objectives. In fact, creators can decide to provide for navigation and also provide several tours through the same information to achieve different objectives.

It may be extremely valuable for someone other than the original creator of a particular body of information to organize that material, either as one or more tours or as navigation. For example, suppose that students have access to a CD-ROM disc that contains pictures of an art gallery's paintings, in the order in which the museum obtained the paintings. Students could become familiar with the museum's collection by organizing the paintings into a tour that would appeal to a particular sort of visitor. Alternatively, students could organize the paintings by date, material, school, artist's name, artist's national origin, and other properties that a user could use to find a particular painting. This is one of many examples of how multimedia projects blur the line that divides creators from users.

Organizing the Creators

A typical multimedia project is a group effort. For efficiency, individual members of the group must be able to take responsibility for well-defined portions of the total effort and carry out those portions more or less independently of one another. Some rework is inevitable when different students or subgroups combine their efforts to complete the project. However, careful organization of the information and the people can minimize that rework.

One useful organization matches topics to students. Each authoring system, as Chapter 3 described, has its own collection of multimedia information, which may be a folder, a card stack, or a book. Using a folder as an example, it may be most efficient to organize a group so that all but one individual or subgroup prepares one folder on one subject. The remaining individual or subgroup prepares a folder that is composed primarily of links to the other folders, combining those folders into a coherent project.

Another useful organization matches media or functions to students. For example, if each topic within a project requires an audio clip, it may make sense to set up a subgroup to write and record the audio for all topics. Several of the examples in following sections note successful ways to organize creators as well as information.

Theory

In the absence of any complete or accepted taxonomy of ways to organize information, this section illustrates and describes ten useful organizations. For a project in which a teacher asks students to select a suitable organization, the students might decide that one of these organizations is optimal, might decide to use a combination of several of these organizations, or might devise an organization that differs from all of these. You could coach students by mentioning several possible organizations, to avoid the common misapprehension that only one organization is possible for a given subject.

We have assigned an arbitrary name to each organization. For example, we call the first one the Shakespeare organization because Shakespeare was the subject of a particularly effective project that used this organization. We do not mean to imply that this organization is the only one or the best one that students could select for a project about the Bard. Moreover, we do not mean to imply that this organization is suitable only for a project about Shakespeare. In fact, Chapters 7 and 8 suggest essentially the Shakespeare organization for their respective projects that relate to different subjects. For each organization, the figure is generic and the discussion relates the generic organization to the specific example that gave rise to the organization's name.

Shakespeare Organization

A teacher suggested that students start to create a project about Shakespeare by drawing a screen similar to the one labeled Main Menu in Figure 5-2. This screen is a simple concept map. The creators used this map to identify the principal concepts that they would include in the project. They decided that Part 1 would be theater costumes; Part 2, the configuration of Elizabethan theaters; Part 3, the life of Shakespeare, and so on. They then divided the work of creating this project among members of the group by assigning each part to one student. Each student developed her part as a separate folder that

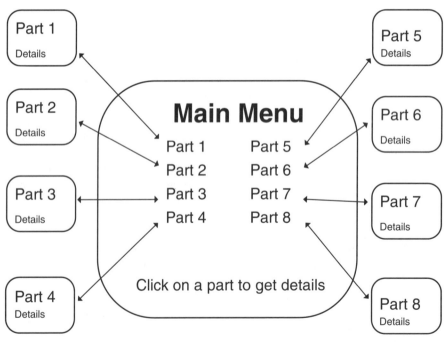

Figure 5-2: The Shakespeare organization

contained text, pictures relevant to the topic, citations, a picture of the creator herself, and whatever links she thought were useful within her part of the project.

The students brought their folders together on one personal computer and cooperated in creating the main menu screen, which was in its own separate folder, with its links joining the main menu to the other parts of the project. Instead of labeling the buttons with words, the students created a consistent set of picture icons that represented the information contained in the respective parts. A person who is using the completed project can thus select an icon that looks like a costume to navigate to the part of the project that shows and discusses costumes.

Within each part, a user can explore information about the corresponding concept. Each page of each part's folder has a button at the bottom of the screen that, when selected, causes the user to return to the main menu. A user can select another button to return to the beginning of the part. Each screen has an identical set of such controls, on which the students decided before separating to create their individual folders in parallel. A small version of the part's icon appears at one corner of each screen in that part, to remind the user where she is. All the screens appear sufficiently similar to form a coherent project, yet each screen contains a clue about where the user is within the project's body of information. Each student could create a part of the project, yet the only way a user links from one part to another is by way of the main menu. The Shakespeare organization is thus a one-level hierarchy.

Hurricane Organization

Creators of a project on Hurricane Hugo, Figure 5-3, began by defining three sub-topics

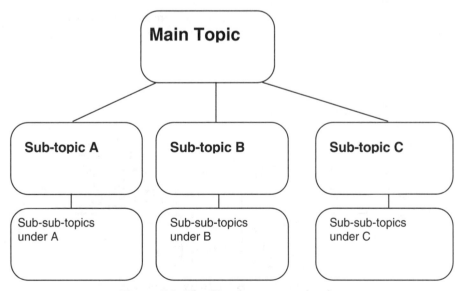

Figure 5-3: The Hurricane organization

of information and assigning one student to plan and create each. The sub-topics were:

- A: Hurricane Hugo, the specific event.
- B: Hurricanes, in general.
- C: Charlotte SC, effects of Hugo.

Each creator developed his entire sub-topic, including an independent story board and timeline. After completing their sub-topics, the creators got together and contributed their results to the total project. They then decided on desirable links between sub-topics. They also decided on a common appearance of controls that would help a user to navigate easily and keep track of the user's position within the project's many-level hierarchy of sub-topics. Allowing each student to select her organization of sub-sub-topics made a complex project manageable. Each sub-topic was many folders with one main sub-topic folder that assisted in organizing for that sub-topic.

Travel Agency Organizations, Tree and Table

A teacher decided to couch a geography lesson as creating a multimedia project for a hypothetical travel agency. Students created a project that tourists could use to explore several cities, select a particular city, and then buy tickets from the travel agency. The creators started by collecting information about three cities: Boston, New York, and Miami. Next, the students spent considerable time devising a classification scheme for the information. They selected choices that tourists could make for each city. Ch1 was the city's climate, Ch2 was scenery, Ch3 was attractions for adventuresome people, Ch4 was attractions for people who like museums, and Ch5 was information on the city's lodging and transportation. The students designed a tree organization, also known as a hierarchical organization, in which a user first saw a main menu containing three buttons that the user could select to specify a city as indicated in Figure 5-4. The user then saw a screen that presented five choices of information about the selected city that

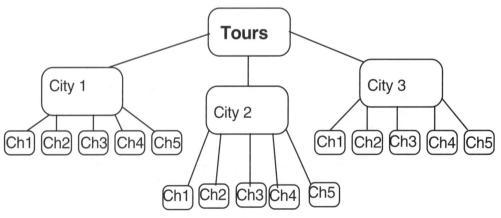

Figure 5-4: The Travel Agency tree organization

the user could elect to see and print.

The creators tested this organization by asking several users to try out the partly completed project. The students found that about half of the users were interested in only one choice and wanted to see information about that choice for each city. The creators realized that their tree organization made navigation difficult for such users. The students therefore changed to an organization in which the main menu showed a table of cities and choices as in Figure 5-5.

	Ch1	Ch2	Ch3	Ch4	Ch5
City 1					
City 2					
City 3					

Figure 5-5: The Travel Agency table organization

The table organization allowed a user to select interesting information easily and quickly. If a user selected Ch1, then the project presented a menu from which the user could select one city after another and see information about those cities' climates. If a user selected City 3, then the project presented a menu from which the user could select one choice after another and see information about Miami, as in the original tree organization. If a user selected the button at the intersection of Ch1 and City 3, then the project took the user immediately to information about the climate of Miami.

The information did not change between these two organizations. The creators simply added links and a new main menu to make navigation more convenient for all potential users.

Columbus Day Organization

A high school teacher organized the subject by dividing students into two teams to prepare multimedia positions for and against celebrating Columbus Day as a good thing. The teacher encouraged the students to use appropriate media to express their views succinctly. The teacher also suggested that each team present their arguments linearly, in whatever order the students thought would be most convincing. The two teams agreed to offer a user the opportunity to enter the user's own views, for subsequent viewers to see and hear after seeing and hearing the students' positions. The Columbus Day organization, Figure 5-6, began with the simplest tree organization, dividing the subject into two natural branches, and then continued with the linear organization, which is suitable for a polemic.

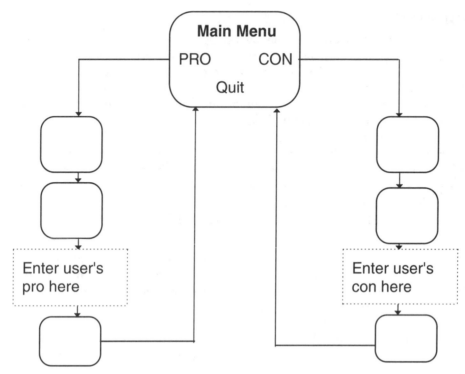

Figure 5-6: The Columbus Day organization

Community Photographs Organization

A community historical society asked a teacher at the local elementary school to help categorize and display several dusty shoe boxes full of historical photographs of the community. A teacher and fourth grade class decided to set up a multimedia kiosk to display scanned images of the photos, along with additional information. The teacher suggested that the students employ a standard form, Figure 5-7, for all the screens, including buttons that a user could select to see a picture, a description, or an opinion. Employing a form helped students collect information individually while working toward a coherent overall project. The teacher set up the form and prepared the multimedia scripts for the hypermedia links that students would require to link from each form to other screens.

The main screen, which a user sees first, is a simple index. It lists names of the photographs' subjects in alphabetical order. Clicking on any name shows the user the

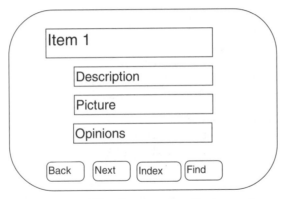

**Figure 5-7: The Community Photographs
organization**

corresponding form. Thus, this organization puts all the historical photographs in parallel. A user can select any photograph with equal ease. The important organizational concept here is the common form that all students employ.

Each photograph's form contains buttons that a user can select to get additional information. For example, Item 3 could contain a picture of a statue in the town square. When a user selects the Picture button, the user sees the corresponding picture and then returns. Selecting the Description button gives a one-sentence description of the statue and returns. Selecting that sentence activates a hidden button that takes the user to a paragraph of information about the statue. The teacher also decided that the form will contain common buttons with which a user could go backward in the sequence of items, go forward, or go to the Index.

Part way through the project, after working with the first 100 photographs, the students found that it took them a long time to find a desired picture in the alphabetized list. They worked with the teacher to implement a Find button on the form, so that this button would appear on each screen. When a user selects the Find button, the user sees a screen that prompts the user to enter a keyword. Then the computer searches all text on all screens for that keyword and displays the first screen on which the word appears. Selecting Find again, without entering a different keyword, tells the computer to search for the next screen on which the keyword appears, and so on. The authoring system made it easy to program the Find button's hypermedia link. The students were pleased that even their rather old and slow computer could search information about all 500 photographs in less than a second. The Find function was a significant improvement to the Community Photographs parallel organization.

School Buses Organization

A Georgia community needed to teach students, including very young ones, how to ride the new school bus system. They wanted visual instructions for the very young, audio instructions for those who learn better with audio, and clear instructions for all. A class accepted this authentic challenge. The teacher and students divided the information into three parts. Part 1 covered catching the bus from home. Part 2 covered catching the bus at the end of the school session. Part 3 covered behavior on the bus and bus safety. They decided that everyone should see and hear all the parts in a carefully selected order. They assigned each part to a sub-group of the class.

After creating the remainder of the project, the students added material designed to attract users to the kiosk; that is, they created a grabber. That material plays as a continuous loop when nobody is using the kiosk. After experimenting with different attraction loops, the students decided on flashing colors, cartoons, and march music. The School Buses organization's grabber was an important addition to the basic organization, Figure 5-8, of a single-level hierarchy with a three-way split leading to three linear presentations.

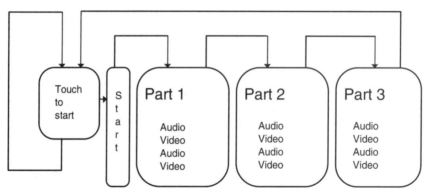

Figure 5-8: The School Buses organization

Police Training Organization

The police vocational training class of a mid-west high school developed a set of multimedia competency-based courseware modules. A module places a user in a typical police situation and asks the user to decide how to handle the situation. Each possible decision invokes a hypermedia link that lets the user see and hear typical results of that decision, which may call for a further decision. The user never returns to a previous screen without seeing some reminder about what has transpired since the user last saw that screen. That is, the module changes each scene as a result of either the user's actions or the passage of time. The module eliminates all such changes when each new user begins.

Such a network of linked scenarios, as shown in Figure 5-9, is particularly effective for training. Developing these modules helped the students who created the modules to become expert in this sort of training. Their expertise involved learning to use an organization that is much more flexible than a tree. The Police Training organization is an example of a general network, in which links can run in any desired direction. Contrast that general network to a tree, which is a special sort of network. A tree constrains links to run only from the trunk, out over branches, to a leaf, or back over branches to the trunk. A tree never allows any link to run directly from one leaf to another leaf. In general, we do not recommend that students use a general network organization. Users can keep track of where they are in a tree much more easily than they can find their way through a general network.

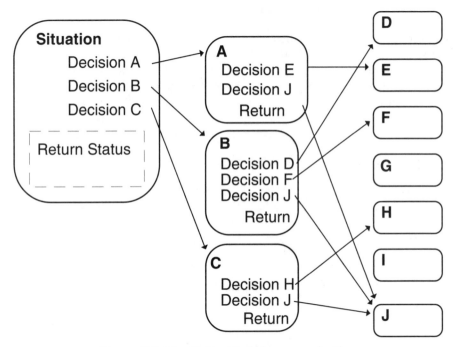

Figure 5-9: The Police Training organization

Encyclopedia of Birds Organization

A biology class used the organization that Figure 5-10 shows to create a project that summarized and organized information the students had collected about birds. The Main Menu shows the name of each species on a corresponding button. When a user selects a button, the user sees a screen that contains a picture of the bird and some

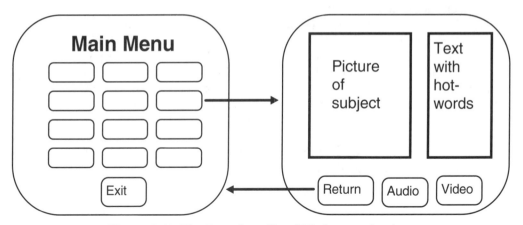

Figure 5-10: The Encyclopedia of Birds organization

detailed description of the bird's behavior and habitat. The screen also contains buttons, on which the class agreed in advance, that a user can select to see video of the bird in flight or audio of the bird's song. Each screen also contains a Return button that a user can select to go back to the main menu. From the main menu, the user may select a button to see information about another species or may select the Exit button to leave the project.

Class Pictures Organization

Eight students created this organization, Figure 5-11, to allow a user to go from a picture of any student to a picture of any other student, at any time, by selecting one button.

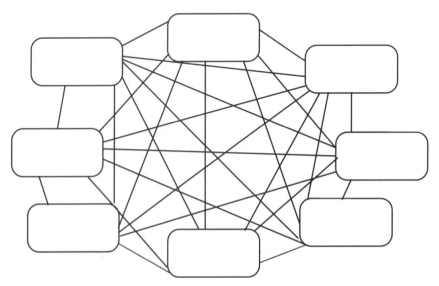

Figure 5-11: The Class Pictures organization

Each student's screen shows eight buttons with the names of all eight students. The students created the eight buttons just once and placed the buttons on a background page so the buttons appeared below all eight pictures. Thus, creating this organization was no more work than creating a main menu page would have been.

However, this organization is unsuitable for an encyclopedia of birds because a user would confuse the buttons for navigating within the information about one species with the buttons for navigating from one species to another. The Class Pictures organization is an extreme example of the general network organization in which a user can link from any screen to any other screen. We recommend that students use this organization only with extreme care.

Origami Ear-rings Organization

Students who were preparing to sell origami ear-rings at a student fair collected many pieces of information about origami. They used graphics to show how to fold paper to make origami, images to show completed origami figures, audio of an interview to tell about origami's role in Japanese culture, and text to discuss origami's place in Japanese history. The students first prepared these media for their multimedia project without creating any links among the pieces. At this stage, the project was not disorganized but rather was completely unorganized.

At this point, the students organized themselves into three groups to utilize their prepared material in three different ways to meet three different objectives. One group's objective was to provide audiovisual aids for live presentations. This group needed a linear motivational presentation with video to display ear-rings in a positive light and background music to set a cheerful mood. This group's organization was similar to the School Buses organization.

The second group's objective was a standalone kiosk. Meeting this objective required a continuously cycling motivational presentation, an attractor or grabber, that links to a navigation session when a user comes up to the kiosk and requests more information. This group used an organization similar to the Shakespeare organization. Each icon represented a specific origami figure or other specific piece of information.

The third group's objective was a project relating Japanese historical and modern culture to the complexities of constructing origami. Meeting this third objective required a video demonstration of constructing one origami figure, then a smooth segue into a discussion of the culture that created the art form, and finally an offer of instructions on how to construct several figures. This group's organization is similar to the Hurricane organization.

Each of the three groups used most of the pieces of information that the class had prepared at the beginning of the project. In addition to adding links among these pieces, each of the three groups of students added screens that contained buttons to invoke the links. Two of the groups found that they needed to add a few new pieces of information in order to meet their differing objectives.

The Origami Ear-rings organization illustrates the important concept that students can organize pieces of information separately from creating particular media that represent the information. This concept allows you and your students to practice organizing information either with or without actually creating projects, as in the next section.

Practice

This section suggests 14 assignments to practice organizing information. A teacher might assign one or more of these to students in appropriate grade levels, facilitate a brainstorming session to help the students consider several possible organizations, and finally participate in reflection to determine whether students selected a suitable organization. As is the case with all this book's practices and projects, the authors recommend that present and future educators play the role of K-12 students and use these assignments for their own practice sessions.

Each assignment involves at least selecting a suitable organization, without actually collecting the corresponding information. It would be possible to use any of these assignments as an actual multimedia project by actually collecting the information, representing each piece of information in one or more suitable media, and implementing the selected organization by means of hypermedia links.

A paragraph about a suggested organization follows the statement of each suggested assignment. Although we drew these suggestions from organizations that we discussed in this chapter's Theory section, other organizations and combinations of organizations may be at least as suitable. Each assignment gives practice in

- deciding upon an organization,
- using one or more navigation options, and
- selecting a unifying visual metaphor.

Women in Engineering, Grade 9

Organize information about several women professionals in different branches of engineering. Indicate what navigation options you would provide and what unifying visual metaphors would you use.

Consider using the Encyclopedia of Birds organization with buttons for different engineering disciplines in alphabetical order.

Events on Timelines, Grades 8 or 9

Devise a concept map that uses a timeline to organize information concerning at least 10 major geological events in the earth's 4.6-billion-year history. Make each event a button that allows users to link to a page that presents more details about the event. Provide buttons on this page that allow a user to link to the causes and effects of the events. Make sure that the user does not get disoriented or lost.

One possibility is the Shakespeare organization. The real creativity required is figuring out how to represent such a large span of time in a visually effective way.

How a VCR Works, Middle School

Devise an overall visual metaphor to serve as the main menu that users can employ to learn how to use a VCR works by navigating to appropriate information.

Consider modifying the Travel Agency Table organization so that each choice becomes a VCR control such as the "Play" button, and each city becomes a task such as "Play a prerecorded tape." This organization makes it easy for a user to determine the function of a particular button as well as which sequence of buttons performs a particular function.

Describe a Cell, Grade 9 or 10 Biology

Organize a multimedia project summarizing what the class is learning about cells.

The Shakespeare organization is one of several good possibilities. In this organization, an image that shows the parts of a generalized cell could be covered by invisible buttons. When a user selects one of these buttons, the user sees a screen that contains a detailed description of the corresponding part.

Favorite Pets' Characteristics, Elementary School

Organize information derived from a brainstorming session about how pets differ in behavior, appearance, and necessary care.

The Travel Agency Tree organization is a possibility. A type of pet could take the place of each city and a characteristic could take the place of each choice.

Hole in the Body, High School

Organize the many ramifications of the hole in a shooting victim. Indicate what navigation options the resulting project would give the user and what visual metaphor would unify the project.

The Hurricane organization is a possibility. This organization's challenge is to decide on suitable sub-topics and sub-sub-topics such as medical and legal ramifications and ramifications of death, including the funeral's costs to the family and society.

Multimedia Equipment Handbook, High School

Set up a handbook, in multimedia form, that describes how to use the school's multimedia equipment. Use appropriate media to explain simply and effectively how to perform a wide variety of tasks. Include at least the tasks of plugging a laser disc player into the television monitor and creating a video clip. Put several of your own favorite multimedia tasks in the catalog and then ask others what they can contribute or what they need to know how to do. For inspiration, find a Radio Shack store containing a kiosk that describes how to use equipment that they sell. Include directions so that others can add additional multimedia techniques easily, as they obtain new equipment and techniques.

The Community Photographs organization would fit this purpose. One challenge is devising a common form that applies to all tasks.

Creative Journeys, High School

As a role-playing assignment, organize a multimedia project to apply for funding for a research grant. Propose a trip to the Arctic for the purpose of learning about the Sami people. The granting organization, of course, has limited funds. They have shown strong interest in evidence that a potential recipient has the ability to plan an efficient trip that will optimize travel time and money. They have asked for a proposal that poses a few well-thought-out questions and presents a plan for answering those questions. If necessary, find out who and where the Sami people are located and telephone a friendly travel agency or reindeer-rental company for some suggestions on how to get to where the Samis are. Develop a multimedia presentation of your travel plan and why you selected that plan, what you will take, and what you hope to bring back. Remember that the granting agency's people's time is limited. You need to attract their attention. You also need to leave some simple images in their mind, so that after looking at many applications they will remember yours and award the grant to you.

The School Buses organization is a good possibility, although the goal here is to convince rather than to instruct. You want to make sure that a user sees and hears all of the important points in the order that you select.

Health and Safety for Driving at 0° F, High School

Organize information about the possible choices and outcomes for a group of high school students. The students want to try out their new drivers' licenses by braving cold and hazardous driving conditions to attend a football game in a nearby town. Include the safest choice, staying home, as well as other scenarios.

The Police Training organization is a possibility for giving the information emotional content, especially if the organization allows a given choice to have different possible outcomes.

Commentaries on Stories, Elementary School

Organize students' opinions about several selected stories. Decide on a classification scheme such as funny, sad, adventurous, science fiction, mystery, historical, and so on. Include comments on how each story compares to others in the same classification.

Consider the Travel Agency Tree organization, where the classifications take the place of cities. Consider devising visually significant icons to represent each category of stories, such as an android for science fiction stories.

About Me, Elementary School

Organize multimedia autobiographies by all of the students in a class.

The Class Pictures organization's free navigation may be ideal to allow a user to navigate from any student's autobiography to any other student's. However, if the class contains more than about eight students, the Community Photographs organization would probably work better.

Whither Garbage, High School

Organize many types of information that relate to the very general topic of what happens to garbage after it leaves students' homes. Select what is important for users to know about garbage in their community from the variety of information from newspapers and other sources.

The Shakespeare organization is less applicable than it may first appear; the Hurricane organization may work better. Useful sub-topics include the current situation, future plans, and companies' products produced or services performed.

Catalog of School Activities, Elementary School

Organize information about extracurricular activities for a multimedia kiosk in the school lobby.

The Encyclopedia of Birds organization could be suitable. Deciding that basic screens will look similar would allow members of the class to divide up the required work on a continuing basis.

Destination for a Class Trip, High School

Describe and present pro and con opinions relative to visiting Washington, Toronto, and New York on a class trip.

Consider combining the Columbus Day organization with the Community Photographs organization.

Summary

Organizing information is an important part of many learning experiences, both inside and outside classrooms. Multimedia projects help teachers give students meaningful opportunities to select organizations and to place pieces of information within those organizations. The opportunity to use hypermedia links to create many different organizations is at least as important as the opportunity to use several different media to express information. A multimedia project may include several different organizations of the same information, just as pieces of information may relate to one another in several different ways. Useful project organizations range from tours, in which creators specify an ordering in advance, to navigation, in which creators provide links that give users total control of what to see and hear next.

It is possible to teach, learn, and practice using hypermedia links to organize information. For those purposes, this chapter suggested ways to help students learn to organize information, provided useful examples of organizations, and suggested challenging material that students and educators can practice organizing.

References

Beasley. "A Methodology for Collecting Navigation Data Using IBM's *LinkWay*, A Hypermedia Authoring Language." *Journal of Educational Multimedia and Hypermedia*. Vol. 1, No. 4, pp. 465 - 470, 1992.

Blattner, and Dannenberg, eds. *Multimedia Interface Design*. Reading: Addison Wesley, 1992.

Harris and Grandgenett. "A Developmental Sequence of Children's Semantic Relationships: Implications for the Design of Interactive Hypermedia Materials." *Journal of Educational Multimedia and Hypermedia*. Vol. 2, No. 1, pp. 83 - 101, 1993.

Laurel, Brenda, ed. *The Art of Human-Computer Interface Design*. Reading: Addison Wesley, 1990.

Lee and Lehman. "Instructional Cueing in Hypermedia: A Study with Active and Passive Learners." *Journal of Educational Multimedia and Hypermedia*. Vol. 2, No. 1, pp. 25 - 38, 1993.

Meyers. "Interdisciplinary Multimedia Learning Using Anchored Instruction." *Empowering People Through Technology*, Conference Proceedings of the 34th International Conference of the Association for the Development of Computer-Based Instruction Systems (ADCIS). Norfolk, Virginia, pp. 73-79, November 8-11, 1992.

Nelson and Palumbo. "Learning, Instruction, and Hypermedia." *Journal of Educational Multimedia and Hypermedia*. Vol. 1, No. 3, pp. 287 - 300, 1992.

Ross, Tweed W., College of Education, Bluemont Hall, Kansas State University, Manhattan, Kansas 66506-5318. "Bloom and Hypertext: Parallel Taxonomies?" *ED-TECH Review*. Autumn/Winter 1993.

Sims, Ron. "Interactive Multimedia Courseware: A Perspective on Competency-Based Training for the Hospitality Industry." *Empowering People Through Technology*, Conference Proceedings of the 34th International Conference of the Association for the Development of Computer-Based Instruction Systems (ADCIS). Norfolk, Virginia, pp. 363-372, November 8-11, 1992.

Small and Grabowski. "An Exploratory Study of Information-Seeking Behaviors and Learning with Hypermedia Information Systems." *Journal of Educational Multimedia and Hypermedia*. Vol. 1, No. 4, pp. 445 - 464, 1992.

Zhu, Xiaoming. "Strategies for Utilizing Hypermedia Instruction vs. Information Access." *Empowering People Through Technology*, Conference Proceedings of the 34th International Conference of the Association for the Development of Computer-Based Instruction Systems (ADCIS). Norfolk, Virginia, pp. 223 - 232, November 8-11, 1992.

Chapter 6

Process and Projects

In this chapter, we explore:

- a practical and effective four-step process for planning a multimedia project, assigning the project to students, coaching students through creating the project, and reflecting on the results.

- an approach to selecting projects by making and using tables that record projects' characteristics.

The Background section introduces the process and suggests sources of assistance for carrying out the steps. The Theory section then describes each step in detail. The Practice section provides tables that record characteristics of the six multimedia projects that you will read about in the next six chapters. It suggests a practical way you can extend the tables to other projects.

Background

Process

A multimedia project can be a substantial undertaking. A successful result depends on time you invest up front in thoughtful preparation, particularly in selecting a project that will help your students achieve the goals that you set. One of the most important ways in which you can help students achieve your goals is by clearly assigning what you expect them to do as they create the project. Because it is the students who actually create the project, you act as their mentor as they carry out your assignment. Finally, reflecting on the students' project and on the extent to which the students achieved your goals is key to a successful result, both for a single project and for a succession of projects.

These considerations led us to suggest the process that Figure 6-1 illustrates.

A process is a succession of concrete steps that produce a desired result. Our process is typical in that it includes loops. The loops from the reflection step back to earlier steps indicate that, as you and your students follow the process, you feed back changes. These changes continually improve both the current project and future projects. A process acts as a checklist that you use to make sure you have not forgotten important items and to help you decide what to do next if you get stuck.

Table 6-1 shows some typical activities in each of the process steps. The Theory section discusses many of these activities in detail. Of course, you may decide to include only some of these activities, and some additional ones, in a particular project.

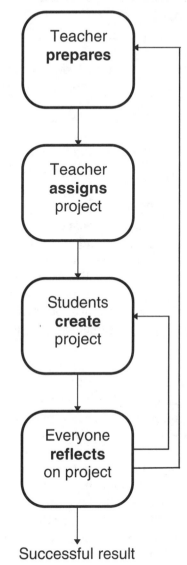

Figure 6-1: Process for multimedia projects

Table 6-1: Process steps' examples of activities

Teacher prepares

- Goals, specific project topic, and anchoring task
- Required and available skills and required and available equipment
- Multimedia tools, organization, and research resources
- Content that teacher will provide and content that students will develop and discover
- Organization of information and who selects it
- Grouping of students
- Requirements for successful completion of project
- Characteristics of outstanding projects

Teacher assigns project

- Anchoring task and optional discussion of goals
- What teacher provides and what students are expected to provide
- Requirements for successful completion of project
- Demonstration of illustrative examples
- Working arrangements, responsibilities, and equipment logistics
- Sources of information in various media
- Suggested tasks, interim milestones, and sizes of media
- Due date

Students create project

- Understand or clarify assignment
- Bring together materials, make plan, organize information
- Determine links among related pieces of information, develop small samples
- Perform group critique as a key interim milestone
- Decide on additional work and modifications needed to existing work
- Prepare final exhibition of project
- Demonstrate project
- Prepare for other users to enjoy the project later
- Teachers record experiences, improvements, and student feedback
- Teachers add results to class portfolio

Everyone reflects on project

- Student self-evaluation is continual part of creation step
- Teachers finalize reflections on the project, the process, and records
- Public performance provides additional feedback
- Class provides final formal evaluation
- Feed back improvements to earlier steps

Sources of Assistance

A multimedia project can be such a substantial undertaking that the prospect can leave you wondering when you and your students would ever have the time to do these four steps, let alone learn intricacies of new hardware and software. Indeed, few would say that a multimedia project is easy, especially the first time around. However, before diving into the process, here are some suggestions on sources of assistance that others have found helpful. These suggestions thus form the broader context in which you and your students execute the four-step process.

- Think about possible projects when you are driving, walking, showering, or going to sleep. Preparing for such projects includes a strong creative component with which your subconscious mind can be a big help.

- Brainstorm on the subject of what you are doing with people you encounter in academic and business contexts.

- Use resources in your school, district, community, and state. A local professional photographer, newspaper person, university media specialist, or legal expert might be a great deal of help in the preparation step, as well as be an interesting guest speaker during later steps.

- Become familiar with Internet forums on which experts and other users answer questions. There are several forums dedicated to general use of technology in education or to specific multimedia authoring systems and tools. Teach your students to communicate directly with experts and users. Learning how to get answers to their own questions may be more important than learning the answers themselves.

- Tap willing retirees and college students. Many educators have found wonderful assistance from such people not only because helping students is a worthwhile activity but also because multimedia projects are especially interesting, challenging, and intellectually rewarding.

- Leverage the students. We constantly hear of educators who admit that they underestimated students' abilities to scavenge and set up equipment, to learn to operate equipment, and to teach new skills to other students and to teachers. One Georgia educator made an informal survey of his students. He found that his students were quite adept at using their televisions, camcorders, VCRs, audio equipment, and video games. They were not at all overwhelmed at having to deal with such equipment in an integrated environment. We continually hear of educators who take young students with them to skill-building workshops. These students later teach other students and teachers.

- Set realistic goals. A project need not be completed in two periods. Allow twice as long or three times as long. What is most important is getting started.

You will often want to think about the activities involved in all four steps of the process in parallel. For example, you start with a wonderful idea and a set of goals for a project.

You know that your high school students come from a middle school that exposed them to multimedia. However, you realize that the students now must use the high school's Intel-based computers, whereas they used Macintoshes in the middle school, or perhaps vice versa. You decide to revise the project to provide some quick tutoring to help the students convert their extensive skills from using one type of computer to using the other. Rather than belaboring hypertext, with which they are familiar, you devise a project that helps them build basic skills on the unfamiliar computer and then moves on quickly to cover additional multimedia skills.

Sometimes thinking about all four steps will lead you to revise a project to take advantage of an opportunity rather than to circumvent a deficiency. You might discover that your students created a multimedia archive of current events using hypertext last term, but then heard that another class used audio. You might be surprised to find that your students insist on using audio.

Theory

Although you will often need to consider all four steps together, along with considering their wider external context, this section discusses each step individually.

Teacher Prepares

A multimedia project, like any other significant classroom activity, requires careful advance preparation. Preparation begins with identifying the goals you want your students to achieve. You then proceed to select an existing project, refine an existing project, or define a new project from scratch that will allow your students to meet all your goals. Then reality sets in. You balance your goals against available projects, hardware, software, skills, and time. The next sections discuss some details of these considerations.

Selecting Goals

For convenience, we divide goals into the four categories that Table 6-2 shows.

Table 6-2: Goal categories

- Higher-order thinking skills
- Group and interpersonal skills
- Content or discipline skills
- Technical skills

Table 1-1 in Chapter 1 shows examples of typical goals, within each of the above categories, that you may elect to help your students achieve by creating multimedia projects. Each of this book's Chapters 7 through 12 includes a discussion of the corresponding project's specific goals. We encourage you to think about these and other projects primarily with regard to the goals your students could achieve by creating the projects. This is the key to integrating student creation of multimedia projects into your curriculum.

In practice, a given project may contribute to many goals. In some situations, you may select a project primarily to help your students meet a particular subject's content area goals, such as learning a particular continent's geography. In other situations, you may give more priority to achieving higher-order thinking skills, interpersonal skills, or technical skills.

For this book, we devised a sequence of six multipurpose projects, to meet specific goals in higher education, as well as meet different specific goals in K-12 schools. Our six projects will help you learn multimedia technical skills and also help you learn to facilitate your students' creation of their own multimedia projects. Our projects are equally suitable for your students to create in schools, to meet particular academic goals, as well as to learn multimedia technical skills.

The way you prepare and assign the project determines which goals are primary, which are secondary, and which are incidental. One positive characteristic of student multimedia projects is that there are likely to be surprise benefits for which you did not plan. Serendipity may take the form of inspired student research leading to an elegant display of a significant connection among seemingly unrelated events or ideas. It may be a wonderful set of pictorial icons in which a student captured the essence of the assigned issue.

In some cases, you may decide on a particular orientation for a project simply because your students have access to particularly relevant source materials. For example, your school's library might acquire *Mammals*, which is a specialized multimedia encyclopedia that covers such animals, and *Microsoft's Encarta*, a much more general multimedia encyclopedia, which also includes information about mammals. You want your students to become familiar with using such references on CD-ROMs. You also want them to learn specifically about mammals. You could devise many different projects based on these goals.

The key is to ask the students to find something specific or to articulate the sides of a specific issue, rather than merely telling them to browse through information and prepare a report. A task that you ask students to accomplish is the multimedia project's anchoring task. Sometimes a very open and general anchoring task will meet your goals. At other times, you may require a more precise anchoring task. You can decide between the general and specific alternatives by analyzing the goals that you want students to meet by creating the project. In either case, students who are creating a multimedia project benefit from having an anchoring task in mind.

Two examples of assignments follow. These assignments use significantly different anchoring tasks to make significantly different uses of the same references, namely *Mammals* and *Encarta*. The assignment in Table 6-3 is less specific than that in Table 6-4.

Being more specific may imply a much more difficult assignment, although a general task need not be easy.

Table 6-3: A general anchoring task and goals

> Assignment: Select one mammal from *Mammals* and *Encarta* and describe it in a multimedia essay.
> - **Higher-order thinking skills goal**:
>   Zero in on one animal and decide on relevant, interesting, and major characteristics on which to report.
>   Organize the selected information.
> - **Content and concepts goal**:
>   Review many facts about mammals such as their sounds, colors, and modes of locomotion.
> - **Technical skills goal**:
>   Use alternative references such as CD-ROMs.

Table 6-4: A more precise anchoring task and goals

> Assignment: Prepare a multimedia presentation representing both sides of the issue "Should alligators be on the endangered species list?" Use Mammals and Encarta as well as any other desired references.
> - **Higher-order thinking skills goal**:
>   Navigate through large quantities of information using multimedia tools for analysis.
>   Identify major issues and summarize them.
>   Assess quality of reasoning and logic behind student's final position.
> - **Content and concepts goal**:
>   Learn about alligators and issues involving endangered species.
>   Analyze and present distinct perspectives of individuals and groups.
> - **Technical skills goal**:
>   Create and present complex multimedia composition.
>   Use additional research materials such as other CD-ROM references.

In many cases, you can modify an existing project so that it comes closer to meeting your goals. Sometimes changing from a specific anchoring task to a general one, or vice versa, suffices. As an example, Chapter 8's Critics' Circle project involves criticizing one specific movie, either positively or negatively. You could change the anchoring task to the more general assignment of criticizing movies in general. Chapter 7's Current Events project is general. Changing to a very specific topic, such as a recent local election, might make the project meet your goals more closely.

Some educators tell us that, unless they take extreme care to state a precise anchoring task to make an assignment concrete, their students find multimedia tools too tempting and become too creative. Although they have nothing against creativity, these educators find that students tend to lose track of the high-priority goals. Other educators find that they stifle their students by too-tight constraints and too-specific assignments. It may help considerably to discuss your projects with fellow educators who can help you steer the fine line required here.

Living with the Environment

As you select and prepare a multimedia project, you must consider the environment you have available. Preceding chapters discuss general aspects of the hardware and software that your students use to create multimedia projects in general. Subsequent chapters include descriptions of hardware and software that you need for particular projects.

As part of preparing for a project, you decide on the extent to which students will participate in selecting and setting up hardware and software. For example, should the students unpack equipment from original packing boxes, place the equipment on tables, connect cables, and install software, or should they walk up to a running system? Should they turn on the computer and invoke the authoring system as one of many possible programs, or should they immediately see the authoring system's main screen? If your primary reason for using a succession of multimedia projects is to help your students learn about multimedia itself, you are likely to encourage them to work up to performing a great deal of the required setup. In the more normal cases, where you are using multimedia as a tool for achieving traditional academic goals, you probably will want to provide an environment in which someone sets up hardware and software for students.

A recent phenomenon is that students are increasingly likely to encounter multimedia computers first outside the classroom. They may want to set up equipment. The experience may help them deal with equipment they encounter elsewhere. We must remain sensitive to students who have no access to computers at home or elsewhere outside the school. For such students, it is especially important to make classroom multimedia computers available to students outside class hours. A major advantage of student multimedia projects is that, for example, calling forth their own voices and images from a computer motivates students to voluntarily spend more time on task than they would tolerate being required to spend. Your students can benefit from this only if you make it reasonably easy for them to spend discretionary time on their projects. In some cases, availability of support personnel is the primary limitation on making computers accessible after normal hours.

Curricular requirements and mandates are another part of the environment that affects your selection of projects.

Deciding What You Will Provide

One of your key decisions about any project is whether to suggest that each group of students use a template, as Chapter 4 defines and discusses. Using a template is an attractive alternative to starting from scratch, especially for novices, but also for experienced creators when you want them to focus on content rather than multimedia techniques. For experienced creators, you have to consider why they should reinvent what they invented or used in previous projects. They might better spend their time on other features of their current project instead.

The primary purpose of giving students a template for their early projects is to allow them to concentrate most of their attention on achieving academic objectives, rather than struggling with details of operating the multimedia software. An important secondary purpose is that templates teach by example. A template can include a printable cookbook telling what keystrokes and pointing device motions students can use to modify the template to create their own new project. Experience indicates that both students and educators ignore such cookbooks whenever possible but use them appropriately when all else fails. Using a template not only decreases the average time that groups of students require in order to complete projects, it also decreases the maximum time that any group requires, because a slow group can catch up by doing what the cookbook says to do and understanding why later.

You may or may not have a template available for a project that you select. In some cases, you may have a specially prepared template. In other cases, you may have a template that happens to be a student project that you have saved from a previous year or have gotten from a colleague. In still other cases, because a template is specific to one project, to one hardware and software platform, and to one authoring system, you may need to create your own template as part of preparing a given project.

There is nothing magic about a template. For example, each of this book's next six chapters describes a particular project in sufficient detail that you could create the project from scratch, by using some imagination but not using a template. The results would be perfectly suitable for subsequent use as templates, provided only that you do not include a password to prevent such use, and that you do not change to a new authoring system. In fact, because our projects are quite generic, they become templates with potential for a great deal of reuse. Moreover, once you create one set of templates, you will find it much easier to create another set for different hardware or software. After some experience, your students, too, will be able to create templates for other students to use. Creating templates with exceptional pedagogical value is also a suitable role for educational technologists.

A second key decision is what role you should play in suggesting an organization for a project's information. With younger students, you could jointly decide on how many categories to divide information among and decide what designs and styles to use for each category on a computer screen in order to implement that organization. You or an educational technologist could then create a template that contains the resulting designs. Students can then use the template, placing information into the selected categories on the multimedia screens, with little help from you.

A third key decision is what role you should play in deciding how the project will look and what media it will include. Chapter 13 on Advanced Techniques discusses some possibilities for using media effectively. This is another area where you must take care to follow a fine line between stifling students' creativity and helping them be more effective. Experience with student multimedia projects indicates that students come to appreciate advice and counsel on how to improve the quality of their media and the look of their screens, but only after they have gone through a phase of uncontrolled initial experimentation.

Grouping Students

An important part of preparing a project is to organize the class into groups of students who are to work together on a particular computer. Experience indicates that students genuinely benefit from working on multimedia projects in groups of between two and five. A single student does not form an optimal group. In this respect, multimedia projects differ from some other uses of computers in education, where one computer per student is ideal, and where larger groups are a concession to an inadequate supply of computers. If a group becomes larger than five, however, not all members can see one computer screen, even to review work in progress. Having a larger group also increases the difficulty of reaching the many decisions on which a successful multimedia project depends.

The group size that is optimal for a given project depends to some extent on the natural number of roles that students can play while they create that project. A large project may have many roles and thus may require a large group, as Chapter 14 discusses. Of course, a large group will require access to more than one computer.

Over a sequence of projects, you are likely to want each student to take on many roles, rather than becoming stuck in a specialty such as collecting information, creating art work, performing videotaping, or setting up organizational structures. Varying groupings helps prevent any student from being consistently over specialized or consistently left out. Different students excel in performing different functions on different media, sometimes in ways that will surprise you. All students should spend some time on activities in which they are strong and more time on activities in which they are weak. You may find it useful to define interpersonal goals for each activity in the context of student and class development. Whereas having students create projects individually may be the only way to assure that they play all roles, avoiding groups altogether is an instance of throwing out the baby with the bath water.

You may know more about grouping students than we do, in general. However, in particular, we want to emphasize that multimedia student projects provide a significant motivation for students to make groups work well. Working in a multimedia group may help:

- prepare students for real work environments,
- weaker students obtain peer tutoring, as a group strives to meet common objectives,
- stronger students reinforce their skills and knowledge by helping others,

- direct toward constructive goals students' natural tendency to socialize,

- give previously unrecognized students a chance to excel publicly,

- create new friendships, and

- create results, sometimes stunningly compelling, not easily achievable by a single student working alone.

Multimedia projects do not erase the negative features of groups, such as increasing the difficulty of controlling and monitoring multiple activities and sometimes allowing strong performers to carry weaker ones. You will need to deal with negative features as they occur.

Example: Tony and Barry worked many summer evenings on Tony's new multimedia computer. They experimented with many special effects but were disappointed in the overall result. They were puzzled about how to create animation. They wanted some help. They looked forward to Mr. Stevens' history class in the fall because they knew he would include creating a multimedia project. However, they were disappointed to be placed in separate groups with students who were multimedia novices, although they were history experts. Tony and Barry discussed the situation with Mr. Stevens, who changed them to a group with two other students who also wanted to try to make special effects work for conveying information. Mr. Stevens promised to give them some special help using these techniques, and they agreed to help some of the novice students.

Preparing for Pitfalls

As for any complex situation, we recommend that you hope for the best but plan for the worst. Although you hope that each multimedia project will be an unqualified success, you plan how you will handle difficulties that your students may encounter. Such planning can make you more ready to facilitate their work by coaching them on how to climb back out the pits. Some examples follow.

- Devoting an excessive amount of time to perfecting one interesting detail can prevent students from finishing a project in the time you allot. You may decide to teach students to think about rationing their time by not alerting the students to the risk and letting the worst happen. Experience indicates that your most advanced students are most likely to fall into this pit and be memorably discomfited by feeling left out as other students present attractive finished projects. Both advanced students and the others can find this situation memorable.

- Some students may surprise you by bringing in exquisite media from parents or other sources. This can be either a wonderful opportunity for the whole class or a cause of extreme jealousy to some members of the class. Think about how you would handle such a situation.

- You may find that equipment or resources that your students counted on is suddenly unavailable. Helping your students learn to deal with such situations is an important part of the learning process.

- After setting up a group of students, you may find that one student does not come through with his part of the assignment, thus disappointing the entire group.

- Combining the last two pitfalls, a student may wait until the final due date before mentioning that the scanner he was going to use at the local university was unavailable, so he did not scan the pictures. Establishing interim milestones can help eliminate such occurrences. More importantly, milestones give students a sense of responsibility and group cooperation and give experience in working around such problems in a timely fashion.

Defining Minimum Requirements

You will need to decide what every successful project must include. This will allow you to make clear to your students what minimum requirements each group must meet in order to complete the assignment, achieve your goals, and receive credit. A list of minimum requirements is your strongest weapon in the war against substitution. In industry, government, and perhaps even education, people tend to substitute enjoyable activities for required activities. Multimedia projects, unfortunately, provide many opportunities for substitution. If you fail to make requirements clear, for example, you will lack grounds to reject a project that includes stupendous artwork, but which students completed without meeting your goals. (The corresponding example in an art class might be a project that has stupendous artwork of the sort that the class studied the previous month.) You might plan to demonstrate previous students' projects, including one that does meet minimum requirements and one that does not despite being highly attractive.

In order to meet goals that emphasize learning multimedia techniques, you might require that students:

- record and play digital audio,

- use a reference from a specific CD-ROM,

- make the project usable, such as by including enough instructions on each screen so that someone other than the creators knows how to interact with the project,

- lay out screens consistently, throughout the project,

- supply text that abides by rules of grammar and style, and

- meet the project's final due date.

Defining Criteria for Outstanding Projects

In addition to completing required parts of a project, you probably want to suggest ways in which some groups of students can make their projects outstanding. An outstanding project is not simply one with more overall quantity or even one with higher quality artwork (unless the main goals are artistic ones). Instead, an outstanding project is one that demonstrates that its creators met and exceeded the specific requirements and goals that you set for the project. Again, examples may be very effective in motivating students to create outstanding projects. You might plan to show some of the best projects that previous classes have created. It is possible to overdo this, however. You will want to avoid giving students the impression that they have no chance to do projects as good as the ones you demonstrate.

We find that students' projects get better and better as students gain experience, receive feedback on their projects, and see what their peers have done. Your expectations should rise accordingly. Just as we found that teachers underestimate students' abilities to handle seemingly complex hardware and software, we find that teachers underestimate students' abilities to organize information in complex structures, deduce logical relationships, and then express the results of their analyses using appropriate media. By defining criteria for outstanding projects, you nudge in constructive directions the efforts of groups that will meet your minimum requirements quickly and easily.

Deciding on Organization of Information

As Chapter 5, Organizing Information, discusses at length, students can benefit from organizing different projects' information in significantly different ways. For example, a multimedia encyclopedia is by no means limited to a paper encyclopedia's alphabetical organization. If students create a multimedia encyclopedia, they can use a timeline to organize their information chronologically, use a map to organize information according to geographical area, and also organize information alphabetically.

If your students have never considered using any organization other than placing one item after another in a linear order, you might want to prepare to demonstrate several projects that illustrate other organizations. For example, you might show a project that covers three main subjects and starts out with a screen that contains three buttons. Noting that a user can select one of these buttons to see information about one of the subjects may inspire your students to think about other simple nonlinear organizations.

To help students complete their first few projects quickly, you can specify the organization that you want them to use. For later projects, you can consider whether a project will best meet your goals by including the requirement that each group of students must devise what they think is the best organization for the project's information. That is, one of the major choices that you make while preparing a project is deciding whether to specify an organizing principle or to make selecting a good organizing principle a major part of your students' challenge.

Deciding on Sources of Media

In kindergarten projects through graduate writing assignments, a significant part of students' total effort goes into finding and absorbing sources of information. While preparing a project, you will want to ensure that students have available material that suffices for them to meet the project's minimum requirements. You may decide to tell them where to find input material or may make finding material be one of the requirements that they must meet to complete the project. You can consider the following sources of input.

- Research in paper libraries with traditional library materials
- Research in CD-ROM discs and on-line services
- Photographs, including photographs of students themselves
- Scanned pictures and diagrams from books and magazines
- Segments from commercial video sources
- Media from prior projects
- Media from nearby content experts in business or academia

Making Changes for Young Children

A project that works well with older students may or may not work well in early elementary school grades. Experience indicates that young children can benefit from creating multimedia projects that include text, graphics, images, audio, and video particularly in the form of animation. We hear that even preschool children use home computers to create audio annotations for animations and create slide shows of art work on their favorite topic. We discuss variations of some of the projects for younger children in the six chapters that describe projects and in Chapter 15 on Variations. In Chapter 3, we have already noted that a few authoring systems provide audio help for creators who are too young to read instructions.

Preparing to Announce Project

Finally, you need to prepare how you will announce the project to your class. As the next section discusses, this can strongly affect how well the students achieve the goals you defined at the outset.

Teacher Assigns Project

Teachers have found that students respond well to a gradual introduction to multimedia projects, particularly to the first project, such as the following.

- Sprinkle multimedia vocabulary and concepts into earlier classes. Teachers in New York City start during the preceding term. They begin using words such as linking, selecting, and images. They talk about alternative ways of organizing information. They talk about visualizing a picture to represent a subject's most important concept.

- Use part of an earlier class to give a hint of what is coming. Several days before you give details, and before you expect students to start using computers, announce that there will be a multimedia project and start discussing its topic. Give the students time to think about possibilities.

- Finally, assign the project to your students during class time, emphasizing the group assignments, anchoring task, and mandatory requirements.

We suggest that you summarize the most important instructions on assignment sheets and give a copy to each group. Consider creating the sheet jointly with the class. Such a sheet could look like Table 6-5, in which we have left some items blank and have partially filled in other items. For example, after making copies with most items filled in, you would personalize a copy for each group by specifying the group number, the equipment that the group can use, and any comments that you feel apply only to that particular group.

Your discussion with the class, in this step of the process, covers the items that you prepared in the previous step. You will probably spend most of the discussion making the anchoring task clear. To this end, you may want to demonstrate some positive and negative examples. In a typical negative example, you might show a project in which a previous student included a very well thought-out optional animation but did not include the required digital audio. To counter the strong motivation to substitute, you may also want to indicate clearly what happens if the students do not meet minimum requirements.

Some of the other items that you prepared may require special discussion. You may provide a special alert to each student on the critical importance of meeting individual responsibilities to their groups. You may have some discussion on how to the group can conduct constructive critique sessions or how the group can brainstorm ideas. You may mention resources that students can use when problems arise.

How Long Should the Project Be?

Although your students may know approximately how long to make an essay, you should not assume that they have any feeling for whether to record a twenty-minute audio or video interview as a single stream of consciousness. You may want to suggest appropriate lengths for a project's text, audio, and video, as well as specifying a suitable number of images or graphics. You need to make the point that, when listening to and watching an interactive project, a user expects to select new information several times per minute. One good way to make this point is to demonstrate a project that, once you have started an interview playing, you can stop only by turning off the computer. Several ostensibly professional multimedia titles can serve as horrible examples in this regard.

Table 6-5: An assignment sheet

ASSIGNMENT SHEET

Project Name:

_____

Group number:

_____

Students in group: Responsibility (if known)

_____   _____
_____   _____
_____   _____
_____   _____
_____   _____

Equipment and Software to use: Equipment to find
    Rooms   _____   _____
    Machine   _____   _____

Minimum requirements for project:
    ___   Draw icons for ...
    ___   Select group members who will ...
    ___   Find pictures to digitize of ...
    ___   Record audio of ...
    ___   Create multimedia pages containing ...
    ___   Summarize ...
    ___   Be sure it is possible to use your project to ...

Outstanding projects can have:
    ___   Additional references in ...
    ___   Links among items ...

Complete project by:
_____ period on _____. No late work will be accepted.
Comments on project:

You might mention that students should keep projects' oral parts relatively short for two reasons. First, listeners lose track of oral information that contains more than three or four different points. Second, digital audio occupies significant disk space on a computer. This is particularly important if students intend to save their completed projects on diskettes. We have seen that fewer than five minutes of voice-grade audio can fill a diskette.

You may need to discuss suitable lengths for text, as well, if your students are unfamiliar with roles that hypertext plays in a multimedia project. Text often guides a user through a project or summarizes information that other media, such as audio interviews, express fully. In either usage, each piece of text should be brief. Moreover, whereas students may have learned to save paper by filling pages, you may have to dissuade them from packing as many characters as they can fit on each screen. You can show them that it is far easier for everyone to read a screen that contains 100 characters than a screen that contains 1000 characters. Even when students need to express a lot of information in text form, you should encourage them to break the information into small pieces, put the text for each piece on its own screen, and provide meaningful links from one screen to another. Recognizing important points and summarizing them succinctly are important intellectual activities. Creating hypertext gives your students an excellent opportunity to practice these activities.

Q: How long do professionals make audio and video clips?

A: One useful exercise for you and your students is to pay close attention to scene shifts in a television drama. Each time a new scene starts, begin counting seconds, such as muttering "asparagus one, asparagus two" until the scene changes again; then write down your last number and start over at one. You may be surprised to find that typical scenes often last only a few seconds and almost never last over 20 seconds. Another related exercise is to check out the total duration of typical television commercials, which tell complete stores in a fraction of a minute.

How Much Time Should the Project Take?

Two key parts of assigning the project are telling students how long they have to complete their work and coaching them on how to allocate that available time among the many tasks that they need to perform as part of completing the project. Projects can take as short a time as one 40-minute period or as long as an entire semester. Work on a typical project may occupy parts of one to five days per week for several weeks, with appropriate homework and preparation.

The time that students require obviously depends on the project, its goals, and the class. As in many learning experiences, a significant benefit comes from trying something that does not work, finding what went wrong, and using that information to devise something that does work. Achieving this benefit requires additional time and adds considerable uncertainty to the time that any given group requires. Some groups simply take much longer than others. You can discreetly monitor that each group is moving forward and not getting bogged down on a detail.

Multimedia projects provide particularly good opportunities to work with students on developing and monitoring schedules. Students will appreciate the importance of taking the last few steps that complete a project before, rather than after, a scheduled presentation time. It is up to you to decide whether students must meet your due date in order to achieve the objectives that you set for the project. Our experience is that, in the absence of a quite firm due date, students tend to work endlessly on a succession of small improvements without ever getting the one large satisfaction that comes with completing the project.

Goals

You may or may not elect to explain a project's academic goals as you assign the project to your students. Especially in elementary grades, it may be more effective to skip such explicit discussions or save a discussion of goals for the reflection step. In any case, the goals and associated minimum requirements are the most important things to keep in mind throughout the step of assigning the project to your students. For example, it may take several projects to convince all your students that they cannot meet the goals by doing an exceptional job on only one or a few parts of the project and slighting other required parts.

Students Create Project

By the nature of student-created multimedia projects, students take over center stage for this step of the process. It is very important that you give up the role of "sage on stage" with all the answers, and take on the role of coach. You need to be unobtrusive about facilitating, monitoring, and reinforcing your students' creative activities. What makes this possible is that, at any one time, most of your students will not need your help. What makes this demanding is that you must determine which ones do need help and must decide what sort of help they need.

As a part of coaching, you may review and reinforce the following.

- Organization, process, and relations
- Content area subject matter
- Group dynamics
- Technical skills

Coaching the groups is a continual activity. In many cases, the most effective approach is to keep quiet. A multimedia project is sufficiently authentic to give students a direct feeling for whether they are succeeding or failing, without necessarily noting how you feel about the project. In other cases, especially with young children, you may find that an active role is more effective. Students may not recognize new opportunities that multimedia offers unless you give them a hint or a demonstration. For example, until you show them a nonlinear organization, students may think that the only way to organize a body of information is to place one item after another in a linear sequence.

Student Creation Activities

During this step each group of students performs a wide variety of activities, many of which depend strongly on the particular project they are creating. A few typical activities are as follows.

- Bring together initial ideas and materials.
- Hold brainstorming sessions.
- Generate a work plan, organization, and story board.
- Decide which members of the group will do what major parts.
- Hold critique sessions to evaluate the plan.
- Determine additional work required.
- Decide when previous work requires modifications.
- Solicit comments from other groups or from people outside the classroom.
- Implement the plan, test the result, and repeat as required.
- Complete separate parts of project independently.
- Assemble parts and check that they work together.
- Refine parts to remove undesirable inconsistencies.
- Present the completed project to the class and others.

The length of this list, which is by no means exhaustive, indicates that some students may need to make a list of concrete tasks. A written list will help prevent them from forgetting any tasks and help them to schedule tasks for which other tasks are prerequisites. The following six chapters that describe individual projects include task lists. You may want to make up such a list for any project, to help yourself check each group's progress. You may want to lead a discussion in which one or more groups of students make up and write down such a list. You may even want to make creating such a list be one of the required parts of a particular project. In the latter case, students should include their task list in a section of the project that has a title such as "How We Made It." Encourage your students to put such side information in the project itself, rather than on a scrap of paper that they will lose.

Student Decision-Making and Fulfilling Responsibilities

In a complex project with a fixed deadline, members of a group may find that they have to make so many choices that they need a formal mechanism for making decisions. If one of your goals is for the students to discover such a mechanism, then you need to watch carefully and nurture the discovery process. If discovering a mechanism is not a major goal, then you may want to provide a few words about this in the beginning. You could suggest that each group elect a leader or establish a voting method.

Planning for completion is important. A group can easily get bogged down in drawing a perfect illustration, deciding on a perfect caption, or performing some other fascinating activity that does not contribute to achieving your goals. Groups may need to establish and track formal intermediate milestones. Of course, allowing some group to experience a conspicuous failure to complete a project may be more educational than nagging all groups enough that all groups finish on time.

Groups often identify particular members as specialists. For example, you may see that you need to coach a group to select one member who will be responsible for collecting images and select another member to undertake particular library research. It is a small step from such specialization to making one person responsible for monitoring schedules, making sure that members of the group know when they are nearing intermediate milestone checkpoints, and generally keeping track of progress toward completion. Different groups may disagree about whether the specialist who manages the group's schedules is the group's manager and most prestigious member or is the group's bean counter and least prestigious member.

The remaining major activity in this step is continual reflection, which the next section describes. At appropriate points throughout the time when students create the project, you need to reflect on what each group of students is doing and feed information back to them. While students are still in the creation step, they can take advantage of such feedback to improve their projects. You probably will want to coach students to reflect on their own work and on each other's work, and to accept and desire peer critiques as part of the creation step. Students may need further coaching on how to provide tactful and helpful criticism, both positive and negative. For example, either "It's awesome!" or "It's awful!" is less helpful than, "I really liked the beginning, but have you considered the possibility of ... ."

Groups need to plan ahead, in order to avoid finger-pointing at the end of unfulfilled assignments and other unpleasant surprises. We emphasize this by showing a loop between the last two steps in our process diagram. Continual reflection as students create their projects is usually significantly more important than assigning grades after students finish presenting their completed projects to the class.

Chapter 14 breaks down the Creation and Reflection steps into seven sub-steps that are appropriate when you organize students into an amateur production company. The Theory and Practice sections of Chapter 14 thus provide more detail on these two steps of the process.

Everyone Reflects on Project

Reflection is an ongoing process that many people perform at many levels. An individual, a group, the entire class, the class teacher, other teachers, an entire school, the surrounding community, and any combination of these can reflect meaningfully on multimedia projects. Chapter 17 on Assessment provides a more detailed discussion of this topic.

> "I am very satisfied with the results of using student-created multimedia projects. Attendance improved from 40 percent to 98 percent. The students must have learned more because they were here more!"
>
> The authors have heard so many teachers make comments such as this that we must respect its importance. However, we believe that multimedia student projects have more fundamental long-term benefits, especially when well integrated into curricula. Reflection is the key to achieving those benefits.

It is important to reflect on every project and to use the results of reflection to achieve ongoing, continuous improvement. It is also important to base reflection on some objective measures, including your original list of minimum requirements. This is the key to making multimedia projects an integrated and respected part of the curriculum. Ideally, students will make reflection a personal habit of mind and will correlate this personal habit with increased feelings of self-esteem.

Reflect on the Process, Too

One major purpose of reflection and feedback is continual improvement of the students' successive projects, the project definitions, and the creation process. To accomplish this, you reflect not only on the students' projects and on the extent to which students met your goals but also on your own part of the overall four-step process. During the creation step, you can reflect on how well the students performed and also on how well you prepared and assigned the project. To improve your preparation for subsequent groups of students, you can note your students' misconceptions, misinterpretations, and common mistakes, both in creating the project and in working in groups.

During the reflection step, you can engage students in a discussion of the entire activity, including process and content. For example, after all groups complete their projects, it may be appropriate to discuss how different groups performed the task. This may produce a consensus on a process, either the one we described here or a better one. Students may be especially receptive to discussing the process just after completing their projects. If you did not discuss your goals beforehand, you might want to do so at this point, when students have the lessons most firmly in mind.

> Example: Mrs. Michaels has planned and executed a project for her tenth through twelfth grade honor students.
>
> The project involved each student's creating a multimedia album on a mutually agreed subject. Mrs. Michaels first intended to require the album to have 15 screens and to contain animations, images, and audio. At the last moment, she decided to make the project more meaty by increasing the number of screens from 15 to 40. After reflecting on the results, she found that this was a mistake.
>
> After completing 15 screens, each student had achieved the intended academic benefits. After completing 25 screens, the students had worked through any quantitative organizational challenges. What she created was unnecessary busywork for her students. Being conscientious, they struggled to complete the project during lunch hours and before and after school. The authoring system she provided, while excellent for helping younger students get started, exacerbated her advanced students' problems with producing large volumes of content efficiently.
>
> The projects turned out wonderfully. Her students put their projects in the portfolios that they included in their college applications. However, for next time, Mrs. Michaels has decided to cut down on the number of pages and to provide her more advanced students with a more advanced authoring system.

Role of Audiences

Creating a multimedia project benefits the project's creators, whether or not anyone else ever uses the project. The major learning is in the creating. On the one hand, having a real or imaginary audience in mind during the creation step gives a project an explicit purpose and thus tends to increase students' motivation and sharpen their focus. On the other hand, having a real audience present during the reflection step is optional. Presenting projects to the class, to a school open house, or to a community center gathering may or may not help your students meet the goals that you selected. If you do decide to invite a large audience, you should try to make the reflection step enjoyable. Comparing a sequence of similar projects on the same subject makes reflection relatively easy, objective, fair, and boring. Comparing a wider variety of projects is more stimulating. As usual, the key to success is to focus reflection on goals rather than on mere appearances. Different groups can meet identical goals by creating projects that are sufficiently different to hold an audience's interest. In fact, we are continually amazed by the different insights into information structures that our students present in their multimedia projects.

Performing a multimedia project publicly may contribute significantly to achieving a project's overall goals. A scheduled performance at least encourages students to meet the completion date. Developing public speaking techniques, including deciding what to say and what visual and audible aids to provide, may be one of your major goals. Public presentation can contribute to self-esteem, as the creators note that others listen to and watch what they created. A presentation may allow group and student personalities to shine through. Most important for reflection, students can benefit from the authenticity of how their peers and others react to a project.

Whenever possible it is desirable to send students' projects home so that their parents and others can become part of the audience. More and more homes have computers that can play digital audio, display images, and show some video from diskettes. It is worth asking how many students have computers that can play back their projects at home. The bad news is that using a multimedia project requires more effort than fastening an essay to a refrigerator with a magnet. The good news is that more people want to use a project than want to read an essay.

Many homes have VCRs. Students, teachers, or support staff could use a scan converter (as we describe in Chapter 14's section on Demonstrating a Project in a Speech) to put sequences of computer displays and audio onto videotapes. In this context, it is important to realize the difference between a diskette and a videotape. Using a diskette, a parent can interact with the project, selecting any of several different alternatives at each point. Using a videotape, a parent remains a passive spectator, viewing the particular sequence of choices that the person who made the videotape happened to select. Watching a videotape requires a parent to imagine what interactivity would mean. Thus, sending home videotapes works best after a parent has come to the school to interact with one or more previous projects.

Measurements

The goals, minimum requirements, and characteristics of an outstanding project that you determined in the preparation step determine the measurements you will use in this reflection step. Less obviously, if you must assign a single grade, you must decide on how to weight different measures. If you prioritized your goals, you will know how to weight your measures.

Measurements may apply to an entire school, not just to one class. In some cases, a school's staff develops a rubric of standards that range from saying what it means for students to complete a task to saying how to determine whether they achieved the required depth of understanding.

Independent of the selected measurement model, it is important to keep experience records. Records facilitate comparing a student's or group's successive projects and documenting their development formally.

Recording Results of Reflections

Both teachers and students can use multimedia to store their reflections on each project. Teachers and students can add written or spoken comments to each project. They can use a common format for buttons that link to their comments. Such reflections can become parts of individual students' portfolios, remaining available for later comparisons. Recording results of reflection as part of a project is an important illustration of the interactive nature of multimedia projects. Even users can add to a project and make it more valuable.

Reflecting on Long Projects

Some projects may extend over an entire term or even an entire school year. It is important to establish major milestones for such projects and reflect on individual milestones. Each milestone is an opportunity to add students' contributions to student class portfolios.

Class Evaluation

Encourage and plan class evaluation, feedback, and improvement sessions. Before beginning a project, you discussed what makes a good project, what makes a good team member, and what you expect students to have learned from previous projects. Just before an evaluation session, discuss evaluation criteria and encourage positive feedback. Be careful to manage the feedback during the class evaluation. Encourage groups to invite outside critics as appropriate. Watch for changes in content knowledge and thinking skills after the project and evaluation are completed. Watch for and encourage subjective feelings that everyone contributes to producing a project of which they are proud, and that is better than previous projects. Members of each group should not stop with reflecting on and refining their own group's project. You will want to encourage members of each group to circulate enough to see other groups' work.

Student Self-evaluation

Multimedia projects provide students with opportunities to become increasingly capable of self-evaluation and assessment. More or less independently of your smiles or happy faces, students can see whether their projects work and can compare their projects to other groups' projects, to professional multimedia titles, and to other media content such as television. Students can increase their understanding of the need to strive for continual improvement as a life-long practice. They can gain knowledge of, and interest in, doing better. Projects give them opportunities to demonstrate their ability to improve. They obtain criteria for assessing themselves and others. They can learn the extent to which media can influence them, by seeing how they themselves can use media to influence others. They can gain knowledge, comfort, and experience with issues of tools, content, and resources. They can get experience with issues of separating content from form and see the role that form plays in making content make sense. Feelings of doing something worthwhile, both individually and as part of a group, can be very important, particularly to students for whom the feeling is unusual. Self-assessment, including assessment of an individual's role in a group, contributes to overall group functioning and to achieving multimedia projects' goals.

Built-in Testing

A multimedia project can help its users evaluate themselves. A project's creators can insert into the project some questions for users to answer. Especially in the case of true-false or multiple choice questions, creators can make the project evaluate individual answers, prompt users appropriately in case of wrong answers, and provide a user with a summary of all answers. This capability blurs the dividing line between student-created multimedia projects, which are mainly intended to educate their creators, and courseware titles, which are mainly intended to educate their users. When students create a project that includes questions, they learn to ask good questions and they see how users respond to questions, both of which can be significant learning experiences. Chapter 10 describes a Science Quiz project that majors in built-in testing.

Practice

Selecting a Project

Selecting multimedia projects is arguably the most subtle part of the four-step process. You need to select a project that your students can create in order to meet particular academic goals without exceeding the carrying capacity of your environment. If you had nothing else to do all day, you could memorize the characteristics of all available projects. You could then use what you remember to select the best project for any situation. Of course, instead, you must snatch information whenever it whizzes past you and use whatever you know to select a project when you need one. We suggest that you create tables of project characteristics, to help you:

- select specific projects,
- categorize projects that you observe or invent, to see how they compare and to see if they really do what you want them to do, and
- customize projects to better meet your goals or to accommodate your environment.

We use the six particular multimedia projects that the next six chapters describe to provide examples of tables of projects' characteristics. Creating these projects can benefit not only you who are reading this book, but also K-12 students. You and your students can create these projects in order to meet technical goals involved in learning multimedia. More important, your students can create these projects in order to meet traditional academic goals. Most important for the purposes of this book, therefore, you can create these projects in order to meet the goal of learning how to help K-12 students create these and other multimedia projects.

You may want to review Chapter 1's thumbnail sketches of the projects. Those sketches show that the projects differ by:

- involving different content topics,
- progressing through successively more demanding multimedia techniques and technologies,
- expressing organization of information in different ways and involving students in selecting the organizations to different extents, and
- involving quite different combinations and prioritizations of different categories of goals.

The following tables organize information about these projects' characteristics. You can use the tables themselves to practice selecting one of the projects to meet a particular set of goals. You can then generalize from these examples to record, in similar tables, information about projects that you invent, observe, or modify. Using and sharing such tables will help you prepare for projects.

Table 6-6 shows each project's topic goal. You would use this information to select a project that your students could use in order to master particular subject matter.

Table 6-6: Projects' topics

Project (chapter)	Topic, which affects subject area goals
Current Events (7)	Relate current news articles by creating links.
Critics' Circle (8)	Express and summarize opinions about a movie.
Trailers (9)	Create a movie trailer to make a movie appealing to a specific audience.
Science Quiz (10)	Learn from preparing a science quiz on motion.
Memoirs (11)	Obtain, organize, and draw conclusions about adults' personal memories of significant historical events.
Research Magazine (12)	Create a multimedia research magazine in cooperation with geographically dispersed creators.

Table 6-7 shows the multimedia technologies that the projects employ. You would use such a table to eliminate projects that exceed the capability of your school's hardware, software, and skills. You would also use such a table to select a project that would help your students to learn one or more additional multimedia technologies. For brevity, the entry for each project assumes that students have met the technology goals of preceding projects. That is, the goals are cumulative. This illustrates a major extent to which these six projects form a progression.

Table 6-7: Projects' technologies

Project (chapter)	Technology goals
Current Events (7)	Create hypertext links. Scan and digitize pictures.
Critics' Circle (8)	Create digital audio and graphic icons.
Trailers (9)	Create and control video clips from a laser disc (or CD-ROM). Create digital audio voice-overs and control sequencing and timing of the clips, audio, and text.
Science Quiz (10)	Create scripts to handle quiz questions and users' answers. Capture video and create digitized video clips of experimental observations of people's motion. Match graphs, digitized clips, and text.
Memoirs (11)	Record video and audio of interviews with adults, digitize this video, and obtain related historical data from CD-ROMs.
Research Magazine (12)	Acquire multimedia data. Select and use appropriate telecommunications. Use on-line databases.

Table 6-8 shows three roles in supplying and using a project's information organization. The three roles are those of the teacher, the project's creators, and the project's users. Note that students play increasingly large roles in selecting organizations for later projects. This is another respect in which students could achieve more demanding goals by creating these projects successively.

Table 6-8: Projects' suppliers of organization

Project (chapter)	Teacher	Creators	Users
Current Events (7)	Supplies organization.	Summarize and create links.	Navigate links.
Critics' Circle (8)	Supplies organization.	Select and represent opinions in several media, then summarize and reconcile differences.	Navigate links and read summaries and conclusion.
Trailers (9)	Supplies organization.	Select clips from movie, record voice-overs, and select order of clips.	Follow a fixed tour.
Science Quiz (10)	Shows examples of multimedia content illustrating multimedia techniques required.	Organize experimental results and science facts, and address issues of understanding content.	Follow fixed tour of quiz but use links for clarity.
Memoirs (11)	Shows examples of content illustrating retrieval and other multimedia techniques, e.g., databases.	Decide on information structure and content for class-sized project.	Select tours or navigate freely.
Research Magazine (12)	Shows examples of multimedia magazines.	Decide on information structure and content, and consider file sizes and transmission costs.	Select tours or navigate freely.

Table 6-9 shows group or interpersonal skills that your students could gain and exercise by creating each project. It also shows typical users for each project. Note that successive projects broaden the range of intended users. You will see that there is a great deal of flexibility in defining the scope of these projects. The skill and time required can vary significantly.

Table 6-9: Projects' group and interpersonal skills and intended users

Project (chapter)	Group and interpersonal skills	Intended users
Current Events (7)	Individual students make separate contributions to a class archive and also link to others' contributions.	The class.
Critics' Circle (8)	Group members strive to perfect each speaker's oral presentation, then summarize all the opinions.	The class.
Trailers (9)	Group members cooperate to persuade a specific group of people.	The class.
Science Quiz (10)	Group members cooperate to prepare a quiz.	Individual students in the class.
Memoirs (11)	Groups work together and with community adults to bring back material for a cooperative effort.	Members of the community.
Research Magazine (12)	Groups and class work with physically remote classes and subject experts.	People around the country.

Table 6-10 shows what we had in mind as we described the projects in Chapters 7 through 12 relative to each project's skill level required and approximate time for completion. Dedicated time is the actual time that students could spend specifically working on this project. Elapsed time is the calendar time from beginning to completion. For instance, Current Events could require only a few minutes of actual student work each week for an entire year. "Medium" might mean approximately a week of 40-minute periods. "Long" could be a term or even an entire year. In workshops for educators, we complete all six projects in a week, along with discussing related topics.

Table 6-10: Projects' skill levels and times

Project (chapter)	Skill level	Dedicated time	Elapsed time
Current Events (7)	Easy	Short	Long
Critics' Circle (8)	Moderate	Medium	Short
Trailers (9)	Moderate	Medium	Medium
Science Quiz (10)	Advanced	Medium	Medium
Memoirs (11)	Advanced	Long	Long
Research Magazine (12)	Advanced	Long	Long

Table 6-11 shows estimates of the extent to which students could use each project to attain selected higher-order thinking skills and content-related skills. This table's rotation merely reflects the fact that there are more such skills than there are projects and the fact that pages are higher than they are wide. You might extend the table still farther down, as well as add more projects. The subjective entries reflect the fact that what students learn in these areas depend as much on you as on the projects. For example, when you read Chapter 9's description of Trailers, you might consider whether you agree that creating this project might possibly help students acquire facts and content skills, probably would help students relate to life experiences, but probably would not lead students to a new mental model.

Table 6-11: Projects' higher-order thinking and content skills

Project Skill	Current Events	Critics' Circle	Trailers	Science Quiz	Memoirs	Research Magazine
Acquiring facts and content	Yes	Possibly	Possibly	Yes	Yes	Yes
Life experience	No	Yes	Yes	No	Yes	Yes
New mental model	Yes	Yes	No	Yes	Yes	Yes
Synthesis	Yes	Yes	Yes	Yes	Yes	Yes
Analysis	Yes	Yes	Yes	Yes	Yes	Yes
Define information structure	No	No	No	Yes	Yes	Yes
Put provided information into structure	Yes	Yes	Yes	Yes	Yes	Yes
Define information needed	No	Yes	Yes	Yes	Yes	Yes
Collect information from reference	Yes	No	Yes	Yes	Yes	Yes
Get information from people	No	Yes	No	Yes	Yes	Yes
Creativity	No	Yes	Yes	Yes	Yes	Yes
Deal with complexity	Small	Small	Medium	Medium	High	High
Decision making	Small	Medium	Large	Large	Large	Large
Group work	Low	High	High	Medium	Medium	High
Persuasion	Low	High	High	Low	Low	Low

Selecting a Progression of Projects

You will not select individual projects in isolation. Rather, you will select a sequence of projects that forms some sort of meaningful and useful progression. The preceding section noted some respects in which our six projects form a progression. If your main objective is to introduce a wide range of multimedia technologies and skills, and if your school has all the necessary hardware and software, you might select all six of our projects in the order given.

There are, of course, many other options for selecting sequences of these and other projects. For example, if your students already know the techniques that our first several projects use, you might begin with the third or fourth project. For an opposite example, if your school is not endowed with the equipment that our last several projects require, you could make good use of several variations of each of the earlier projects. In general, if your particular objectives do not place a high priority on learning technical multimedia skills, you might select only one or two of our projects and select or invent other projects that meet your requirements. You would then select your own progression of projects.

Modifying Projects

The following six chapters include quite specific project descriptions. Being specific clarifies exposition. For example, Chapter 8 describes the Critics' Circle project. It contains a sentence in which "students record their opinions about the selected movie" because that is easier to read than a sentence in which "students or other selected critics record their opinions about whatever topic was selected for discussion." Despite our specific description, you and your class are quite likely to modify the content of each selected project so that it better fits your particular purposes. For example, you could modify Critics' Circle to record and analyze opinions on any of a wide variety of topics, including deadly serious social issues, rather than using a movie as the topic. The people whose opinions your students record can be authentic voices from the surrounding community, rather than members of the class. Chapter 15 discusses this variation and a good many others. Still other variants may occur to you and your students as you go along. Please do not feel that the specificity of our descriptions limits you to using the projects exactly as described.

You can adapt our projects and most other projects for multiple grade levels with minimal effort. This is why our tables of projects' characteristics did not include a column such as "Suitable grade levels." However, if you make and share your own tables of characteristics, you might want to include such a column.

You can use a given project repeatedly, even in one grade, by modifying the project's topic or subject matter. For example, you could chose to run the Current Events project all year to help your students summarize successive topics of study.

A particular group of students could continue using the same general project through several academic years with increasing sophistication. For example, students could create a particularly well-documented class archive of opinions about the meaning of the history of their times. Similarly, in Chapter 12's Research Magazine project, you could change the magazine's topic from health care to global warming, crime prevention, expanding world populations, recycling, or the school's sports teams, without significantly changing the other aspects of the project.

Summary

This chapter describes a four-step process, of which actually coaching students as they create a project is merely one step. It discusses a wider context that includes important sources of assistance in carrying out the steps of the process. The Practice section provides a practical method for recording information about many possible projects that will enable you to select individual projects and progressions of projects to help your students meet objectives that you set.

Armed with basic information from Chapters 1 through 5, and with this chapter's information about a process and a way to select projects, you are now well prepared to embark on the chapters that describe six projects in detail. Ideally, you will actually play the role of a K-12 student and create the projects. Even if you do not actually create each project, you can benefit from reading each chapter's description and thinking about how students could benefit from creating such a project.

As you work through the next chapters, we encourage you to see if you agree with the entries that we put in the tables in this chapter's Practice section. We also encourage you to invent your own new projects and add these projects' characteristics to the same tables.

Part B - Progression of Projects

- How can my students relate new items to time frame, to geography, and to each other?

- How can my students use different media to convey and synthesize different peoples' feelings on controversial issues?

- How can my students use different media to appeal to different groups of people?

- How can I help my students organize information from different sources?

- How can students prepare an on-line quiz.

- How can my students use the Internet for their multimedia magazine ?

Chapter 7

Current Events

In this chapter, we explore:

- building a class archive on news events.

- the first project in the progression, a suitable first choice for you and your students.

- how to instruct and guide your students in the use of hypertext, including how to set up menus for time and place.

- the requirements for setting up a process for a class project.

The Current Events project introduces the fundamental multimedia technology of hypertext. Hypertext is the capability of organizing content so that users can navigate through the material in multiple ways. The principal medium of this project is text. The creators may also scan-in photographs or import images associated with an article. Although you may do this project for all the reasons traditionally associated with current event assignments, some additional benefits arise from the new technology. This project helps student exercise higher-order thinking, analyze events of the day, and practice writing.

This chapter describes the project itself, the academic outcomes that it can help students to achieve, the initial process of beginning the archive, and the ongoing process of adding to it and using it.

This chapter describes a project based on the familiar assignment to students to bring in a newspaper article on any topic of current events. The teacher establishes the range of generality or may choose a narrower focus. Elementary school teachers and social science teachers at the middle, junior, or high school levels would probably choose the general assignment. Science teachers may choose to require science articles, or articles in health, environment, space, energy, or some other area. Mathematics teachers may guide students towards survey and polling results, sports statistics, economic news, projections of health demographics, and product analyses. English teachers may choose the general assignment, with the focus on expository writing and bibliographic citations, or may direct the students to articles on literature, plays, or films.

Background

In Current Events, the entire class creates, updates, and uses a computer archive of news stories, an organized collection of entries compiled over time. The students prepare summaries and citations for articles that they select from newspapers and place the material in the archive according to the time and place of the event. The students also make connections between each new entry to the archive and the articles already present. As the project continues over the course of the school year, the archive becomes a resource for the class. You can modify the assignment to vary the challenge to the students and to cover specific topics in the curriculum.

The class works as a whole to produce and maintain one News Archive. You can initiate the project by describing the assignment and giving a schedule. Students individually select articles, write summaries, and prepare citations, using a format defined by the teacher and appropriate for the grade level. If the article has an accompanying photograph or diagram, the student scans the picture for inclusion in the archive. Students must determine where and when the event occurred in order to place their articles in the archive. They must also peruse the archive to see if their new article possesses a strong relationship to one or more prior events.

Making do

Scanners (and pictures) are not essential for this project. The critical tasks are summarizing the story and linking it appropriately in the archive. An alternative way for students to illustrate stories is to have them use clip art or make their own drawings and diagrams using commercial draw programs.

Teacher Defines the Project

You prepare the initial archive by setting up the menus shown in the figures or whatever you devise. The first menu shown in Figure 7-1 offers the user the option of turning to articles already in the archive or adding a new article. The user finds articles through the use of a timeline or one of two maps.

Time and place are clear and fundamental organizing concepts

WELCOME TO OUR CLASS NEWS ARCHIVE
Click here to search for news stories from
[national map]
[global map]
Click here to search for news stories from a [time line]
Click here to [add a new story]

Figure 7-1: Opening page with buttons for timeline and two maps

---

that can and should be represented graphically. Time is one-dimensional and, until the technology improves to the point of being able to project holographic images, two-dimensional maps will serve to indicate place. Teachers can ask the students to compare these organizing principles with others. We indicate in this chapter, and also in Chapter 15, Variations, other organizing principles for this project. Computer drawing programs provide teachers and students with the facility to prepare their own timelines. Similarly, teachers and students can search out and acquire maps from commercial multimedia sources as indicated in Chapter 4.

The maps indicated in the menu pages assume that the articles and the students' interest would split between national stories and global stories. You may decide if a local map of the town is appropriate in addition to or instead of the national map. You can weigh current familiarity versus the opportunity to expand students' interests.

Instead of preparing the menus ahead of time, you may choose to lead a class session to design the menus. Students would design and produce the timeline and locate suitable maps from a commercial source. The timeline should correspond to the schedule for assignments. Teachers and students use the basic functions of adding text and boxes to a page or use the draw program associated with the multimedia authoring tool to produce the timeline drawing. Chapter 4 describes how commercial products such as on-line atlases are available that contain maps appropriate for inclusion in student projects. We emphasize that "appropriate" means both suitable in content and legal to copy.

If the menus prove inadequate for the articles collected, the class can design and produce new menus as replacements or as additions. They can produce a new menu page and build new links from this page to each article. This is one of the benefits provided by the technology (see Chapter 5, Organizing Information). Science teachers may choose to begin the project with a menu giving topics such as the one in Figure 7-2.

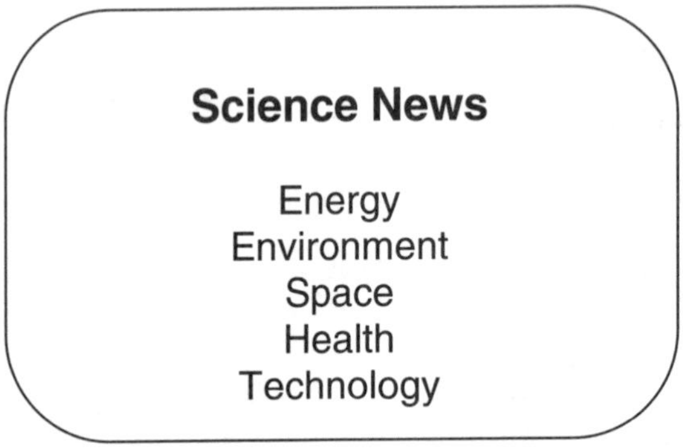

Science News

Energy
Environment
Space
Health
Technology

Figure 7-2: Science topics

Similarly, social science teachers may choose to begin the project with a menu of topics relating to politics or other social science issues.

Students Make Contributions

When students decide to add a new article to the archive, they add a new page and write text summaries. You may treat this as you would any piece of composition. In this case, however, many people will read and re-read these summaries and, as a consequence, student writing may improve.

Technical Note

As part of the initial preparation of the archive, you may guide the students' work at each step by the use of the facilities of the authoring system. For example, the button on the first menu, Figure 7-1, that says, "Click here to add a new story," can ask the person at the keyboard to type in his or her name, generate a new page, link the page to previous work by that student, and guide the student creation of the entry. Similarly, you can arrange that the entry would not be stored in the archive unless a citation was given and links created to at least one of the main menus. You may need to ask a technical support person for assistance or give it as a challenge to a student. Alternatively, you may decide that it is not appropriate to set up these controls. You may want the students to have the challenge of following instructions.

Requiring the students to insert a citation as a pop-up text field exercises the research skill of properly giving citations. Students may also include an image, placing it on the page directly or as a pop-up.

Picture: Yes or no?

We pose here a question on pedagogy. At what age and maturity level can you make the assignment "include a picture if and only if it is important to the story?" Many students will try to bring in a picture and choose their articles based on the existence of a picture. Since the existence of a striking photograph can affect the placement of a news story, it is not surprising that students find it difficult to make these judgments. Over time and through class discussion of many stories, you can invoke thoughtfulness in your students on this subtle issue. Techniques include comparing the coverage by different newspapers and asking students to express their reactions to photographs independently of the text.

Next, the person adding to the archive establishes the event in time and place by constructing linking buttons from the timeline and map pages to the article page. One possible task at this point is to invent a short, evocative name or phrase for the article. This will go in the correct spot for time and for place. These are similar to the "slugs" used by working journalists to label news copy. Last, the student builds links between the new article and one or more articles in the existing archive. Labeled buttons or icons indicate the links, with the label or symbol indicating the relationship. Some articles may give rise to multiple links, whereas others may be relatively isolated events.

Contributors to the archive link any follow-up article on a story to the most recent, relevant article. They do not link the follow-up story to the map menu. The first article on this evolving story is linked directly to the map. These concrete decisions are worthwhile challenges to the students. You may need to provide guidance, but it is important to give students the opportunities to exercise judgment. Figure 7-3 shows a mock-up of a story page with a button for pop-up text for a citation and a button for a pop-up photograph too big to include as a fixed part of the page.

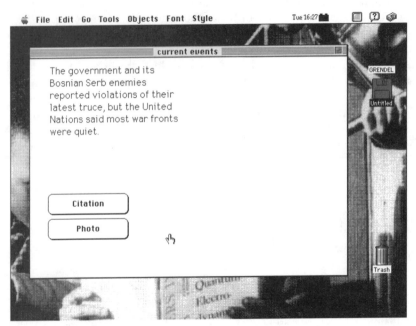

Figure 7-3: Screen dump on Bosnia story

Figure 7-4 and Figure 7-5 show the effect of a user clicking on the citation button and clicking on the photo button, respectively.

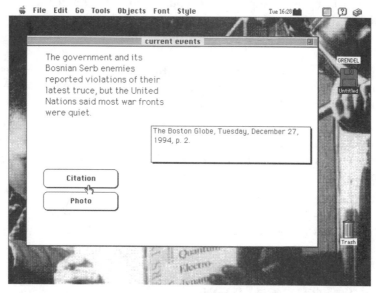

Figure 7-4: Screen dump on Bosnia story, pop-up citation

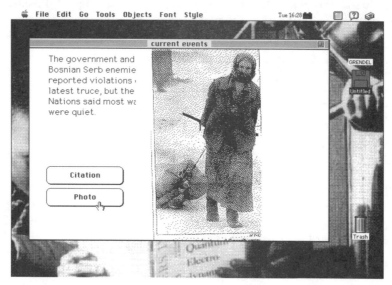

Figure 7-5: Screen dump on Bosnia event, picture pop-up

It is up to you to decide how students will identify their work.

- They can sign each news article page.

- They can bring their summary to you, written out longhand or prepared at home or school on a word processor with the article attached. This would provide a mechanism to check the work before they sit down at the classroom computer.

- They can link their articles to a page with their names on it (and perhaps even their pictures) in order to maintain a record of their personal work. A class page would hold buttons for each student.

The latter two methods each ease the task for the teacher of locating students' work while avoiding putting a student's name on the page. This relative anonymity means that other students have a chance to read the article without any preconceptions of what to expect. This can serve to break up patterns of relating among the students.

The design of Current Events given here requires students to take turns making their additions to the single News Archive. In the Practice section, we offer suggestions on managing the logistics for efficient operations and also invoking responsibility on the part of the students.

News Archive Grows

Figure 7-6 shows a story board for the News Archive at one stage of development. The story board diagram indicates that there are currently three article pages, with a link between two of the articles.

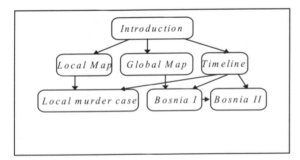

Figure 7-6: Story board for Current Events

You also can turn periodically to the archive to see what is new, and students can use it as a reference source for particular topics.

The look of the menus and the articles changes over time. Figure 7-7 and Figure 7-8 show two screens, months apart, showing a map representing the globe. In this example, the buttons are plain, with no labels or graphics.

You can use the evolution of the Science or Social Studies News Archive and its menu page as the basis for discussions on the interrelationships of categories. The class can then generate a concept map of the subject area. The concept

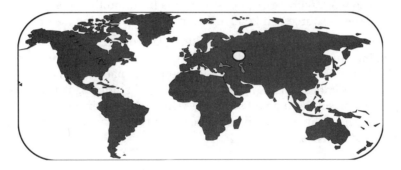

Figure 7-7: Global map with one button for one story

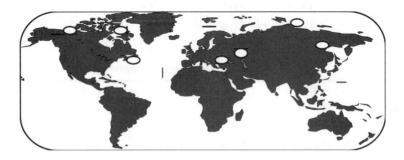

Figure 7-8: Global map with buttons for more stories

map and the hypermedia structure of the multimedia archive are different representations of the same thing.

This multimedia version of a common, traditional assignment offers the following benefits:

- The News Archive is attractive and robust in comparison to a bulletin board. It can hold more articles and indicate complex relationships. It will last the whole school year. It frees up the bulletin board for transitory uses.

- The requirement for crisp phrases for article buttons and relationship buttons invokes a discipline on the students. Similarly, the repeated requirement to position events in time and place and relationship to other stories provides for substantial learning.

- Because of the robust nature of the archive, the project can last the whole year and can change based on the circumstances of the class. The project enables students to work with descriptions of events from multiple perspectives, from a variety of news sources, and with different students making the summaries.

- As with other student-constructed multimedia projects, Current Events provides a genuine audience for student writings because everyone is continually engaged as both user and contributor. The public nature of the students' work product is a critical factor in the motivation of students. It also facilities the discussion of subtle and not-so-subtle issues of relationships and journalistic practices. The archive grows both in the quantity of content and in the quality of writing and analysis.

Theory

The Current Events project is a traditional activity supported and enhanced by new technologies. In this section, we indicate the educational goals that this project addresses, following the framework given earlier. In the summary, we indicate what the technology-assisted version provides as additional benefits. Table 7-1 summarizes goals students may achieve by creating this project.

Table 7-1: Goals for Current Events project

Higher-Order Thinking Skills
- Summarizing
- Relating distinct events to each other
- Selecting and naming important events
- Recognizing and analyzing distinct coverage of the same event
- Organization

Group and Interpersonal Skills
- Participating in a large group project
- Sharing tools

Content Material Learning
- Awareness of current events and how they evolve
- Expository writing
- Locating events on a map
- Bibliographic citations

Technical Skills
- Writing and entering text into a multimedia folder
- Scanning photographs
- Building buttons
- Following cookbook instructions

The Current Events project encourages students to read and understand what is happening in the world as described in newspaper articles. They must summarize the text in a written form, which has the advantage of ensuring that they understand the material well enough to restate it in their own words. Inventing the short name or phrase for the button exercises a more precise ability for analysis, especially as the archive grows and students want distinct labels for their articles.

The student adding to the archive must locate the event on the timeline and the maps. This task appears fairly straightforward. However, reports on United States children's ignorance of the most basic geography justify requiring practice with this task week after week. Students also may make use of the timeline and maps to identify other articles to link to their new articles. This exploratory use reinforces the sense of time and place. You can also guide students to ask questions: "What was going on around my town, the country, and the world at this time? What was occurring in the very same place last week, last month, or back at the start of the year?"

If a main menu represents categories of events, such as the example for the Science News Archive or Social Studies Archive, then students must choose the appropriate category. Real learning occurs when there are ambiguities. Is an oil spill an environment story or an energy story? Is a story about taxes an economics story or a political story? Adults may find it easy to say, "Of course, it is both." Young students tend to start off with categories. It is when ambiguities and conflicts occur that significant learning takes place. Making categories is useful, but understanding interconnections and so-called gray areas is also important. The concrete nature of the task of adding to the archive brings out these learning opportunities.

Similarly, you can encourage students to bring in news stories that relate to topics not on the list. When this happens, the students decide first if the article is appropriate. Then they must decide if they should add a new topic to the menu or place the article in a catch-all category. The access to the archive is facilitated by these decisions. These are issues of judgment and usability.

The continuing requirement to relate new articles to previous ones encourages students to examine differences in coverage and varying aspects of causality. Both teacher and class can generate and codify a set of buttons for relationships as shown in Table 7-2.

Table 7-2: Sample outcome of brainstorming on connections

Relationship of one article to another
• More detail
• Overview or analysis
• Other point of view
• Contradictory coverage
• Follow-up to event
• Outcome
• Explanation

Current Events is a group project in which students work by themselves. The students are working with each other's writings and share a sense of pride in the growing product.

As we have described, you may choose to modify the archive by adding a new menu sometime after the project begins. This provides significant, additional learning opportunities for the class. The students exercise the higher-order thinking invoked by defining an organizing principle. This is considerably more profound than being given a scheme, such as time, place, or a set of several categories, and then doing the sorting. The class instead reviews all the articles from this new perspective. This provides reinforcement for the initial learning.

News events themselves may inspire a change in the archive. For example, you may decide to focus all attention on one or two stories as they evolve. You may assign students to specific news sources. Teachers may also adjust the assignment based on increased capabilities on the part of the students. We believe that "raising the bar," that is, raising the standard of performance, is a valuable tool for improving self-esteem.

Practice

We next discuss each step of the process introduced in Chapter 6. Issues touched on in the Theory section appear again in the context of the process. The application of the process will be somewhat different for Current Events than for the other projects because Current Events is ongoing and the others have defined completion points. For example, we refer to ongoing reflection. Table 7-3 indicates the steps.

Step One - Teacher Prepares

The authors devised and selected the Current Events project as the first in the progression because it makes use of the most basic of multimedia technologies and because it is similar to a common classroom activity. These same reasons may make it an appropriate first choice for classroom teachers. The first step of preparation is to determine the educational goals.

You determine the focus of the assignment. This could be any current event or any event within some category, as indicated earlier. You can also define the acceptable range of publications.

You can pick from a spectrum of strategies for initiating the project. At one extreme, the teacher prepares or acquires a template containing embedded code for guiding the student in each step of entering a new article. The teacher demonstrates the use of this template for the class and can seed the archive with two or three articles. At the other extreme, you and the class start off with nothing and define and build the structure as you go along. Students produce the article pages from "scratch" each time. The archive will not have a consistent look to it and it will be more likely that some students forget to do the citations and complete the links.

Table 7-3: Process steps for Current Events

Teacher prepares project
- Select goals
- Define range of topics for articles
- Assess technical environment
- Determine strategy for start-up

Teacher assigns project
- Announce topic and goals
- Describe and demonstrate time and place menus
- Establish weekly routine
- Devise and announce new topics and conditions, as appropriate, over time

Students create project
- Students (individually) make additions
- Teacher monitors work

Students and teacher practice ongoing reflection
- Student self-evaluation when using system
- Scheduled class reviews of archive
- Teacher and class propose changes and additions to structure
- Teacher raises standards

You can operate with a strategy between these extremes by using class discussion to get ideas and agreement on menus and formats and then assigning a small group of students to prepare a template for the class or create a written set of instructions posted near the computer workstation. Alternatively, you can kickoff the project using prepared menus for time and place and later, when the students are more familiar with the system, initiate a discussion of adding a new menu.

You may also want to determine how the writing aspect of this assignment fits in with your general plan for achieving objectives for composition. We offer some suggestions, when we describe the assignment step.

After determining goals and focus, the next critical part of preparation is assessing the available equipment. This is simple for this project. The basic requirement is one computer loaded with a multimedia authoring system. To scan-in photographs, the class requires access to a machine connected to a scanner and a supply of reusable diskettes if the computers are not on a network. You can establish the procedures for individual students to go to the location of the scanner.

Step Two - Teacher Assigns Project

The teacher establishes Current Events as a permanent weekly assignment. You can initiate the project and define the weekly routine using whatever start-up strategies are appropriate for your class. For the early grades, or in an environment that has rigid schedule constraints, you may schedule specific times for each student to prepare and enter her weekly articles. In other circumstances, you may give the responsibility to the student to get the job done. You may need to monitor this process, assessing and intervening as appropriate, as when someone complains that she "did not get a chance at the computer."

Many people, including young children, have become adept at composing on the computer, although others prefer to write out their work longhand and type it in. Each multimedia authoring system has a facility for entering text, but they differ in word processing capabilities such as spell-checking. Teachers determine the standard and the routine or set of routines that the students are to follow to produce their written summaries. This is "writing for a purpose" and "writing for publication." We emphasize that the students will review each other's writing when they use the archive.

At the time of the initial assignment, you can indicate what the schedule will be for reviewing the archive. One approach is to schedule two different reviews:

- a weekly review as part of a classroom discussion on current events and
- a monthly review by the teacher and individual student (see reflection step) .

Step Three - Students Create Project

The students produce their additions to the archive following the weekly routine. They bring in an article and write a summary in school or do this step at home as homework. They can use the multimedia authoring system directly to type in their story summary or use their normal word processor and import the file. It may be advantageous to use the second approach if students are familiar with the word processing application. It is also more likely that the word processing system includes a spell-checker. The multimedia authoring system may not. This approach may also relieve congestion on the computer holding the class archive.

If members of the class have selected a story with an accompanying picture, they scan the picture, saving it on a diskette or using the network. Scanning involves the following sequence of steps.

1. Attach a scanner to a computer and install corresponding scanning software. Place the picture on the scanner, as you would place the original on a copier. Use the software to choose appropriate settings, such as selecting a color, gray scale, or black-and-white image and zooming in to capture only the picture.

2. Many formats exist for digital images. Some scanners can produce more than one format of an image file and, conversely, some authoring systems can accept multiple formats. Users of the scanning software specify the format in which to save the file. Teachers and school support staff need to determine how to achieve the best match between scanning software and authoring system. This may involve a separate format conversion step.

3. The students adding images to the archive then bring their image files produced by the scanner over to the computer holding the class archive and import the pictures into the authoring system. Generally, this requires them to clip the image or piece of the image they want and bring it onto the page with the written summary.

Each student determines the time, place, and any other category and creates the buttons linking to his story. The student then reviews other stories, using the menus, to see if there is a story to link with the new entry.

The exact mechanics for the addition of new article pages depends on the features of the authoring system, the skills of the students, and the predisposition of the teacher. Roughly speaking, there are three possibilities:

• As we have said, you may, with possible help from technical support people, prepare a program that leads the students through the steps from the time they click on "Add a new story" to when they are done. The program, built using the scripting language of the authoring system, creates new pages, fields of text, and pop-ups. It may, for example, display the message, "Type in citation," and not go on until that is done.

• At the opposite end of the spectrum, the teacher may instruct the students in the basics of the authoring system, and leave them on their own to create pages, create and fill fields of text, and create buttons.

• Another strategy is to show the students how to locate the page for one of the stories you have put into the archive, copy it, and make changes in place. This strategy is easier than developing a working program but also establishes some uniformity to the look of the total archive. It is also what many professionals do when creating multimedia.

You need to determine how much individual autonomy to allow each student and, hopefully, increase this over the course of the year. Initially, especially with younger children, you may monitor the whole process, approving the article, reviewing the summary, and confirming that the student can identify time and place. As the year unfolds, students should flourish under less supervision. You can guide students towards more sophisticated articles and can also suggest seeking out unusual publications, including newspapers in different languages.

> **Technical Note: Aspect Ratios**
>
> The aspect ratio of a picture is the ratio of the horizontal dimension to the vertical dimension. Some scanning and format conversion programs will attempt to achieve a certain aspect ratio and, in the process, distort an image. One technique to prevent this is to make the image scanned fit the aspect ratio for the whole screen and then clip the resulting image to what you want. Actually, students enjoy seeing pictures distorted as done by the mirrors in the Fun House at an amusement park. However, it does take away from the intent of the assignment.

> **Technical Note: Palettes**
>
> Some picture formats work with an associated palette file of colors, similar to the artist palette. However, you must make sure your students copy the palette file along with the image file when they move files between systems.

The creation step requires attention to classroom and school logistics. If the archive computer is not in the classroom, then individuals or groups may be assigned times in the computer lab, media center, or library. If the computer is in the classroom but the scanner is elsewhere, then you need to determine if they should do the scanning themselves, assign it to a special working group, or schedule students in groups to visit the scanner.

The benefits of adding multimedia technology to this common assignment will quickly become apparent. Students enjoy relating their article to place and prior events. They concentrate more on their work because it will be read. The computer archive remains attractive and accessible and does not become tattered and torn as would an aging bulletin board display. Teachers can lead the class in discussing modifications of the News Archive, such as a focus on a new set of topics or attention to a specific geographic area. The class then implements the modifications with their technical hypermedia skills.

Step Four - Ongoing Reflection

The Current Events project has an intrinsic role for reflection. The student adding a new article asks herself, "What does the archive tell me about what has been happening? How does this new article fit? How can I position it in time and place?" Students see their work and that of their peers in use every time they access the archive.

To invoke wider circles of people in reflection, you may schedule periodic reviews for the class and showings for the school and parents. These are performances, and students can participate directly or observe how an outside audience responds to their product.

You can also use the periodic reviews to encourage more profound work. You can point to particular events and suggest that students seek out articles to reveal the rest of the story over the coming weeks and months. The periodic reviews are also the time to discuss new organizations for the archive.

It may happen that students or teachers may notice a pattern of media coverage. Newspaper A always has a different slant from Newspaper B. Newspaper A has more articles on topic X than does Newspaper B. The class can design and perform experiments to test their theories. Figure 7-9 illustrates an assignment sheet for this experiment. This experiment is an example of reflection leading to investigation and, presumably, deeper learning. The coverage assignments shown in Figure 7-9 can be the basis of an additional menu for the archive.

Newspaper	Student
NY Times	Daniel
Reporter Dispatch	Aviva
Wall Street Journal	David
Amsterdam News	Tommy
El Diario	Bernardo
Newsweek	Debbie

Figure 7-9: Coverage assignments for news sources experiment

Teachers and students may also engage in assessment directed to the objective of ongoing, continuous improvement. The following are questions to consider on Current Events.

- Are the weekly assignments complete, with clearly written summaries, correct spelling and citations, and appropriate pictures? Does the student tell "who," "what," "where," "when," and "why?"
- How do other students respond to the work? Is this student's work read?
- Is the writing improving? Is the choice of story changing in a positive way? Does the student respond to suggestions to seek out more complex issues? Teachers can ask students, "How do you think you can improve?"

The archive provides excellent material for parent teacher conferences. Parents can browse through the archive and pick up a general sense of what the peers of their children are doing.

Summary

Current Events is a good initial project for student-constructed multimedia. Its equipment requirements are modest. It is mainly an exercise in hypertext, that is, devising and producing distinct ways for users to navigate through material. You have great flexibility on how much to prepare in advance for your students and how much to make their responsibility. During this ongoing project, you can coach your students and modify their interactions as appropriate.

The technology provides a variety of significant functions for this very traditional assignment. These include both prosaic matters and issues of higher-order thinking and interpersonal behavior. One purely utilitarian factor is that a computer archive is neater and hardier than anything on a bulletin board. The mechanics of hypermedia and the ease of computer drawing support explicit attention to abstract relationships. Students read other students' work and know that their work will be read. This stimulates improvements in performances.

Chapter 8

Critics' Circle

In this chapter, we explore:

- a project in which students take the role of movie critics.

- a project requiring teamwork in which teams identify and present differing opinions.

- how to guide your students in the use of digitized audio and digitized images.

- how distinct media are used together for distinct effects.

The Critics' Circle project introduces several important multimedia technologies: digital audio, digitized images (still pictures), and symbolic icons. You can select this project to help students learn these technical multimedia skills and to gain insight into the effects of juxtaposition of distinct media. Involvement in this project helps students acquire the key higher-order thinking skill of recognizing that different people can hold a wide spectrum of different opinions about exactly the same subject. Successful completion of the project also requires both expository writing and oral expression, which are standard components of all levels of the English curriculum.

This chapter describes the project itself, the academic outcomes that creating this project can help students achieve, the four process steps for creating the completed project, and practical suggestions to help you achieve the desired outcomes.

This chapter describes a particular form of the project in which three members of a group of five students record their own opinions of a movie. Of course, you are likely to modify this to meet particular requirements for different size groups. Instead of a movie, you could select a novel, a poem, a picture, or even a controversial political issue.

Background

In Critics' Circle, members of a team of students play the role of critics and record their oral opinions about a movie. Other members provide pictures of the critics, design symbolic icons denoting distinct viewpoints, and prepare a written summary of the opinions. Students or others who use the completed project can choose to listen to the critics' opinions while viewing images of the critics and read the summary, in any order.

Groups Create Their Critics' Circle

To begin Critics' Circle, you first select a movie and divide the class into groups of five students each. Each group begins by holding a roundtable discussion of the movie in which everyone gets a chance to be heard. The group then makes a collective decision on which three members will be critics. The group proceeds to create its own multimedia project by modifying its own copy of the Critics' Circle template provided by the teacher.

The three critics use the template to record their opinions about the movie, as follows. They open the template and see a "Welcome" page, similar to the one shown in Figure 8-1, with icon buttons for the three critics and their microphones. Of course, their icons are arranged around a critics' circle. Each critic in turn records his opinion by selecting one of the microphone icons. For example, selecting the microphone icon in front of Critic Three invokes the link that goes from the "Welcome" page to a page "Desk of Critic Three," similar to the one shown in Figure 8-2. When Critic Three sees this page, he selects the "Record" icon (on the image of a tape recorder), tells what he thought about the movie, and then selects "Stop." The critic checks the result by selecting "Playback" and may repeat the process until satisfied with the result.

These icons are not merely pictures on the computer screen; they are actually button objects that tell the computer's audio adapter to start recording, stop recording, or play back what the critic recorded. Employing a multimedia authoring system's facilities to create these pages and buttons from scratch would not be particularly hard, but employing the template allows beginning students to concentrate on forming and recording opinions. More advanced students can use the templates to learn by example. That is, they can look inside any of the objects that make up the templates, modify the objects in many ways, and copy useful objects as parts of entirely new projects.

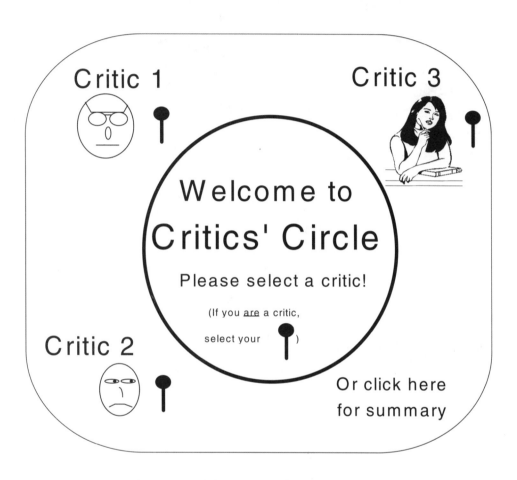

Figure 8-1: Welcome page for Critics' Circle

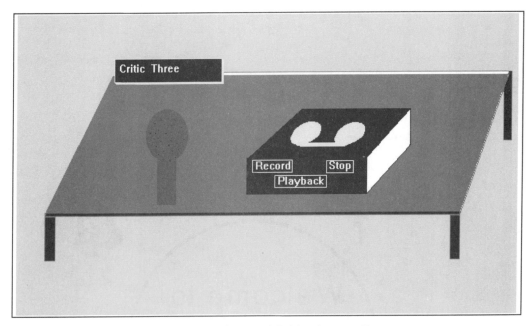

Figure 8-2: Screen dump of Critic 3's recording page

Figure 8-3 shows the completed "Opinion" page for Critic Three. One member of the group is responsible for placing a digitized image of the actual student critic on her corresponding page. The group members also create icons that they think illustrate the respective critics' opinions such as the scowl that Figure 8-1 shows for Critic Two. They then substitute their icons for the place holder icons of faces that are provided on this "Welcome" page of the template, Figure 8-1.

Figure 8-3: Opinion page for Critic Three, incorporating a digital image produced using the Logitech Fotoman Plus camera

Finally, the group agrees on a written summary of the opinions and enters that summary on the template's "Summary Page," like the one that appears in Figure 8-4. How the group interacts to accomplish this and the standards for assessment are covered in the Practice section of this chapter.

Summary

Our three critics represented a wide range of opinions

All seemed to think that the movie contained a significant amount of sex and violence, but their conclusions from that fact ranged from enjoyment to disgust.

Their opinions, in turn, seem to be so completely stereotypical that our group thought that the opinions themselves were disgusting.

Figure 8-4: Summary page

Audiences Use Each Project

Teachers, staff, parents, and other students play the role of users of the group's completed project. They listen to and analyze the critics' opinions of the movie and read the group's summary of the opinions. A user begins at the "Welcome" page and selects one of the three icons that represent the three critics. This invokes a link that takes the user to the corresponding "Opinion" page so that the user can see the critic's image while hearing the critic's voice. Then the user selects the page's "Return" button to go back to the "Welcome" page. The user can select other critics' icons and the summary, and also go back to confirm the stereotypical opinions reported in the summary. You can view each group's work individually, schedule showings one after the other, or arrange a time when students and visitors to the class can circulate around the room. The Critics' Circle project can be a culminating event for a portion of the curriculum or can initiate a unit of study. In either case, you may wish to gather the students together to discuss all the projects. Table 8-1 indicates the distinct roles taken in this project. One person can take on multiple roles.

Table 8-1: Roles people play in Critics' Circle project

- Teacher selects projects, executes four-step process, facilitates creation.
- Students create projects in groups, playing the role of critic, image and icon specialist, analyst.
- Users enjoy and evaluate the projects.
- Support staff assists the teacher in setting up equipment and installing templates.

Internal View of Critics' Circle

Critics' Circle uses an appropriate selection of different media for different purposes. It uses voice, drawings, and images to present informal information that captures each critic's emotion and mood. It uses an image to emphasize that each critic is a real individual whose opinion deserves a respectful hearing. Finally, it uses text to present a formal analysis and summary. The definition of this early project prescribes the roles for the respective media. In subsequent projects where students themselves select the media, you may remind the students how Critics' Circle used each of the media.

Critics' Circle uses icon buttons that invoke links that go from one page to another. These links allow user-driven navigation so that a user can hear the opinions in any order and can go back and review previous opinions to analyze their differences and similarities. For such analysis, user-driven navigation is preferable to a creator-driven tour that proceeds through the information in a fixed order. Other projects, where students attempt to convince users of something, use fixed creator-selected tours to present their material in the most persuasive order.

Experienced students could complete Critics' Circle from a description without using a sample prepared by the teacher. However, starting with a template allows even beginning students to complete the project without paying too much attention to the software or to the equipment. With this preparation, student creation of the project can be compressed into three to five hours, if desired, with high confidence of success.

A story board such as the one shown in Figure 8-5 helps students keep track of the structure of a project. As described in Chapter 3 and in detail in Chapter 13, a story board

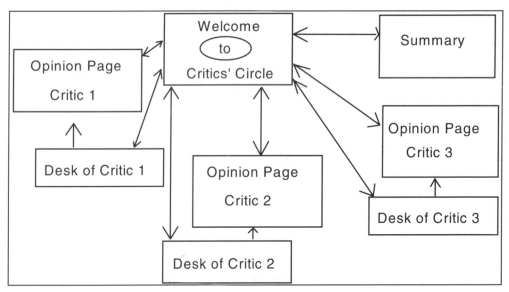

Figure 8-5: Story board for Critics' Circle

is particularly useful if someone is creating a project from scratch rather than using a template. Each box in the story board represents one page in the project. An arrow such as the one from the "Welcome" page to the "Desk of Critic 3" page means that there is an icon on the "Welcome" page that links to the "Desk of Critic 3" page. We have seen that the icon that invokes this link is the microphone in front of the representation of Critic Three. Where an arrow between two boxes has a head on each end, it means that there is an icon on each page that invokes a link to the other page.

Theory

The major goals that Critics' Circle can help students meet appear in Table 8-2. Meeting such goals can represent an important cognitive and interpersonal experience. Note that this project can achieve serious objectives even by using an arbitrary movie as the topic for the project's opinions. Of course, to use this project to help teach particular content, you would instead select a topic that relates to that content.

This project requires a team effort resulting in a presentation in front of the whole class. The fact that certain members of the team held specific opinions may fade in significance with the effort to put together a presentation on the whole topic.

Creating Critics' Circle includes selecting a subset of the group members' views that represent a complete spectrum of opinion and are individually and collectively interesting and engaging. The group strives to express these distinct opinions using a combination of speech, image, graphics, and writing. The project gives the group an opportunity to use multiple media to express, analyze, and possibly reconcile the opinions.

Group members must come to terms with the experience of performing different roles such as giving their own opinion or helping others to give their opinions. Members may consider role-playing to present a view different from their own, particularly if they see an interesting opinion that none of the critics happens to actually hold.

On occasion, you would select Critics' Circle to meet the particular technical goals that are listed at the bottom of Table 8-2. For example, it would be reasonable to select a project that introduces voice recordings and digitized images in between a project that concentrates on hypertext and a project that produces motion video clips. In fact, we first designed this project primarily for its ability to help high school teachers to meet those technical goals.

You would probably select Critics' Circle because of the higher-order thinking skills, interpersonal skills, or content material learning that it can promote. For example, you might decide that a given class is ready to explore the concept of honest differences of opinion or that the students are ready to experience working and making decisions in small groups in which they may play distinct roles. The project's requirement to produce a tangible and attractive result, one that peers, teachers, and others will use, can strongly motivate students. It instills self-discipline on the part of the group to produce a complete result.

Table 8-2: Goals of Critics' Circle project

Higher-Order Thinking Skills
- Formulating viewpoints
- Choosing among different viewpoints
- Analyzing and meaningfully communicating contradictory opinions
- Synthesizing and composing a concise summary
- Articulating and refining an oral statement
- Imagination and empathy
- Role playing to cover a range of opinions

Group and Interpersonal Skills
- Recognizing a spectrum of different, valid opinions on the same subject
- Working successfully in a group, including choosing roles
- Noting what different people react to in the selected movie

Content Material Learning
- Expository writing (speakers' scripts and text summary)
- Deeper understanding of tensions involved in content
- Dramatic and production values
- Content of movie or other subject discussed

Technical Skills
- Recording voice (digital audio) to convey informal opinions
- Creating and recording images
- Linking to provide coherent and logical organization (hypermedia)
- Express opinions in text, graphics, and speech
- Creating expressive graphic icons
- Using text for a formal summary of opinions
- Modifying a template, perhaps following cookbook

Current curriculum standards call for attention to the different kinds of communication skills. Critics' Circle provides such attention, both to scripts for the spoken comments and to the written summary. The project requires students to go through a process that includes brainstorming, exposition with feedback, writing, editing, and publishing or performance. This project invokes higher-order or metalevel skills that include recognizing differing points of view and organizing distinct views into a framework. It also invokes using distinct modalities of expression or media, namely oral in the audio recordings, symbolic in the icons, representational in the images of the critics, and text in the written summary. Completing this project helps students develop the skills to organize and present recorded speech, written text, images, and graphics in an integrated and compelling fashion.

The skills involved also include basic teamwork involved in cooperative learning. Successfully creating a Critics' Circle project requires visible performance by each group member as well as recognition and integration of individual contributions into something produced by the team. In one way or another, these skills are required by many jobs and by life itself. Although the project's movie topic may be innocent and fun, students should be able to achieve significant objectives by creating these projects.

Classroom example

Mr. Delgatos is starting to teach eighth grade social studies in Miami, Florida. His class includes many ethnic groups, of which the largest is Hispanic. He has noticed that some students take extreme positions on various subjects, believing that any opinion expressed is either completely right or dead wrong. He is looking for a way to teach, vividly, the reality that different people can have different but valid opinions about the same subject. His students are at a restless age and are unusually restless near the beginning of the school year. Thus he also needs a way to break the ice with his class and help them to focus on school work. He wants to give the students some practice in working in groups that cut across cultural lines.

Classroom Example

Mrs. Jameson adopts Critics' Circle for her middle school English class in order to achieve greater understanding of *Much Ado About Nothing*. She wants the class to explore a variety of interpretations of the play as well as the language used in the play. She wants to emphasize well-articulated opinions. She requires that the oral opinions must use a language style similar to that used in the play.

Although she has digitized images of the class already, she will allow the class to use a digital camera to prepare additional images of themselves dressed in period costumes.

She plans to set up a computer in the school's auditorium on which visitors can use the resulting project. She will title it "Mrs. Jameson's Middle School English Class takes you to Shakespeare's Court."

Practice

We next discuss each step of the process introduced in Chapter 6 as it applies to Critics' Circle and show how preparing, assigning, creating, and reflecting on this project can meet the objectives discussed in the previous section. The steps for this project appear in Table 8-3.

Table 8-3: Process steps for Critics' Circle project

Step One - Teacher prepares
- Select goals and movie or other topic to be discussed
- Determine groupings of students
- Select items required in all projects
- Define characteristics of outstanding projects

Step Two - Teacher assigns project
- Announce topic, educational goals, and exhibits
- Present organizing principle, template, and story board
- Decide sources of images of critics
- Suggest subtasks
- Allot time for completion

Step Three - Students create project
- Brainstorm
- Select the three critics
- Rehearse stating the opinions
- Record each critic's opinion
- Design icons that represent the opinions
- Put in each critic's image
- Analyze the arguments and write the summary
- Assemble and test the complete project

Step Four - Reflection
- Student do self-evaluation as they create project
- Teachers reflect on the project
- Review any public performances
- Conduct class evaluation

Step One - Teacher Prepares

A multimedia project, as any other significant classroom activity, requires careful preparation beforehand. As noted, you start with the goals that you want to achieve.

You then select a project that can help students achieve those outcomes using the available equipment.

Table 8-4 shows the teacher, computer coordinator, and students what equipment they will need for Critics' Circle (equipment not required is shaded).

Table 8-4: Media input and output in Critics' Circle project

Media	Input	Output
Text and Data	Computer keyboard; CD-ROM	Computer display screen; Printer
Graphics	Draw program & Mouse; CD-ROM	Computer display screen; Printer; Plotter
Still image	Paint program & Mouse; Video camera & Digital video capture adapter; Camera & Scanner; Digital camera; CD-ROM	Computer display screen; Printer
Audio (voice & music)	Microphone & Audio card; CD-ROM; MIDI	Digital audio adapter and Amplified speaker
Analog video video	Video camera; Cable; Laser disc; or VCR	TV monitor; Computer display screen and Video window card
Digital slow-frame video	Video camera; Cable; Laser disc; or VCR and Digital video capture adapter; CD-ROM	Computer display screen
Digital full-motion video	Video camera; Cable; Laser disc, or VCR and Digital video compression card; CD-ROM	Computer display screen and Video decompression card

Figure 8-6 describes a typical setup for Critics' Circle. It shows two systems. The first is suitable for each group to use. The other provides the means to digitize students' images, which many groups can share. For example, a computer containing a digital video capture adapter and a video camera or a digital still camera could be available in a school library or media center for various classes to check out and use. Chapter 2 discusses each of the media that this project employs. Chapter 13 gives some details in its sections on Audio and Audio Techniques.

Computer for each group, with
- screen, keyboard, mouse, and system unit;
- digital audio adapter;
- microphone wired to audio adapter; and
- amplified speakers wired to audio board.

Computer shared among all groups containing
- digital video capture adapter and
- video camera wired to digital video capture adapter.

Diskettes or network for carrying images to groups' computers.

Figure 8-6: Equipment needed for Critics' Circle project

Making Do

If no audio adapter cards are available, a teacher may choose to use an audio cassette tape recorder. Students would then present the text and graphics on the computer along with on-screen instructions to manually place the correct cassette tape for each critic's opinion in a player at the appropriate time.

If no digital video capture adapter or equivalent is available, students could hold up photographs as instructed by written instructions on the computer screen.

As part of preparing for this project, you need to determine the extent to which students should participate in selecting and setting up the hardware and software. For example, should the students connect the cables or walk up to a running system? Should they create objects from scratch or modify objects in a supplied template? If this is only their second multimedia project, then you might want them to concentrate on meeting the nontechnical academic goals rather than worrying about the hardware or software. However, if you use Critics' Circle later to help students collect and analyze opinions on more serious topics, then you might expect them to set up the equipment and forego a template.

You also might want to arrange to make multimedia computers available to students outside the hours when students must be in class. A major advantage of using multimedia projects is that they often motivate students to insist on spending more time on task than they would normally tolerate being required to spend. Having their own voices and images called forth on demand has a remarkably long-lasting appeal and can bring out dormant tendencies toward perfectionism.

The last part of preparing for Critics' Circle is to determine the grouping of students who are to work together. We suggest that you put five students in each group. Because each group records and summarizes three opinions, this challenges the group to decide which three members of the group go "on stage" and which two members play supporting roles. If it is necessary to get around equipment constraints or to make things come out evenly, you can pick a different number than five, and you can also choose groups of different sizes. However, three opinions is about the smallest number that can show the diversity of opinions and five to six students are about as many as can easily view one computer display. As already discussed, offstage students have important and suitable roles, such as ensuring that the images get into the appropriate critic's "Opinion" pages and being responsible for the "Summary" page.

You can vary the grouping in several ways over the course of several projects. For one project, you may group arbitrarily. Try combining the first five students in alphabetical order. Another method, counting off, tends to separate students who sit together. The opposite extreme is to allow students to select their own groups. In some cases, you will want to hand-tune each group for a particular purpose such as putting the more technically adept together where their discussions will not confuse or annoy other students or spreading them out to provide all groups with their skills. The considerations for any group activity apply here. For example, it is important to avoid isolating minorities.

Varying the groupings helps prevent any student from being consistently over specialized or left out. Different students excel in different roles relative to different media. Each student should spend some time doing things in which he or she is strong and some more time doing things in which he or she is weak. It is better to achieve balance by using different groupings for different projects and define interpersonal goals for each activity in the context of student and class development.

You might want to use Critics' Circle to teach the mechanics of producing the required images using whatever method is available. This activity will occupy significant time. It is important to keep track of which students have had a turn using the equipment, as well as which have had their images completed. We suggest that this is something that you orchestrate over several projects, beginning with a small coterie of students who then teach the others, but including periodic accounting to make sure that all students master the basics. Having available digitized images of each student is convenient throughout the year. Students are amazed and motivated by manipulating images of themselves and their classmates. One of the ideas in Chapter 16, The Idea Book, is to have students sign their multimedia term papers with their own digitized images.

Step Two - Teacher Assigns Project

The teacher assigns the Critics' Circle project to the students during class time. In an earlier class, you would give a hint of what is coming and either show the selected movie or assign the students to go see it as homework. If learning to deal with differences of opinion is an important objective, you should introduce that subject in advance by means of a few examples of role playing with the class. You can use this opportunity to show that students can deal with differences of opinions respectfully and without insulting each other.

While assigning Critics' Circle, you should emphasize that each group should strive to produce an engaging show, as well as one that accurately exhibits the range of viewpoints. You might point out that many people read and listen to movie reviews and book reviews and that most people enjoy hearing different opinions. Moreover, people often enjoy a movie more if they have heard different people's opinions of it. In this setting, divergent points of view are to be encouraged and conformity is not desirable. Of course, each group can decide if they want to give an overall impression that they themselves enjoyed the movie and would encourage users of their project to actually go see the movie.

The teacher should challenge the groups to use the media in an effective and appealing way, using symbolic, oral, and textual forms. You can point out how informal speech differs from formal writing and how symbolic forms such as the graphic icons can convey specific messages.

You should also discuss appropriate lengths for the project's oral and textual material. The summary text, by its nature, should be concise. Students should not reiterate the oral opinions but rather distill the essence of how the opinions relate to one another. Similarly, they should keep the oral parts relatively short for two reasons. First, users lose track of oral information that contains more than three or four different points. Second, digital audio occupies a great deal of disk space on a computer.

Technical Note

Q: How much storage space do images and audio occupy?

A: Here are some examples.

- **The image in Figure 8-3 is 280 by 280 pixels, and has 4 bits (or 1/2 Byte) per pixel, so it occupies 39,200B.**

- **Table 2-3 notes that a 320 by 240 by 1 Byte color image occupies 76,800B.**

- **Table 2-3 also notes that a one minute opinion's audio can occupy 480,000B of disk space.**

Two key parts of assigning the project are telling students how long they have to complete their work and coaching them on how to allocate the available time among the many tasks that are required for completion. Different groups may require opposite sorts of coaching. Some groups tend to get stuck on a single task and not realize that they must ask for help in order to have time to do the remaining tasks. Other groups tend to become too interested in perfecting one task and use up the time they need for completing the other tasks.

Important skills are involved in learning to avoid both sorts of schedule problems. Multimedia projects give teachers particularly good opportunities to work with all students on developing and monitoring schedules because the last few steps of completing a project make it so much better than an unfinished project. This is also an opportunity to introduce the idea that one group member keeps track of which tasks are complete and which checkpoints are approaching.

Creating icons for the "Welcome" page can vary in importance to the overall project. You can offer some examples, such as happy or sad faces, or encourage the groups to come up with their own novel representations. In an art class or in a cross-disciplinary activity that includes art, creating evocative icons could be a major reason for doing the project. Alternatively, students can select from commercially available sources of graphic designs called "clip art" from diskettes, CD-ROMs, or networks.

Q: How can I handle a student who says "But I am not good in art?"

A: It is easy and common for people to use statements such as "I can't draw" and "I can't sing or play music" as reasons not to try. Although most of us will never be renowned writers, we still accept that writing is important enough to deserve attention and practice. We accept that this practice will produce results. Artistic expression is also essential to our lives and can contribute to life-long enjoyment and perhaps even to long lifetimes. If teachers accept low self-esteem in these areas as a reason for students to avoid them, they allow those capabilities to atrophy unnecessarily. Many students who cannot avoid ruining pictures with pencil smudges and tears find that computer paint programs and draw programs help them to start by producing neat images and graphics, and they then go on to produce genuinely attractive results.

Students can complete their Critics' Circle project relatively quickly if the equipment is already set up, if they build on components of the system prepared ahead of time, and if their images are already available on diskettes. At the elementary school level, an afternoon of creation, with some time the next day for reflection and touch-up, should suffice. At the middle and high school levels, three or four periods should be sufficient. In any case, you might tell the class that they will have an opportunity to use more time to improve the result after the deadline. Adult teachers in workshops, including some with no personal computer experience, have completed this project in a couple of hours.

As part of assigning the project, you can demonstrate a sample Critics' Circle in order to show how one possible finished project might appear to its users. You might also show an example of using cookbook instructions to make or modify the sample, in case students get stuck, lose the thread of what they are doing, or do not achieve the results they expect.

We suggest that you write down who is in each group, what computer is assigned to each group, what features of the project are absolute requirements, and what features an outstanding project might have. Figure 8-7 is a suggested assignment sheet.

Project: Critics' Circle		
Group number:	**Student Name:**	**Responsibility:**
Computer to use:		
Required tasks		**Date/Time complete**
	Select 3 critics	
	Get digitized image of each critic	
	Draw icon for each critic on "Welcome" page	
	Record opinions	
	Put images on critics' pages	
	Summarize conflicts and range of opinion	
	Check navigation through project	
	Reflect on project and improve it	
Suggested additional tasks		
	Add space for a fourth critic's opinion	
	Create links from summary page to critics' pages	
	Complete project by:	o'clock on
	Comments on project:	

Figure 8-7: Assignment sheet for Critics' Circle project

You may elect not to explain the project's academic goals to the students as part of assigning the project. Especially in elementary grades, it may be more effective to save such discussions for the last step, "Reflection."

Step Three - Students Create Project

The groups next create their projects. Critics' Circle is inherently a group project, so the members of each group must learn to work together effectively. Although only three of the group's members get "time on stage," the group as a whole is responsible for the success of the total activity, including the creation of the summary. Group dynamics are highly variable. Your guidance can range from letting the students devise their own method for completing the project to suggesting a particular formal process. Optionally, you can facilitate a class discussion that results in agreement on a series of steps that each group should follow and a time frame in which they should strive to accomplish each step. One possible set of steps for a group to follow is as follows.

1) Hold a group discussion to brainstorm about the movie and crystallize all of the group members' opinions of it.

2) Select three group members whose opinions represent the entire spectrum of thinking about the movie. This involves understanding the reactions the movie invokes both emotionally and intellectually, although this may not be the terminology in which a teacher would express the idea to young children.

3) Let each of the three selected critics speak in turn without recording. Some critics may find that they need to write out scripts for themselves. The group may then give feedback to each critic with coaching by the teacher.

4) Decide what graphics to use to replace the sample icons on the template's "Welcome" page. Also jot down the issues to address on the "Summary" page while thinking about the different opinions. Use a paint or draw program to create the icons representing the critics and their remarks. Note that planning and creating simple but vivid icons requires creativeness and some technical skill. Icons are most evocative if they are consistent across the group; therefore, the choice of icons should be a group activity even if a team specialist ends up creating the icons for all three critics.

5) Record each critic's opinion. The group must be supportive and attentive to the technical details while critics record their speeches. Other groups in the room must cooperate by being silent on request.

6) Locate each critic's image and use it to replace the corresponding sample image that was included as a placeholder in the template.

7) Discuss the issues that the group wants to include in the "Summary" page and agree on the basic content. Creating this page is an important part of the project because the students need to come to grips with differences and similarities of opinions and then synthesize these in concise text.

8) Assemble the complete project and make sure that a user, who is not a member of the group that created the project, can navigate from page to page.

9) Reflect on the total project and improve or enhance it as time and imaginations allow.

> **Technical Note**
>
> Q: Why did the speaker howl and disrupt the whole class when I tried to record my opinion?
>
> A: That howl is called "audio feedback." You left the amplifier and speaker turned on when you were trying to record what you spoke into the microphone. What you recorded came out of the speaker and fed back into the microphone. Either turn off the amplifier or turn down its volume control.

> **Technical Note**
>
> Q: What is digital audio and why does this project use digital audio rather than an audio cassette recorder? Why do we scan our photographs and store them in digital form in the computers?
>
> A: Everything stored on a computer is digital. We store words and numbers on disks so that we can access them rapidly, edit them, process them, and make accurate copies of them. We convert sounds and photographs to digital form so that we can store them on the computers and get the same advantages.

The title of this step, "Students Create Project," understates the teacher's vital role in this part of the process. At one extreme, you need to recognize when one group is so hung up on an early activity that they will not be able to achieve the project's major objectives. At the other extreme, your judicious and timely suggestions can help a group convert an acceptable project into an outstanding one. However, make sure that the group members continue to feel that they, rather than you, own the project and are responsible for its success. If a group or individual lacks certain technical skills, encourage the students to help each other. However, we recommend giving direct assistance only if a group or student asks for specific help or if they are foundering too deeply to realize that they should ask for help. Inevitably, some groups will complete their projects ahead of others. One of the teacher's roles in this step is to suggest additional activities to such groups. You can also read Variations, Chapter 15.

You may suggest that students

- add a title page ahead of the "Welcome" page that contains text and images pertaining to the movie with a background of the movie's theme music;
- add appropriate background music along with a critic's spoken opinion;
- illustrate and annotate the "Summary" page;
- create links from the summary text to particular critics' pages;
- give the critics' pages smaller photos to leave room for some graphics or text pertaining to their respective opinions about the movie; or

- create a new "Opinion" page in the project for a fourth critic's opinion.

Step Four - Reflection

For the Critics' Circle project, groups should have time to do their own reflection and refinement and should then have time to circulate and see each other's work. Assessment can include asking and answering the following concrete questions.

- Did the group complete the project's requirements? For each critic, is there an audio recording with an appropriate image called out by a suitable icon? Is there a text summary, and does it elucidate the similarities and differences between the opinions? Do the selected opinions cover a reasonable range of possible opinions? Do the commentaries express significant ideas about the movie rather than trivialities?

- Is the multimedia project appealing, attractive, entertaining, and convincing? Are the views expressed reasonable rather than contrived? If the group chose to present something silly, is it genuinely amusing? Do the graphic icons and the written summary indicate how different people can hold divergent opinions?

- Are the oral and written commentaries at an appropriate level for these students? Is there adequate depth of expression? Is the language evocative? Is it suitably concise? Oral remarks can have a certain informality that is inappropriate for written comments. Did this point occur to the students?

- How did the creation process actually unfold? For each group, was everyone engaged in productive work? Were any group members overlooked? Did each group member contribute to the extent of her abilities and talents? How did the students manage themselves? How did they react to unforeseen problem situations?

- The students, groups, and entire class are in an ideal position to do their own reflection. They can address questions such as How could we improve our work? Did we choose speakers well? Would a user of our multimedia project be prepared to see the movie, or would he think we were talking about something else? Can we improve our aesthetics and style? Can we say something more to express our opinions? Is the oral language compelling and not too rambling? Could we use more imagery or other media?

Note that both teachers and students can use multimedia mechanisms to store their reflections on each project. They can amend the project with written and spoken comments using a common format for corresponding buttons. Such reflections can become parts of individual students' portfolios where they will remain available for later comparison and for noting improvements.

During the "Reflection" step, you can engage the students in a discussion of the entire activity, process, and content. For example, after all groups complete their projects, it may be appropriate to discuss the ways the different groups performed the task. This may produce a consensus on a process, either the one detailed earlier or a better one. Students may be especially receptive to discussing the process after the fact. You can also encourage the entire class to expound on the total range of opinions expressed in all of the projects that they have seen. This would be a suitable time to ask whether any students have noticed other people with whom they tend consistently to agree or disagree and whether they think that some people consistently agree or disagree with a clear majority of opinion.

This project, like the others described, is intended to produce its major learning in the doing, even if no one else ever uses the completed project. However, it is always advantageous to give class work an explicit purpose and to have an authentic audience in mind. To make the projects more appealing to a larger audience, teachers might encourage different groups to address different movies. This makes the class collection more suitable for use at a school open house, library, or community center. Another possibility is to send projects home for parents to admire. A few parents may have computers equipped to play digital audio, so you could send home diskettes. Many more parents have VCRs, so teachers or support staff could use a scan converter to turn computer displays into video and record several typical navigation sessions on tape. We discuss this in Chapter 13's section on Presenting a Project.

Summary

Since Critics' Circle incorporates sound clips and images, you may consider it as a good introductory multimedia activity for your students even if they have not done a project such as Current Events. Digital audio adapter cards are now standard on many personal computer products. Similarly, packages preloaded on computers typically include draw programs. The requirement to produce icons, speech, and written summaries can invoke deep thinking on how to portray opinions. The choice of subject matter is yours and it can range from serious to silly. The activity can serve as the culmination of a unit or as a stand-alone event.

The possibilities of recording speech and designing icons mean that students must grapple with these distinct modalities along with written text to produce an orchestrated final product. This provides an advantage over having one unit on public speaking and another on written composition. The group dynamics suggested by this activity, both within the teams and between the team and the audience, also motivates respect for the views of others and attention to aesthetics and detail.

Chapter 9

Trailers

In this chapter, we explore:

- building movie trailers, advertisements that feature clips of the movies.

- an activity that puts students in the role of creating products for which there is a professional counterpart that they have viewed as consumers in movie theaters.

- how to instruct and guide your students in the use of laser discs.

- how to challenge groups of students to perform an authentic task.

The Trailers project introduces the multimedia technologies of control of a laser disc and synchronization of audio clips with video. Although the technical aspects of the project require attention on the part of the teacher, they are quite feasible. The challenge to the students is to produce a trailer that meets the high standards we all have in terms of persuasion and aesthetics.

This chapter describes the project itself, specifically, a suggestion for the challenge to the students. In the Theory section, we elaborate on the educational goals for the project. Lastly, using the same process referenced before, we provide practical advice for teachers on how to guide the learning experience for this project.

Background

In the Trailers project, the class, working in groups, produces an advertisement for a movie in the form of clips (sequences of video frames or screens) and audio voice-overs. The term "trailer" is based on the old practice of showing advertisements for future movies after the main attraction. Producing trailers is an important and respected part of the marketing of a movie. Students can study commercial trailers as well as read about them.

Challenge

Film producers make trailers with the purpose of getting customers to want to see a movie. This involves selecting portions of the movie that would appeal to the market segments targeted for the movie's success, independent of whether these clips represent the movie. With this model in mind, teachers begin the Trailers project by identifying a set of movies appealing to the students and available on laser discs. (CD-ROMs may be an alternative.) The challenge for the groups of students is to select a market, for example, teen age girls, and produce a trailer that makes the movie attractive to this market.

Creation of a trailer involves stimulating a response in an audience. Success depends on understanding the audience to the point that creators know what moves their target population and successfully implementing a strategy based on that understanding. The latter involves skills of artistry and persuasion. Aesthetic factors include

- choice of clips,
- ordering of clips,
- nature of transitions from one clip to another,
- use of additional audio recordings in combination with sound from the clips themselves,
- use of graphics for titles, and
- total orchestration of video, audio and graphics.

An important component of the project is group and class reflection on the stereotyping that is inherent in this process. You may encourage this reflection at all phases of the activity.

You may also choose to encourage "tongue-in-cheek" projects such as a trailer that portrays the movie *The Birds* as the perfect entertainment for the Audubon Society. Another potentially thought-provoking angle to pursue would be to produce a pair of trailers: one appealing to parents and one for children or teenagers. More generally, you can give any film to several groups so that the resulting trailers can be compared.

It is also possible to move away from the advertising rationale for the project and assign students the task of constructing commentary on a literary movie. The set of clips could

---

Classroom Experience

In one workshop for teachers, everyone was told ahead of time to see one of the Indiana Jones movies. One group made an advertisement for an invented amusement park. Another made a trailer called "The Dating Game." Most of the groups chose to do something entertaining as opposed to a purposeful trailer.

---

document stages in the development of a character or the enfolding of the plot. The final product would be closer in nature to a critical review than an instrument of advertising. However, it would be similar in structure and process to the trailers described in this chapter.

Creating a trailer using a laser disc or CD-ROM of a movie requires the group of students to locate short segments of the movie and write appropriate scripts for voice-overs for some or all of the clips. The actual project created by the students consists of a programmed set of instructions that cause the laser disc player to play the segments synchronized with instructions to replay digitally recorded audio clips.

Creation

Authoring systems differ in the facilities provided to synchronize video and audio. Because the audio playback proceeds independently of the playback of a video clip, it is necessary to ensure pauses so that control does not proceed to the next audio clip in advance of what is showing on the screen. The mechanism for doing this varies depending on the authoring system. Some systems may require the creator to time the different segments and explicitly introduce pauses. Others may require the creator to arrange events on a timeline where pauses can be put in explicitly. In other approaches, creators can insert commands corresponding to "wait until this completes." The run-time system executes the indicated operation. In any case, the student groups must identify each video clip and record each audio clip first and then put it all together using the multimedia software tools available.

The completed trailer proceeds from start to finish with continuous presentation of video with its own sound track, plus any added audio recordings of voice-overs. This multimedia project does not allow the user to choose how to navigate through the material. Creating the trailer involves developing a very specific sequence of events. During the production phase, the creators may make temporary buttons that invoke each video clip, audio clip, and image.

Let us consider a plan for a trailer aimed at convincing the stereotypical young boy to come to a movie. The trailer consists of six parts:

Historical Note: Jargon

As would be expected when two technical fields come together, there is overlapping jargon. We have used the term 'scripts' in the proceeding paragraph in the movie industry sense as the text prepared for use by a performer. At other points in this chapter and in this book, we refer to the script language that exists as a feature of authoring systems. This internal programming language can create special effects in the multimedia project.

---

an introduction, shooting scene, a clip of a car chase, a clip of a second shooting, a clip of a second car chase, and finale. Each of these parts is a clip from the movie. Some of the clips have audio voice-overs. We describe later how the choices could have been made for this particular sequence of the parts.

The complete trailer is produced by the authoring system's script facility for sequencing these distinct parts together. The terms event or scene are also used to refer to parts of the trailer. Note that a part could also be a still image or title page. Special effects can be used for transitions between the parts. We use "script" in its common English meaning here, but it also applies to the use of the programming language.

Before indicating how these events are combined, we will indicate in a very general way how each medium is created. To create a part or event that involves playing a section of video, students preview the material and determine the starting and stopping frame numbers for each clip. The previewing is done by using the laser disc player in stand-alone mode or by using the multimedia authoring system. If just the laser disc player is used, the creators must take notes on the frame numbers. Most authoring systems provide a facility to mark the start and end points and, subsequently, copy them into the definition of a clip. The screen for doing this often resembles the controls on a standard VCR, as Figure 9-1 illustrates. The resulting video clip is an object that can be referenced from the students' own folder. Digital audio has been described in earlier chapters. Students choose the quality of recording and control its length.

Students can also construct still pictures for titles at the start and the close of the trailer and, if they wish, interspersed throughout.

The information stored in the computer referring to the video clip is essentially two numbers, the starting and stopping frames. The video itself is stored on the laser disc. In contrast, the audio clip is an object, made up of digital data and stored on disk, representing sounds. These audio clips can take a substantial amount of storage space, and if the computers used do not come with sufficient disk space for everybody's project, you will need to assist the students in managing files and handling diskettes for backup purposes.

Making Do: Do you need audio?

The invention and planning required when voice-overs are included in this project exercises important cognitive skills. However, it is possible to have a computer with a connection to a laser disc but without a digital audio adapter. A scaled-down version of the project is certainly feasible.

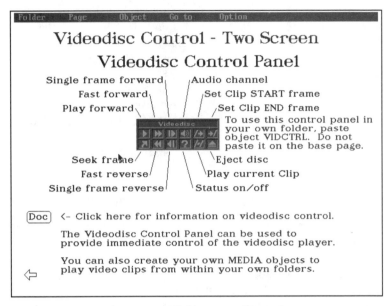

Figure 9-1: Video control panel

The Trailers project has an additional requirement that the previous project does not have. In Critics' Circle, each audio clip plays by itself while the display shows a still photo. Viewers can interrupt the audio and jump to other pages. In contrast, for a trailer, each audio clip is a voice-over to one video clip in a sequence, and you want the trailer to advance to the next pair of events in a smooth fashion. To achieve this, students must time the audio and video clips, ensure that the video clips are longer than the corresponding audio clip, and use the authoring system to make sure that the audio and video are synchronized.

We indicate schematically the two general ways that authoring systems handle sequencing the parts. In Figure 9-2, we see what looks like a programming language.

```
do Intro_picture;          --show introductory picture
wait 3;                    --pause 3 seconds
do Shooting1;              --start 1st shooting video
do Shooting1_A;            --start 1st shooting audio
wait 20;                   --wait 20 seconds (for video & audio)
do Car_Chase1;            --start 1st car chase video
do Car_Chase1_A;         --start 1st car chase audio
wait 14;                   --pause 14 seconds
do Shooting2;              --start 2nd shooting video
wait 10;                   --pause 10 seconds
do Car_Chase2;            --start 2nd car chase video
do Car_Chase2_A;         --start 2nd car chase audio
wait 5;                    --pause 5 seconds
do Finale;                 --start finale video
do Finale_A;              --start finale audio
```

Figure 9-2: Sample generic script programming for trailer sequence

The timeline or graphical method would look similar to Figure 9-3 using the symbols defined in Table 9-1. These authoring systems featuring the timeline approach often use a graphic or icon symbol instead of a name to represent the part or event. For digital audio clips, laser disc clips, or CD-ROM clips, the authoring system may assign this symbol. For digital video, which is not what we are discussing here, the assigned symbol may be a small version of the first frame of the video clip.

Table 9-1: Symbols for events in sample trailer

Event	Symbol
Intro	1
Shooting1	LV1
Shooting1_A	A1
Car_Chase1	LV2
Car_Chase1_A	A2
Shooting2	LV3
Car_Chase2	LV4
Car_Chase2_A	A3
Finale	LV5
Finale	A4

Figure 9-3 does not show the complete representation of the trailer. The authoring system provides this mechanism so that the creator can scroll back and forth in time and set out the events on the timeline.

Time	│ │ │ ││ │ ││ │ ││ │ │ ││ │ ││ │ ││ │ │ │ │ │ ││ │ ││ │ │ │ │ │ │ ││ │ │ │ │ │
Seconds	0 5 10 15 20 25 30 35 40 45 50 55
Events	1 LV1 LV2 LV3 LV4
	A1 A2 A3
	→

Figure 9-3: Trailer as sequence of events on a timeline

Technical Note: What is a Trailer?

Students employ an authoring system to create the project as several disk files. The contents of one file tell a computer when to present the following media to the user:

- a title image and a closing image,

- a set of digital audio files containing the students' voice-overs, and

- a set of analog video clips (ranges of frame numbers) from a laser disc.

Except for the digital audio files, the project is relatively small. Chapter 2 tells how to estimate the file sizes for images and digital audio.

Purpose

The preceding example may look complex, but in practice it is not the particular method of synchronizing the events, but the task of deciding what clips will accomplish the job of persuading the audience that is difficult. One approach is to plan at a gross level first and then refine it, perhaps in stages. The following sequence of steps suggests what might have happened for the case described here.

- Boys like violence and action.
- We will show shootings and car chases.
- These two shootings and two car chases seem appealing.
- We will add comments and scary music to these scenes.
- Let's alternate shootings and car chases.
- The music and sounds for the second shooting are great as is.
- Now we decide exactly when to cut.
- We prepare titles for the start and the finish.
- Let's put it together and see what needs adjustment.

For the final stages of refinement, many people prefer the timeline approach. In all cases, there is bookkeeping work to do, such as recording the starting and stopping frame numbers for different clips and keeping track of the elapsed time, which is part of the challenge of the activity.

The Trailers project is a demonstration of what is now feasible for classroom work because of rapidly evolving multimedia hardware and software tools. The students manipulate video content prepared by others and add audio content of their own creation. This experience can help them be knowledgeable viewers rather than passive consumers of the voluminous manipulated images shown to them in their daily lives.

The construction of the trailer requires attention to fine detail, technical skill, and aesthetic sense. It also exercises broad and detailed awareness of the content of the video material and understanding of the specified audience. We discuss these matters more in the next section.

Theory

The Trailers project challenges students to produce a familiar product. Even though these advertisements appear more often before the main feature than as a trailer after it, most people, particularly children and teenagers, recognize the format. Trailers have a specific objective: to induce people to come to the movie. Occasionally, reviews of movies make note of unusually effective trailers of movies that do not fulfill the expectations that their trailers raise.

The combination of these two aspects of the project, its familiarity and its specific objective, makes it easy to make the activity an authentic task. If representatives of the target market are in the classroom, the creation group can hear an authentic response to their efforts. The task requires

- role playing: creators put themselves in role of the target audience using the empathy they have with this population;
- aesthetic sense: creators devise a trailer that invokes the desired response; and
- attention to detail and continuity of purpose: creators produce a trailer, performing all the subtasks without being distracted from their objective.

It is natural for all viewers of the students' trailers to compare them to what they see in theaters. You can establish a high standard for this project by announcing that reactions from members of the target audiences will be solicited. You may also choose to specify an exact length for the trailer and enforcing a strict schedule.

Students are not creating their own video material, but they are manipulating video for their own purposes. The power to manipulate video, audio, and images is important for students to appreciate because they are the targets of manipulation of media by advertisers and news broadcasters.

Table 9-2 lists the major educational goals for the Trailers project.

Table 9-2: Educational goals

Higher-Order Thinking Skills
- Role playing and empathy
- Confrontation with stereotyping
- Continuity of purpose
- Persuasion
- Respect for and wariness of power to manipulate media

Group and Interpersonal Skills
- Working in a group with tight deadlines for a fixed purpose
- Sharing tools

Content Material Learning
- Identifying significant, attractive segments of film
- Aesthetic skills in filmmaking

Technical Skills
- Editing within tight time constraints
- Scripting and producing audio voice-overs
- Public speaking

The planning and editing required to produce a trailer are demanding. We recognize this by including under higher-order goals the attention to detail and continuity of purpose; under group skills, working in a group under tight time constraints; and under technical skills, the technical experience of doing video editing (cutting and arranging), audio production, and synchronization of audio and video.

Because the students are working with commercial movies, one might think that the students do not have to work very hard to make their trailer look good. Such is not the case. Our standards are very high for video in general and for movie advertisements in particular. For example, audiences grow restless if a scene continues for too long. This means that this project stimulates the students to high levels of performance.

> **Do you have to watch the whole movie?**
>
> In our experiences in workshops, groups do not have to watch the whole movie to get the small number of very short clips required to make up a successful trailer. Of course, some groups of students may forget the assignment and just view the movie. However, we find that most people want to begin selecting clips right away. It may be beneficial to suggest that students set a deadline for considering the task as a whole and deciding on the clips they want. This deadline should not be too soon nor too late. The setting up of interim checkpoints is valuable for any project work.

When the groups present their completed trailers to the class, members of the audience share their reactions. This gives everyone a chance to discuss reactions to the trailers. This can make discussions of stereotypes less personal and less threatening. You can use these activities to initiate or complement ongoing classroom discussions about different groups in society and the perception of those groups by others and by themselves.

If groups choose a "tongue-in-cheek" goal, such as portraying the horror movie *The Birds* as being suitable for bird-watchers, they still face an authentic challenge. Is it genuinely funny? Is there a sense of drama? Is it quick-paced, or does it drag? A good test for any of the trailers is whether audiences enjoy seeing them several times.

Content or discipline-specific goals are dependent on the choice of movie. It is common in many classrooms to show a movie version of a book assigned to the class. You may use the Trailers project as a culminating activity to this unit of study. You can modify the assignment from creating commercials to featuring the important literary or historic aspects of a work of art. The class can show their trailers to audiences outside the class, including other students and parents.

In Chapter 15, Variations, we describe other approaches to making trailers that will cause the students to exercise different skills.

Practice

We next discuss each step of the process introduced in Chapter 6. The application of the process will be similar to Critics' Circle. This is a project of fixed, short duration, unlike Current Events. Table 9-3 shows some suitable process steps for this project.

Step One - Teacher Prepares

In preparing for the Trailers project. you need to determine the goals, review the equipment, and plan the logistics. We have reviewed the potential educational goals in the Theory section. You may choose one or any combination of the following:

- focus on the higher-level skills of persuasion and empathy, taking the objective of trailers as a serious objective;

- concentrate on providing students an opportunity to work with a movie of important content, viewing it thoughtfully; and

- encourage exploration of the technologies.

Your decision regarding goals will guide you in the rest of the project. We now focus on equipment and logistics.

Table 9-3: Process steps for Trailers

Teacher prepares
- Select goals
- Define set of available, appropriate movies
- Assess technical environment
- Determine strategy for grouping and assignment of movie and audience

Teacher assigns project
- Announce project, define objective of trailers
- Oversee and adjust student grouping
- Monitor and approve choices of movies and target audiences
- Describe and demonstrate a sample trailer
- Establish schedule

Students create project
- Groups create trailers
- Teacher monitors work

Performances and reflection
- Student self-evaluation when using system
- Presentations of trailers to class and class reflection
- Presentations to wider audiences with sharing of reflection

The additional equipment introduced for this multimedia project is a laser disc player. Laser disc players are often available in schools for the delivery of specific lessons such as health and safety. The computer controlled laser disc player provides quick jumps to different points in the movie, which is not possible using videotape. In Chapter 2's section on Analog Video we discussed the following three alternative ways to display the clips from the laser disc, depending on what equipment is available.

- In a two-monitor configuration, the laser disc player is connected to its own television monitor.

- In a picture-in-picture configuration, the video image is shown on the computer monitor but takes up only a portion of the screen.

- In a full-screen configuration, the computer monitor shows only video.

Groups may choose to use one or both of the first two alternatives, if available, while creating the trailer and then use the last alternative for the presentation. It is, of course, possible to present in the two-monitor configuration.

Chapter 14 contains relevant sections on Setting Up a Laser Disc Player, Selecting Suitable Laser Discs, and Combining Two Sources of Audio.

You prepare for the Trailers project by collecting a set of appropriate movies in a suitable laser disc format as discussed in Chapter 14. An important factor is whether the students have seen and remember the movies. Because trailers are typically two minutes in duration, it is not necessary that students remember the whole movie. However, it is important that they appreciate the task of promoting a full-length movie by a very short trailer. Students who have not seen the movie will feel that they are at a disadvantage even if this is not true, so you may have to arrange for showings.

The next preparation task is to determine the strategy for grouping. In other projects, teachers determine grouping based on factors independent of the project. Is it time to get different abilities working together? Is it acceptable to let friends work together? It is time to break up cliques? The Trailers project includes a specific focus on how one set of people, the producers of movies, view and seek to persuade market segments. For this reason, you may choose to let natural groups form and work together. Of course, the groups may coalesce around common choices of movies. You may let the groups form in this manner and then give the assignment.

The technical environment may force certain scheduling arrangements on the activity. If only one laser disc player is available, then only one group can work at identifying and making video clips and on final construction of the project. However, it is possible to do meaningful work away from any equipment. This includes overall planning and writing scripts. Groups can record the audio voice-overs on computers without laser disc players. Students can draw pictures for opening and closing titles on any computer that has an appropriate drawing program.

> **Making do: Without a laser disc player or CD-ROM player**
>
> It is possible to do this project without a laser disc through careful, patient use of audio tapes and video tapes. Some schools are equipped with editing equipment for video tapes and sound tracks. We recommend that you seek out the laser disc player so the students can concentrate on the creative and communication aspects of this challenging assignment and not the mechanics of editing.

Step Two - Teacher Assigns Project

You assign the Trailers project by asking the students to recall advertisements they have seen for movies and to share their initial reactions and their reactions after they saw the movies. You then tell the students that they will work in groups to produce their own trailers and show them the available movies. You can spread the laser discs out on a table. You carry out the strategy for grouping you have planned.

For a smooth-running trailer, the students should make all of their video selections from one side of one disc. Full-length movies take up two or three disks, which means that two or three different groups can work on the same movie without sharing materials. You then make the assignment and set the schedule. In the spirit of making this an authentic assignment, we recommend that the schedule be enforced. Figure 9-4 shows a typical assignment sheet for this project.

Project: Trailers
Group Name: _____
Students in Group:

_____
_____
_____

Movie: _____   Disc: _____
Computer to use and Schedule:

_____   _____
_____   _____

Target Audience: _____

Figure 9-4: Assignment Sheet for Trailers

You can proceed in making the assignment by demonstrating a completed trailer produced using the authoring tools available for the class. The next steps are to demonstrate the distinct tasks of making a video clip and an audio clip and then synchronizing the two. You accomplish this as we have indicated previously by adding commands to a script program or placing events on a timeline. If the class has completed projects such as Critics' Circle, teachers can omit the audio clip demonstration or ask volunteers from the class to do it. The groups can have copies of the sample trailer to use as a model for their projects.

Step Three - Students Create Project

If you are the creator of the sample trailer, you can model the thought process for the students. This can include statements such as

- "I wanted to include something that showed...."
- "I thought of this scene."
- "I then had to decide where to begin."
- "This seemed to be soon enough."
- "This was a good (scary or sweet) ending."
- "I decided that this clip worked well by itself. "
- "But for this clip, I wanted to say something that distracted you from what was going on, so I said this."
- "I changed the order here and put something that happened after this scene, before it."

Real trailers are sometimes made from the so-called "out-takes" of the movie. These are pieces of film left over from the editing by the director and do not appear in the movie. Sometimes trailers are shot separately. Students can report on what they remember from trailers viewed in theaters.

The making of a trailer requires attention to a process (see the creation step), but you can decide how much direction to give the groups ahead of time. Table 9-4 shows a possible guide.

As we have indicated before:

- Teachers can develop their own detailed process and present this to the students as a requirement.
- Teachers can lead the class in a brainstorming session to develop a process that everyone agrees to adhere to.
- Teachers can suggest that groups begin by defining their own process.
- Teachers can choose to step back and observe, making process suggestions only in special situations such as groups failing to make progress.

Table 9-4: Creation steps for Trailers

- Decide what features target audience likes.
- Identify approximately locations in movie that fit these features. You may choose more than will be in final version.
- Decide on general content of voice-overs for some or all clips.
- Write scripts for voice-overs.
- Select video clips and time segments.
- Choose speakers.
- Make audio recordings of voice-overs.
- Program the script to synchronize audio and video. This may lead to adjustments in length of video and rescripting and rerecording of audio.
- Work on project. Consider flow for the over-all effect. Make adjustments.
- Create titles. Create initial and final voice-overs. Again, consider overall effect.

The groups of students now create their projects. They must agree on a working plan, or they will not operate effectively. They have to balance the enjoyment of viewing the movie with the responsibility to get the job done. Failure to complete the job will be highly visible.

As we indicated in the assignment step, you decide how much guidance to offer students in terms of formal process. You can amend the list of steps shown in Table 9-4 to include a scheduled time for completion of each step. Requiring the groups to "report in" after each step makes a minimal requirement on the students for project management. In contrast, allowing the groups to work out their own arrangements and interim schedules is putting the most burden on them and is appropriate for mature students or as an activity to test and stretch the students' abilities. This may not be apparent in the final product, but it is something to keep in mind.

The student groups go through the steps of defining clips, writing scripts for the voice-overs, and putting it all together. There may be a tendency to jump to the controls too soon and not spend enough time planning. Scarcity of resources, such as a limited number of computer stations, may be an advantage here because it forces students to spend time away from the equipment. Whether there is a prescribed process or not, it is appropriate for teachers or any technical staff to look around and see what the groups are doing. If they are working on subsecond editing or very fancy titles and the deadline is approaching, you can remind them of the time.

Step Four - Reflection

The presentation of the completed trailers to the whole class is a grand event. We think that this project has the appealing nature that all, or practically all, efforts are good, and some are great. This means that it will be rare for a group or an individual to feel ashamed of their performance, but some groups will feel very proud.

You can choose between two approaches for the presentations:

- Groups announce their target audience and their strategy.
- Members of the audience guess target population after seeing the trailer.

After the presentation, the groups can ask the audience if their trailer had the desired effect. Is the movie an exciting action thriller? Is it romantic? The representatives of the target market segment can say what they really look for when they go to a movie. This is similar to movie producers or advertising agencies holding focus groups on the perception of their products. The people in the target group will also demonstrate how any group is made up of distinct individuals. It may not be a uniform group at all.

The groups can also respond to each other's work. Hopefully, there will be shouts of praise and "we could have done ... ." You can build on these responses to ask the students how they would do better next time.

You can also use this reflection period to ask students about the effect of montages of images and voice-overs. This inoculates students for protection against manipulation of media by teaching them how to manipulate media themselves.

Classroom Experience: Voting as assessment

Once when doing a workshop for teachers, we had planned to hold a vote for the best trailer. To our surprise, the class rebelled. The participants said: "We are having a good time. We don't want to be judged." "Some people had more experience than others. It won't be fair." The workshop leaders did not think there was an obvious winner. We felt that the final products were quite similar. Our rationale for the vote was to provide an experience of a direct holistic assessment. However, the change in plans led to an unexpected success. The incident provoked a moving open discussion, as well as many side conversations, about assessment, judging teachers, judging students, paranoia, safe havens, protecting and nurturing students, and letting them grow.

Summary

The Trailers project provides students with a significant and appealing challenge. It is not a multimedia enhancement of a traditional assignment; it stands by itself. However, the project does contribute to traditional goals. These include refining communication skills, practicing persuasion and empathy, attending to aesthetic effects, and working cooperatively and effectively on a difficult task.

An important goal of all multimedia projects, but particularly Trailers, is to provide students with the opportunity to manipulate media so that they will be more resistant when they themselves are the targets of media manipulation.

Chapter 10

Science Quiz

In this chapter, we explore:

- building a multimedia quiz.

- a project that is challenging in terms of group work, subject content, and technology.

- how to guide your students in the use of digitized video and screen capture in order to incorporate activities into multimedia.

- how to guide your students in the use of an authoring system's scripting language to handle users' answers to the quiz's questions.

- suitable content areas for multimedia quizzes.

The Science Quiz project introduces three distinct multimedia technologies: digital video, screen capture, and use of a scripting language which is part of the authoring system. You can select this project to help students learn these technical skills and to continue the process of exploring the orchestration of distinct media.

Science Quiz demonstrates that multimedia can be used for something beyond the presentation of information and that serious subject matter can be handled in a rigorous fashion with multimedia tools. We include two versions of the quiz and describe each in a precise way. The chapter provides ideas and information for teachers of all subject areas, not just science teachers. For more ideas on quizzes, see Chapter 15, Variations.

This chapter first describes the project itself, then elaborates on the academic outcomes that creating this project and others like it can help students to achieve. Finally, using the four process steps, we provide some practical advice on how to guide the creators in the production of the whole quiz.

Background

Science Quiz is an example of a student project that uses multimedia technologies to enhance and extend the learning process initiated in another activity. Because the project requires a group of students to create and assemble a quiz, the project demonstrates the principle that a good way for students to learn is to ask them to teach.

The questions in the quiz involve viewing alternative representations of motion shown as student-made video, graphs, and text descriptions. The quiz-taker is asked to match corresponding representations. The quiz-makers must prepare the materials and provide help through an artful ordering of the questions and by providing hints.

An essential component of scientific and mathematical thinking is the representation of the same information or phenomenon in alternative ways. Multimedia technology is extremely well suited to the creation and presentation of alternative representations and the correspondences between them. The Science Quiz project would not be possible without these capabilities.

Representations

In this case, the phenomenon being represented is the movement of a person. This movement is represented visually, symbolically, and descriptively through the use of video (movies), graphs, and text, respectively. When considering other subject areas for multimedia quizzes, ask yourself if there are aspects with similar multiple representations. To describe Science Quiz, we begin by describing how the act of a person moving is recorded in three ways.

Video Clips

A student camera crew using a video recorder shoots a movie of the target subject and then uses functions of the multimedia authoring system or other multimedia tools to digitize it and then incorporate it into their project. A silent video clip is incorporated into the project as digitized, partial screen, slow-frame video. Figure 10-1 shows a sketch of a page of the quiz, indicating a small (1/9th screen) window and buttons for returning to the questions or obtaining hints.

Figure 10-1: Sketch of movie screen page

Time versus Distance Graphs

The target subject moves back and forth in front of a position probe that measures the subject's distance from the probe. This sensor is part of a Micro-Based Lab system that records and graphs the distance against time.

The exploration we suggest here uses a position probe built with the same technologies employed in autofocusing cameras. The software connected to the probe produces a graph of position versus time, indicating the relative position of an object moving in front of it. Distances are posted as dots on the graph in "real-time," that is, as the motion occurs. When the exploration is complete, the micro-based lab software connects the dots and displays the graph on the personal computer's screen. This screen is available for screen-capture. The MBL can also record velocity versus time or acceleration versus time in a similar manner.

In the motion represented in Figure 10-2, the initial, horizontal segment of the graph indicates that Jane, the actual participant in this exercise, was standing still for several seconds. This is indicated by the fact that distance is constant while time varies from zero to about seven seconds. The graph then shows that she moved slowly toward the probe, which is indicated in the graph by distance decreasing with time. The fact that the segment approximates a straight line indicates that she walked at a fixed speed. Toward the end, the graph indicates that she moved away from the probe faster and faster, shown by the graph curving upward.

Narrative Descriptions

Students must also compose a narrative that describes the actions of the participant during the event. They then add this narrative to the multimedia project. Note that the teacher can establish the style of the narrative description in terms of grammar and technical language. In the example shown in Figure 10-3, the creator has used whole sentences, and the term "speed" is used instead of "velocity."

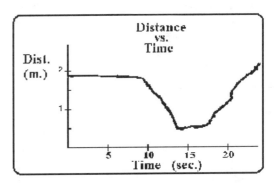

Figure 10-2: The MBL computer screen

TEXT A

The subject stands still for several seconds.

The subject then walks quickly towards the probe.

The subject then walks away from probe, starting slowly, but increasing in speed.

Figure 10-3: Example narrative

The Quiz

The task of the creators is to compose an on-line quiz that requires the quiz-taker to match corresponding representations of the same event. Although the quiz-makers could present the task in a variety of ways, we present specific quiz formats that we have used, a simple one and a more complex, adaptive version.

In our simple version, the quiz-takers are asked to examine three different types of representations of three different events and then try to match corresponding representations. We call one set of three events a unit. The quiz takers first view three video clips of fellow students moving toward and away from a position probe. The quiz-takers then look at position versus time graphs of these same events. They also read narrative descriptions of the three actions. They can review these in any order and as many times as they wish. When they feel ready, they attempt to match up a given representation, for example, the video of a certain student, with the correct corresponding graph or narrative. The Science Quiz tells them either that they are correct or should try again.

The quiz-makers produce general hints for the quiz-takers to read at their discretion, such as the one shown in Figure 10-4. Hints may also be linked to specific graphs, video clips, or narratives, so that the creators can add different hints associated with the different representations. The example shown in Figure 10-5 refers to a specific movie and attempts to direct the quiz-taker to observe and interpret what she sees in ways that would relate to the matching graph.

> **Video Tools**
>
> **Creators can use the LWMovie or Photo-Motion tools with LinkWay Live!, AVI Movies with Video for Windows, or Apple's Quicktime with HyperCard or other Macintosh authoring tools to produce a slow-frame, partial-screen video. Similar capabilities exist for all platforms in many other commercial products. See Chapters 2 and 3.**

General Hint

When a subject stands still, the position doesn't vary with time. This corresponds to a horizontal line segment on the graph.

Moving at a constant velocity, rapidly or slowly, means the changes in position are the same for each time unit. This corresponds to a straight line segment, sloping up or sloping down, depending on whether the subject is moving toward the probe or away from the probe.

Figure 10-4: General hint

Movie Hint

Notice in the movie that Bob walks away from the probe slowing down at the end and then is still for a time.

He then moves away and back very quickly, waits and then away and back again before waiting. Then he moves towards the probe.

Look for a graph that has these parts:

1. walking away slowly
2. standing still
3. moving away and back quickly, twice
4. walking towards probe

Figure 10-5: Hint for movie

The quiz-makers work in groups to produce the materials for each unit. They then work together or hand the materials they produced over to another group to merge into the final product. Our decision to have them compare three motions in each unit is arbitrary but appears to offer the right intellectual challenge. Classes can start off with two units and work up to more, as appropriate.

The user who is taking the multimedia quiz sees a screen naming all elements of a unit on a single page. The one shown in Figure 10-6 has three categories of buttons or hot words, with three choices within each category. The categories of representations are graphs, texts, and movies.

In this example, the first column gives evocative names for the graphs. Clicking on any of these will produce a full-page presentation of one of the graphs. For example, clicking on "ski-jump" would cause a display of the graph shown in Figure 10-2.

The hot words in the second column in Figure 10-6 cause screens of text to be displayed. For example, clicking on "a" invokes the narrative shown in Figure 10-3.

The third column holds buttons of people's names. Each invokes a short movie of the motion performed by the person named. A sketch of this type of page is shown in Figure 10-1. The slow-frame partial-screen video is more than adequate for the quiz-taker to view and compare with the graphs and the narrative texts.

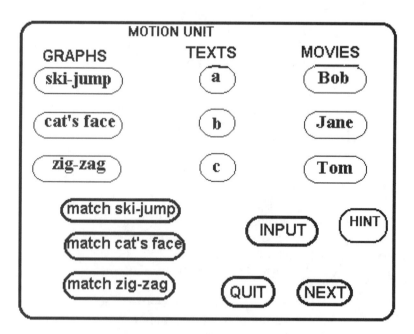

Figure 10-6: A unit page screen

Making Do

What if you don't have a micro-based lab? The groups can still produce video clips and hand-drawn graphs using stopwatches and tape measures. These often tend to be idealized representations, but this also introduces the concept of data sampling. Similarly, classes can still do something without a video camera, because the quiz-takers can have the challenge of correlating narratives with graphs.

At the bottom of the unit page are buttons that invoke dialogues with the users. These are the actual questions of the quiz. There are many strategies you could choose. We have chosen to require the user to match each graph to a text and each graph to a movie as Figure 10-7 shows. We also go beyond a multiple-choice format to include a facility for free-form input. The button labeled "input" in Figure 10-6 opens up a file for the user to enter his or her own description of the movements shown in the movies. Users type their names so that they can reuse this file for other units and so the rest of the class, including the teacher, can identify their input.

Figure 10-7 describes the dialogue for the "Match Ski-jump" button. The quiz-makers must program this interaction for the quiz-takers. The quiz poses a question and examines the response. The examples here make use of what programmers call "pseudo-code," a stylized form of expression intended to convey what the appropriate programming language would do for each step.

Pop-up text:	**ski-jump matches A, B or C?**	
Pop-up text response to correct answer:	**Fine.**	*JUMP to CLIPS*
Pop-up text response to incorrect answer:	**Try again!**	*EXIT Dialogue and SWITCH to Graph A*
CLIPS: Pop-up text:	**ski-jump matches BOB, JANE OR TOM?**	
Pop-up text response to correct answer:	**Great!**	*EXIT Dialogue and ADVANCE to harder Unit*
Pop-up text response to incorrect answer:	**Try again!**	*EXIT Dialogue and SWITCH to Graph A*

Figure 10-7: Action of dialogue boxes

The simple version of the Science Quiz project is a collection of stand-alone units, each covering three movements, with quiz-takers getting only right or wrong for feedback. For the advanced version, the class builds an adaptive tutorial.

Scripting Languages

Most multimedia authoring systems provide basic functions through menus and more complex functions through the use of a scripting language. In the case of LinkWay Live!, the programming language is called SCRIPT and is unique to it. This is also the case for Hypertalk for HyperCard. In MicroWorlds, the programming language is Logo, a language in its own right. Visual Basic is in the process of being adopted as the embedded programming language for various tools offered by Microsoft.

The advanced version of Science Quiz is built up of units of the simple version. Again, each unit consists of three motions, each represented by three forms of data. These units are arranged according to difficulty. The program counts the number of hits and misses as the quiz-taker attempts to match up corresponding events within the unit and offers hints and makes changes in difficulty level according to the quiz-taker's performance. The adaptive approach requires more effort on the part of the quiz-makers, both in programming and in organizing the questions. The strategy described here is to keep track of the number of failures and the number of successes and move the quiz-taker up and down in level of difficulty, accordingly.

The units have a common format, which means that although constructing the first unit may be time consuming, subsequent ones follow the same structure and can be produced easily. This scripting task is exacting, but is doable if enough time is allowed. Chapter 3 describes the variety of scripting tools embedded within most multimedia authoring systems.

```
Set up variable x for holding inputs;
display the question "ski-jump is A, B,
  or C?", input x;
if x = "B" then display "Fine.";
display the question "ski-jump
  matches Bob, Jane or Tom?", input x;
if x = "Tom" then display "Great"; exit;
if x not="Tom" then display "Look" and
  show SKIJUMP; exit
```

Figure 10-8: Program for dialogue, simple version

The dialogue for the simpler version is shown in Figure 10-8. It is executed by clicking on the "match" buttons on the screen shown in Figure 10-6. A variable, x, is used to hold the user's response and x is compared with the correct answer.

The advanced version requires a program to be executed at the start of each unit plus a more complex program for each dialogue. Figure 10-9 represents the program that initializes variables. The programs for the questions update these variables for failure and success. When quiz-takers have supplied all three answers, they move ahead. If they fail more than 4 times, that is, if the variable "fail" is greater than 4, then they are moved back. Figure 10-10 shows the program for the dialogue. Success advances the quiz-taker to the first unit of the next higher level in difficulty, unit31. Failure takes the quiz-taker back to unit11.

```
setup variables fail(3),
   got1(2), got2(2), got3(2) ;
--
set fail to 0; set got1 to 0;
set got2 to 0; set got3 to 0;
```

Figure 10-9: Unit initialization program, adaptive version

```
setup variable x;
display "ski-jump is a, b, or c?", input x;
if x = "b", display "Fine";
   display "ski-jump is Bob, Jane or Tom?", x;
   if x = "Tom", display "great"; set got1=1;
   else increment fail by 1;
   if fail > 4 link unit11;
   else display "Look"; do ski-jump;
else  -- answer to x = "b" was wrong
increment fail by 1
display "Look"; do ski-jump;
if got1^got2^got3 then link unit31;
-- returns to same unit screen
```

Figure 10-10: Program for dialogue, adaptive version

Navigation

We explain navigation in Science Quiz first for a unit and then for the quiz as a whole. You can use the device of story boards, written on the black board, as a focus for class discussion.

A unit in Science Quiz contains three events, with each event represented by one video clip, one narrative, and one graph. For each unit, quiz-takers have the option to look at all representations in any order and as many times as they want. Whenever they choose, they can invoke the match buttons. They also can invoke buttons for the hint, quitting, or moving to the next unit. Figure 10-11A is a story board describing the navigation in a single unit. Figure 10-11B is a story board describing the overall structure of the more advanced, adaptive version of Science Quiz.

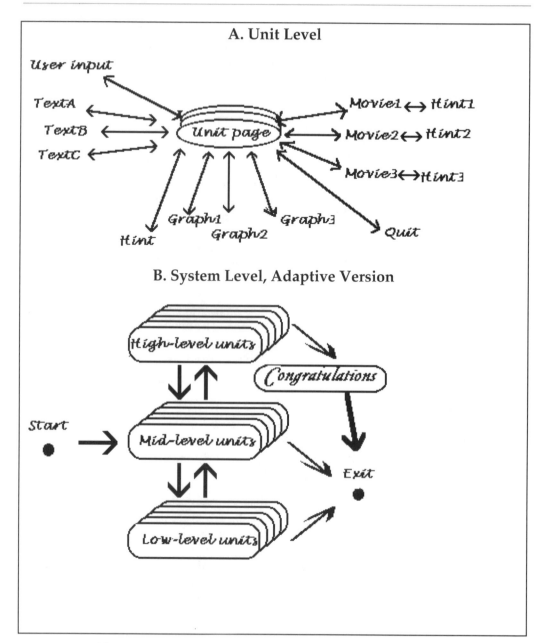

Figure 10-11: Story boards for single unit and for entire quiz

Movement from one unit to another differs for the two versions of Science Quiz. In the simple version you have the option of ordering the units according to difficulty, but the program does not control the movement to harder problems.

In the adaptive version, the system controls movement. Quiz-takers who answer the questions correctly will advance and those who do not will be shown units at the same or lesser difficulty. In the simple version, the quiz-taker chooses to go on or to quit.

In the adaptive versions, Figure 10-11B indicates that the users begin with a set of units of middle level of difficulty. They can move up or down, or they can quit. If they have completed all units successfully, they reach a CONGRATULATIONS screen. The story board does not indicate that some of this navigation is not under the user's explicit control. Notice our use of two story boards to express navigation at the unit and the system level. When developing or explaining navigation for more complex work, you may find it convenient to follow this approach.

Theory

This project features the use of multimedia to build student-constructed quizzes based on explorations using micro-based labs. In this section we indicate the benefits of the multimedia enhancement over and above the considerable advantages of the active learning enabled by the basic micro-based laboratory. Table 10-1 indicates the educational benefits in terms of our framework of goals.

The multimedia enhancement of the micro-based lab activity is beneficial for learning because of the following factors.

- The subject matter for the quiz, representations of movements through video recordings, position versus time graphs, and text descriptions, intrinsically requires multiple media. This subject matter is generally acknowledged to be difficult, and the assistance rendered by the multiple representations may make the difference in understanding for many students.

- Designing and producing quizzes for one's peers reinforces understanding. The multimedia quizzes are appealing for both quiz-makers and quiz-takers. The students are the ones doing the hands-on activity, and they are the ones producing the materials.

- The project is a challenge both in the attention to detail needed and the overall organization required. This is an advantage, not a drawback. Under these circumstances, successful results are obvious.

The project is feasible because the short video clips contain enough movement to compare with the graphs. If longer or higher quality video were necessary, it might be too large a burden on the storage capacities of current classroom computers. The script programming is exacting, as is all programming, but is within the reach of students.

The Science Quiz project demonstrates how multimedia can extend and sustain the learning experience in an activity. The critical notion is the motivating device of students teaching students by designing, developing, and producing a quiz or a self-study review system.

> **Mark Off the Distances?**
>
> Simple motions back and forth in front of the position probe can yield good questions for the quiz takers. It is not necessary to ask them to distinguish between a move to a position three meters from the probe versus four meters from the probe. However, if teachers want to exercise quantitative as well as qualitative understanding, this is possible. It may be useful in the early stages to mark off distances with cones or tapes visible on the video.

The system derives its appeal, both to creators and to users, through the use of multiple media and the interactivity of hypermedia. This approach will be beneficial whenever the original activity has visual and graphic components.

The content area learning provided by this experience is clear. Students work closely with the graphical and visual representations and generate the textual narratives. The requirements to produce hints and to order the units force the quiz-makers to reconstruct their knowledge of time and motion. Creating this project makes students use their cognitive and interpersonal skills when putting themselves in the mind of the taker of the quiz. The project requires group work and produces a significant result that audiences can and will appreciate.

The creators of Science Quiz, the quiz-makers, must plan and execute a series of micro-based lab explorations to produce the correlated materials for the quiz. The production of materials requires several roles: operators of the micro-based labs, subjects doing the movements, and students doing the videotaping. The creators must keep track of what has been taped and what remains to be done. They must manage videotapes, image files, and files of digitized video.

The quiz-makers must devise the feedback strategy to use when the quiz-taker makes a mistake. What hints are appropriate? Content understanding and expository and pedagogical skills are all intertwined.

Quiz-makers may reason, for example, that one unit of questions must include the subject standing still, which would produce a constant line graph of position versus time, a straight line parallel to the horizontal (time) axis. Moving toward or away from the probe at a fixed velocity produces roughly straight line segments, whereas starting off slowly and then speeding up produces a curved segment in the graph.

The comparisons should be on broad qualitative grounds, as we have indicated previously. For example, it would be appropriate for the quiz-makers to ask the quiz-takers to distinguish standing still, moving toward the probe, moving away from the probe, and constant versus accelerated movement.

Distinguishing between rates of movement or exact positions should be avoided or relegated to higher levels of difficulty. Interpreting velocity versus time graphs or acceleration versus time graphs is difficult for most people, so these questions also should be assigned to the highest levels. Both the quiz-makers and the quiz-takers will gain considerable experience with these concepts. In particular, the kinesthetic experience of measuring and seeing representations of one's own movement facilitates understanding.

Table 10-1: Educational goals

Higher-Order Thinking Skills
- Organizing subject matter according to difficulty
- Devising strategy for responding to quiz-taker's performance
- Planning a major production
- Completing a project for authentic use

Group and Interpersonal Skills
- Participating in a large group project
- Sharing tools

Content Material Learning
- Position, velocity, and acceleration
- Qualitative versus quantitative differences
- Expository writing for descriptions of movement
- Use of instrumentation (skill in the science discipline)

Technical Skills
- Creation, capture, and manipulation of screen images
- Videotaping
- Digitization of video clips
- Management of image and movie files
- Programming script commands for responses

Practice

Next, we discuss each step of the process as outlined in Process and Projects, Chapter 6, and specified for this project in Table 10-2.

Step One - Teacher Prepares

We selected the Science Quiz project for this position in the progression of projects because it introduces student-made video clips and programming responses to user action. This project also demonstrates a productive synergy between constructing multimedia and hands-on science. You would select this project to focus the students on the subject matter in order to raise the bar on the depth of understanding required. It also serves to give the class experience operating the video cameras in a simple setting. This would provide practice for more complex taping at a later time.

Table 10-2: Process steps for Science Quiz

Teacher prepares
- Select goals and determine strategy for start-up
- Introduce and practice using micro-based laboratories
- Prepare parts of project for quiz-makers to build on
- Assess environment and arrange for use of equipment
- Arrange space for videotaping
- Partition task and assign groups

Teacher assigns project
- Announce project
- Discuss and establish schedule with benchmarks
- Demonstrate technologies

Students create project
- Class as a whole brainstorms and plans
- Work is assigned to groups
- Groups assign roles or a system for rotating roles
- Group previews, reflects, and modifies
- Class or editing group compiles whole package

Reflection
- Student self-evaluation when using system
- Public performance
- Assessment for content
- Assessment for multimedia skills

Chapter 13, Advanced Techniques, contains relevant sections on Video Techniques, Planning Video Shots, Composing Video or Images, and Lighting Video or Images. Chapter 14, Production Company, has sections on Selecting Video Connections and Making Projects Look Good on Television.

You should prepare for the project by identifying requirements for equipment and other resources. Table 10-3 shows a list of staples. Figure 10-12 shows a feasible layout for the video camera and lights.

Table 10-3: Equipment requirements

- micro-based laboratory equipment (computer, MBL software, and probes)
- video camera and tripod
- space for MBL work and videotaping
- lights
- computer with digital video capture adapter
- supplies of diskettes and videocassettes
- standard classroom or laboratory computers

You must decide how much of the structure of the quiz you will define ahead of time and how much you should leave to the class or to individual groups. The manner of grouping students is connected to this decision. You can divide the class into groups, with each group doing everything to produce one unit of questions, or set up a production company for the implementation of the entire project. The production company approach sets up specialists such as camera crew, operators of the micro-based labs, file librarians, programmers, writers, and producers and directors. We describe the features and benefits of this approach in Chapter 14. Here we describe the whole group approach, each group bearing responsibility for a whole unit, with the teacher supplying the programming required for an individual unit.

You should also arrange for the making of the videos. This involves reserving the equipment and arranging space. The micro-based lab equipment and the video equipment may each be shared resources in the school. There are certainly benefits in giving each group of students practice setting up the micro-based lab, positioning lights and the tripod for the camera, and connecting all the cables. However, we recommend that a space be reserved to set up and leave the equipment for the duration of the project to reduce the required set-up time for each group.

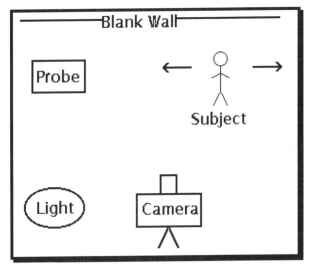

Figure 10-12: Scene layout

This project involves many different files and, probably, several computers. You should gather a supply of diskettes for holding the captured screen files unless all the computers are connected on a network. Teachers and students need to agree on naming conventions and storage places for diskettes and video cassettes.

Step Two - Teacher Assigns Project

The Science Quiz activity takes place after the teacher introduces the micro-based lab and the position probe. You would assign each team (group) of three or four students a specific unit to produce for the quiz. The team must perform the motions, do the video taping, capture the screens holding the resulting graphs, write and enter the text narratives describing the motions, keep track of all these files, and put them together in one folder. The worksheet in Figure 10-13 indicates the subtasks involved, with spaces for file names as well as scheduled and actual completion dates.

We recommend such a worksheet as a guide to the teams. The teacher would complete one worksheet for each team, covering the tasks to complete one unit. Note that if one student is the subject for the video taping, the other team members share responsibility for operating the micro-based lab and for doing the videotaping. The worksheet would contain descriptions of the exploration's movements in a terse form (for example: "mainly standing still," "moving steadily away") or in a detailed form that could be the narrative in the final quiz. If the teacher chooses to produce a structured quiz, the actual three motions for each unit would be defined during the all-class planning session. Otherwise, teams can plan their own three movements. The worksheet can also be used to record the scheduling. You should probably provide time for retaping.

Step Three - Students Create Project

If you choose to produce the adaptive quiz, the project begins with an all-class planning session, defining types of movements to be teamed into units and then categorized into levels of difficulty. The intellectual activity of this planning session is the science and the mathematics of graphs.

For both the simple and adaptive versions, the teams producing a video tape of a movement and the associated graph begin with a plan for the movement. The graph will automatically match the videotape. At this point, the team must decide if the movement is close enough to the plan to include or if they want to do another video take. In either case, they write the detailed narrative describing the movement after the fact.

The team must decide if the actual movement as captured by video and graph is close enough to the plan to fit the requirements of the quiz. This will constitute an important exercise in evaluating real-world variability as opposed to textbook examples. The writing of the narratives and the hints require creators to focus on the major features of the movements, that is, to concentrate on forests not trees, on gross movements not wiggles.

The videotaping required is exacting but feasible once someone sets up the scene, lighting, and camera position. Use a tripod for the camera. The background should be as clear as possible. The authors once found out that the straight lines of a white-board produced a disturbing pattern of so-called "jaggies" when recorded in the low-resolution of one form of digitized video. The use of one or two lights greatly improves the quality of the video produced. Look again at Figure 10-12.

Acquiring the images of the graphs from the MBL program requires use of screen capture. Some authoring systems such as LinkWay Live! include their own screen capture program. Others rely on procedures built into the operating system or provided by other packages. The micro-based laboratory package may include a facility for saving the images of the graphs. Usually the user needs to determine a particular sequence of key strokes to capture the screen. It may mean that before starting the micro-based laboratory program, the creators must load and invoke the screen capture program or procedure for their authoring system or platform. Subsequently, when the complete graph is on the screen, the creators invoke the screen capture program by pressing a specific combination of keys. The system gives the user a chance to name the file with the image. We caution again that the management of all these files requires agreement on names beforehand.

Screen Capture

"Screen capture" is the generic name for the process of making an image file of the current contents of the screen. Screen capture programs are typically resident programs, that is, they 'reside' in memory with system programs while the applications are operating concurrently. Please be warned that some products are designed in such a way that a specific screen capture program or procedure will not work.

Group name:	Students		
	Tasks	Target Time / Date	Done?
Movement 1.			
	Taping: subject		
	Movie: file name prefix		
	Graph: file name		
Movement 2.			
	Taping: subject		
	Movie: file name prefix		
	Graph: file name		
Movement 3.			
	Taping: subject		
	Movie: file name		
	Graph: file name		
Create Folder:	folder name		
Enter texts for narratives & hints			
Copy and link files			
Test			

Figure 10-13: Science Quiz worksheet

Digitizing the video is a separate operation that you can schedule for later than the videotaping. For each of the authoring systems, the make-a-movie operation involves a distinct interface screen. The creator proceeds through the following set of steps:

- Attach video camera or videocassette player to digital video capture adapter in computer.

- Locate start and stop of clip using the playback facility in the camera or by viewing the video on a separate, attached television monitor.

- Using the video frame capture interface, acquire the first frame from the selected video. Adjust the palette of colors using this frame for the movie clip.

- Using the interface, set up start and stop points and digitize video. You may be prompted for the value of certain parameters such as the type of compression. You may refer to Chapter 13's section on Making Suitable Analog Video.

- Name and save the video clip. Because the amount of data is large, it may be divided into smaller files. The user name may be a short prefix.

The groups of students bring the files from the videotaping session to the main computer system and assemble their portion of the quiz. They must link the images to the appropriate buttons and generate or modify the script programs.

Palettes

Many computer systems have the potential of displaying a large set of colors with the limitation of being able to display only a small subset of colors at one time. Palette is the term for this subset of colors. An appropriate palette for an outdoor scene with trees and plants would not be appropriate for an indoor scene with people and furniture. The process of digitizing video may involve the creator selecting or customizing a palette.

Step Four - Reflection

The creation stage of the project has many opportunities for reflection. Is this the movement we wanted to record? Does the text match the movement? How good are the hints?

When the Science Quiz is produced, quiz-takers are assessing the work when they are using it. Are the navigation paths correct? Do movies, graphs, and text appear in the right place? Can the quiz-takers distinguish the movements? Are the texts understandable? Are the choices of movements appropriate?

This role of quiz-takers as assessors of quality applies to all testing but is easy to accept when the students are the quiz-makers. If the quiz-takers flounder, then the quiz-makers must reassess their work. Quiz-makers and teachers can read the free-form input to see how the quiz-takers describe the action and react to the quiz in general. Quiz-makers are also quiz-takers, because students in one team can try the units produced by other teams.

The class can offer the quiz to other students and to adults. The fact that the subject matter is not trivial will provide the students with opportunities to display their expertise. This will invoke even deeper challenges to explain what is going on to siblings and parents.

You can use this project as scaffolding in the interpretation of other graphs. The kinesthetic experience of producing a specified motion while getting immediate feedback is very powerful. The quiz making challenges the students to plan and produce multiple recordings of multiple movements, reinforcing the learning experience.

The project is also scaffolding for other activities involving videotaping. In Science Quiz, the setting is fixed and the subjects are team-members. In the next project,

Memoirs, students must leave the classroom to go out to interview adults in their homes.

Summary

Both the science content and the technical production make the multimedia Science Quiz a challenging project for students. The best way to invoke and confirm understanding of the correlation of distinct representations of any phenomenon is to produce those representations. This activity does that for representations of movement. We propose multimedia as a complement to exploratory, hands-on science, an activity vital to our students.

The quiz-takers gain benefits from using the final product, but the primary beneficiaries are the quiz-makers. The multimedia technologies provide the students with a presentation vehicle that supports graphics, video, text, and, in other projects, audio. Multimedia also provides a structure for representing simple and complex events. This can enhance and sustain the learning produced by the hands-on experience.

Chapter 11

Memoirs

In this chapter, we explore:

- how creating a multimedia project can help students understand the effects of historical events on people's lives.

- the advantages of a project that employs all five media, involves an entire class as creators, and involves adults in the community as participants.

The Memoirs project looks quite different to creators and to users. The Background section describes the project from these two viewpoints. The Theory section discusses computers' unique contribution to this project and indicates the goals that creating this project can help students achieve. The Practice section provides detailed suggestions for applying the four-step process to this project.

Background

In this project, students ask what public events have most strongly affected adults' lives. The students videotape some of the interviews, analyze all of the answers, and combine the results into a memoir of the interviewees' lives and times.

This project's position near the end of our progression of six projects justifies its being complex and challenging. However, you can use the underlying idea for much simpler projects than the one we describe here. For example, you could suggest that students summarize interviews in text form and complete this project using no media other than hypertext.

Students prepare digital video of selected interviews, use CD-ROM encyclopedias and almanacs to find background information about events that interviewees mention, categorize the events, use a database to analyze the events and categories, and employ several media to present the results in a meaningful fashion. Memoirs is thus significantly more challenging than Critics' Circle, in which students used digital audio to record each other's opinions about a subject, showed images while the audio played, and used text to summarize their opinions.

Use of computers to store data

Q: What is a database and how does it relate to multimedia and education?

A: A database is an organized way of storing information in a computer. The information can contain media in addition to text or can point to media in addition to text. Deciding on an organization, putting information into an organization, and studying the results helps students understand the meaning of information. A computer database makes it easy and quick to get different views of stored information. A project such as this one encourages good organization of information, which is important to education. Because this project's database involves tables, a spreadsheet program may be used for maintaining some of the information.

A User's View of the Project

A user might encounter this multimedia project in the lobby of the school, in the public library, or in city hall. The user would first see a screen such as the one in Figure 11-1.

A user can select one of three screens to see next by clicking one of the three buttons labeled Choices, Tour, and Summary. Clicking on Choices takes the user to the screen shown in Figure 11-2, at which point the user can select among the buttons shown on that screen. Four of these buttons allow a user to see a list of the events in one of the four categories into which the students decided to separate the events they collected. The categories happened to be Sports, History, Culture, and Science-Technology. Selecting

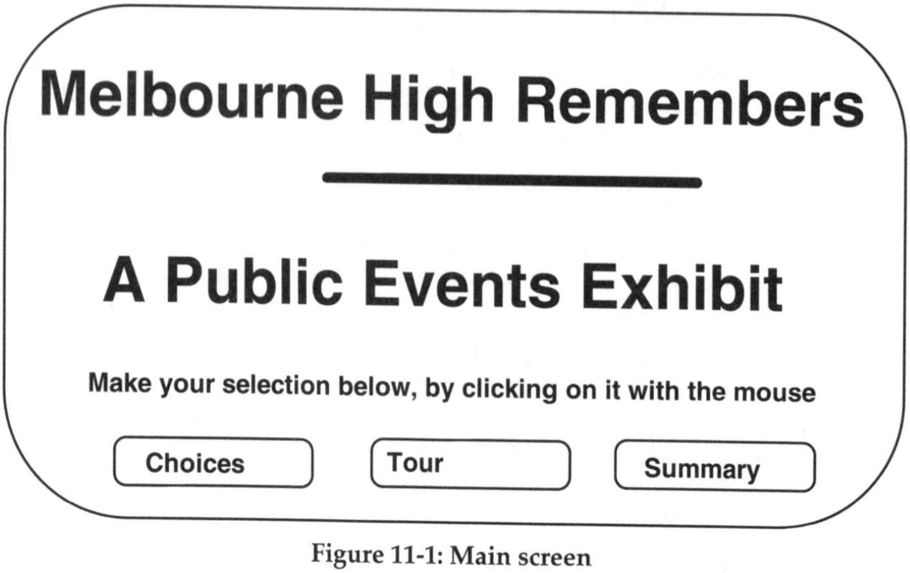

Melbourne High Remembers

─────────

A Public Events Exhibit

Make your selection below, by clicking on it with the mouse

| Choices | Tour | Summary |

Figure 11-1: Main screen

the button for a category takes the user to an alphabetized or chronological list of events in that category. Selecting the first event in the History category might take the user to Berlin Wall Falls, shown in Figure 11-3. A user can instead select the Top Ten, All Events, or Summary button. Selecting the Add On button allows users to add their own comments on events.

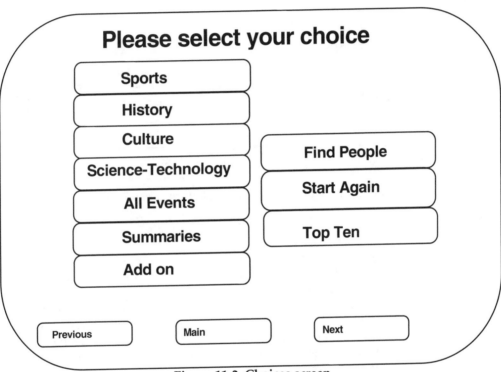

Figure 11-2: Choices screen

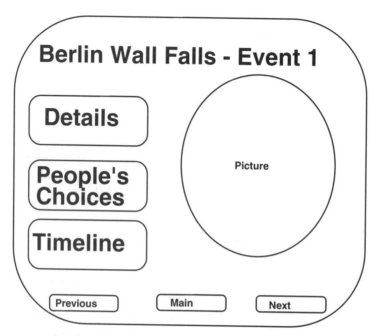

Figure 11-3: One Event in the History category

If a user selects the Find People button on Figure 11-2's screen, the user sees a screen similar to the one that appears at the top-left in Figure 11-4. At this screen, the user can select a button to see a particular interviewee's picture and other information, as Figure 11-5 shows. A user can select buttons on that screen to see and hear that interviewee's contributions, as Figure 11-6 indicates. In this case, there is no audio associated with the Agnews. Clicking on the audio button, which is standard across all the people screens, gives the user a spoken message explaining that there is no audio. A user may, however, select a short video of the Agnews.

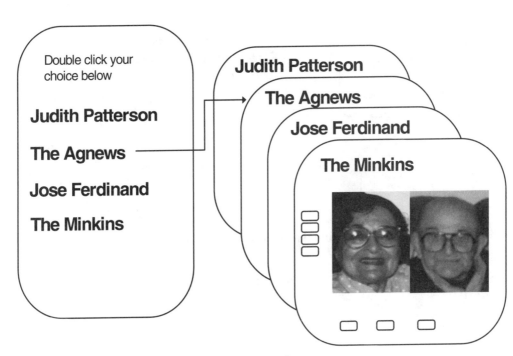

Figure 11-4: People screens

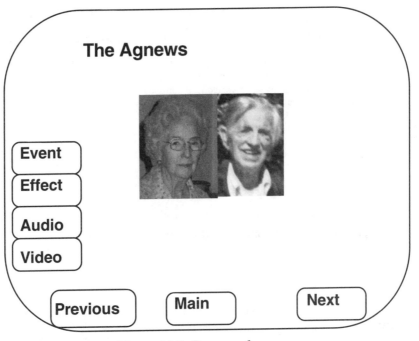

Figure 11-5: One people screen

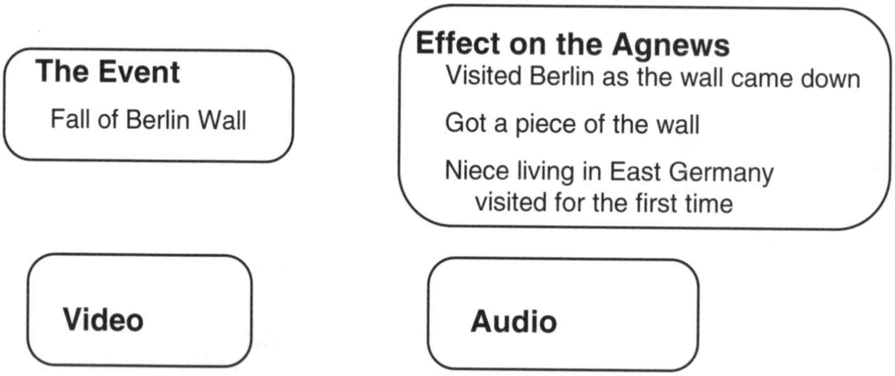

The Event

Fall of Berlin Wall

Effect on the Agnews
Visited Berlin as the wall came down

Got a piece of the wall

Niece living in East Germany
visited for the first time

Video

Audio

Figure 11-6: Additional screens associated with the Agnews

If the user selects Details from the screen in Figure 11-3, the user sees the screen in Figure 11-7.

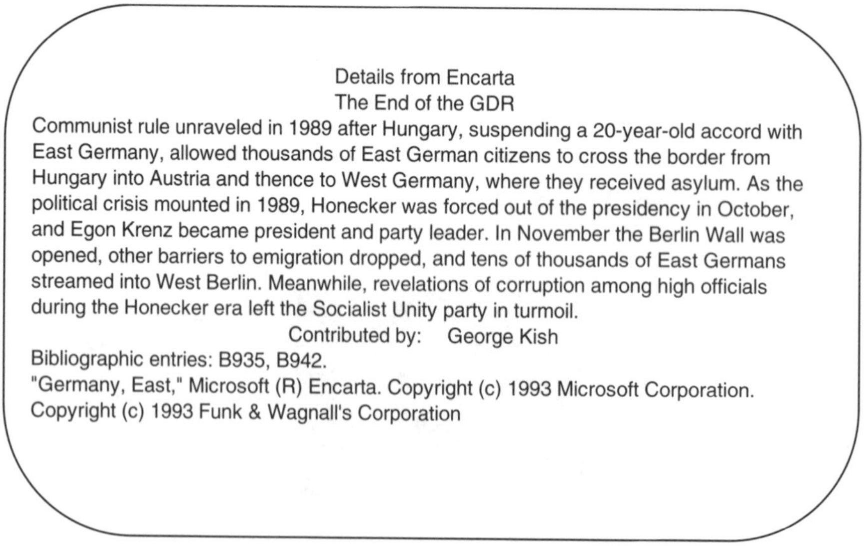

Details from Encarta
The End of the GDR
Communist rule unraveled in 1989 after Hungary, suspending a 20-year-old accord with East Germany, allowed thousands of East German citizens to cross the border from Hungary into Austria and thence to West Germany, where they received asylum. As the political crisis mounted in 1989, Honecker was forced out of the presidency in October, and Egon Krenz became president and party leader. In November the Berlin Wall was opened, other barriers to emigration dropped, and tens of thousands of East Germans streamed into West Berlin. Meanwhile, revelations of corruption among high officials during the Honecker era left the Socialist Unity party in turmoil.
Contributed by: George Kish
Bibliographic entries: B935, B942.
"Germany, East," Microsoft (R) Encarta. Copyright (c) 1993 Microsoft Corporation.
Copyright (c) 1993 Funk & Wagnall's Corporation

Figure 11-7: Associated event reference with citation

The user goes to the screens shown in Figure 11-8 after selecting all events from the screen in Figure 11-2.

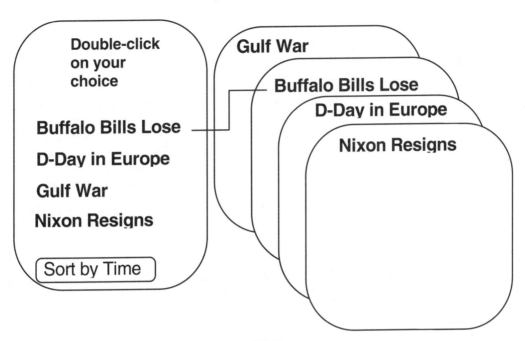

Figure 11-8: All Events screen

The students need to give careful consideration to what they want a user to see when the user selects Summaries from Figure 11-2. One possibility is a table such as shown in Table 11-1 with options to click on the various entries. As an example of how to read this table, note the row that has Women at the left. This row indicates that women mentioned a total of 20 sports events but that the students' analysis indicated that there were only 10 unique events in what they mentioned.

Table 11-1: A possible summary table

Event Categories	Sports		History		Culture		Science and Technology	
Demo-graphic categories	Unique	Total	Unique	Total	Unique	Total	Unique	Total
Men	10	30	10	15	5	10	10	20
Women	10	20	10	30	6	15	5	10
Students	1	1	2	2	1	1	1	1
Teachers	8	10	2	3	3	5	4	7
Total								

A Creator's View of the Project

Students who create the Memoirs project create the screens, buttons, and links that the preceding section described. The students spend significantly more time collecting the underlying data than creating the screens that present and summarize the data.

Each student interviews a parent or some other adult. The student asks the interviewee to identify the five events that have most strongly affected the interviewee and then asks the interviewee to discuss these events' impacts. We have picked five events arbitrarily. You may want to limit the number of events to as few as one per interviewee or even ask for more per interviewee. The class practices for these interviews by identifying what they consider to be the five most significant events in their own lives. They then ask five teachers to specify the five events each that have been most significant to them.

The students analyze the events that interviewees discuss by deciding on a few categories and placing each event in a category. Table 11-2 shows some of the possible events.

Table 11-2: Sample events

1. Dissolution of the Union of Soviet Socialist Republics
2. Mets win the 1986 World Series
3. Personal computers become pervasive
4. Jet aircraft travel becomes widely available to the public
5. D-Day in Europe
6. Magic Johnson announces he is HIV-positive and retires from basketball
7. Nixon resigns because of Watergate
8. Mike Tyson goes to jail for rape
9. Buffalo Bills lose the Super Bowl three times
10. Arthur Ashe wins Wimbelton and dies of AIDS
11. Hurricane David wreaks havoc on the Caribbean
12. Hurricane Andrew wreaks havoc on Miami
13. Mississippi floods Midwest
14. Snow storms of the century hit the east coast
15. Earthquake in Los Angeles
16. Vietnam War
17. Assassination of JFK, RFK, and Martin Luther King, Jr.
18. Moon Landing
19. Camp David Agreement
20. Palestine and Israeli signing
21. Gulf War
22. End of World War II
23. End of Korean War

The class attempts to associate interviewees' specific demographics with tendencies to name specific events. The class saves the information that they collect in an organized way, such as by using a spreadsheet to create tables. Table 11-3 shows a sample of such a database.

Table 11-3: Entries for interviewees and events

Record number	Demo-graphic category	Event category	Summary	Effect on interviewee	Unique event number	Name of interviewee
1	Women	Sports	Gymnastics Olympic award for an American	Had children sign up for gymnastics	4	James Jones
2	Women	Sports	Cathy Rigby wins Olympic medal	Watched more Olympics	4	Corey Johnson
3	Women	Sports	Bowling successes	My bowling team goes to the State championship	3	Anne Wright
4	Teacher	History				Mr. Albert
5	Teacher	History				Mr. Minkin
6	Teacher	Sports				Mr. Minkin
7	Teacher	Culture				Mr. Minkin

The class thus creates a multimedia project that not only identifies the important events but also records how many of the interviewees included each event in their own lists. Without asking each interviewee to undertake the difficult and unsatisfying job of ranking his or her events in order from most significant to least significant, the class will nevertheless end up with a rank of the events' importance, based on the frequency with which interviewees mentioned the events.

Creators can use a common technique that allows users to peruse a screen that contains a long list of events. If the list is so long that not all of the events fit on the screen at one time, the creators can allow a user to scroll through the list. After the user finds the event she wants to select, she can click or double-click on that event to go to the page or perhaps a folder, stack, or toolbook that describes the event. Different authoring systems have different names for this technique. Asymetrix ToolBook calls it using a listbox with hot words for each line in the list box. Each hot word has an associated script that contains the linking statements.

The completed project includes a written summary of the extent to which different interviewees did and did not identify the same events and of other significant items that come up during the interview. Table 11-4 shows one possible representation. We have only partially filled out this table. For example, looking in the Totals column shows that eight people chose unique event 3. To make Table 11-4, students number the unique events and assign each event to a category. They then count the number of men, women, teachers, and students who have indicated that each event was significant for them and total the number of people who selected each event. Students then use this table to determine which events were most frequently selected within each category and within the overall sample. The students supplement each unique event with a detailed discussion, supported by research from on-line references and other sources, as Figure 11-7 illustrates.

In a class of 30 students, each student collects five events from one interviewee. The class adds their five events and interviews five teachers who contribute five events each. The class thus has 180 events to work with. One of the challenges is determining which of these events are unique. For example, one interviewee may mention "Watergate" and another may mention "Nixon resigns." The students must note that both interviewees referred to the same event. Similarly, the conversion of the Soviet Union into the Former Soviet Union might fail to make the top dozen events if a class insists on recording the change in each former satellite as a separate event.

Ideally, the creators would include digital video of each interview in the completed project, in order to allow a user to select any desired interview and see and hear that interview within seconds. However, available disk space will probably limit most classes to including a few very short interviews as part of their multimedia projects. Decreasing price and increasing availability of disk space will gradually allow classes to include more and more digital video in their projects.

Table 11-4: Event selection frequencies

Category	Unique event number	Men	Women	Teachers	Students	Totals
Sports	1	6	0			6
	2	1	0	2	1	4
	3	2	5	1		8
	4	3	1			4
	5	4	1			5
History	6					
	9					
	10					
	11					
	12					
	13					
Culture	33					
	34					
	35					
Science	43					
	44					
	45					
	49					
	50					

Students may ask about the possibility of putting their Memoirs project on a CD-ROM. One CD-ROM could hold up to an hour of video interviews. Although the price of equipment that can write CD-ROMs had decreased to less than $3000, few schools have access to such equipment. A school might arrange for a service bureau or find a local college with this equipment to make a CD-ROM. Perhaps by the turn of the century, and certainly within the lifetimes of today's students, it will be feasible to include in a Memoirs project a screen such as Figure 11-9.

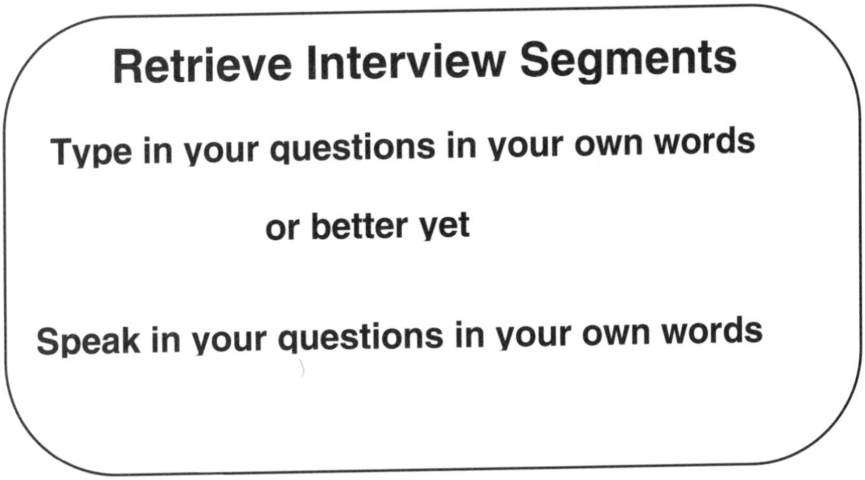

Retrieve Interview Segments

Type in your questions in your own words

or better yet

Speak in your questions in your own words

Figure 11-9: Query screen

To make use of such a screen, students would index each significant segment of video by keywords. The computer would attempt to match keywords with words that a user typed in or spoke.

Because this project deals with the impacts of events on interviewees' lives, we strongly recommend videotaping all the interviews. Video and audio of facial expressions and vocal inflections express emotions more vividly than typical text can do. Students could complete the project by capturing interviews on audio cassette recorders, but emotions would be considerably less evident without video. Another reason for videotaping each interview is that tape allows students to study and improve their interviewing techniques.

Even if disk space prevents digitizing the interviews and incorporating them into the project, students can benefit from having a library of videotaped interviews. If digitized video is out of the question, a Memoirs multimedia project can replace links by specifying the name of the videotape that contains each interview. This would make the interviews available, although it would require several minutes for a user to find a selected tape.

Not all people will agree to come to the school for interviews. The teacher must decide whether to loan out video camera equipment or to use video produced by equipment that the school does not own. Figure 11-10 shows several of the screens in a typical Memoirs project, along with links among these screens.

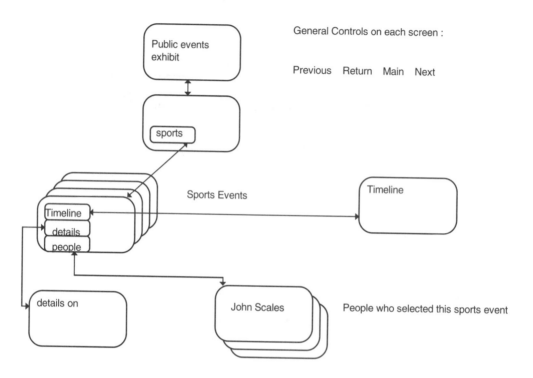

Figure 11-10: Part of a story board

Theory

The Memoirs project's critical notion is that understanding history includes understanding how events affect people. Using multimedia helps students to explore, organize, understand, and document the ways in which historical events affect people. Creating multiple media offers students the opportunity to convey significantly more information, including information about peoples' emotions, than they could express with text alone or with any other single medium. Creating hypermedia links helps students to understand relationships among people and events. This project introduces the technologies of using digital video, finding supporting information in on-line sources, making good use of limited resources, and analyzing information by means of spreadsheets.

Table 11-5 summarizes some goals that a teacher can help students achieve by creating the Memoirs project.

Table 11-5: Goals for the project

Higher-order thinking skills
- Insights into history experienced by family and friends
- Appreciation of diversity of views
- Categorization of many events
- Combining differently phrased references into the same idea
- Analysis of quantitative data
- Responsibility for carrying out a complex, detailed project
- Preparing and carrying out interviews with adults
- Selection and preparation of multimedia information to make a specific, compelling, and interesting multimedia project for a general audience

Group and interpersonal skills
- Working cooperatively and synergistically to complete a complex project
- Relating to and accomplishing specific tasks with older generations

Content material learning
- Relationships among events
- Detailed information about events, perceptions, and facts

Technical skills
- Constructing and using databases and spreadsheets
- Collecting and digitizing media
- Providing users their choice of information to be viewed
- Using video to record interviews
- Planning and carrying out a large, complex multimedia project

The fact that multimedia is not only multiple media, but also hypermedia links among the media, is particularly valuable in the Memoirs project. A cardboard box overflowing with text on index cards, sketches on paper, photographs, audiotapes, and videotapes would contain multiple media. Multimedia allows your students to use a computer to organize the multiple media into a coherent project, which they and others can use to learn from and enjoy the interviews and summaries.

Using multimedia for Memoirs is technically and economically feasible because reasonably affordable multimedia computers are capable of recording and playing back all five media, including digital audio and digital video. The amount of digital video that students can employ is small in the mid-1990s but will increase rapidly in subsequent years.

A teacher can use Memoirs to meet a wide variety of objectives by specifying the sorts of events about which students ask interviewees. A teacher might limit the subject to health issues, to events of the last ten years, or to events in the interviewees' own community. In Chapter 15, we discuss variations of this project that you could use to meet other objectives. For example, instead of producing a memoir of the past, students could ask interviewees to forecast the most significant events of the next 10 years. Younger children can gain special benefits by categorizing information and summarizing results in a table. Subjects could include friends' and relatives' favorite foods, colors, pets, or weekend and vacation activities. Even very young children can use video, with suitable help.

Practice

This section divides the project's practical aspects into four steps. We present the material in the form of one of many possible scenarios. These four process steps are summarized at the end in Table 11-9.

Step One - Teacher Prepares

The teacher plans for a relatively large number of students to create several different media and combine the media into a single project. The teacher also plans for playing back the completed multimedia project, which includes video, in a suitable location such as the school lobby. Table 11-6 lists typical hardware that creators and users may need. Students who create the project need a way to both put in and get out each medium. Users who play the project need to get out each medium and need to put in enough media to make their selections. If the creators provide for users to put in text comments, the users may need additional input hardware.

Table 11-6: Media input and output

Media	Input	Output
Text	Computer keyboard; CD-ROMs for reference	Computer display screen
Graphics	Draw program and Mouse; CD-ROMs for maps, timelines, and so forth	Computer display screen
Images	Paint program and Mouse; Video camera and Frame-grabber; Camera and Scanner; Digital camera; CD-ROM for clip art	Computer display screen; Printer
Audio	Microphone and Digital audio adapter; CD-ROM; MIDI source	Digital audio adapter and Amplified speaker
Analog video	Video camera	VCR; Television monitor or Computer display screen and Video window card
Digital video	Video camera; Digital video capture adapter	Computer display screen and optional Video decompression card

The teacher decides that students will use two types of computers to create the Memoirs project. Table 11-7 indicates what these computers contain. Students use several computers of the first type most of the time while they are creating the project. Many students share one computer of the second type, which is equipped for digitizing images and video. The shared computer might be in a school library or media center. The first type of computer suffices for users to play back the project, perhaps in the school lobby.

Chapter 13 contains relevant sections on Video Techniques, Planning Video Shots, Composing Video or Images, and Lighting Video or Images. You might also refer to Chapter 14's sections on Selecting Video Connections and Making Projects Look Good on Television.

As part of this preparation step, the teacher needs to make the following decisions.

- Will the playback computer be a stand-alone kiosk or simply a project that someone will come up and start?

- What is the relative priority of the many goals that this project can accomplish?

- Is managing a fixed amount of disk space (which digital video could easily exceed) an important goal of the project?

- What is the size of the project? For example, how many adults will students interview and how many events will they ask for?

- Will some students have specific assignments?

With these and other decisions made, the teacher is ready to assign the project.

Table 11-7: Typical equipment to use

Computers for students containing
- Screen, keyboard, mouse, and system unit
- Digital audio adapter
- Microphone cabled to audio adapter
- Amplified speakers cabled to audio adapter
- CD-ROM drive and reference discs

Shared computer containing
- Digital video capture adapter with cable to video camera or VCR
- Digital audio adapter with cable to video camera or VCR
- Video camera (or separate VCR to play camera's tapes)
- Television monitor if video capture adapter requires one
-

Several diskettes for carrying digitized images and video to the other computers if no network is available.

Step Two - Teacher Assigns Project

The teacher describes the project. He asks students to observe techniques that interviewers used on television news shows. He may demonstrate some multimedia projects created by prior classes to inspire the students. He emphasizes that they have 30 MB (or whatever he decides is appropriate) of free disk space available for this project. He invites them to determine how many minutes of text, graphics, images, audio, and video will fit in that space.

He also demonstrates some CD-ROMs that students may use for background on events. Examples are *Microsoft's Cinemania* and *Encarta* and CNN's *Events of the Year*. He gives the students time to explore these CD-ROMs on their own. He asks for volunteers to demonstrate how to find a reference and prepare a clip with a citation to paste into their multimedia projects. Besides using CD-ROMs that contain almanacs or encyclopedias to provide details of the events, he may suggest that students visit a public library to review microfiche headlines of the *New York Times* for the past 50 years.

Although the class is anxious to get started, the teacher makes one last suggestion that students decide how to record all the information on the computer. He is not sure that the students appreciate these remarks now; but he is sure that they will later.

The teacher arbitrarily divides the class into smaller groups and asks them to brainstorm about topics such as how to organize the material, what users would want to see, how members of the class should organize themselves, and how to apportion the available disk space among the five media. Although he has an organization, responsibilities, and milestones ready to suggest, such as those in Table 11-8 and Figure 11-11, he wants to see what his class comes up with. He is more than willing to be flexible. Although he has information from Figure 11-12 about how much of each medium can fit into a given amount of disk space, he thinks that it is important for the students to perform this bit of investigation and calculation themselves and then come up with a plan to use their assets well.

Note that the numbers in Figure 11-12 vary widely, so the teacher and students do some experiments to see what numbers actually apply.

The teacher decides to turn the students loose to work on their own, except for spending part of each day's scheduled class period in discussions about planning for milestones and preparing and performing interviews.

Table 11-8: Assignments for students

Assignment	Number of students
Design introductory grabber	2
Design look and feel of all screens	2
Maintain spreadsheets, event sheets, and people sheets	6
Video interviews	Each student
Set up people screens	Each student
Manage sizes of media	1
Create timeline	2
Set up event screens	2
Assemble entire project	2

Project: Memoirs

Responsibility:

- Design introductory grabber
- Design look and feel of all screens
- Maintain spreadsheets, event sheets, and people sheets
- Conduct video interviews
- Set up people screens
- Set up event screens
- Assemble entire project

Computer to use for digitizing images and video:

Room   _____

Machine   _____

Compulsory parts of project:

Suggested Milestones:

- 3/11   Interview questions prepared and tested with teachers
- 3/15   Interviews conducted and events brought in
- 3/20   Preliminary story board, spreadsheets, forms completed
- 3/20   Screens designed for all sections
- 3/18   Events categorized
- 3/25   Story board and navigation plan completed
- 3/26   Assembly plan completed
- 3/30   Video interviews completed
- 4/10   Project assembled and tested

Complete project by _____ o'clock on _____

Comments on project:

Figure 11-11: Assignment sheet

Q: How much storage space do digitized media occupy?

A: 30 MB of free space on a disk can hold approximately:

- 3000 typical black-and-white scanned line drawings, or
- 1071 color images created with a computer paint program, or
- 600 images digitized from analog video with no compression, or
- 62 minutes of audio, or
- 3.3 minutes of digital video compressed using Intel's Smart Video Recorder.

Figure 11-12: How much media can fit on 30 MB of disk?

Some of the students report that they have difficulty being taken seriously by their friends and relatives. The teacher helps the students become confident and effective by suggesting that they practice some of the following.

- Know the purpose of the interview.
- Ask open-ended questions.
- Probe for further information, such as saying "Tell me more about ..."
- Don't be afraid to ask for clarifications, such as "I don't understand; could you explain?"
- Follow-up on what the interviewer says, such as "How or why or when did you do that?"
- Prompt the interviewee to keep talking, by your using such comments as "I see. Um hmmm. how interesting. Go on please."
- Feed information back to check on its accuracy, such as "Let me try to summarize. Please correct me if I am wrong."
- Check for completeness, such as "Is there anything else that I should know or ask about?"
- Ask a generative question, such as "If you needed to interview people to get their five most significant public events, what questions would you ask?"
- Make certain all areas are covered and that the conversation does not wander off.

The teacher also suggests that the students do the following.

- Make videos of practice interviews.
- Review the Advanced Techniques chapter's suggestions.
- Give constructive criticisms of other interviewers.
- Continually reassess new information and revise the plan appropriately.
- Make observations and conclusions from data and from sources of data.
- Consider whether the sample of interviewees represents the community.
- Do not get carried away with insignificant facets of this project.
- Have a realistic assessment of what is possible.

Step Three - Students Create Project

The class carries out the following tasks, partially overlapping in time.

- Reviews the teacher's demos in smaller groups.
- Brainstorms on what users need to see and want to see.

- Brainstorms on what is practical to prepare, as opposed to what they might like to do.
- Decides on categories for the events.
- Decides on categories for demographics of interviewees, such as men or women, age ranges, native or non-native born, high school graduate or college graduate, and occupation.
- Decides on interview questions by having a few students prepare a tentative list of questions and then review the questions with the class.
- Practices using the selected questions to interview some teachers in the school.
- Makes plan revisions based on data collected so far.
- Decides on preliminary event categories.
- Revises these categories as necessary after the interviews.
- Prepares a letter or fact sheet for interviewees, such as the one in Figure 11-13.

Dear _____,

The eleventh grade class of Melbourne High School is studying the significant events that affected the lives of some important people around us. We would like to interview you at a convenient time and place. In general, we will ask you the following questions.

What were the five most significant public events that happened in your lifetime? How did each these events affect your life?

We will assemble the information, including some very short selections from the videotapes of the interviews in a multimedia kiosk that you will be able to see.

If you are available, please contact the school office at 777-3444.

Very truly yours,

Figure 11-13: Sample letter to prospective interviewees

The students conduct interviews and bring back the results. The class meets as a group to modify the event categories and demographic categories as appropriate. In parallel, others develop other pieces of the project.

The students decide to dedicate 20 MB to video interviews. They realize that they have space for only the most illustrative answers. They decide that there is no reason to show video of people listening to questions, so they use text to show the questions. They experiment with some of the practice interviews and find that 20 seconds is enough for a meaningful answer. Thus, they have space for digital video showing about seven answers.

The class:

- collects details on events using CD-ROM encyclopedias such as *Microsoft's Encarta*,
- prepares screens and links and assembles the entire project,
- decides to add background music to the introduction or grabber, and
- decides not to add background music to the other parts of the project.

The students ask some teachers and students from other classes to test their project. They find that the music is too distracting. They change the music to other more suitable music. They get several requests for printed copies of the events that interviewees mentioned most frequently and of some of the screens of specific interviewees. They discuss some options for adding this additional feature but decide not to do so now.

Step Four - Reflection

After the students complete the project, the teacher suggests that each student should write a short essay answering the following questions.

- What surprises did you encounter while creating this project?
- What worked well as you worked on this project?
- What would you change the next time you do a similar project?
- How would you add to the result, if you had more time?
- What five events were most important to you?
- Did your interview change your relationship with the interviewee?
- Did the project cause you to become particularly interested in some specific event? If so, which one and why?

The teacher encourages each student to make sure that the adult whom the student interviewed gets a chance to interact with the completed project. This is more than common courtesy. It gives the student a chance to observe whether the adult has difficulty operating the project and whether the adult feels that the project correctly reflects his or her feelings about events. The best choice is for the student to arrange to meet the adult at one of the sites where the public has access to the project. Another choice is to invite several interviewees to the classroom to take turns using the project. Because the project is interactive multimedia, rather than being an audiovisual presentation aid, either of the above choices is better than hiring a hall and demonstrating the project to many interviewees all at once.

Table 11-9: Process steps

Teacher prepares
- The teacher writes a short description of the project such as "the class obtains, organizes, and draws conclusions about adults' personal memories of significant historical events."
- The teacher decides she needs to coach or refresh video skills and coach interviewing skills.
- The teacher decides that the students can determine who works on what and with whom.
- The teacher delegates most responsibilities to the students.

Teacher assigns project
- The teacher announces the topic and demonstrates some possibilities.
- She facilitates a discussion on tasks and possible milestones and provides coaching in hands-on video and interviewing.
- She recommends some sources of reference materials in various media.
- She discusses some suggested tasks.
- The teacher and students create the Assignment Sheet of Figure 11-11.

Students create project
- The students brainstorm in smaller groups.
- They bring together information, make plans, and develop samples.
- The group carries out a critique and generates some modifications.
- They determine additional work.
- The students reach the milestones and then complete the project.
- The class tests the project and then invites volunteers including some of the adults who were interviewed to perform a thorough test.
- The class installs the kiosk in the public library.
- The teacher records all significant creation experiences.

Reflection
- The students perform self-evaluation as they create the project.
- The teacher reflects on the project and talks to some interviewees and, when the project is complete, to some library users.
- The class evaluates the effort.
- The teacher reviews all feedback, makes an assessment, and then updates the process.

Summary

Mrs. Esther Weber, the computer science teacher, visits Jacksonville High School for a conference. She is very impressed with a multimedia kiosk in the lobby of the high school on a 20th Century History of Health Progress. She would like to have her students develop a kiosk to make practical use of the multimedia tools that she has been teaching. She decides that she will partner with a subject teacher. On returning to her school, she finds that she has ten volunteers. After thinking about it for a while, she decides to have her class teach a short workshop for the volunteers and then to have a couple of students work with each of the teachers on separate projects. The principal is so pleased that he decides to have an exhibit and award some prizes. To everyone's surprise, Mr. Gindel's third grade wins big.

Chapter 12

Research Magazine

In this chapter we explore:

- creating a multimedia project in which students electronically publish a magazine containing the results of their substantial interdisciplinary research.

- using a network to link students over a wide geographic area, as they collaborate on creating and distributing the magazine.

- delegating primary responsibility for success to the students themselves.

The Research Magazine project emphasizes using a computer network to create and distribute an authentic result. The Background section describes the magazine's structure and discusses how using a network enhances the project. The Theory section discusses goals that the project can help your students achieve and discusses how you can vary the magazine's topic in order to achieve different goals. The Practice section discusses how you can motivate and empower your students to solve significant problems in conjunction with students across the network.

Background

This chapter presents the book's last and most demanding project. The project is a multimedia magazine on which students in far apart high schools collaborate by using a network. The students use this magazine to report on their research into teenage health issues. The students use many of the techniques that previous chapters discussed, including brainstorming, interviewing, discovering and creating information, soliciting and expressing opinions, and summarizing. This project introduces using a network to apply such techniques across a wide geographical area. Students collaborate by traveling the Internet or one of the other precursors to the proposed national information infrastructure or information superhighway.

Students organize their magazine as a hypermedia document. Student contributors in different sites communicate extensively by way of electronic mail (E-mail) to plan and implement the magazine. Although upper-class high school students at one site lead the project, younger students can contribute as well.

Creating a magazine dedicated to a single serious topic encourages students to research facts in depth, obtain people's opinions, and then form opinions and draw conclusions. This format differs significantly from either a multitopic magazine or a newspaper that offers frequent high-level updates on what is new.

Users' Views of Project

To be concrete, we describe a project initiated by Owego High School.

During the summer, the teacher, Mrs. Torres, sent out a general inquiry from her home computer to some of the on-line forums to which she subscribes. She found that there was enough interest to initiate the project.

The teacher decided that she wanted a multidisciplinary research project of which the students would report back the results by using multimedia. She thought of a couple of topics that she considered suitable. She reviewed the topics with fellow teachers to be sure that others felt that her topics would be a good educational experience and lead to life-long skills. They selected teenage health issues as the topic.

The students have set up their completed magazine on a personal computer in Owego's public library. The magazine operates as an unattended kiosk. That is, people from the community can walk up to it and operate it without any additional help. The public library has provided an Internet service for the community to use on the same personal computer.

A user who approaches the kiosk encounters a main menu screen that presents choices, as shown in Figure 12-1. The user chooses Volume 1 of the Research Magazine and sees the screen in Figure 12-2.

The user also sees that the magazine's creators can provide diskettes that enable people to install the magazine on their own personal computers. Eventually, the creators would like to be able to send updates of the magazine to the kiosk and to users' homes over networks such as Internet. Eventually it will be possible to publish the entire magazine on the World Wide Web (WWW), which we discuss in the Appendix..

Selecting "What's in this issue" links the user to the screen in Figure 12-3. A user can select the button for any section and thereby link to the selected section. For example, selecting Facts and Surveys Index brings up the screen shown in Figure 12-4.

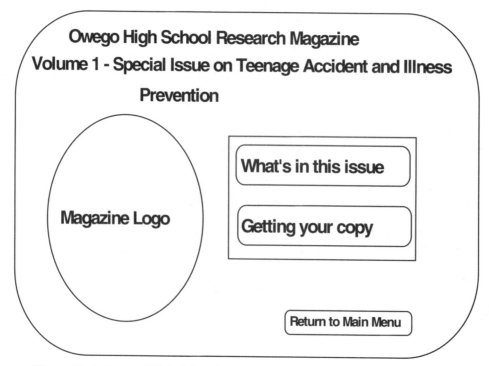

Main Menu

Community Calendar

Community government information

Owego High Remembers

Owego High Research Magazine, Vol 1

Owego High Research Magazine, Vol 2

Owego Elementary Critics' Circle

Academic Honor Role for First Quarter

Internet Access

Click on your selection

Figure 12-1: Main Menu

Owego High School Research Magazine

Volume 1 - Special Issue on Teenage Accident and Illness

Prevention

Magazine Logo

What's in this issue

Getting your copy

Return to Main Menu

Figure 12-2: Owego High School Research Magazine's introductory screen

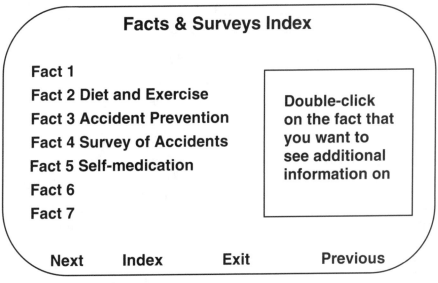

What's In This Issue

FACTS & SURVEYS INDEX

OPINIONS

CALENDAR & TIMELINE

STUDENT EDITORIAL

SOURCES, CITATIONS, CONCLUSION

Previous   Main Menu   Next

Figure 12-3: Contents screen

Facts & Surveys Index

Fact 1
Fact 2 Diet and Exercise
Fact 3 Accident Prevention
Fact 4 Survey of Accidents
Fact 5 Self-medication
Fact 6
Fact 7

Double-click
on the fact that
you want to
see additional
information on

Next   Index   Exit   Previous

Figure 12-4: Facts & Surveys Index screen

Figure 12-4's screen uses the list box technique that Chapter 11's Memoirs project used. This is an open-ended structure that allows creators and perhaps even users to add to the Facts. Once a user selects a specific Fact, the user goes to a screen such as the Fact 2 screen shown in Figure 12-5.

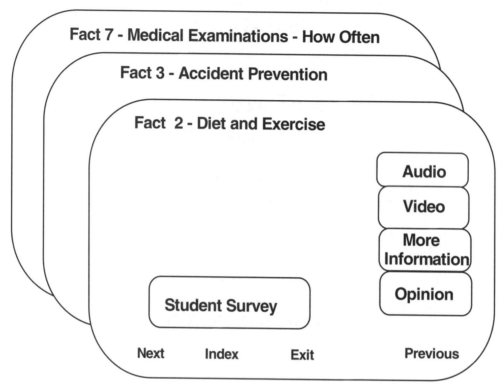

Figure 12-5: Facts screens

The magazine reports on several student surveys that accompany the Facts and Opinions. For example, for Diet and Exercise, there is a student survey that divides students attending the collaborating schools by age and sex, by who is on a diet, and by who exercises regularly. There is also a survey on availability of cardiopulmonary resuscitation (CPR) and other first aid classes along with a statistical sample of teens who have taken such courses.

Choosing Opinions instead of Facts on Figure 12-3's screen takes the user to the screen shown in Figure 12-6. On this screen, a user can specifically request opinions from professionals in the field, members of the community, or the students themselves.

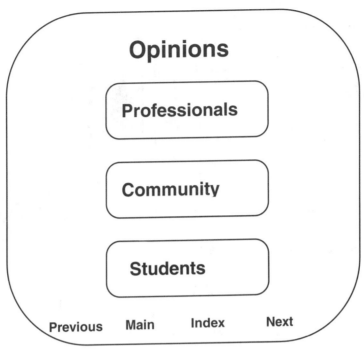

Figure 12-6: Opinions screen

Specific opinions are available through the Facts screens in Figure 12-5, as well. Here, however, the opinions are matched to the appropriate specific Facts. The information is the same. However, it is associated with other information in a different manner.

The Calendar and Timeline and Student Editorials are selections that the user might request. Last come the Conclusions, Sources of information, and Citations. These entries require more than one screen. Figure 12-7 shows the skeleton of a citation screen. It is highly desirable to have pictures of the students who contributed material.

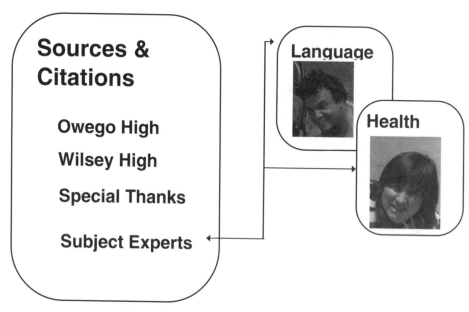

Figure 12-7: Sources and Citation screen

Creator's View of Project

The creators organize their effort according to the sub-topics shown in Figure 12-8. The students set up separate sections for these sub-topics. A section would be a ToolBook if the students are using Asymetrix Multimedia ToolBook, a folder if they are using LinkWay Live!, or a stack if they are using HyperCard. The students then construct and start using a skeleton set of sections. Initially, the sections are sparse, with only a title page and buttons that link the sections together. Soon, however, the sections grow as suggestions come in and as students make decisions on attractive icons, backgrounds, color schemes, and button layouts. The students exchange E-mail about what kinds of navigation and common controls they want. They decide that almost every page should have NEXT, PREVIOUS, MAIN, INDEX, and EXIT as navigation and control buttons. After some debate, they decide that EXIT will not take a user completely out of the project but rather take them to the screen that offers sources, citations, and conclusions. They decide that each Fact sheet will contain controls for audio, video, more information, and opinions. They decide that both the Opinion and Fact sections will be built around the list box technique that Chapter 11 employed. A user will be able to select any item in an alphabetized list. A user will also be able to go from a specific Fact sheet to a related Opinion. The students decide to use Multimedia ToolBook, although any authoring system such LinkWay Live!, HyperCard, or HyperStudio would also be suitable.

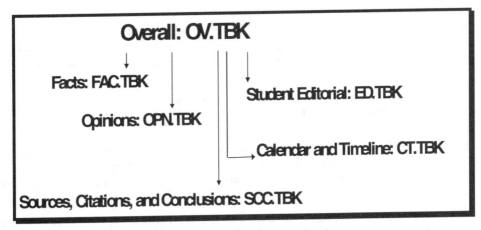

Figure 12-8: ToolBook organization

Project Networking

Students who collaborate on creating a Research Magazine project employ computer networks in three ways.

- Students use networks to communicate with collaborators and other people by way of electronic mail (E-mail).
- Students use networks to access on-line databases for information to include in the magazine.
- Students use networks to distribute portions of the completed magazine.

Even without a formal network such as Internet, students in two widely separated classrooms could use modems to exchange E-mail. A modem, which means modulator-demodulator, is the hardware that allows a computer to send and receive information over the normal voice telephone network. In some schools, a modem connects directly between a computer and the telephone network. In other schools, a modem connects to a local area network that, in turn, connects to several computers.

As an example of sending E-mail without a formal network, students in one classroom could use their computer to write a message and then use software that comes with a modem to tell the modem to dial the telephone number of the computer in a second classroom. The second classroom could be in a neighboring town or could be a continent away. Students in the second classroom could leave their computer's modem in the mode in which the modem automatically answers the telephone to receive the first class's message.

A formal network such as the Internet facilitates such E-mail in three important ways.

- Students can often reach anyone in the country or even anyone in the world without making a long-distance telephone call.

- Students in one classroom can place messages in a specified electronic mailbox. Later, students in a second classroom can retrieve the message from that mailbox. That is, the students need not have their computers available at the same time.

- In many cases, students can connect to a world-wide network without going through the slow part of the telephone network, to achieve high data rates.

A formal network also facilitates using on-line databases. Students can connect their computer to one network and gain access to databases in computers all over the world. Without a formal network, students would need to establish separate connections between their computer and each computer that contained data that they wanted.

Finally, a formal network greatly facilitates electronic distribution. Students may send portions of their completed magazine to the mailbox that belongs to each subscriber. Alternatively, students may place their completed magazine in their own database and tell subscribers how to come and get it electronically over the network. In either case, the students are participating in an important trend toward on-line publication.

On-line Publication

Many companies and institutions, including some major newspapers and magazines, are experimenting with on-line publication. Three examples follow.

- Access Atlanta, launched by Cox Newspapers and Prodigy Services, is a commercial service. It features an electronic neighborhood, which is an electronic way to catch up on news and discuss issues. It includes electronic distribution of news and other information using graphics, images, and other media. It offers more in-depth coverage and earlier availability than most newspapers or magazines can provide. It continually updates the news. It provides for easier user selection of specifically desired classified ads. There are on-line forums of community discussions about daily issues and interests. It encourages on-line discussions by having guest celebrities, educators, and publishers actively participate in the discussions.

- Francisco Bravo Medical Magnet High School in Los Angeles has had a multimedia newspaper for several years. The newspaper is distributed to all members of the school community over the school's token ring network.

- CompuServe, one of the oldest on-line services, now offers a multimedia magazine on a CD-ROM. It covers topics from entertainment to travel and shopping.

General Networking

There is much discussion about the Information Superhighway and a version called Internet. Other efforts that appear to be somehow related to the Information Superhighway discussion involve being on-line and using on-line service providers. There is discussion about the importance of making sure that every school is attached, somehow, to the Information Superhighway by means of some network or gateway to a network. As this decade moves on, this discussion will not only continue but increase. There is good reason for this.

This highway offers the potential of access to vast quantities of information and people all over the world. However, to take advantage of this potential, students need more than connectivity to the highway. They need to know how to work with on-line information, how to discover or find it, how to generate it, and how to manipulate it. They need to learn how to operate constructively and synergistically with people using this Information Superhighway.

In addition to Internet, students may have access to a commercial provider such as Prodigy, CompuServe, or America Online. Some students who have a connection to one or more of these services in their homes will want to know how to connect to whatever the school set up.

Research Magazine is a project that you can do now that deals with some of these aspects. Doing this project can help develop some important skills. We are in the early stages of what can be accomplished reasonably on the Information Superhighway. It is the intent of this chapter to alert you to some possibilities as opportunities that may come along in the near future as well.

The Information Superhighway is a metaphor that refers to using a computer that is connected in some way to a series of networks to access other computers' information and using this computer to also send information over these networks to other computers. There is a set of vocabulary associated with the Information Superhighway. Some important words and definitions follow.

- Internet is a huge network of smaller networks where people from many walks of life are connected. Internet is subsidized by the government. Many colleges and universities have host nodes on Internet and are places to go for more information.

- Other networks such as Prodigy, CompuServe, and America Online have many users and even offer access to each other's and Internet's services.

- Forums, lists, conferences, and user groups are all on-line bulletin boards where people can ask questions, answer questions, and make comments for all who participate in those groups to see.

- E-mail is generally a one-to-one communication from one user to another although several users can be copied. You write a note, submit it, and then come back later for answers.

- Real time or chat mode is a variation of E-mail in which you send a message to someone whom you expect to read the message immediately and answer the message almost instantaneously.

- A video conference uses a television camera that takes moving pictures of you and sends them out for another person to see, as you simultaneously see the other person.

- Being on-line, in general, means being connected to one of the service providers.

A network can help students to find subject matter experts with whom to discuss research activities. For example, the University of Texas at Austin sponsors an Internet-based service called the "Electronic Emissary" that brings together students, teachers, and subject matter experts. Each electronic exchange begins with approximately two weeks of project planning by way of electronic mail between the subject experts and the teachers. Thereafter, students communicate with the experts for up to ten weeks.

Examples of Connecting to Internet

Many schools have some sort of Internet connection. One common data rate is 9600 bits per second (bps). However, some schools are involved in pilot projects with telephone companies that provide substantially faster data rates. Two real examples follow. The first example paraphrases a response to a message we sent over Internet and is from Mike Diamond of Summerville, South Carolina.

Example 1:

"Our school has Internet access through a local college. We have a 9600 bps modem connected through a direct telephone line to the college's remote access system. Every student who has access has a private account name. Access requires a VAX Terminal Emulation (using Reflections4 for Windows) so access from homes is not directly available. I conduct a two-hour training session on using the system, the various services available, and access restrictions. We have only E-mail, Gopher, Telnet, and FTP services due to the college's hardware limitations to command line only. We do not have any multimedia access using Mosaic or Netscape which require a PPP or SLIP connection. Our system is an IBM compatible 486. So far, the students have used Gopher, E-mail, and FTP with good, self-directed success. By the way, not everyone can get an account on the college system. Their hardware disk space is at a premium and we have limited (nonprime time) usage. Thus, for our students, access is a privilege based on need and faculty recommendation. The local college has provided the access at no charge, but our school pays for the telephone line, installation, modems at both ends, and terminal emulation software. It has cost us about $1000 for one terminal this year. Because of the growing needs and access, we are attempting to add two more lines for next year. Hope this helps."

Example 2:

The IBM Yorktown Project is a more futuristic pilot project. However, it is important for you to know about it and projects like it. You might have the opportunity to participate in a pilot project of this nature. Also, this kind of thing may be widely available within the next decade.

ARKNET is a joint program between IBM Research and Cablevision Systems of Yorktown, New York. It is a prototype community computer network established by creating a digital network over the television cable infrastructure. The community network will connect schools including Yorktown High School, homes, libraries, museums, the IBM Thomas J. Watson Research Center, and the Internet. The focus is on collaborative work. Because the data rate is significantly greater than 9600 bps, simultaneous multimedia document sharing is possible between students located at different schools.

Finding Collaborators

A significant part of the Research Magazine project involves finding teachers and students across the country who might be interested in using a network to participate in such a project. Two of many approaches follow.

One way is to prepare a description, a call for collaboration, following a prescribed template for the Global SchoolNet on-line list. Guidelines are available not only on how to make this description effective, but also on how to design a successful project that involves using on-line communications. For further information, send an E-mail message to info@acme.fred.org and request information about "HILITES." To actually submit your proposal, send your description to HILITES@ACME.FRED.ORG. This group is also a conduit to international mailing lists. Another way is to prepare a concrete but brief proposal and send it by E-mail to one of the educational forums such as EdTECH of which the E-mail address is Edtech@msu.edu.

Theory

The critical notion of the Research Magazine project is that communicating with students in distant cities helps students to deepen their comprehension of a topic. The topic of teenage health issues has the desirable property that students in different states or countries have enough problems and solutions in common to make communication easy, yet have enough different problems and solutions to make communication interesting. Many other topics, but not all, have this desirable property. Students learn more about any such topic when they have the opportunity to see their own problems through other students' eyes, and when they have the opportunity to think about other students' problems.

Multimedia is highly desirable for a magazine about teenage health issues because this topic contains many sub-topics that students must see or hear in order to understand fully. For example, images or a video showing a CPR technique are truly worth thousands of words of text. The emotional content of health issues benefits from expression in audio and video even more than technical issues benefit.

Sending multimedia over networks is becoming feasible in the mid-1990s as networks become increasingly capable of carrying other media, in addition to text. Whereas live video conferences may remain expensive and scarce, networks such as Internet are becoming adept at transmitting files that contain audio and video. A file can flow overnight from a sender's computer's disk to a receiver's computer's disk, so that the receiver can see and hear the results in the morning. Interim measures, such as mailing VCR tapes, are available for use when necessary. Chapter 13's section on Making Suitable Analog Video discusses what your students can do to help video compression produce the smallest possible digital video files.

You can have your students create a Research Magazine project in order to achieve some or all of the goals that Table 12-1 shows.

Selecting Other Topics

You can use a project similar to Research Magazine to achieve different goals, particularly in the area of learning different material content, by using a topic other than teenage health issues. In fact, you could help students achieve a succession of goals throughout a school year by having the students publish several research magazines on different topics. For subsequent magazines, students can use the first magazine as a template in order to concentrate more on the issues and less on the multimedia techniques.

Although a multimedia magazine could have popular topics such as school or community events, we suggest selecting fairly serious topics. A magazine should not provide a survey but rather provide in-depth information about a particular topic for the users of the magazine. Creating the magazine provides an in-depth research, analysis, and synthesis experience for the students.

Table 12-1: Goals

Higher-order thinking skills
- Identifying a topic's most important issues
- Focusing on, articulating, and answering questions about the most important issues
- Designing a project with achievable goals
- Logical planning and thinking that results in expressible conclusions
- Organizing a work effort
- Preparing concise questions that can result in good answers
- Researching using a variety of possible sources of information, including on-line resources
- Selecting information, making conclusions, and presenting effectively

Group and interpersonal skills
- Working cooperatively and synergistically across geographical regions
- Completing a complex project on time
- Utilizing different sites' unique skills and providing for their unique needs

Content material learning
- Facts and opinions on topics selected
- Scientific method and thinking

Technical skills
- Difference between technical and economic feasibility
- Selection of and use of various delivery options including networking
- Construction and assembly of a complex, attractive multimedia project

We suggest that teachers and students agree on a question or set of related questions to develop and address in a magazine. Working on this project is meant to be both interesting and challenging for the students.

Some suitable topics are as follows.

- Do we have an energy crisis and, if so, what should we do about it?
- What are our health care responsibilities?
- How real are environmental concerns for our community?
- Hispanics are the fastest growing minority. What are their major issues and what impact will they have on society in the United States?
- Should we be spending money for manned space exploration?
- Is there computer equity and if not what should we do about it?
- Should there be universal access to the Information Superhighway and, if so, how should this happen?
- What role should the United States play militarily?

- How can the United States become economically competitive in a post-cold war world?

- What should the United States do about problems in South America, China, and Africa?

- How has the crime scene changed in your community and what are you doing about it?

We suggest such subjects for this multimedia on-line magazine for the following reasons.

- Our society is now dealing with these current issues. These issues are important for the students, their families, and friends. A project of this nature encourages and motivates the students to spend time researching, analyzing, and synthesizing information relating to these issues. The techniques of finding out how to prepare this magazine and work with others in a distributed geographical location are valuable life-long skills. Students are likely to maintain some of their friendships with other students who are far away, long after the project is over.

- These issues are multidisciplinary and can be best articulated using media in addition to text.

- The issues affect people in different parts of the country in different ways and to different extents. Using E-mail to find out about and appreciate the differences and similarities among peer students across the country by first exchanging information and then exchanging formal conclusions can be effective.

- Much of what people are discussing about these issues is not yet published. Students can gain well-deserved self-esteem and confidence from preparing an attractive and unique multimedia publication.

- These issues as yet have no well-defined right and wrong answers. As students delve into such topics, they discover additional tough questions to consider. Some examples are as follows. How much should California taxpayers pay to provide health care for illegal immigrants? Should we have a policy that everyone has equal access to something as vague and nebulous as the Information Superhighway if many classrooms lack basic essentials such as enough textbooks for all the students?

Although a teacher could select the topics, a second possibility is to have the students jointly agree with fellow contributors on the topics from a suitable list. A third alternative is to assign the students the job of identifying some significant community issues. One way to start identifying issues is to count inches of columns that local newspapers dedicate to specific topics over a couple of weeks. Another way is to consult with the community's leading public figures.

Practice

This section divides the project's practical aspects into four steps. We present the material in the form of one of many possible scenarios. These four process steps are summarized at the end in Table 12-7.

Step One - Teacher Prepares

We now return to Mrs. Torres, whom we introduced briefly in the section on Users' Views of Project. Mrs. Torres verified the feasibility of her class's gaining access to the Internet during the prior spring. Her district computer coordinator and principal were supportive and promised to provide her with network access from at least one computer by the fall. They discussed whether this access would have to be in her classroom or whether it could be in the library. She indicated that she would prefer access from her classroom but would be willing to have one student monitor and use a computer in the library. The school installed an additional telephone line into the library and equipped a library computer with a modem. They arranged to have Internet connectivity through the local community college. This means that the school's library computer calls the local community college's computer. This computer is connected to the Internet.

Mrs. Torres met with the computer coordinator to review her equipment and software lists. She asked for recommendations on software for E-mail that is able to send out files that contain control characters. She also requested additional disk space. Her students had taken and digitized video in a prior class. She reconfirmed that the video digitizing setup still worked and was available to her and her students. Because she has as a major goal that the students do the bulk of the planning and organization, she did not complete any arrangements with collaborators or other people during the summer.

A significant part of the project is for students to find efficient and pleasant methods for collaborating on the magazine with students at remote sites, for accessing remote databases, and for distributing the various media that make up the completed magazine. Students may elect to send some media over an electronic network and send other media by way of the post office, using diskettes or videotapes. Such decisions have strong effects on the project, so students should seek suggestions and guidance from the teacher. This is the opportunity for teachers to create authentic experimentation and decision possibilities for the students. What students learn about finding the best way to communicate will become life-long skills.

Mrs. Torres prepared to help students determine what media are reasonable to send over a computer network and what media require other means such as using the post office. She prepared Table 12-2. She left it for the students to fill in the actual cost numbers when they began the project in the fall. She noted that commercial providers of on-line service, such as Prodigy and CompuServe, cost about $20.00 per month and charge additional fees for E-mail, file transfer, and information access. She decided to ask her students to investigate these services' charges. There are several possibilities for sending the results of students' multimedia projects over wide area networks to people in other states or countries. The good news is that all the projects are likely to be of interest to others and that others' interest sparks and widens the creators' interest. The bad news is that there is no single economical way to send large amounts of multimedia, particularly interactive video, over long distances on-line.

Table 12-2: Cost of sending information

Network Provider	Cost
Post office	Two pounds cost $2.90 with priority delivery
Telephone	After 5:00 PM, about 10 cents per minute
Telephone teleconference	$4.00 per person and 53 cents per minute. This drops to 49 cents per minute outside prime business time. For five schools, five minutes would thus cost $28.25.
Internet	A modem costs less than $100.00. A telephone line costs about $20.00 per month. The school need not pay for access.

Students will probably decide to exchange some media by mailing diskettes back and forth. This method of transmission is economical and retains interactively once installed. However, using only a few disks limits the content to hypertext, a few images, a very small amount of video, and short audio clips. If recipients need any commercial CD-ROMs or laser-discs, the creators can advise the recipients to obtain them locally.

Sending large quantities of information through the network

Q: We have an Internet hookup with a modem that sends bits at 9600 bits per second. Why can't we send all media through this modem?

A: As an exercise you might have the students experiment with how long it takes to send a 3 MB file from their personal computer until Internet says the transmission is complete. The actual data transfer rate will be less than the modem's rated speed. Experiments are important to determine realistic numbers for planning purposes.

Time to tie up a modem

Q: How long is it reasonable to tie up the modem sending large files?

A: This depends on who is paying and who else is waiting to use the modem.

> Q: Who pays for Internet?
>
> A: The general answer is the taxpayers. However, a specific service provider may charge fees for your connection option.

Step Two - Teacher Assigns Project

Mrs. Torres discusses the following items with her class.

- The importance of the issues discussed, possible questions of interest and debate, some facts, and possible sources of reference.
- The desired output of the project.
- Good methods for collecting results.
- The time students have available to complete the project.
- The mandatory requirements of the project.
- Using E-mail with Internet or an equivalent access facility.
- The various roles the project requires and who might be interested in some specific roles.
- Some demos of on-line magazines. This is the first time she has used this project, so Mrs. Torres cannot demonstrate samples from last year's class's magazine.

She passes out some reading materials and gives a library assignment. She asks the students to bring back at least five references and five relevant facts. She suggests they look at back issues of the newspapers as well as other reference books. She allows a day for the students to complete this assignment, to discuss the project among themselves and with friends, and to think about it. She tells them that tomorrow she intends, with their help, to decide on who performs what functions. She shows them Table 12-3, into which they will record their decisions.

Table 12-3: Heads

Areas	Name of student who will head the area
Editor	
Asset Manager	
E-mail Coordinator	
Project Manager	
Department 1	
Department 2	
Department 3	
Department 4	

The column labeled Areas shows the major responsibilities for the project. She intends to get buy-in from the students on the table's partition of effort and to have students volunteer to head each area. She plans to wait until hearing back from other schools before assigning heads for the Departments. She hopes that other schools assume those responsibilities.

Mrs. Torres brainstorms with the class to determine the tasks for which each of these heads will be responsible. The class comes up with Table 12-4. They note that they can perform many of the tasks in parallel.

Table 12-4: Responsibilities and number of students

Task	Number of students including head	Head
Design overall structure and initial skeleton toolbooks	2	Editor
Design look and feel of screens	2	Editor
Coordinate communications	1	E-mail Coordinator
Prepare and maintain files of information as received	3	E-mail Coordinator
Conduct video and audio interviews	3.	Asset Manager
Get facts and survey information and set up these screens	6	Project Manager
Get opinions and set up these screens	6	Asset Manager
Manage sizes of media	1	Project Manager
Create time line and calendar	2	Department
Assemble entire project	2	Production

Mrs. Torres hands out assignment sheets similar to Figure 12-9.

Project: Research Magazine Assignment Sheet
Head:

Responsibility: Students in Group
Computer to use:
Compulsory parts of project:

Suggested Milestones:
- 9/9   Kick off
- 9/12   Agree to and assign heads
- 9/15   Send out solicitation to get collaborative schools and subject
           experts
- 9/17   Present plan for who will do what at lead school
- 9/20   Reviews subject, topics, questions, focus areas
- 9/25   Complete preliminary story board, spreadsheets, record forms
- 10/5   Get agreements with schools, send packages with sizes
- 10/15   Design screens for all sections and exchange them with schools
- 11/15   Report on facts and opinions collected, new information desired,
           observations, and so forth
- 11/20   Complete story board and navigation plan
- 12/01   Turn over all information to Owego High by E-mail or post office
- 12/04   Conclude discussion, circulate draft
- 12/15   Assemble project
- 12/18   Start distributing magazine
- 1/15   Reflect on feedback and plan for updates

Complete project by:
- 12/16 at 2 o'clock
Comments on project:

Figure 12-9: Assignment sheet

For the media input and output hardware that students will require for the Research Magazine project, Mrs. Torres refers to the chapter on Memoirs. She notes that students can develop this project using any available computers. Although it is possible to mix different types of computers, she seriously considers the resulting complexity. She decides to allocate about 30 MB of space for the magazine. She decides to have the students plan how to allocate that space.

The only new piece of equipment that the Research Magazine project requires is a network connection. For these connections, she specifies a 9600 bps modem with supporting software for sending E-mail and transferring files that contain text and data with control characters.

Although Mrs. Torres intends for this to be an on-going interdisciplinary project lasting a term or so, she knows that she must make sure that the students do not get carried away and spend so much time on the project that they neglect the rest of their studies.

Mrs. Torres could make very specific assignments. However, students can meet important goals by deciding for themselves what tasks are necessary and agreeing among themselves who will be responsible for each task. Thus, Mrs. Torres decides that she must coach the students toward understanding that they need to communicate well among themselves about who will do what and when they will do it. Mrs. Torres suggests that each student write down what they will do. She suggests that each of the Editor, E-mail Coordinator, Asset Manager, and Project Manager write down what they expect others to do, who they expect to do these things, and in what form they expect to receive the results.

As part of the collaboration process, Mrs. Torres encourages the students to begin by discussing the conclusions. This is a very important part of this project. Owego High creates and circulates a final draft for collaborators at other schools to review. Teachers involved communicate about the project's status and about what they can do to maximize the extent to which their students meet their respective goals.

A scaled down project could differ as follows.

- Eliminate collaboration across sites.

- Use a template that is simply the list as in Figure 12-4 and only do facts and opinions.

- Only do facts with no opinions.

- Don't do video or audio, just text and images.

If no Internet facilities are available, then this project can be carried out by using only the US Mail. Another alternative would be to find a willing parent who has some sort of E-mail service.

Step Three - Students Create Project

Each of Mrs. Torres' students participates in performing the following tasks.

- Reads the assigned library materials and researches the project.
- Goes over the goals of the project again with the teacher and demonstrates clear understanding of the goals of the project.
- Participates in the assignment of people.
- Reviews the teacher's demonstrations and project requirements in a smaller group.
- Reviews and reports on commercial on-line services to which they may have access.
- Brainstorms on what users need to see and want to see.
- Brainstorms on what is practical to prepare as opposed to what users might want to get.
- Helps decide on a division of labor to get started and how to allocate work as additional schools join the project.
- Works on plans to contact other schools.

After this planning period, the students prepare to send out their description by E-mail to Internet's EdTECH forum and the Global School Net forum. Together with Mrs. Torres, they agree on minimal conditions to participate and include this information in the E-mail message, Figure 12-10.

> **Call for E-mail participation**
> - Proposal: Call for contributing writers, subject experts, and researchers
> - Project: Research Magazine, Volume One, Accident and Illness Prevention; Volume Two, Information Superhighway
> - Dates: 10/15 to 12/15 for first magazine and 2/15 to 5/15 for second magazine
> - Purpose: Utilize media, on-line information, and personal collaboration to create a living reference on two critical issues facing society
> - Subject: Multidisciplinary science, technology, English, demographics, social studies, and current events
> - Grade Levels: 10 to 12
> - Number of participants desired: At least three remote sites
> - Project Coordinator: Mrs. Corey Torres
> - Roles: Owego High School has overall coordination and organization; other schools have department heads, writers, and subject experts
> - Expectations: Meet deadlines, edited quality work of specified size and formats, some video, audio, and images desired
> - Equipment needed: Internet connection, 30 MB to hold the final magazine, digital audio adapter card, S-VGA monitor, Windows, and ToolBook
> - Skill level: On-line text processing is required and prior multimedia experience is desired but not necessary

Figure 12-10: E-mail message asking for participation

In Owego's case, Mrs. Torres decided on issues and questions ahead of time. These decisions were included in the E-mail message. However, another option is for the students to include a list of possible issues as part of the E-mail message and invite other schools to indicate their preferences. The students can then decide which issues to answer and choose the exact phrasing of the questions.

The students then

- obtain teacher's approval to send the E-mail,
- prepare a videotape of introduction,
- review some E-mail responses, and
- send out answers to E-mail and also clarifications along with the videotape.

Students in the collaborating schools agree on what is included in accident and illness prevention for the first volume, which is scheduled to be published in three months. They agree on how people can best be equipped to use the Information Superhighway for the second volume, which is to be published in six months. Mrs. Torres decides to wait before doing more work on the second topic because she knows that what she will learn from the first experience will significantly affect the second one. Owego is delighted to find continued interest from several schools even after the clarifications and answers to their E-mail questions. Owego initiates a discussion with the other schools to refine and narrow the first topic to health care for persons between the ages of 12 and 20 as in Figure 12-11.

Accident and illness prevention focus areas

- Focus on ages 12 to 20
- Community programs for preventative care for teens - sample survey
- Cost of preventative care - sample survey
- Cost of not having preventative care
- Preventing common teen accidents
- Survey of common teen accidents - sample survey
- Preventing common teen illnesses
- Self treatment
- Importance of preventative care - interviews with public officials, school officials, hospital officials, and teens

---

Figure 12-11: Project topic refinement

The students must also agree on assignments, responsibilities, and schedules for people in several schools. Owego decides to establish an organization that consists of an overall staff of an Editor, E-mail Coordinator, Asset Manager, and Project Manager, along with four departments representing the major sections of the magazine. They agree on the Heads for each.

- Department 1 manages the collection and preparation of the Facts section, including the subject matter experts and information from newspapers.
- Department 2 manages the collection and preparation of the Opinions, including the editorials section.
- Department 3 develops the Calendar and Timeline.
- Department 4 manages Sources, Citations, and Conclusions.

Owego High School is delighted to accept Branson High's and Wilsey High's volunteering to handle Department 1 and Department 3, respectively. Willow Creek High decides to be an active contributor to all the sections rather than direct any one section. Willow Creek also agrees to find subject experts as required. Figure 12-12 shows the resulting organization.

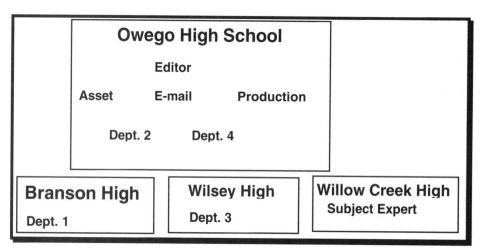

Figure 12-12: Overall organization

Each participating school creates video and audio clips and images, collects survey data and opinions, conducts interviews, and performs the school's unique responsibilities.

Owego High students, facilitated by Mrs. Torres, decide the information flow.

- The Editor sends overall specifications on the look of the magazine and the overall structure of the magazine to each of the heads. This includes an example of how the Editor expects students to send back information.

- The departments in the various schools develop the information in the desired format and then send the information to the E-mail Coordinator either by the post office or E-mail.

- The E-mail Coordinator categorizes the information or otherwise acts on the information and sends what is appropriate to the Asset Manager.

- The Asset Manager further customizes the information for the project and then passes it over to the Project Manager.

Owego asks each school's teacher to send an E-mail note indicating what their school commits to do for the magazine. Owego High impresses on them that this is a serious commitment and urges them to think carefully about what they sign up to do. There can be a strong tendency to agree to do too much, especially the first time around. Each school, as appropriate, may choose to have a formal learning contract with the students involved. It is important that the contributions become part of a student's academic responsibilities and not just an extracurricular activity.

For example, Willow Creek High School makes the assignments indicated in Table 12-5.

Table 12-5: Willow Creek High School's assignments

Assignment	Number of students
Collect data from city's newspapers for Facts section	1
Interview school nurse, a subject expert, and make a short video	2
Six fact reports	6
Three opinions with audio reports	3
Set up screens	all
Manage assigned sizes of media	1

Owego High School's Editor then

- sends out an organization chart specifying who will do what,
- sends out preliminary toolbook skeletons and other related information,
- agrees on weekly status reports, and
- draws some conclusions from their results so far and sends these out as the first week's status report.

Mrs. Torres tells her students that they have 30 MB on a disk allocated for the project. She requires that the magazine have at least one video clip, one audio clip, one animation, and several images. However, she does not specify actual numbers for any of these clips. She leaves it for the students to figure out how to make the effective use of the allocated disk space. She suggests that the students perform some experiments to determine what distribution mechanisms they will use for the different media.

The staff decides to send text, images, and some compressed audio through the Internet. However, they decide to send short video clips by way of two-day mail on diskettes. They also plan to send out the completed project using diskettes.

The Editor, Asset Manager, and Project Manager agree on the allocation of media across the departments, as shown in Table 12-6. They do not set a limit on text, because text occupies so little space. Images can be up to half the area of the computer screen. Video can occupy up to one quarter of the screen.

This is an example of how to read Table 12-6. Department 1, headed by Branson High, can have 15 images with 16 colors or less, 15 with 256 colors or less, and 1 video clip of 30 seconds or less. As you might expect, students want to be able to use more space.

The E-mail Coordinator conveys these allocations to the collaborating schools over the Internet along with the skeleton toolbooks. The Editor supervises preparation of these skeletons, for all schools to fill in and send back. These skeletons contain only text and are thus quite small. It is quite reasonable to send them out over the network. However, there may be problems with sending control characters.

Table 12-6: Media allocation

Media	Overview	Dept. 1: Facts	Dept. 2: Opinions	Dept. 3: Calendar-Timeline	Dept. 4: Sources, Citations, and Conclusions
Text	No limit	No limit	No limit	No limit	No limit
Images with 16 colors		15	10	10	
Images with 256 colors	8	15			7
Video clips, 15 seconds		2	4		
Video clips, 30 seconds		1	2		
Audio clips, 15 seconds	4		1		
Audio clips, 30 seconds	1		4		1

Problems sending skeleton toolbooks with control characters

Q: When I send my skeleton toolbooks, word processing documents, and images as E-mail, the person on the other side cannot read them. Help!

A: You need to send out your files as binary files rather than as text files. Your word processing files contain control characters that you want preserved. Your other files are not text files in any sense. You may need to check with your local service provider to find out how the students can send binary files. You then need to warn the receiving schools that they will be receiving binary files.

The two schools that have department head responsibilities design screens for their respective sections. However, they must do this around the skeleton that Owego High sends. Owego High School asks each school to rename their toolbooks with the first three initials of their school and with a unique sequence number. This helps Owego High to help keep track of updates. The Asset Manager and Project Manager know that they will have work to do when the toolbooks are sent back despite these preparations. Initially, there is a little confusion over who does what. However, Mrs. Torres knows to merely watch and observe and allow these people to work out the details themselves, if possible.

> **Using network messages**
>
> Q: When a student receives an E-mail message, what does he do with it? It does not look nice enough to include in any kind of document, let alone a multimedia document.
>
> A. The student ultimately will need to import the E-mail document into a word processor to clean it up by removing the E-mail routing information. However, he need not retype any of the information. Copying text from the word processor to an authoring system can be as simple as copying the text into a clipboard and pasting it into the authoring system, or dragging the text from the word processor and dropping it into the authoring system. The student may also save the word processing document as a file and then import that file into the authoring system.

Next, the students:

- plan information organization and design and work on a sample,
- develop story boards, navigation, and screen design,
- hold local peer reviews and then send results to other schools to get their opinions,
- collect information and assemble initial drafts of the project,
- brainstorm, based on new information,
- draw some conclusions from their results so far, and
- make plan revisions.

In parallel, others develop other pieces of the project. Finally, the students assemble all the data to make up the entire magazine. They send the result to the participating schools on several diskettes. Although the schools may already have the final version, this ensures that everyone has the same pieces. The diskettes are carefully labeled as the project version. The schools using these diskettes arrange with their local libraries to set up kiosks using the magazine as the main attraction. Two schools arrange for kiosks in an airport lobby and in a mall.

Branson High sends E-mail to the Owego E-mail Coordinator reporting that they have been unable to find any CPR classes for teenagers to take. The E-mail Coordinator sends E-mail to the other participants and subject experts asking for suggestions. Suggestions soon pour in. One subject expert volunteers a set of videotapes along with a qualified first aid specialist to answer questions. The speed with which this is accomplished using E-mail and collective ideas amazes all involved.

Branson High School discovers an on-line forum on preventing car accidents in the snow. Although this does not apply to Branson, Florida, Owego adds it to the additional sources of information Fact references for accidents. Several students who drive in winter check out this forum.

A student at Wilsey High School finds that she can send E-mail messages to her aunt who is working for an HMO in Ohio. Her aunt not only sends back some interesting facts, but also tells her about tools that will help the student to hunt for specific information on the Internet. These tools have names such as Gopher, Veronica, and Mosaic. Mrs. Torres observes the students' interest and excitement. Although she had not intended to get into this level of detail, she does invite a college instructor over to explain some possibilities. Another student discovers some royalty-free digital images to use in the magazine.

Getting Fancy

Q: What are some suggestions for making the magazine even more appealing?

A: Add background music to the introduction or grabber and to other selected parts of the project. Add backgrounds of images in blue and gray for each section.

Step Four- Reflection

After her class and their collaborators complete the magazine and install it at the school and public library, Mrs. Torres asks the students to write their impressions of what worked well and what did not work well. She suggests that other teachers who have been involved make the same request of their students. Each class summarizes class members' impressions. All the collaborating classes exchange their summaries.

Table 12-7: Process steps

Teacher prepares project
- The teacher begins by writing down a brief statement of the project, such as noting that the class organizes multiple geographically distributed students who will then prepare a multimedia magazine on a research topic.
- The teacher determines that her class has sufficient skills and equipment, but she notes that she may need to refresh their video skills.
- The teacher decides to let the students determine organization and grouping, but with her subtle suggestions.
- The teacher identifies and refines some of her goals.
- The teacher plans to delegate most responsibilities to the students.

Teacher assigns project
- The teacher announces the project and demonstrates some possibilities.
- The teacher facilitates discussion on possible milestones and then coaches some hands-on experimentation in video and in using the Internet.
- She suggests some sources of reference materials in various media.
- She helps the class identify suggested tasks and ways of encouraging and monitoring progress.
- Together, the teacher and students create the Assignment Sheet of Figure 12-9.

Students create project
- The students brainstorm in small groups.
- They bring together reference materials, make plans, and develop samples.
- They plan a group critique at a fixed time.
- They determine additional work, integrating the other sites into their efforts.
- The students pay critical attention to milestones.
- They reach their milestones and finally complete the project.
- They then test the project and invite volunteers to test it also.
- They distribute the magazine, mostly by way of the post office.
- The teacher records experiences and asks opinions of other sites' students.

Reflection
- As the students are working, the teacher asks them to reflect on their own efforts and how they might be more effective.
- The teacher reflects on the project and also consults with the remote participants.
- All participants evaluate the effort and the results. They plan for updates and possible use of CD-ROMs for the project in the future.
- The teacher reviews all feedback, makes assessments, and updates the process and the students. She especially stresses the importance of a team effort toward not just this project but other activities as well.

Summary

A remote user hears about the magazine from a subject expert who has helped provide information to the students for the magazine. She sends a request for the magazine to the magazine's editor through E-mail.

Handling requests for copies of the Research Magazine

Q. Our magazine, counting the audio and video, occupies 20 diskettes. We cannot afford to send out many copies of that many diskettes. What do we do?

A: Many requesters are willing to provide diskettes or money for diskettes.

Another option is to reduce the number of diskettes by compressing the information. With PKZIP, you may be able to reduce the number of diskettes by 15 percent to 40 percent.

Compression is important, because video files occupy a large fraction of the project's 30 MB. Computer scientists are making progress on compressing video, as we discussed in Chapter 2. You can experiment with compression techniques for AVI files or Apple video files. If you explore your Video for Windows or QuickTime menu, you will see optional compression formats. If compression makes your magazine's files sufficiently small, you may reconsider sending them all through the network. A compression standard called MPEG may be a viable choice in the late 1990s. MPEG compression may save significant amounts of space.

Still another option is to approach your local college or university and ask if they would be willing to set up a listserv, which is a special Internet database to contain your magazine or, as described in the Appendix, place some Web pages on their Web server containing parts of the magazine. If so, you can merely advise requesters of the location and name of your listserv and leave the getting to the requester.

Part C - Advanced Topics

- How do I help my students make their projects more effective?

- We want a multimedia project to help anchor our thematic unit. How can I organize this?

- I have limited equipment and time. How can I modify some of the basic six projects , know what I am left with, and still get value?

- How can multimedia help me keep track of my own ideas?

- How do we assess projects?

- What's next?

Chapter 13

Advanced Techniques

In this chapter, we explore:

- a wide variety of advanced techniques that you can coach students to use in order to achieve better overall style and quality in their multimedia projects, usually without spending more time in the process.

- when and how to introduce these techniques to your students.

- how students can improve their projects' interface designs, including screen layouts, colors, and fonts (appearances of letters and numbers).

- ways in which students can use each of text, graphics, images, audio, and video even more effectively after their first few projects.

- ways in which students can finish projects for formal use, present projects to audiences, and use story boards to plan their work.

- ways to practice advanced techniques.

This chapter's Background section discusses the why, who, when, what, and how of advanced techniques. The Theory and Practice sections discuss general and specific techniques that your students can use to create successive projects that are more satisfying and more motivating.

Background

In previous chapters, you have read about the theory and practice of multimedia hardware and software. You have read about our six projects. We hope that you have created some or all of the projects. You are familiar with all the media, including digital audio and digital video. You are familiar with some of the ways to distribute media, including using networks. You have seen how to select, invent, and customize multimedia projects that will help your students meet particular academic goals.

This chapter is about helping your students create even better projects in order to meet successively higher goals. The Theory section presents lists of useful techniques. The

Practice section suggests activities for your students to learn advanced techniques. Many of the techniques deserve their own books or courses. The References section suggests some books. For courses, see your favorite college's catalog.

Most of this chapter's techniques help students improve by working smarter and more efficiently, rather than by working longer. Nevertheless, learning such techniques does involve time and effort. Why should students make the effort? Which students can benefit most from learning the techniques, and when should they learn the techniques? What sorts of techniques will students find most valuable? How can you help students learn such techniques most effectively? Those are the subjects of this Background section.

Why?

Why should students learn advanced techniques for creating better projects? To repeat a familiar refrain, the reason must be that learning the techniques will help the students meet the goals that you set for the projects. Learning a technique that does not lead toward your goals is an instance of substitution and may even be counterproductive, as Chapter 6 discusses.

Learning new techniques may help students meet goals either directly or indirectly. For example, learning how to improve image composition obviously helps meet objectives of an art, video, or media class. In other classes, learning advanced techniques may have less obvious but equally strong benefits. For example, improving the composition of images that illustrate an English project can make students more proud of their results and can thereby motivate students to work harder to understand the English content. Making an animation that shows an ecological process more clearly can clarify the creators' understanding of the concepts involved. In general, students benefit from learning to produce a high-quality product. If students happen to expect their project to have real users, then anticipating the users' admiration will motivate the students to apply more time and effort to the whole project, learning more in the process.

We have received several requests for information about advanced techniques from educators and students. Educational consultants from several locations have recommended that we make such information available even to people who do not know why they need it.

Who?

Which students should learn advanced techniques? The students who most need a technique are those who cannot quite produce acceptable and satisfying results without knowing that technique. Multimedia projects are sufficiently authentic to motivate such students to improve, rather than hiding behind a lack of talent. The students who least need to learn how to make an incremental improvement in a project are those who are just beginning their first multimedia project, are concentrating on coming to grips with the software, and are satisfied by any success. Other students who can benefit are those who already produce very good results, without knowing the techniques, but who might produce excellent results if they knew more. In summary, all students are candidates for learning any given technique, but not all at the same time.

When?

When should a student learn a particular technique? When the student has a burning interest in the question to which that technique is a satisfying answer. In this respect, multimedia is the same as any other sort of education. In general, a student tends to go through the following stages.

1. Learning to create individual pieces of projects and settling for whatever works
2. Completing a couple of projects and settling for whatever hangs together
3. Applying fundamental techniques, such as expressing each piece of information in the right amount of the right medium, and providing useful links among pieces of information
4. Discovering and experimenting with many additional possibilities, such as making text that blinks, changes color, rotates, and slithers off the screen, and setting up excessively complex structures of links
5. Observing that not all projects and other multimedia titles are equally effective and starting to notice what characteristics make a project work well
6. Learning to use advanced techniques that significantly improve projects

Rather than hurrying students through the first four stages, you can be most helpful by recognizing when students are ready to enter the fifth stage. Students may tell you they have seen television shows, CD-ROM titles, or friends' projects that work better than their own projects. If not, you might want to demonstrate particularly effective multimedia titles. Students then have only a small step from the fifth stage to the sixth stage.

What?

What sorts of techniques will help students create better projects? Many advanced techniques consist simply of having students think about topics they previously ignored, consider using options other than defaults, and do something other than the first thing that comes into their heads. For example, one of the most important techniques for improving images is to look beyond the subject. If a student has never thought about the possibility that a tree limb might be growing out of the subject's ear, the student might never think to look. Other techniques involve coming to grips with the surprising fact that some things that are possible are undesirable. For example, a student must learn that having 38 different fonts available is not a hint to use all 38 on each screen. Most techniques involve thinking ahead and getting better results on the first try, but others involve improving partially completed projects. For example, students should strive to get the desired content in audio or video, but students may also need to know how to edit audio or video, at least to select a good short part of a long recording.

How?

How can you teach an advanced technique to all the students who need to know it? A good way is to help one student who needs the technique learn the technique and then let other students see the benefits she gains from the knowledge. In many cases, a student learns a technique best if you give a hint about the direction in which she can find her own answer, rather than giving the complete answer itself. In fact, particularly in questions of taste, answers may be right only if they come from the student and peer group.

Stopping an entire class from working on their projects to answer a question only once, for everybody, may seem efficient. However, stopping work wrecks students' trains of thought. Asking the students to concentrate on an answer that does not interest them at the moment tends to be ineffective.

Perhaps the worst way to coach students is to give them laundry lists of things to do and things not to do. However, the lists in the following Theory section will help you suggest directions and answer students' questions.

Theory

We are now in the mature years of the desktop publishing revolution. After years of being restricted to documents that could use only one text font and no graphics, we quickly learned that it is a lot of fun to use every available font and a lot of images. It took most of us considerably longer to learn that using restraint yields far better results. Multimedia, which can be viewed as the next step up the personal communications ladder from desktop publishing, gives us a chance to learn and teach restraint from the start. The most important advanced techniques that creators of multimedia projects need to understand are keeping projects simple, realizing that less is more, being consistent, and aiming at specific objectives. A multimedia project may be a constant battleground between the tendency toward excessive variety and the need for focus, simplicity, and consistency. Multimedia gives students wonderful opportunities to exercise creativity and spontaneity. It also gives them opportunities to learn to eschew surplussage, as Mark Twain advised us all. The trade-off is delicate, but important.

We first present general techniques that apply to an overall multimedia screen interface. We then move on to techniques that apply to individual media. Finally, we present advanced techniques for preparing projects for public display, techniques for conducting the presentations, and techniques for planning a project by using a story board. For these techniques, we draw on personal experience, on some results of cognitive research, and on references, which we show in parentheses and specify in detail at the end of this chapter. We urge you to add useful techniques to this far from exhaustive list and to share your additions with colleagues.

Q: How do schools help students learn more advanced techniques?

A: We have found that some schools start by teaching students to use camcorders, VCRs, and a video monitor. They then advance to using laser discs and digital cameras. They access parts of the laser discs with bar code readers. They then go on to computers and finally to multimedia projects. At each point, the students are expected to become quite adept at using a specific medium's creation device. Most schools, though, start with word processing on computers, then jump into elementary multimedia projects, and then move on to more advanced projects. Both approaches work well, although the latter is more common.

One particularly advanced high school in California has piles of brief reports that describe advanced techniques. When the students ask for the techniques, the teacher goes to the corresponding pile and presents the students with specific information to read and apply.

Another high school gives out style sheets and hints to improve the appearance and effect of multimedia projects. They always summarize a project's requirements in a short set of instructions. They have cookbooks available and have set up an idea file. Teachers participate in periodic short idea meetings. In this school they stress quality of style. One reason they have made this an important goal is that they find that working on style helps many students whose native language is not English become more verbal and have more confidence in their ability to communicate.

Some schools have defined levels of competencies for students that include multimedia and include advanced techniques. Students acquire these competencies by completing specialized sessions or projects within their standard courses.

Some schools have formal courses for advanced multimedia techniques.

Overall Project Style

- Design with the real or imagined users in mind.
- Consider the intended environment, including hardware and software. Must the project look good on a television monitor? Must it flow over a network?

- Identify the main points and summarize using the best media for each piece of information. Stick to the crux of the story without irrelevant items, no matter how cute or tempting they may be. Concentrate on content rather than style or form. If an image contains a strong idea, the image will look strong.
- Be consistent throughout the project.
- Use consistent formats in all screens or in each major section of a project.
- Use the same fonts, button designs, colors, border styles, backgrounds, methods of interacting with text boxes, control panels, and special effects such as transitions.
- Don't introduce an oval button in one place and then use a square button elsewhere, unless you have a real reason for the change.

Screen Layout

- Provide a title at the top of every screen.
- Provide a comfortable place to start scanning the screen, a place to go next, and a place to finish.
- People read English from top to bottom and left to right. Try to organize a screen the same way, even if the screen contains graphics and images as well as text.
- Put information that users need first in the upper left. Put what users need last, such as buttons to select what screen to see next, in the lower right.
- Concentrate critical information in the center of the screen. Color critical information in red and green.
- Divide all screens into the same zones or grids and place similar functions in similar locations on all screens.
- Avoid placing important objects or text near outer borders of the screen. Doing so would require separate eye focusing and additional eye movement. Doing so would also risk that a television display will cut off important information.
- Center text on screens that are primarily text screens.

Boxes

- Boxes around text and other objects help separate objects and help emphasize what is in a box.
- A box draws your eye to what the box contains.
- A box interrupts the flow of the page, for good or for ill.

Buttons That Invoke Links

- Provide meaningful interactivity.
- Provide a superb Help facility that contains answers to all questions that might occur to users. Let the computer take the memory burden off the users.
- Provide users with the feeling that they can control where they are going and know where they have been. Never expect users to keep track of more than three successively deeper paths taken with hyperlinks without providing substantial assistance, such as a graphical map depicting the structure.
- Prepare buttons carefully.
- The fewer buttons, the better.
- Use at most a dozen buttons on any one screen.
- Use the same style for buttons that provide the same controls throughout a project.
- Use meaningful labels for each button rather than a cryptic label or no label at all.
- Use button colors and locations as visual hints about what buttons do.
- Minimize the number of keystrokes a user must enter.

Colors

- Use at most five colors on a screen.
- Be consistent in coloring different screens. Do not alter the coloring scheme in the middle, without a very good reason.
- Use colors that match familiar meanings, such as red for stop or danger.
- Select screen colors that are pleasing to the intended audience.
- Use beige or blue tones at the edges of the screen.
- Use blue tones for backgrounds.
- Use bright reds and yellows when you want users to respond quickly.
- Present alphanumeric information in the spectrum of red, white, and yellow.
- Use only quiet colors, such as green or blue, if a project is likely to appear on television screens. Bright colors are attractive on computer screens but not on televisions.
- Note that natural images, that is, pictures of the real world, have opposite color requirements from graphics. Whereas graphics require a maximum of five colors, a natural image requires a minimum of 256 colors and benefits greatly from having as many as 16 million colors.

Backgrounds

- Use a background that is more interesting than a plain color, to add a professional touch.

- Do not make a background too complicated or it will distract users from the foreground's content and may make text unreadable.

- A close-up photograph of a piece of granite or a gradual shading from one neutral color to another are good backgrounds, but an aerial photograph of a city or a page of text are not.

Getting Attention

- Put images and audio that will attract attention at the start of a project. One glance at this grabber must draw a user into the project and motivate the user to continue. Make one keyword in the grabber **HUGE**.

- Use motion on the screen to attract instant attention. Consider starting a screen with motion in the upper left corner and later, when its time for a user to leave the screen, initiating motion in the lower right corner.

- Attract attention to important text with a flashing border. Note that making the text itself flash makes the text hard to read.

- Alternatively, flash an important message a few times to attract the user's attention to it, then stop the flashing so the user can read the text.

- Consider putting important material near where red touches blue. A user's eye goes first to the area of highest contrast, unless something on the screen is moving.

- Put a list's most important items at the top and bottom. A user's eye goes to the top item in the list first, then skips to the bottom item.

Synergy among Media

- In general, play audio of a voice along with a screen that contains video, image, or graphics, but not text. Do not expect people to both read and listen at the same time.

- Play a voice simultaneously with displaying text only if both media use exactly the same words. Even using an abbreviation in the text, and a complete word in the voice, destroys a user's concentration. Adding a spoken summary that plays while a user is reading a detailed explanation on the screen prevents a user from concentrating on either the summary or the details.

- Consider delaying the start of audio for a few moments to allow a user to read text without being distracted with audio.
- Consider letting the user decide when to start audio.
- Never make narration the primary way of conveying important information, in a sight-and-sound medium.
- Use narration and visual materials to reinforce each other.
- Do not present any sort of video, including animation, when you expect people to either read or listen to unrelated material. Motion is too distracting. Of course, playing audio and video of a speaker is fine.
- Use transitions such as wipes and fades to avoid abrupt changes between media.
- Use a few types of transitions consistently, sparingly, and with a definite purpose, rather than using all types of transitions for the glitz.

Text Techniques

- When in doubt, use large white characters on a pale blue background.
- White characters on a blue background may not be most effective for attracting attention or being convincing.
- Make sure text is readable, quickly and easily, on any display that must show the project, not only on the display used to create it. If the project must show on a television monitor or projection television, be sure to test it.
- Emphasize simplicity. In particular, use few different fonts and sizes.
- Use a sansserif font for titles and bullets. (Serifs are short lines added to some letters. A font with no serifs is called sansserif.)
- Avoid large blocks of text, but if you must use a lot of text, use a serif font.
- Use an appropriately sized font. Be sure the text is large enough to read. Consider centering the text.
- Use active verbs.
- Use parallel constructions.
- Be cautious about any use of alliteration, simile, or metaphor.
- Avoid pronouns.
- Round off numbers to indicate their accuracy.
- Avoid imperatives and personal interpretations.
- Use simple, everyday words whenever possible.
- Use upper and lower case. NEVER USE ALL UPPER CASE.

- Don't forget the fundamental hypertext techniques of using few characters per line, using few lines per screen, and using links to give the information a comprehensive and comprehensible structure.

Graphics Techniques

- Use graphics to guide users to important information, as opposed to distracting them toward unimportant information.
- When possible, tie words to graphics. For example, if a screen's title contains the word circle, consider basing the screen's design on a circle.
- Use graphics that are relevant to the objectives and ideas communicated in text.
- Make graphic objects concrete and meaningful and consider users' familiarity with the specific area.
- Consider how users interpret individual graphics, along with their ability to perform required interactions.
- Use particular graphic objects that interest specific user groups.
- Rather than trying to convey too much information in one image, use several simpler images.
- When graphics must contain a lot of information, emphasize the important information on which you want users to focus their attention. Use visual cues, such as labels or arrows.

Audio Techniques

- Clipping a microphone to a speaker's lapel gives far better results than using the microphone that is built into a video camera. Be sure that the microphone points at the speaker's lips. Place it far enough to the side so that the speaker does not blow air directly at it when she says "popcorn" or "telephone." This will avoid recording the sounds of moving air as lip blast.
- For best results, the interviewer and the person being interviewed need separate microphones on their lapels. If at all possible, route both microphones through an inexpensive audio mixer box and listen to the mixed result through headphones to be sure that you are recording both people at the same volume. However, merely using a cheap adapter that has two inputs and one output and connecting that output to video camera is far better than using the camera's built-in microphone.

Video Techniques

It is important to realize that creating a few minutes of professional quality video usually requires hours of work and several techniques that may not be at all obvious. The skills involved in creating excellent video do not come naturally. Although becoming truly professional requires years of experience, you and your students can create much better video by learning a few techniques. The payoff is very large.

Video records time sequences. Video can be particularly effective for showing how a person feels or how a machine works. Video of an interviewee's body language, including facial expressions, can provide far more information than a text version or even an audio version of the interview. For example, an ironic expression can reverse the meaning of spoken words. Video showing a machine, such as an animation of an internal combustion engine's cylinder and valves, can make the machine's operation clearer than any verbal description or sequence of still images could do.

Essentially everybody has internalized a standard for high-quality video production (although perhaps not of high-quality content) by watching television shows and commercials. Students quickly learn that users judge students' video against television standards. If video in a student's project contains major blunders, then users remember the blunders rather than the content of the project. Fortunately, students can create acceptable video without spending as much time and money as go into a Super Bowl commercial.

Planning Video Shots

Planning for effective video requires thinking about ideas and images in order, showing shapes, colors, wholes or parts, objects in motion, time sequences, different perspectives, shifts in perspective, and time relationships among events. It is possible to do a good job of all of this, just by pointing a video camera at the right subjects at the right times. However, selecting desired sequences from video made at different times (called nonlinear editing) makes it possible to do a better job more easily. Students need not dissolve from one scene to another on two faces of a rotating cube, but they can benefit from the ability to cut cleanly from one scene to another, rather than leaving a second of torn and shattered video between the two scenes. Many digital video editing tools make this possible. Editing is worth doing only if students plan ahead to obtain suitable video.

Making Suitable Analog Video

Students can create excellent digital video by first using a camcorder to create suitable analog video and then using a digital video adapter to capture the analog video in compressed digital form. Suitable analog video makes use of what the capture process does well and avoids what the capture process does poorly. Even people who are accustomed to using video cameras need to understand techniques that will lead to better quality digital video.

You will want to be prepared to suggest setups with which your students can produce suitable analog video and also to suggest changes to setups with which students have produced unsuitable analog video. Most students need not consider the details that follow, although some advanced students find the details fascinating.

The goal of the capture process is to produce good quality digital video with the smallest possible data rate and, for a given number of seconds of video, with the smallest possible number of Bytes of storage space. Video capture software gives students the opportunity to specify capture options that meet this goal. To reduce the data rate and file size, students select options that tell the capture software to:

- use a low resolution, suitable for a small video window,
- use a small number of colors, often 256,
- compress digital video within each frame, and
- compress digital video among successive frames such as by storing only the differences between one frame and the next frame.

We next discuss consequences of each of the above selections.

Whereas analog video fills a television screen, digital video often fills only a small window on a computer screen. A typical video window fills only 1/3 of a computer screen's width and 1/3 of the computer screen's height. This leaves the rest of the screen for text and other media. Since each member of a group of students usually needs a clear view of the digital video, it is important to create analog video in which the principal subject fills most of the frame. For example, when making analog video of an interview, students should concentrate on the interviewee's head and shoulders.

Moreover, because the captured digital video will be no sharper than the original analog video, students should focus carefully. For this purpose, it is highly desirable to set up a television monitor that shows what the video camera is recording. This allows students to focus by looking at a large color screen, rather than by relying on automatic focus or by squinting into a tiny viewfinder. Another advantage is that using a television monitor to show what the camera is recording allows all the members of a group to participate.

Whereas analog video may use as many different colors as a human eye can distinguish, digital video may be limited to only 256 different colors. To reserve most of the available colors for the principal subject, it is important to use a background that is a solid color. Because different brightness levels always count as different colors, it is also important to adjust the lighting to illuminate the subject and background reasonably evenly on all sides. However, allowing some shadows helps make a subject look rounded and interesting. Similarly, subjects should wear solid-color clothing, rather than plaids or stripes.

Whereas analog video can show an arbitrarily complex frame that contains lots of small details, digital compression can store a simple frame in fewer Bytes than a complex frame requires. Compressing one frame at a time is technically termed intraframe compression, because it operates separately on each frame. However, this is easier to remember by the name space compression, because it works by noting similarities among pixels in different parts of the frame. Space compression is another reason to use plain backgrounds and solid color clothing, so that digital video can use only a few Bytes to store unimportant parts, and can use more Bytes to store important details of the principal subject.

Whereas analog video can show arbitrarily large changes between one frame and the next, digital compression often stores only the differences between one frame and the next. As a result, lots of changes mean storing lots of Bytes. Compressing groups of frames is termed interframe compression, because it operates between frames. However, this form of compression is easier to remember by the name time compression, because it works by noting similarities among pixels at different times. Using time compression is extremely important, because by using time compression you can produce far smaller video files than you can produce using only space compression. However, time compression works best with a background that holds still. If the background holds still, then digital video can use more of its Bytes to store the principal subject's motion, such as a changing facial expression. Time compression is also a reason to hold a camera steady and not pan the camera from side to side or zoom the camera lens between wide angle and telephoto. Jiggles, pans, or zooms create motion all over successive frames and thus can require many Bytes on a disk. Suitable video requires either a heavy, solid tripod with a smoothly rotating head or a camera with electronic or mechanical motion suppression.

To summarize the above suggestions for creating analog video that is easy to capture as good compressed digital video, consider the following horrible example.

- Part of a football stadium is in strong sunlight with the rest of the playing field in a dark shadow.
- A distant announcer in a plaid jacket is squinting into the sun and narrating a play in which 22 other important subjects are running madly in all directions.
- The camera person is jiggling the camera, panning the camera from side to side, and also zooming in on the announcer.
- Small text scrolls across the bottom of the frame, giving statistics.

Designers of Direct Broadcast Systems, HDTV, and other compressed digital television systems say that football requires about twice as many Bytes per second as any other major subject matter. One way to think about making suitable analog video is be as unlike the above football game as possible.

Composing Video or Images

- Position any horizontal line, such as the horizon or a roof top, either 1/3 or 2/3 of the way from the top to the bottom of the scene, rather than across the middle of the scene.

- Similarly, position any vertical line, such as a tree trunk or the wall of a building, either 1/3 or 2/3 of the way from the left side to the right side.

- Place a small but important object, such as a distant person, at a 1/3 or 2/3 point, both horizontally and vertically, rather than at the center of the frame.

- Think of dividing a scene into an even tic-tac-toe pattern with two horizontal lines and two vertical lines. Place a strong linear object along one of these lines or place a small important object at one of the four intersections. These are all examples of using what is called the rule of thirds. Figures 14-10 and 14-11 apply this rule.

- Avoid juxtaposing a subject with a distinctive object behind the subject. In life, this does not look at all strange. In a picture, however, it can look as if a branch is growing out of a subject's ear.

- Place a subject far enough from the background that the subject's shadow is not visible on the background.

- Frame an image to avoid cutting off the subject at the eyes, nose, mouth, chin, or any major joint such as knees or wrist. Cut the subject off either below the shoulders, at mid thigh, or below the feet.

- Leave the subject some head room inside the frame.

- If the subject is facing or moving to the right, leave more space on the right than on the left, so the subject appears to look or move into the picture.

- Whenever possible, use a television monitor to see clearly what a video camera is recording. That is, you can connect the video camera's output to a television monitor. You can watch what the video camera is recording on the monitor rather than in the eye piece of the camera. This is an especially useful setup for videotaping interviews. Try not to rely on a camera's tiny black-and-white viewfinder for framing or focusing, let alone for involving a group in the activity. However, you may want to avoid placing the television monitor where the subjects can see the screen.

Lighting Video or Images

A single intense light, such as bright sunlight or a spotlight mounted on a video camera, makes unappealing pictures. It is far better to use diffused sunlight outdoors or use three-point lighting indoors as Figure 13-1 illustrates.

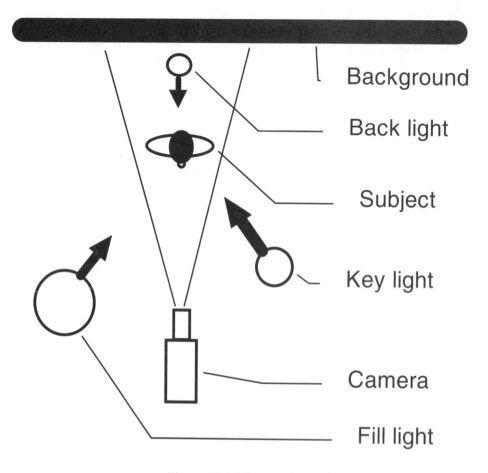

Figure 13-1: Three-point lighting

For three point lighting, proceed as follows.

- The main source of light is called a key light. Place the key light in front of the subject, but off to one side and above eye level. The key light will cast strong shadows and emphasize that the subject is not flat.

- Use a dimmer and softer light, called the fill light, to partly fill the key light's shadows. This will avoid excessive contrast. Place the fill light farther away from the subject than the key light is, in front, but off to the opposite side from the key light. The fill light is particularly important for de-emphasizing wrinkles and lines in an older subject's face. A neutral color wall that reflects other light is a perfectly suitable fill light. Avoid a sharp, bright fill light that creates a second set of highlights in a subject's eyes or on a subject's glasses.

- Use a back light directly behind the subject, but sufficiently high to be out of the camera's view. The back light brightens the subject's hair and sets the subject off from the background. Avoid an extremely strong light behind the subject, unless all you want to see is a silhouette.

- Be sure that there is some light on the background, too. This may require a fourth light. Try for a background that is plain beige and is several feet behind the subject to avoid shadows.

Try to avoid using outdoor light from a window as the key light, fill light, or back light. Outdoor light, particularly from a blue sky, is much bluer than is light from a bulb. (Technically, the sun has a higher color temperature than does an incandescent tungsten lightbulb.) Mixing lights that have different color temperatures produces unpleasantly colored shadows. A video camera can adjust automatically for either sunlight or tungsten illumination, but cannot compensate for a mixture. For the same reason, avoid bouncing light off any brightly colored surface onto the subject.

Editing Video or Images

The techniques that we mentioned previously will enable your students to capture useful video and images from the outputs of video cameras and digital cameras. Nevertheless, students may eventually choose to learn techniques of editing images to improve the images in various ways. Paint Shop Pro, for Intel-based computers, and Adobe Photoshop, for both Intel-based and Macintosh computers, provide sophisticated functions to enhance, revise, and customize digitized images in many formats. Many other tools provide similar functions

We help our students take each other's pictures with a video camcorder. We or our students then digitize the taped video to get individual images. The students import their images into Paint Shop Pro. Then they remove unwanted edges (called cropping), enhance colors, enhance other features of the image, reduce the number of colors to make their files smaller, and perhaps convert the image to black-and-white for printing. The students then use their images throughout the semester in their projects and, they tell us, continue to use the images long afterward, such as in party invitations and holiday greetings.

For example, one student wanted to include in her autobiography a picture of herself as a new-born baby. The best photograph that she could get from her mother showed more blanket than baby and showed her face sideways. After she digitized the photograph, she used Paint Shop Pro to crop just her face and then to rotate her face upright, as shown on the left side of Figure 13-2. She then explored other image editing functions including the Emboss function in Paint Shop Pro's Special Filters menu. She used this function to produce a background that set a subtle mood for her autobiography, as shown on the right side of Figure 13-2. Students may also choose to learn techniques involved in video editing. Some suitable video editing tools are VideoShop, for Macintosh computers, and Adobe Premiere, for both Intel-based and Macintosh computers.

Original

Original

Cropped   Rotated

Embossed

**Figure 13-2: Cropping, rotating, and embossing
images**

These tools work in conjunction with QuickTime on Macintosh computers and with
Video for Windows on Intel-based computers. With such editors, students can add
special effects, such as fades to and from black and dissolves from one clip to another.
Students can also import frames, animations, or images from other tools; import sound
files; and use nonlinear editing to assemble the video and audio in any desired order.
Students can then export results as QuickTime or Video for Windows digital video.
Figure 13-3 shows a screen that displays some of the effects students can achieve with
Adobe Premiere. Students can achieve similar effects with other digital video editing
tools as well.

Your students may well ask you about morphing. Morphing appears to convert, for
example, a chicken into a frog. You can obtain morphing tools for less than $100.00.
What you end up with is a sequence of images that start showing the chicken and
change smoothly to show the frog. Morphing is thus a source of synthetic video, that is,
of animation. With a morphing tool, all a creator must do is specify matched pairs of
points on the chicken and on the frog, such as corresponding eyes, ends of feet, and top
of head. The tool then creates the intervening images. Playing back the images
sufficiently rapidly gives video's usual illusion of motion.

Story Boards

A story board is a valuable tool students can use for planning, organizing, and keeping track of a developing project. Students may put the following information on a story board.

- Rough sketches of the screens, such as Figure 13-4, from a story board for a multimedia project about a Binghamton, New York blizzard

- Links that will take a user from one screen to another, such as the links that Figure 13-5 represents as arrows

- Notes about work they need to do to implement the corresponding screen on a computer, and other related tasks

- Identifications of the screens, such as by page numbers, to help the creators keep track of where the screens are in their project

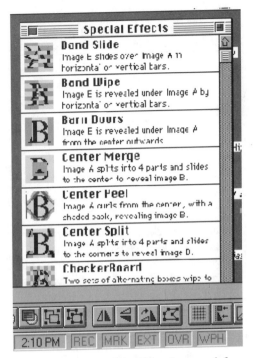

Figure 13-3: Adobe Premier special effects screen

Teachers and students may select any useful format for a story board. There is no official story board format. Students may want to start with blank copies of a sheet that simply shows a dozen empty screen-shaped boxes. Alternatively, they may want to start putting each screen's sketch on a separate index card, arrange these on a large sheet of paper, and draw lines among the cards to represent the links among screens. Students need not put highly detailed sketches on the cards, as long as they can recognize the sketches. A story board is a tool to ease the students' work.

Students may elect to use a draw program to create a story board as graphics on one or more screens. A story board does not become a normal part of the project that it describes. A user must not need to see a story board in order to use a project. However, including a story board in a project is especially convenient for others who later employ the project as a template or a source of techniques. It is good practice to make every creation self-contained and self-documenting. Multimedia makes this easy by allowing students to use graphics as just another one of their media and to store the media all together as the completed project. They might include a button labeled "For curious users only" that calls up the story board screens either directly or by way of a menu of such material.

Screen 12 - A Car Covered in Snow

Instructions to photographer: Take a photograph before the snow melts! Get a car covered in snow. Get several views; we will pick the most suitable one.

Digitize pictures and place in files named car1.bmp, car2.bmp, car3.bmp.

(Peter has checked out the camera and will take the pictures.)

Audio narration needs three buttons:

1. Discuss blizzard in Binghamton - Blizzard Button, bliz.wav.
2. Discuss effect on motorists - Motorist Button, mot.wav.
3. Discuss recovery process - Recovery Button, rec.wav.

(Rhonda will place the audio in the three .WAV files.)

Plan each audio segment to last no more than 20 seconds.

Instructions:

Snow covered car picture with Binghamton Blizzard title.

Three buttons for optional audio prepared by Rhonda.

Button for text pop-ups of description of day, car, and photograph credits.

Have standard buttons at the bottom of the screen.

Use Jan's background and fonts.

Figure 13-4: Story board sample

You may choose to require a group of students to prepare a story board as an interim milestone that demonstrates that the group has done thoughtful planning, rather than just diving into creating their project. Alternatively, you may refrain from mentioning story boards until students begin to notice that they have trouble keeping track of their project's structure in their heads. At this point, students will be eager to learn about story boards to solve a problem that faces them. Learning the technique of making and using story boards achieves the useful goal of learning to use graphics to represent complex relations among ideas and objects.

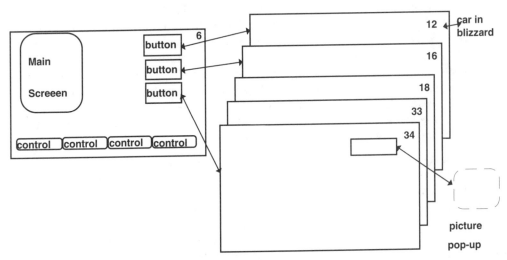

Figure 13-5: Story board showing navigation

Finishing a Project

Occasionally, it is important for your students to finish a project beyond the point that suffices for demonstrating it to other members of their class. In some cases, they need to prepare a project for a polished presentation to an outside audience. In other instances, the students plan to install the multimedia project in a kiosk in a library, send it to several schools located outside their city, or even send it as part of their portfolios to a college or job recruiter. We must emphasize that, in general, creating a project is more important to achieving its goals than is presenting the project to an outside audience or distributing it far and wide. However, there are times when students will want to prepare a version of their project for public consumption. This version should look as simple, uncluttered, and attractive as possible, in order to convey information well. It goes without saying that you and your students want to make the best impression possible.

In a similar vein, the most useful form for a completed project is a form that others can explore, augment, and change. That is, users should either be able to see menus, status bars, and all active parts of a screen, or else they should be able to retrieve these parts by using normal authoring system functions. Nevertheless, sometimes your students need to put finishing touches on a project that make sure that no one user can destroy it for other users, either accidentally or deliberately. That is, they need to know how to make it bullet-proof. Examples are setting a password, putting the project in a reader mode and preventing users from changing to author mode, and physically covering parts of the computer's keyboard.

As an example of a case where students will want to make their project uncluttered and bullet-proof, suppose your class set up a continuously running unattended kiosk near the main entrance to help visitors find their way around the school. Because the purpose is to guide visitors, rather than demonstrate underlying multimedia techniques, students should hide as much of the underlying structure as possible. Seeing the structures would confuse casual users, no matter how much seeing the structures would help another multimedia creator. Moreover, students should set a password in the copy of the project that runs in the kiosk, to prevent other students from experimenting to see how much wrong information they can insert in place of the correct information.

Most authoring systems provide some sort of script statements for the creator to not only accept input from users and then to act on that input by executing appropriate parts of the multimedia content but to perform initial screening on the user input. In more advanced projects, particularly ones that run in a public environment, your students may want to perform such a screening on whatever a user enters and ask the user for different input if there are obvious misconceptions, typographical errors, or nonsense entries. For example, if your students ask the user to enter her name and she enters 254.6, then your students may want to prompt her to enter a name rather than a number. Most authoring systems allow you to check whether a user has entered expected keystrokes. For example, in Asymetrix Multimedia ToolBook's script language, you could use statements such as those in Figure 13-6.

The second line of Figure 13-6 merely tests to see if the user pressed one of the keyboard's numeric keys. It tests for the numbers 48 through 57, which are the ASCII codes for characters 0 through 9. If you want your students to do some such function, you look at the authoring system's reference manual under keyboard, keystroke input, or user input to find the exact script to use.

Your students may also want to provide a way for the user to enter an answer and for

```
to handle keyChar key
if (key > 47) and (key < 58)
  request "please do not type any numbers."
else
```

Figure 13-6: A script to check for numeric input

the project to test whether the answer is approximately correct. For example, LinkWay Live! provides a MATCH statement in which you can use an asterisk to indicate that you accept any character in the asterisk's position. Thus, as Figure 13-7 shows, you could ask the user to enter the capital of New York state and use the MATCH statement and an IF statement to test the answer.

```
INPUT "What is the capital of New York state?", ANSWER;

MATCH "al***y, ANSWER";

If result>0 MSG "GOOD ENOUGH, ALBANY";
```

Figure 13-7: A script to accept approximately correct input

Finishing up a project can include having the students:

- spell check the project thoroughly.
- remove from the screen all menu bars and other tools that are useful only in author mode.
- put range checks wherever users can enter keystrokes.
- get outside testers to check that they can use it without becoming lost, that is, that they know what to do next at every point when they are using the project.
- create a run-time version if appropriate and possible with the authoring system and tools used. See Chapter 4 for information on run-time environments.
- create instructions on how to install and start the title from diskettes. The best instructions are ones that can be placed on the diskette labels. A good instruction will say what equipment a user requires and will say what a user types after placing the first diskette in a diskette drive.
- create the diskettes and optionally compress the diskettes' content.
- test the diskettes on some system other than the one on which they created the project, to ensure that your installation procedure works and that your students have included all the parts that are needed to run the project.

If creators intend a project for public presentation, we advise them to plan a mansion but build only a room. For example, plan a magazine with six sections but first publish only two sections, if that is the most on which they can be sure to do a high-quality job. Emphasize quality over quantity. If users receive a project well, add more sections later.

Presenting a Project

In general, any user can navigate through a good student-created multimedia project. A project is not primarily an audiovisual aid for the creators to use during presentations. Nevertheless, for authenticity, you may want to encourage students to present their projects to their class and to wider audiences whenever possible. The presentation techniques that the students need to know depend on the type of project they are presenting.

One collection of techniques applies if the creators have organized their project as a simple creator-selected tour with little or no interaction. In this case, the creator typically

- explains the project's purpose and intended audience,
- runs the tour, without trying to talk over the audio portions,
- summarizes the extent to which the project achieved its purpose, and
- answers questions.

The other collection of techniques applies if the creators have endowed their project with significant interactive user navigation. This case presents the creator with the challenge of giving each member of the audience the vicarious experience of interacting with the project. That is, the creator should strive to give members of the audience the feeling of navigating through the project, selecting desired portions of the project's material. Because this challenge is unfamiliar and your students will need considerable coaching, we list these presentation techniques in detail. To demonstrate an interactive project effectively, the creator:

- explains the project's purpose and intended audience.
- brings up the project's first screen.
- allows the audience to listen to the screen's instructions or other audio, if any, rather than talking over the audio or trying to explain the audio.
- gives the audience time to read the screen, such as by reading the screen silently.
- reads important and brief parts of the screen to the audience, and discusses these parts as appropriate.
- emphasizes that the user selects one of several choices that the screen offers, in order to determine what to see next and perhaps hear next.
- states clearly what selection the presenter intends to make, then tells how to make the choice such as by clicking a particular button, then pauses, and only then actually makes the choice so that the audience sees and perhaps hears the

result. The pause is crucial. The pause takes account of the fact that the presenter's hand is, indeed, far quicker than the audience's eyes. If the presenter actually makes the selection as he or she states what the selection is, the audience will not have time to see what the presenter did.

- makes at most one or two more such selections and then solicits subsequent selections from the audience. This technique quickly turns a presentation into an interaction between the audience and the project.

- decides when to end this main part of the presentation, based on time available or audience interest, without necessarily covering all the material in a large project.

- summarizes the extent to which the project achieved its purpose.

- answers questions.

Before beginning any presentation, it is important for the presenter to test whether the audience will be able to read the screens and hear the audio. The only way to make this test is to use the actual equipment, in the presentation room, under the actual illumination that will exist during the presentation. In an optimal setup, the presenter will be able to face the audience, rather than having to turn away from the audience in order to see a screen. This usually requires a separate computer screen for the presenter. It is perfectly reasonable to have different members of a group of creators perform different steps in the above list. Students will find that the most difficult technique is keeping quiet while the audience listens to audio or reads screens. Students will need at least one practice run to use the above techniques successfully and to feel confident about their presentations.

Practice

This section suggests exercises that either you or your students can use to try out some of the Theory section's advanced techniques. Because many techniques involve matters of taste, rather than of fact, they are especially suitable for your class and you to explore as colearners. Although we phrase the exercises with respect to a K-12 class, the exercises are equally suitable for a higher education class, for adult self-study, and for immediate practical application. In particular, to achieve excellent results in the projects that use video, you would be well advised to take a few minutes to practice the Video exercise before setting up lighting that students use. If possible, leave the lighting set up for use during an entire school year. Video or images that students take with normal room lighting may not digitize well. Fortunately, correctly positioned lights are high enough to be out of the way, leaving the space available for other uses.

Overall Style

Have your students divide a large sheet of paper into five rows and five columns. In the left column, ask the students to identify in crisp, short phrases the five most significant events in their lives. In the second column, ask them to write the name of the medium in which they could most effectively represent each event. Mention that text may not always be the best answer. In the third column, ask them to write what information they would express about the event using the selected medium. In the fourth column, ask them to write the metaphor that they would use for the background of each event. Finally, in the right column, ask each student to sketch the first screen the student would use in a project about that event.

Video

Help students set up three-point lighting and take turns making videos of one another. Connect the video camera's video output to a television monitor so that the whole class can see what the camera is recording. Observing the results of turning on only one of the lights, in turn. Note the effects of moving the fill light closer to and farther away from the subject, to create weaker and stronger shadows, respectively. For an interestingly ominous effect, try using only a key light and placing it near the subject's knees, pointing up. Try a silhouette with only a back light.

For each student, digitize a short clip of video and at least one image. Practice changing the contrast and brightness of the image, using controls in the digitizing software or in an image editing tool. Avoid having any part of the resulting images too light or too dark. Consider offering image editing to one or two students as a specialty.

Check your understanding of analog video that will become good digital video by taking analog video of a football game. Also take analog video of a subject that has far less motion, contrast, and detail. Practice capturing both sorts of analog video as digital video, and observe the different results.

Audio

Record an interview using only a video camera's microphone. Repeat the interview using two lapel microphones. Play both recordings back and compare sound qualities. Digitize both recordings, play back the resulting digital audio, and compare the results. Digitize some high-quality music and some voice, trying out different numbers of samples per second and numbers of bits per sample. Note that the higher settings, which produce relatively large numbers of Bytes per second, do improve music quality but do not improve voice quality.

Color

Pass around a large box of crayons. Ask each student to select two crayons at random and then answer the following questions about the colors they selected.

1. Do any companies use your colors in their logos or recognizable products, such as yellow for Kodak film?

2. Are your colors good for elderly people who may have difficulty distinguishing different shades of blue and who benefit from bright colors?

3. Are your colors suitable for color-blind people? Color-blind people may have trouble distinguishing red from black and green from gray. They can read blues and yellows.

4. Are your colors potentially inappropriate for cultural or social reasons? Note that pink, yellow, and black have at times been controversial.

5. Are your colors environmental, such as green for vegetation, blue for water, or yellow for desert?

6. Are your colors strong-reaction colors such as red?

7. Do you have holiday colors such as orange for Halloween or red for Christmas?

8. Are your colors associated with some time frame, such as pink and gray for the 1950s?

9. Do your colors look well together on a computer screen, television monitor, projector, and color printer?

Story Board

Generate a story board for a project, such as one of the six that this book describes. Use one of the three methods discussed in the Theory section, namely sheets with blank screen images, index cards on a large sheet of paper, and computer graphics. Consider making the same story board using the other two methods or a method that you devise and comparing the results.

Screen Design

Figure 13-8 shows sketches of eight screens that illustrate some of the Theory section's techniques. Elaborate on each sketch as the basis for redesigning one of the screens of some project, such as the ones that Chapters 7 through 12 describe. Experiment with alternatives. Do they work as well?

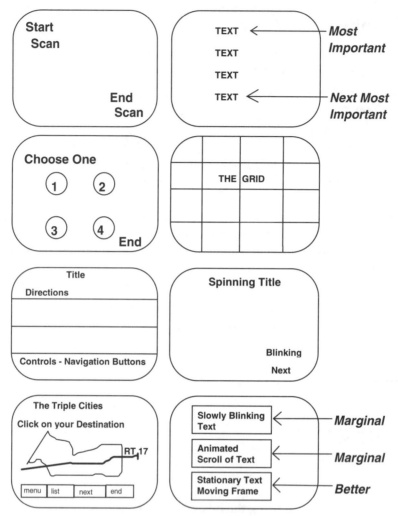

Figure 13-8: Screen layout examples

Buttons and Backgrounds

Using the Theory section's techniques, have your students devise alternatives to one project's buttons and background. What determines whether the alternatives are improvements?

Selecting from Masses of Content

Suppose that your students have almost completed a project. The project has become quite large and has lots of good information spread across many screens. Find a way users can locate specific text phrases or words. See if your authoring system provides a search tool. Is this search available only to creators or can you also allow users of the project to search for particular text?

Capture and Convert

Set up a computer for screen capture, that is, for converting the contents of a selected screen into a file for use in a project. Bring up any interesting application, such as an image editor or any multimedia title. If you are using an Apple Macintosh, use the keys Shift-Command-3 to capture the screen to a PICT file. If you are using Windows, you can use Shift-Alt-Print Screen to capture the screen to the Windows clip board and then paste the clipboard into an application. Other techniques are to use a program such as LwCaptur, which is supplied as a part of LinkWay Live! for DOS, or HiJaak Pro.

Use an authoring system's image conversion utilities or the extensive conversion utilities in a program such as HiJaak Pro to convert the file that you captured to your authoring system's format. Import the resulting image into a project. Write a list of the file formats that the capture program can produce and a separate list of the file formats that your authoring system's utilities can accept. Be on the lookout for screens to capture and for clips that have these file formats.

> **Q: I see that it is reasonably easy to convert between different image types, after I find a good utility. However, a friend brought me some really nifty audio files from a DOS environment that we want to use on our Macintosh. What can we do?**
>
> **A: You have two challenges. One is to convert the DOS environment's audio format, most likely WAV, into the Apple's most common audio format, AIFF. The other is to convert the result to the diskette format that Apple recognizes. The good news is that there are utilities to do both. Some authoring systems such as Macromedia's Director will allow you to save directly to diskette in either format.**

Finish a Project

Have your students experiment with different ways to provide help to different sorts of people who user multimedia projects. Look at some existing titles and report back to the class. Experiment with different methods of getting information from different sorts of users into a project. Experiment with using scripts or other techniques to screen such information. Consider different sorts of users, such as children from three to five years old or senior citizens. For example, suppose the real or imagined users of a project on transportation safety will be in the lobby of the town hall. Consider how your students' project can get users to enter their names and how the project can hint that different users should select different sections of the project.

For additional practice, you might have your students report on what techniques public kiosks such as automatic teller machines use to get desired user inputs.

Summary

The middle section of this chapter is an organized list of techniques that you will want to keep in mind for coaching selected students at appropriate times. The first section discusses how to make decisions such as who needs the techniques and when. The last section hints that you might practice as many of the techniques as possible, to fix them in your mind and to have them ready for use.

References

Badgett, Sandler. *Creating Multimedia on Your PC*. New York, New York: John Wiley and Sons, Inc., 1994.

ChanLin, Okey, and Reinking. "Computer Graphics: Implications for Instructional Design." *ADCIS 34th Conference*. University of Georgia, 1992.

Chapman. "Color Coding and the Interactivity of Multimedia." *The Journal of Educational Multimedia and Hypermedia*. Vol. 2 No. 1, 1993.

Laurel, Brenda. *The Art of Human-Computer Interface Design*. Reading, Massachusetts: Addison Wesley, 1990.

Miller, Crespo, and Kennedy. "An Investigation of the Legibility of a Color Anti- Aliased CRT Typeface." *Technical Report 54.518*. Armonk, New York: IBM, August 21, 1989.

Shelton. "Effective Script Design - How to Make a Film or Video Deliver Your Message." *Photo>Electronic Imaging*, September 1992.

Strauss, Roy. "Multimedia for the Masses: Designing for the TV Screen." *AVVideo*, Vol. 14 No. 2, February 1992.

Yager, T. *The Multimedia Production Handbook for the PC, Macintosh and Amiga*. Cambridge, MA: Academic Press Professional - Harcourt Brace & Company, 1993.

NewMedia. NewMedia Magazine, 901 Mariner's Island Blvd., Suite 365, San Mateo, CA 94404. Telephone (415) 573-5150, FAX (415) 573-5131.

"Premiere 4.0," Adobe Systems, 1585 Charleston Rd., Mountain View, CA 94043, (800) 833-6687.

"VideoShop 3.0," Avid Technology Inc., Metropolitan Technology Park, 1 Park West, Tewksbury, Massachusetts 01876, (800) 949-2843.

Chapter 14

Production Company

In this chapter, we explore:

- how students can achieve academic results and acquire life-long skills by organizing themselves into an amateur multimedia production company.

- details of a process that members of a production company can follow.

- types of multimedia projects and services that members of a production company can offer to their school and community.

- some concrete examples of services that members of a production company can provide for other students who are creating projects that involve video and audio.

- corresponding multimedia hardware and software skills that a school needs, either from a production company or from an educational technologist.

This chapter's Theory section discusses setting up and operating a student production company. The Practice section presents scenarios of projects and services that students can perform as members of such a company. Several scenarios emphasize applying a detailed process that has seven sub-steps. Other scenarios concentrate on actual hardware and software knowledge.

Background

In earlier chapters, you read about multimedia technologies and techniques and about creating several projects. The chapter before this one showed you separate close-up views of how your students can use advanced techniques to make even more effective use of specific media. This chapter shows you a wide-angle view of how your students can achieve significant academic outcomes by organizing themselves into a multimedia production company.

A multimedia production company is a group of people organized to produce demanding multimedia projects over a long time interval, such as a semester or a school year, and to offer multimedia services. Setting up a production company may be part of the regular curriculum, may be the subject of a separate course, may be a summer project, or may be an extracurricular noncredit activity such as a club. Being a member of such a company can offer students extensive experiences in planning, scheduling, making and keeping commitments, taking responsibility, and being of service to the school and the community.

A production company can include students from several classes, several subjects, several grades, and even more than one school. The production company approach applies particularly well to classes that are about to begin open-ended projects studying major themes or issues. Production companies are suitable for middle schools or high schools.

Theory

Setting up and operating a production company provide students with an additional dimension of learning and experience. It can be the means to teach several significant life-long skills, such as achieving high-quality results by cooperative work and continual improvement, understanding the importance of on-time completion in complex environments, and working with the prospective recipient of the students' production efforts.

Roles

The most important feature of a production company is that each student plays a specific role. A production company thus requires a different sort of cooperation from a less formal group in which each student may do a little of everything. Some examples of students' roles in a production company are as follows.

- Director, manager, or producer
- Arranger of performances, sales, and publicity
- Content expert, researcher
- Script writer
- Screen designer
- Graphic artist or animator
- On-screen video personality
- Narrator
- Legal eagle, primarily obtaining permission to use others' work
- Accountant who deals with expenses and income

Matching students to roles in a multimedia production company is no different from matching students to roles in a school play or on a sports team. Because you may know lots more about this subject than we do, we limit our discussion to the following few reminders. Many important roles are off stage, such as the roles of connecting and operating lights, selling tickets, or operating a sound system. You may decide to encourage individual students to play roles at which they have already demonstrated excellence. Alternatively, you may encourage students to try new activities or even to practice activities at which they have demonstrated that they need extensive practice in order to meet minimum requirements. You may or may not decide to interchange students' roles for each successive project. You must decide the extent to which you will encourage the students to determine their own roles. In assigning roles, you may often need to weight the important long-term goal, helping the students to learn, more heavily than the short term goal, producing an outstanding project.

Students do not play all the roles in a production company. One of the most important roles is yours. You help students achieve the optimal academic results from creating large and long-term multimedia projects. You also help students acquire understanding and skills that they can employ throughout their lives. You may elect to help by suggesting specific organizations and processes, by selecting group leaders, and by participating in planning for complete projects. Alternatively, you may elect to motivate brainstorming and critique sessions, ask judicious questions, and otherwise stand well back until your students ask you questions.

With constructive coaching, you can help students use brainstorming sessions to produce useful ideas and use critique sessions to evaluate ideas. Because the students are working toward an authentic outcome, you can easily make the point that the goal of a brainstorming or critique session is to improve the project, rather than to put down students' ideas.

We advise you to encourage your students to use pieces of existing multimedia content whenever doing so is legal, is ethical, and contributes to meeting your academic objectives. You can also encourage your students to prepare their own media in forms that they can reuse. For example, if a project involves categorizing 500 slides, the creators might develop a single multimedia form that several people can use while entering and displaying information about each slide. Using a common template helps to make the creation process efficient and helps to make the result consistent.

Setting up and operating a production company introduces the important role of the client. A project's client is often a different person from the project's intended user. To borrow an evocative metaphor from the advertising industry, dog owners, rather than dogs, select and purchase dog food. Students must learn that clients, rather than users, determine whether the students produced the desired project and determine whether the students' production company will get repeat business. Some examples of clients who commission and evaluate projects are teachers, principals, business people, and parents.

Projects and Services

Students who are members of a production company can create projects for people in the school and for the surrounding community. Equally important, such students can provide multimedia services for other students, for teachers, for nearby nonprofit organizations, and even for local businesses. Students in a production company can conduct one-on-one peer tutoring, can install and set up equipment, and can create multimedia projects for others to use.

We have visited widely separated and diverse cities to discuss large multimedia projects with members of student production companies. Such activities generally run for at least a couple of months. Some examples of students' projects are as follows.

- *The Pit and the Pendulum* is a thematic project in which California students not only explored the literary aspects of Poe's work but also explored the physics of a long pendulum swinging in a stairwell and the biology of the rate at which a rat can chew through a rope.

- *Hospital Kiosks* is a community service project. Students in Georgia produced child safety information for kiosks in a hospital.

- *School Newspaper* tells students at a school in Los Angeles, California, what is going on in their school. Students create daily on-line multimedia articles as well as features that describe current activities. Other students access the resulting newspaper by way of local area networks throughout the school.

- *Call of the Wild* is a California project that explored many aspects of living in the Arctic, using Jack London's novel as a springboard.

- The Academy of Multimedia is a Salt Lake City, Utah student multimedia production company that creates computer-based instruction titles using the QUEST authoring system. The students worked initially under a grant from IBM and Allen Communications.

Development Process

A production company gives students the opportunity to employ a more detailed version of the last two steps of the overall process that Chapter 6 describes. The two steps "students create project" and "reflection" break down naturally into the seven sub-steps that Figure 14-1 shows.

The testing sub-step typically feeds back information to earlier sub-steps, so that students can improve the project on which they are working. The postmortem sub-step (which, despite its name, does not assume that the project died) feeds back information to all steps and sub-steps in future projects, so that students can improve all projects. We discuss this process with regard to a specific example in the next section.

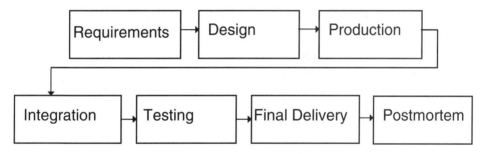

Figure 14-1: Process sub-steps

Practice

This section illustrates a dozen typical activities that a student multimedia production company might carry out. The first activity is a project; the others are services. All are suitable for practical use either in higher education or in K-12, with some subject changes as noted. The descriptions of the first two activities concentrate on the seven sub-steps that comprise the detailed creation step. The remaining descriptions emphasize different high points of the same process. In each case, for clarity, we describe a very specific activity, which educators and students could modify as necessary to meet their own goals.

Alaska Recruiting Project

Suppose that the Alaska Board of Education needs to hire several teachers for its high schools in Juneau, Sitka, and Prudeau Bay. The Board has issued a request for proposal (RFP) for recruiting materials that they can send to potential job applicants. Students in a multimedia production company decide to respond to the RFP with a proposal to prepare recruiting materials in the form of a multimedia project. They decide to follow the formal development process with seven sub-steps.

Requirements

The RFP specifies the client's general requirements. It says that the Alaska Board of Education wants materials that will tell potential applicants about the available jobs, the working environment in the schools, and the living environment in Alaska. The client wants to attract serious candidates who have the necessary qualifications and who would enjoy living in Alaska.

The students in the production company begin the requirements sub-step, Figure 14-2, by writing detailed descriptions about their understanding of the project's objectives, goals, and success measurements.

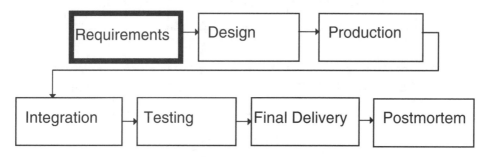

Figure 14-2: Requirements sub-step

The students might find that they require information beyond what the RFP contained. For example, the students might realize that they do not know whether the client is more concerned about attracting too few or too many job applicants. It is better for students to discuss detailed requirements with the client than to proceed on the basis of a questionable assumption about what the client really wants. After the students write what they think the requirements are, the students can make sure that the client agrees, before proceeding to the design sub-step, Figure 14-3.

Design

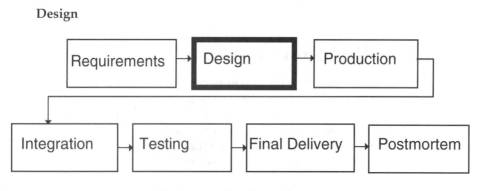

Figure 14-3: Design sub-step

The production company decides to begin designing their project by using brainstorming. Brainstorming is a good way to encourage all students to contribute ideas. Each student needs to understand that brainstorming is nonjudgmental. Unconventional ideas are not only allowed but expected. Nobody criticizes an idea. Asking "What do you mean by that?" stimulates creative thinking, but asking "How could you think of something so dumb?" turns off creativity and inhibits further contributions.

One of the students should record all ideas exactly as the students express the ideas. Suggested questions are as important as suggested answers. It may be useful to write each suggested question at the top of a blank panel and then write suggested answers in a column below the corresponding question. A blackboard has a large area but requires that ideas be erased and rewritten in order to reorganize the ideas. Placing a question and all suggested answers on one flip chart or easel chart facilitates grouping related questions. Writing each question or each potential answer on its own index card makes it even easier to rearrange ideas, by fastening cards to a wall in different organizations. The ability to move individual ideas is particularly helpful when it turns out that a particular column contains suggested answers to two different questions, or two columns contain answers to the same question.

When a brainstorming session's flow of ideas slows down, it is wise to call a break. You can advise your students to keep the project in mind as they talk with other students and with teachers. They can think about the project as they are going to sleep. They can think about the project in the first person singular, using the "I" word, by asking themselves questions such as "How can I make this better?" and "Are there other ways I could do this?" and "What will the resulting project look like and sound like?"

A typical brainstorming session resulted in the following questions and answers.

What information would potential job applicants want to get, and which media are most suitable for giving each type of information?

- Nature of the job - video of a person discussing it
- Formal job requirements - text
- Working environment - images of buildings and offices and also audio of interviews
- Physical setting and nature - video
- Living environment - images of homes and graphics of city maps
- Cost of living - text tables of information keyed to images of homes
- Crime and safety - text of statistical tables
- Health and pollution - graphics showing trends
- Organization of the schools - graphics of an organization chart
- How to apply for the job - text

What distribution method is most suitable for each medium?

- Text - diskette, CD-ROM, network
- Graphics - diskette, CD-ROM, network
- Images - CD-ROM, laser disc

- Audio - CD-ROM, audiocassette tape
- Video - CD-ROM, VCR tape, entire kiosk

How could Alaska distribute the material?

- Mail diskettes to people who answer an advertisement. Assume they have computers with S-VGA displays but without CD-ROM drives.
- Ship CD-ROMs to universities and employment agencies. Assume they have computers or kiosks with video decompression hardware.
- Ship complete kiosks, containing the necessary hardware and software, to selected universities and employment agencies.
- Ship laser discs and diskettes to universities. Assume that they have computer-controlled laser disc players and television monitors.
- Distribute the material over a network such as Internet to anyone who wants to download it.
- Distribute color brochures along with the computer material.

What platform will run the authoring system?

- Use our existing platform.
- Select a specific platform after we know what tools we will need to run.
- Select a specific platform based on the source materials we find.

Where will the project's content come from?

- Client should supply video footage and photographs.
- Get a tape of last year's National Geographic special (investigate legal aspects).
- Contact a school principal's wife who is an amateur photographer.
- Get an audiocassette tape that contains each school's anthem and the state anthem (investigate legal aspects).

As a clearly separate activity from the brainstorming session, students decide which suggested answers to adopt. Students collect together groups of answers that are mutually exclusive from one another and, within each group, decide which answer will form part of the proposed design. When one student's role in the production company clearly covers a group of such alternative answers, that student might decide which alternative to adopt. If the question is too general to fit within any one student's role, discussion may help the students to reach a consensus on one answer. If they cannot reach a consensus, the students can vote.

The design sub-step includes estimating any requirement for additional staff and skills, preparing a budget, and writing a Preliminary Proposal document. This document may include a story board for the proposed project, that is, a sketch of each screen and a graphic showing links with which users will get from one screen to another. Such a document may be a significant writing project and may be either straight linear text or multimedia.

In the real world of multimedia services, the production company would mail its Preliminary Proposal document to Alaska and await a reply. Even if the reply is favorable, the client is likely to request changes. Reviewing a detailed written design is excellent for bringing to mind new requirements or different ways to prioritize existing requirements. The first two sub-steps may thus repeat one or more times before students proceed to the production sub-step, Figure 14-4.

Production

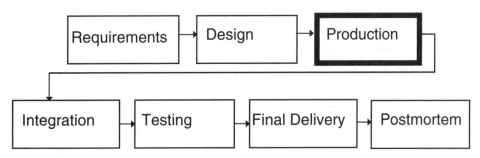

Figure 14-4: Production sub-step

In this production sub-step students create or obtain the project's individual component parts. The parts may include several media and several instances of each medium. A partial list of tasks that students perform in this sub-step is as follows.

- Arrange to get material from others, insofar as this is possible, legal, and ethical. Start a file that contains written permission to use any material that is not the students' own original work.
- Prepare a shot list for images and video.
- Note which shots require the same location, setup, and participants. Then make these shots together, even if they will not be together in the project.
- Digitize, that is capture, images and video.
- Write text.
- Prepare scripts for audio interviews.
- Record interviews and other audio.
- Create graphics by using a draw program.
- Create original images by using a paint program.
- Touch up and edit media as necessary.

- Create libraries of the multimedia objects and make them easy to locate while performing the next sub-step.

Integration

In this integration sub-step, Figure 14-5, students assemble the total project from its component parts and create the hypermedia links that will take users from one screen to another. What makes this sub-step challenging is that a typical project has many different paths. Integrating a multimedia project is very different from integrating a linear presentation, such as an essay, a book, or even a movie. Creators of a linear presentation concentrate on making one meaningful path through their material. At any point, they know exactly what the reader or viewer has already experienced. For example, they can introduce new terminology gradually.

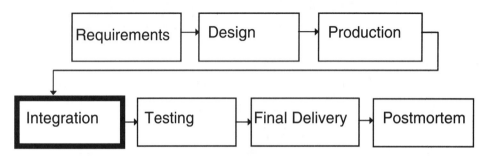

Figure 14-5: Integration sub-step

Creators of a multimedia project allow a user to select successive screens and thus take one of many different paths through the project's material. The creators must assure that each possible path is meaningful. Assuring this may be difficult, because the creators themselves build up a conceptual model of their project's information content and organization. Creators may not realize that users will not have any such model in mind. Users may literally become lost in hyperspace.

Creators must trace all paths that a user could select to be sure that each path is meaningful. A story board is useful for this purpose. By following allowed links through the story board, creators can make sure that a user will be able to understand each screen along a path. Creators may find that they need to add explanatory screens, delete links that could get users into trouble, or add links back to familiar screens that will make a user feel comfortable. The most important links are links that take a user back out of an unintended blind alley and links that take a user out of the project altogether.

Testing

After creators think that they have made every screen on every path comprehensible to users, the creators should test the project, to determine whether users can navigate through the project and achieve successful outcomes. To do this, the creators must think about who the intended users are and what success means to the client, which is not necessarily the same as pleasing the users. Testing, Figure 14-6, determines whether typical users will react to the project as the client desires. If not, then testing requires that students loop back to earlier sub-steps.

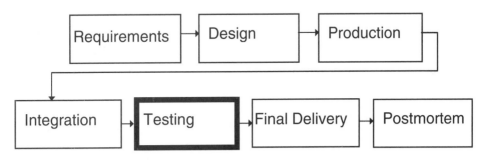

Figure 14-6: Testing

In this case, the client is the Alaska Board of Education. If the client's main problem is getting enough suitable candidates, then a successful test shows that users concentrate on parts of the project that describe how beautiful Alaska is in the summer and how pleasant the people are. If the client's main problem is filtering out applicants who would never actually accept a job in Alaska, then a successful test shows that users concentrate on parts of the project that discuss the length of Alaska's winter nights. After a successful test, students can proceed confidently to final delivery.

Final Delivery

In the final delivery sub-step, Figure 14-7, the students' production company delivers their completed project to their client. In many cases, the client will further distribute the project to end users in various ways. For example, the master for the contents of a CD-ROM could be a digital tape or a removable disk, and the master for a laser disc might be a videotape. The hardest part of this sub-step may be letting go of the final version on time, despite a burst of ideas for improving the result. Instead of endlessly improving this project, students would be better advised to redirect their energies toward improving subsequent projects by means of the postmortem sub-step. In many cases, the client will want one copy of the project that has a password to prevent others from changing the project and want a second copy without a password to allow the client to change future versions. The students must make clear to the client which is the final version, especially if they have sent prior versions for the client's evaluation.

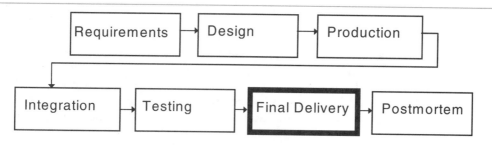

Figure 14-7: Final delivery

Postmortem

After the client and end users have had experience with the completed project, the student production company can take positive action to determine how well the project met the client's requirements. Based on characteristics that the client liked and disliked, the students can discuss how to improve each of the seven sub-steps during the postmortem step, Figure 14-8.

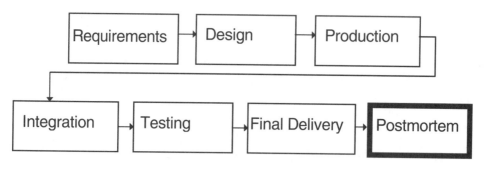

Figure 14-8: Postmortem

A student multimedia production company can perform services, as well as create multimedia projects. The rest of the sections in this chapter illustrate practical services that students can perform as members of a production company.

Setting Up a Laser Disc Player

Ms. Critchlow is a social studies teacher in a school that set up a production company last year. Ms. Critchlow asks the production company to help her select and set up a laser disc player. Students in the production company respond by going through the same seven sub-steps that we just described.

In the **requirements** sub-step, the students make sure that they really understand what Ms. Critchlow needs. She may or may not need to order a computer controlled laser disc player. If her real requirement turned out to be a single presentation on architecture, using some images of famous buildings on a laser disc, she might be well advised to borrow someone else's player. However, because she plans to build a year of study around a family of laser discs, and because no existing player is available for the year, the students find that she does need to order a player.

In the **design** sub-step, the students select a suitable model laser disc player, along with suitable devices for controlling the player and for receiving the player's output. The students start with a stake-in-the-ground design that uses a computer to control the laser disc player, one television monitor to receive the player's video output, and an amplified speaker to receive the player's audio output. Next, they check whether each of these component pieces is really necessary. For example, if Ms. Critchlow had no plans to create a computer program to call up images of buildings, she could get by with a bar code scanner. She could use a book that contains thumbnail versions of the images and then scan the bar code beside a desired image to display that image. Moreover, if she required images but no audio, the amplified speaker would be unnecessary. The students find that Ms. Critchlow plans to use a project that her students created last year to control the laser disc player, so they make sure to recommend a computer that will run that project.

The students find that they must replace their stake-in-the-ground design by a slightly different design. They find that Ms. Critchlow's class contains 25 people, so a single television monitor will not allow everyone to see the video clearly. The students in the production company decide among three possible designs. One design uses two large television monitors at the front corners of the room. Another design uses a special projector mounted on the room's ceiling. The third design uses an LCD panel and an existing overhead projector. The students select the design with two television monitors, which happen to be easily available.

To document the results of the design sub-step, the students draw a connection diagram such as Figure 14-9 and mark the parts that are not easily available. The easiest parts to forget, and some of the hardest parts to obtain at the last minute, are unusual cables and adapters. The students must be sure to mark which of these small but essential parts are not already on hand.

In the **production** sub-step, the students obtain the missing parts that they identified in the design step. The students decide whether to borrow, rent, buy, or even make the parts, and then carry out the decisions.

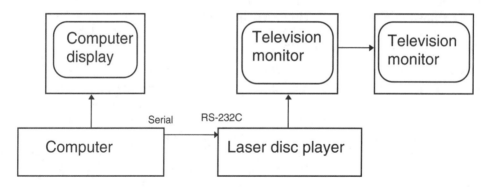

Figure 14-9: Laser disc player connections

In the **integration** sub-step, the students fit the easily available parts together with the new parts that they obtained in the production sub-step. This is mainly a matter of seeing whether the parts will plug together. Usually, the parts won't. The students make several trips to a store that sells adapters between different sorts of connectors. Integration may take longer than production, particularly if the laser disc player's unique serial cable is missing and the students need to order one. Integration covers both hardware and software, such as a multimedia project that runs on the computer and controls the laser disc player.

As always, the **testing** sub-step must refer back to the client's requirements. When Ms. Critchlow specified the size of her class, she was actually specifying the requirement that all the members of her class must have a clear view of the laser disc's contents. The only way to tell whether the integrated system meets her requirements is to test the entire setup with her actual laser disc in her classroom. If the students in the production company missed something significant in the requirements sub-step, then the students may need to go back and repeat the design sub-step. The students are relieved to see that, whereas everybody in Ms. Critchlow's class must be able to see the output of the laser disc player, only Ms. Critchlow must be able to see what is on the computer screen. However, the students find that they need to go back to the integration sub-step to make minor changes, adding room light dimmers and window shades. They repeat the integration and testing phases, with these changes.

The **final delivery** sub-step for setting up Ms. Critchlow's laser disc player includes making sure that she knows how to run the setup and keep it running. An oral description and a tour of the connections is necessary but not sufficient. The production company must deliver a connection diagram that labels each end of each connection with the exact wording that is printed on the box to which the cable connects. For example, the laser disc player may be labeled "RS-232C" near the connector into which the serial cable plugs. If so, the students must deliver a connection diagram that shows that same cryptic label at the laser disc player end of the serial cable. Moreover, the computer may have absolutely nothing printed near the point where the other end of the same cable connects. To handle this, students should write "Serial Port" on a piece of tape, stick that tape near the computer's connector, and write the same phrase on the connection diagram. Moreover, the students should stick a label on each end of the cable, telling what box and port the end plugs into. In the example, the label on one end would say "Computer's Serial Port" and the label on the other end would say "Laser Disc Player's RS-232C port." Such labels will reduce the number of emergency calls to members of the production company to come replace a cable that fell off. The most professional part of the connection diagram is a statement of how to contact the production company in case of more serious problems.

Again, the last sub-step, the **postmortem**, has the largest potential for helping the production company itself, as well as for helping future clients. This sub-step involves not only asking Ms. Critchlow if she was satisfied with the result but also attending a class and seeing whether she should be satisfied with her laser disc player installation.

Selecting Suitable Laser Discs

Ms. Critchlow calls for help again half a year later. She has found a pile of laser discs, has tried using the discs in the player that the production company set up for her, and has found that the discs work in two different ways. Only some of the discs allow her to stop the video or slow the video. For example, she wants to stop at the frame that shows a particular building, to allow her class to study and discuss that building. Moreover, Ms. Critchlow needs to buy another disc. She wants to be sure to buy the type of disc that she can stop. Some of the discs in the pile that she found are labeled "standard play," others are labeled "CLV," and others are not labeled at all. She needs to know which discs in her pile are worth trying. She also needs to know what labels to look for on discs that she is considering buying. Students in the production company understand what is behind the discs' cryptic labels and can even tell which type an unlabeled disc is by looking at the disc itself.

The type of laser disc that is more desirable for use with computers is sometimes labeled "standard play" and sometimes labeled "constant angular velocity" (CAV). As the latter name denotes, a player spins this type of disc at a constant angular velocity that is equal to 30 revolutions per second. As the player's laser beam follows along the disc's spiral track, the laser beam reads one complete picture, called a frame, every 1/30 of a second. The player thus produces video at the standard rate of 30 frames per second, which television monitors require. Because the spiral track can make as many as 54,000 turns around the disc, each side of a disc can contain up to 30 minutes of video. Thus, the disc's two sides total one hour.

The less desirable type of laser disc is sometimes labeled "extended play" and sometimes labeled "constant linear velocity" (CLV). As the former name denotes, this type of disc can contain more video. In fact, one side of such a disc can hold one hour of video, so the two sides of one disc may hold a complete movie. This is a clear advantage if you merely want to play a movie from beginning to end.

So why are CLV discs less desirable for use with computers? The answer is hidden in the name CLV. This type of disc requires a player to start spinning the disc at 30 revolutions per second as the laser beam starts reading the inside of the disc nearest the center hole, just as is the case when playing a CAV disc. However, when playing a CLV disc, the player gradually slows down the disc's angular velocity. The player slows the disc all the way down to 10 revolutions per second, by the time the laser beam reaches the outside of the disc. A full disc is written so that the outside is exactly three times as long as the inside, as you can check with a ruler. The disk contains one frame of video on the inside revolution, contains three frames of video on the outside revolution, and contains intermediate numbers of frames on all the revolutions that are in between. Each of the frames is thus the same length, in linear measure such as inches. Of course, the part of the track that contains one frame must pass under the laser beam in a constant time, namely, 1/30 second. In the process, as the disc's angular velocity changes gradually, the disc's track passes under the laser beam with a constant linear velocity, measured in inches per second.

Having more frames per track allows a CLV disc to hold more frames than a CAV disc. This is why a CLV disc plays for a longer time than a CAV disc. This is also why a CLV disc may be labeled extended play as well as, or in addition to, being labeled CLV.

Although a CLV disc works wonderfully for playing an hour of video linearly from beginning to end, a CLV disc works badly for skipping nonlinearly from one part of the track to another part of the track. The trouble is that a player cannot begin to play a new part of the track until the player's motor has sped up the disc or has slowed down the disc to exactly the correct angular velocity that gives exactly the correct linear velocity that corresponds to the radius of the new part of the track. Whereas a player can move its laser beam to any radius in less than a second, speeding up the disc or slowing down the disc takes significantly longer than a second. A CAV disc works better, because a CAV disc rotates at a constant 30 revolutions per second. Thus, a CAV disc can begin playing as soon as the player's laser beam reaches the desired radius, usually well within one second. This is one reason why you prefer a CAV disc for use with a multimedia project.

What matters more to Ms. Critchlow is that, with a CAV disc, a player can stop the video to show one frame for as long as she wants her class to look at that frame. A player can hold its laser beam at a constant radius to play a single frame over and over, and thereby show a still image. With a CAV disc, a player can also produce slow-motion video. For example, if a player lets the disc rotate 15 times before moving its laser beam to the next frame, the player shows two frames per second, which is very slow motion.

Applying the same techniques to either stop the video or produce slow motion with a CLV disc would fail miserably. Remember that each different revolution of a CLV disc's track contains a different number of frames. Near the inside of the disc, a rotation contains one frame plus a little of a second frame. Near the outside of the disc, one rotation contains two frames and most of a third frame. Holding the laser beam at a fixed radius, so that it reads one revolution over and over, would produce a flickering mixture of several frames and parts of frames.

Even without labels, a CAV disc is visibly different from a CLV disc. Because each track on a CAV disc holds exactly one frame of video, the gaps between successive frames line up with each other and form a band that runs from the disc's inside to the disc's outside. In fact, one frame is composed of two half frames, called fields, so there are two such bands, one on each side of the center hole. The two bands form a bar that runs clear across the video on a CAV disc. A CLV disc shows no bar. Different tracks on a CLV disc hold different numbers of frames, so the gaps between these frames do not line up. Some movies and other titles have a mixture of CAV sides and CLV sides.

We have found that it is almost impossible to memorize the meanings of the four names standard play, extended play, CAV, and CLV, without understanding the meanings behind the names. After members of a production company understand where the names came from, they will have no trouble advising others on which type of discs to obtain. Moreover, they can appear to work magic by predicting that a side that shows a bar will work better in a multimedia project.

Demonstrating a Project in a Speech

Principal Hallas decides to include a ten-minute demonstration of a student-created multimedia project in his speech to a local business persons' club. He calls in Muriel, who is a member of the multimedia production company, to discuss the possibilities. He mentions that the speech is tomorrow.

Muriel describes several of the most creative projects that other students have created in the last few months, in enough detail to enable Mr. Hallas to select a project. She then asks what equipment is available in the hotel where Mr. Hallas will give the speech. The answer is one large television monitor with a video cassette recorder. That completed the **requirements** sub-step. Muriel makes enough promises to get out of Mr. Hallas' office and calls an emergency meeting of the production company.

The students note that running the project that Mr. Hallas selected requires eight pieces of equipment that weigh a total of about 80 pounds and take half an hour to set up. Even worse, the computer display screen is too small for such a large audience to see. In a brainstorming session, one of the students suggests a creative solution to the screen size problem. The students can use a scan converter box, sometimes called a Mac-to-TV or PC-to-TV box, to convert the computer's display output to an analog video signal. The resulting video signal can drive the hotel's large television monitor, replacing the computer's display screen. Then another student suggests an even more creative variation that the production company selects as the conclusion of their **design** sub-step. This design consists of using the scan converter box to produce analog video and using a VCR to record that video on a videotape. This design allows Mr. Hallas to carry a half-pound videotape to the hotel, rather than transporting 80 pounds of computer equipment.

The students are familiar with this design, because they have been helping other students record projects on videotapes to play at home. The students know that they connect the computer's display output to the scan converter's display input jack and connect the scan converter's video output jack to a VCR's video input jack (or to a television monitor's video input jack). For audio, they connect the digital audio adapter's line output jack directly to the VCR's audio input jack (or to an amplified speaker). That is, they do not need to pass the audio through the scan converter. We discuss both video and audio connections later in this chapter.

The **production** sub-step consists of having the student who created the selected project pick one path through some of the project's most interesting material and record the results on the videotape. The students quickly **integrate** that tape with a VCR and test that the taped material shows the project's strong points. **Final delivery** consists of handing Mr. Hallas the VCR tape and politely suggesting that, well before he begins his speech, he should make sure that the hotel's VCR will play the tape through the television monitor.

In the **postmortem**, Mr. Hallas mentions that he liked the demonstration so much that he plans to mail the tape to a colleague in London. A student remarks that, although they were almost certain that the VCR in the local hotel would be able to play the tape, they are equally certain that a VCR in London would not be able to do so. They explain that stations in Great Britain broadcast a different television standard from the one that stations in the United States broadcast.

VCRs in the Americas and Japan play tapes that use the National Television Standards Committee (NTSC) broadcast standard. The NTSC standard calls for scanning a scene with 525 horizontal lines and calls for completing an entire scan 30 times each second. Most of Europe uses a different standard named phase alternating line (PAL) that calls for scanning 625 lines, 25 times each second. The fundamental reason for the different standards is that television frames must occur at one-half of the power line frequency. The power line voltage happens to oscillate at 60 Hz in the United States and at 50 Hz in Europe. The students in the production company had learned about different video standards the hard way, by mailing a tape to a class overseas and hearing that the class had not been able to play the tape.

To avoid a disappointed client, the students also tell Mr. Hallas that a videotape can show only one selected linear path through a project. A tape cannot contain all of the project's hypermedia links. Thus, using a multimedia computer gives a better demonstration of a project than does playing a VCR tape. In particular, when a member of the audience asks to see what selecting a different button would do, a speaker can use a computer to demonstrate the answer. A speaker cannot use a videotape to do so. However, far more rooms and homes are equipped with VCRs than with multimedia computers.

Making Projects Look Good on Television

Dr. Jonas Salk once said that the greatest reward for doing anything is the opportunity to do more of it. Members of our production company find that this reward applies to helping Ms. Critchlow. Ms. Critchlow says that she has a serious problem and wants to come talk to the entire production company.

She explains that she has taught a full year in which members of her class could see the television sets that show video from her laser disc player, but only she could see her computer's small display screen. She has started coaching groups of members of her class as the groups create multimedia projects. She says she wants each group to demonstrate its project to the entire class on screens that all the members of the class can see.

The members of the production company start whispering congratulations to one another. They have already solved this problem. All they have to do is get Ms. Critchlow a scan converter to connect between her computer and her two television monitors. However, the students notice that Ms. Critchlow is still speaking. She remarks that, of course, she tried using a scan converter.

Ms. Critchlow goes on to explain her problem. A project that looked fine on a computer screen did not look so good on her television monitors. Her class could not read the project's text, because the television monitors blurred the characters together. Her class could not see a row of buttons at the bottom of the television screens, although those buttons had been clearly visible on a computer screen. The television monitors made edges of brightly colored regions look fuzzy. Finally, wherever a project used a thin horizontal line, the television monitors made the line seem to flicker on and off annoyingly. Ms. Critchlow asks whether she should get her two television monitors repaired or whether she should put in a request for much more expensive monitors. Either solution will take several months, so she wants to be sure she picks the right solution.

A few members of the production company have enough experience with analog video to know that either of the two solutions will turn out to be a waste of time and money. Instead of repairing or replacing her monitors, Ms. Critchlow needs to help her students create projects that will look good on television.

In fact, only one student or educational technologist needs to know the contents of this section, in order to keep a school from trying to push television beyond the technical limits of analog video. Others can simply use the four rules that we summarize at the end of the section.

You can probably guess how Ms. Critchlow's students can solve their first problem because you read Chapter 2's discussion of how resolution applies to text. Now we discuss how resolution applies to analog video, and then discuss solutions to the second, third, and fourth problems with analog video that Ms. Critchlow's students encountered.

Readable Text

Television screens do not have as much resolution as computer display screens. In Chapter 2, we suggested using only 40 to 60 characters per line, so that each student in a group can read the text on a computer screen. This limitation is even more important for allowing an entire class to read the project's text on a television screen. In most setups, a line that contains more than about 40 characters appears as an unreadable blur on a television screen.

A fuzzy screen is usually not the fault of a scan converter or the fault of a particular television monitor. Rather, a fuzzy screen usually results from the underlying NTSC standard for analog video. Designers intended televisions for casual group viewing from across a room, whereas designers intended computer displays for critical individual viewing up close. Nevertheless, you can purchase television monitors that have different resolutions. Here, then, is the heart of Ms. Critchlow's questions. Can she have her television monitors adjusted so that the television screens will have resolution that is as good as the resolutions of computer screens? Can she buy more expensive television monitors that have resolution as good as a computer screen's resolution?

Here is what makes answering these questions a challenge for students in the production company. Computer engineers and television engineers measure resolution in different ways. We have seen that a typical computer display has a resolution of 640 x 480 pixels. A typical television has about 340 lines of horizontal resolution. You will see lines of horizontal resolution quoted in television catalogs and printed on tags in stores. What does it mean?

Television engineers use a standard test pattern to measure a television monitor's number of lines of horizontal resolution. Their test pattern has vertical lines that are black, then white, then black, and so on. The total number of these vertical lines that a television screen can show from the left side of the screen across to the right side of the screen is essentially equal to the television's number of lines of horizontal resolution.

Note that a television's number of lines of horizontal resolution is a completely different concept from the number of horizontal scan lines. The NTSC specification says that all televisions in the United States will have exactly 525 horizontal scan lines in every frame, no matter how many lines of horizontal resolution a particular television has. A number of lines of horizontal resolution and a number of horizontal scan lines sound sufficiently similar to cause considerable confusion if you do not understand what the numbers mean.

Now, how can we compare a typical television's number of lines of horizontal resolution to a typical computer display screen's resolution? How many vertical black lines and white lines could a computer screen show? A computer screen that has a resolution of 640 x 480 pixels can make one pixel bright, make the very next pixel to the right dark, make the next pixel to the right bright, and so on, for all 640 pixels in one row across the screen. As a result, a computer screen that has a resolution of 640 pixels in each horizontal row can show a clear test pattern that contains 320 bright vertical lines separated by 320 dark vertical lines. A television engineer, counting both the bright lines and the dark lines, would say that the computer screen has about 640 lines of horizontal resolution.

A computer or television tube reproduces one horizontal row of a scene by scanning a beam from the left side of the screen to the right side of the screen. As the beam moves along, the computer or television makes the beam brighter and dimmer. To show alternating white and black vertical lines, the beam quickly turns bright, dark, back to bright, and so on. A display that can show a large number of pixels can simply change from bright to dark, back to bright, and so on, very quickly. That quickness gives high resolution.

Thus, you can compare a computer's screen's 640 pixels across each row to a television's 340 lines of horizontal resolution. For comparison to the resolutions we gave in Chapter 2, note that a 21-inch television screen has an actual display that is about 18 inches wide. Dividing 18 inches into 340 pixels gives 18 pixels per inch. A television's 18 pixels per inch is comparable to a computer's 58 pixels per inch.

Typical television screens thus have significantly lower resolution than typical computer screens have. In fact, the NTSC standard for broadcast television in the United States allows only 340 lines of horizontal resolution. Having more than 340 lines of horizontal resolution would make one television channel interfere with the next higher numbered channel and interfere with the next lower numbered channel. Most VCRs are designed to have only about 240 lines of resolution. Providing more resolution increases a VCR's cost, so only high-end VCRs can produce as many as 425 lines of horizontal resolution. Laser disc players can produce somewhat better resolution than a good VCR. To accommodate expensive VCRs and laser disc players, some expensive television monitors are built to display more resolution than the NTSC standard allows in broadcasts. The most sophisticated consumer televisions have about 550 lines of horizontal resolution. Remember that a sophisticated computer display has 1280 pixels in each row.

You may have read about proposals for high definition television (HDTV). These proposals include improving television to show about 1200 lines of horizontal resolution. In the meantime, students will need to accommodate their projects to analog video that has about half as much resolution as a computer display screen has. The first rule for showing projects on televisions is thus to limit the number of text characters per line to about 40.

Edges, Colors, and Flickers

The second problem with analog video that faced Ms. Critchlow's students was the fact that television screens always cut off a screen's top, bottom, left, and right. Although many of today's television screens have sharp corners, early picture tubes were circular. To eliminate ugly black borders around the pictures, televisions were designed to over-scan, that is, to show only the center portion of the broadcast signal. Students should design screens in their projects so that important items, such as titles and buttons, stay well away from the outside edges of their computer screen. Otherwise, the important items may disappear off the edges of a television screen. Moreover, when you set up a scan converter, you may need to adjust knobs and switches carefully to center the project on the television screen.

The third problem with analog video that faced Ms. Critchlow's students was the fact that television screens blur regions of strong, bright colors. Whereas a computer display signal specifies each pixel's exact amount of red, amount of green, and amount of blue (an RGB signal), an NTSC television signal separates information into brightness (luminance, or Y) and color (chrominance, or U-V). Moreover, television can change the Y signal much more rapidly than the U-V signal. That is, the number of lines of horizontal resolution for color is only about half of the resolution for brightness. As a result, a television screen cannot show a sharp edge of a brightly colored region, such as a box or a text character. Students should design project screens to use pastel colors. For example, bright red text on a bright blue background is hard to read on a television screen, even with 20 characters per line. In general, for easy reading on a television screen, it is best to use white characters on a light blue background.

The fourth and last problem with analog video that faced Ms. Critchlow's students involved thin horizontal lines that flickered. Again, Ms. Critchlow needs to know that this is not a problem that she can fix by buying even the most expensive television monitor. Students can understand what causes this problem if they know about interlace, which is a characteristic of analog video signals.

As we mentioned in connection with the bar across a CAV laser disc, each frame of a video signal is actually composed of two half-frames, called fields. A frame breaks down a scene into horizontal scan lines numbered 1 through 525. However, a television does not actually scan the lines in that order. Instead, it scans lines 1, 3, 5, through 525, in 1/60 of a second. This is called the odd field. Then it goes back and interlaces the even field's lines 2, 4, 6, through 524 in the next 1/60 of a second. The scan thus covers the entire frame 30 times each second. The human eye and brain see an illusion of smooth motion, because the television presents a complete picture 30 times each second.

However, scanning the screen from top to bottom only 30 times per second would produce an intolerable flicker. Interlaced scanning eliminates the flicker by scanning the screen from top to bottom 60 times per second. However, this works only if every feature of the scene appears in both the odd field and the even field. Suppose that students create a screen containing a horizontal line that happens to match scan line 15. Then a television scans that line only during the odd frame, not during the even frame. As a result, the television brightens that line only 30 times per second and the line flickers like mad. Students should use horizontal lines that are at least two scan lines thick, to make sure that each line appears in both the even frame and the odd frame on a television screen.

What does this all this mean to a television's resolution? Because of over-scan, only about 470 scan lines actually appear on a television screen, even though there are always 525 scan lines in each frame. Because of interlace, the smallest usable picture element is about two scan lines high. Thus a television's vertical resolution is about half of 470, that is, 235 pixels. Including the horizontal resolution that we discussed before gives a typical television resolution of 340 x 235 pixels.

A line that is only one pixel high looks fine on a typical computer display, because the computer display does not use interlaced scanning. The computer display scans the entire screen 60 or even 72 times each second. This progressive scanning gives both smooth motion and no flicker. You will see occasional references to interlaced scanning in computer catalogs. Whenever possible, try to get computer displays that use progressive scanning.

In summary, students in the production company assure Ms. Critchlow that her television monitors are working about as well as she could expect. They explain to her why she should encourage members of her class to design projects that follow the four rules of using large text characters, keeping important items near the center of each screen, using pastel colors, and making wide lines.

Selecting Video Connections

Mrs. Green is a self-reliant type. She seems to be annoyed that she needs to ask the production company for help. She says that she saw Ms. Critchlow's classroom and had no trouble setting up a similar scan converter and television. She says that she suggested that her students follow the four rules for creating projects that look good on television. The resulting projects look fuzzy on Mrs. Green's setup, although they look fine in Ms. Critchlow's classroom. Mrs. Green feels especially put-upon because she paid extra for a television that has a larger number of lines of horizontal resolution than Ms. Critchlow's. What could be wrong?

Because a few members of the student production company understand analog video, they can look at Mrs. Green's setup and solve the problem. First, the students make Mrs. Green feel good about doing almost all the work without assistance. Then the students explain that televisions may provide three different kinds of connections and that the kind of connection you use strongly affects your resulting horizontal resolution.

For our discussion of the connections that will yield highest resolution, we use the following terminology. A plug on the end of a cable fits into a jack on a television or on some other sort of video equipment. Inside a plug, there may be one or four pins that carry the signals. The same discussion applies not only to connecting a scan converter, but also to connecting a laser disc player, VCR, or video camera. Using a ruler, along with the measurements that we give, will help you identify the jacks so you can learn to recognize them.

An inexpensive television set may have only an antenna input connection. This input may be a pair of screws 3/4 inches apart or it may be a jack that is 3/8 inches across and has grooves on the outside. It may be labeled antenna input, VHF, or RF for radio frequency. A scan converter may produce a signal that the television set can receive through this antenna input with the television tuned to channel 3 or channel 4. However, using an antenna input gives the lowest number of lines of horizontal resolution and thus gives the fuzziest screens.

A more expensive television set, or a television monitor, has a normal video input jack. This input may be a jack that is 5/16 inches across and is often yellow on the inside, or it may be a jack that is 3/8 inches across and has two small knobs on the outside rather than grooves. It is usually labeled Video Input. Using this normal video connection gives significantly more lines of horizontal resolution than does using an antenna connection.

A still more expensive television set or monitor may have a super video input jack. This input is a jack that is almost 1/2 an inch across and has four small round holes. It may be labeled S-Video, Super-Video, or just S. Using this connection gives the best possible horizontal resolution. Why is S-Video better than normal video? Two of an S-Video jack's four holes accept pins that carry the brightness component of the video signal. The other two holes accept pins that carry the color component of the video signal. A normal video jack has only a single hole that accepts a single pin. That carries a composite signal that includes both brightness and color information. Separating the video components gives higher resolution than does mixing video into a composite signal.

Video cameras and VCRs that have S-Video connectors are called S-VHS or Hi-8. Just as you will get best results by using an S-Video connection whenever possible, so you will get best results by buying equipment that has these connectors whenever you can afford it. Note that the difference is more than the connectors. You cannot get higher resolution by buying a little adapter that converts normal video to S-Video.

The members of the production company simply replace the cable to Mrs. Green's antenna connection by an S-Video cable. They demonstrate that Mrs. Green's setup now shows sharper screens than does Ms. Critchlow's setup. They expected this result, because Ms. Critchlow's television monitor has only a normal video connection and has a correspondingly lower number of lines of horizontal resolution.

Disk Speeds

Mr. Brown installed a digital video capture adapter in a mid-1980s computer and tried digitizing video from a videotape. He was surprised to find that he could play back the video at only eight frames per second. He had recently upgraded the computer with a fast processor. He had selected a video capture adapter that was specified to be capable of capturing 15 frames per second in a computer with such a processor. Mr. Brown comes to the production company to ask what went wrong.

Members of the production company suspect that his relatively old computer may have a slow disk. They try an experiment. They find a large 1.3 MB file on Mr. Brown's computer and they try copying that file to another file with another name. They count "succotash one, succotash two," and so on up to "succotash twelve" during the copy. They conclude that, in about 12 seconds, the computer read 1.3 MB off the disc and wrote the same 1.3 MB back onto a different part of the disk. They divide the total of 2.6 MB by 12 seconds to get the disk's actual data rate of 217 MB per second. They compare their result with the magic single-speed CD-ROM rate of 150 KB per second. Some newer disks are as much as 50 times faster than the CD-ROM data rate.

Note that copying a file from one part of a disk to another part of the disk requires the disk to move to a new location before each read and move again before each write. Nevertheless, this experiment gives a reasonable estimate of the rate at which a disk writes a file of digital video. After significant use, a disk has no large block of unused space, so the disk must write pieces of a new file into a large number of small unused fragments that are located in various parts of the disk. Before writing each piece, the disk must move to the corresponding location.

The members of the production company have two suggestions for Mr. Brown. First, they suggest that he run a program that defragments his disk, so that the disk will have a single large block of unused storage space into which to write a digital video file. Second, they suggest that he move his digital video adapter to a computer that has a faster disk. Mr. Brown takes both suggestions. Defragmenting the disk increases video playback to 10 frames per second. Using a faster computer gives 15 frames per second.

Connecting Audio Devices

Ms. Lee's students have finished creating this book's Critics' Circle and Trailers projects. They had no trouble connecting their microphones and speakers to their computers' digital audio adapter cards. They noted that each adapter card has a jack marked MIC for a microphone and a jack marked SPK for a speaker. Their microphones and speakers came with plugs 1/8-inch across that fit into those jacks. Nothing could have been easier.

Now Ms. Lee's students are creating the Memoirs project. They need to capture digital audio from their videotaped interviews. On the back of their VCR they find a jack that is clearly marked AUDIO OUTPUT. The jack is 5/16 inches across, just like the jacks for normal video. The students have a cable with plugs that fit this jack. They are pretty sure that they can record audio from a videotape by connecting a cable from the VCR's AUDIO OUTPUT jack to the adapter card's IN jack. But the plug on the cable that fits the 5/16-inch jack won't fit into the 1/8-inch jack on the digital audio adapter card.

One of Ms. Lee's students wanders into the room where the production company keeps its equipment, describes the problem, and runs back out holding a finger-sized adapter that solves the problem. In fact, that adapter allows the students to connect their digital audio adapter cards' inputs or outputs to any of a wide variety of devices including CD-DA players, audio cassette recorders, laser disc players, phonograph record players, radio or television tuners, video cassette recorders, video cameras, amplifiers, and even some music keyboards. Figure 14-10 shows this adapter, part of a cable that plugs into the adapter, and part of an audio card into which the adapter plugs.

Members of the production company had previously bought that adapter from an electronics store. They knew what adapter to ask for, because they knew the names of the different types of jacks and plugs. The 5/16-inch jack appeared on phonographs made by Radio Corporation of America. This jack is therefore named either a phono jack or an RCA jack. The 1/8-inch jack on a digital audio card is a miniature version of the jack that human operators plugged cables into, in order to set up telephone connections, before telephone dials were invented. This jack is therefore named a 1/8-inch mini phone jack. (The full size phone jack is 1/4 inches across. There is also a slightly smaller subminiature phone jack that is 3/32 inches across.) A plug is named the same as the jack into which the plug fits. Most cables have phono plugs on both ends and need adapters to plug into any jacks other than phono jacks.

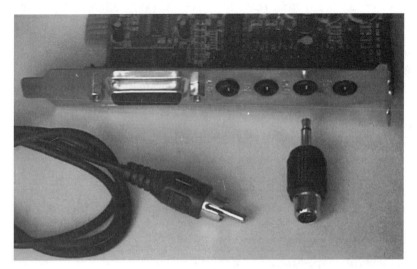

Figure 14-10: A useful audio adapter

The finger-sized adapter that solves Ms. Lee's students' problem has a phono jack on one end and has a 1/8-inch mini phone plug on the other end. A store calls this an adapter from a phono plug to a 1/8-inch mini phone jack. After a half-dozen years in the multimedia business, one of the authors has accumulated two pounds of about 20 types of adapters. A production company would be well advised to do the same.

Actually, when Ms. Lee's students first try using their new adapter to record audio from a VCR, they get absolute silence. In their previous projects, they had been digitizing the signal that came into the adapter's MIC jack. For the Memoirs project, they need to tell the authoring system software to tell the audio adapter card to digitize what comes into the IN jack instead.

Using Stereo Audio

One of Ms. Lee's students comes back to the production company with a slightly more difficult problem six months later. Ms. Lee has obtained a more expensive VCR. Instead of a single AUDIO OUTPUT jack, the new VCR has two output jacks that are labeled LEFT and RIGHT. The student understands that she could connect the VCR to a stereophonic (stereo) music system. The LEFT signal would play through a speaker that is located on the listener's left side and the RIGHT signal would play through a speaker that is located on the listener's right side. The student needs to know whether to connect those two jacks to a digital audio adapter card, which has only a single IN jack and, if so, how to make the connection. Here is what a member of the production company explains.

Most input jacks and output jacks of a digital audio adapter card handle stereo signals. A stereo IN jack can accept both a left audio signal and a right audio signal from the same plug. The card's circuitry can convert both signals from analog to digital at the same time and can create a single file that contains the digital form of both signals. Similarly, playing back digital audio can deliver both signals to the card's OUT jack and can also deliver both signals to the card's SPK jack.

You may be able to purchase a single physical cable that carries both stereo signals. Each end of such a cable has a stereo 1/8-inch mini phone plug. A stereo 1/8-inch mini phone plug has a connection for the left signal on the tip of the plug and also has a second connection for the right signal on a small metal ring. This ring is clearly visible behind the tip of the plug. A useful alliterative mnemonic is "right is ring." If a cable's plugs have rings, it is a stereo cable. You plug one such cable into a stereo input or output jack in order to connect both the left signal and the right signal.

However, you cannot plug a 1/8-inch mini phone plug into a VCR or into any other normal piece of audio equipment. As a result, a stereo cable that has two 1/8-inch mini phone plugs is sufficiently rare that you may not be able to find one to purchase, even if you want one.

In general, you make a stereo connection by using two cables, each of which has a phono plug on each end. To use two cables that have phono jacks to connect stereo audio to a digital audio adapter card, you need an adapter. This adapter has two phono jacks on one end and has a stereo 1/8-inch mini phone plug on the other end. Stores call this an adapter from phono plugs to a stereo 1/8-inch mini phone jack. Figure 14-11 shows such an adapter with cables ready to plug into it. Such an adapter does not usually label its right and left phono jacks. Instead, the right signal's phono jack is almost always red, which continues the alliterative mnemonic with "right is ring is red." The left phono jack is white. A video phono jack is often yellow.

Using Mono Audio with Stereo Audio

Many multimedia projects use only monaural (mono) audio. Mono audio has only one signal, which goes to a speaker in front of a listener. One reason for using mono in projects is that the most common uses of digital audio are student narrations and interviews, for which mono is perfectly sufficient. Another reason is that using mono requires only half as much disk storage space per second as does using stereo. For these reasons, the member of the production company also tell Ms. Lee's student how to use mono audio with stereo hardware.

A mono 1/8-inch mini phone plug has only the tip connection. It has no ring connection. When you plug a mono plug into a stereo jack, the mono plug's tip connection touches the jack's left connection. Thus, you always use a stereo system's left signal for a mono signal. A mono plug's body extends all the way to where a stereo jack is built to contact a ring, so a mono plug's body grounds a stereo jack's right signal.

Grounding the right signal may be good or bad. It is good for an input connection, because grounding the input avoids adding noise to the unused right signal. However, grounding the right signal may be bad for an output connection. Inserting a mono plug into a stereo output that has strong amplifiers may short out and damage the right amplifier. A useful rule is to plug only stereo plugs or stereo adapters into a digital audio adapter's speaker jack.

Most microphones are mono. Hence, a digital audio adapter's microphone input is usually a mono jack that drives both the adapter's left signal and right signal. To avoid wasting disk space by storing two identical signals, whenever using a microphone, students should tell software to tell the digital audio adapter to capture only a mono signal. They should capture stereo only when a source of music actually has two different signals.

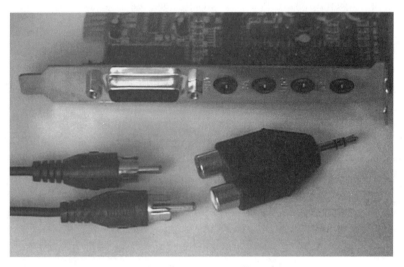

Figure 14-11: A stereo audio adapter

Combining Two Sources of Audio

When a group of Ms. Lee's students created their Trailers project, they simply used two speakers. They used one speaker to play the narrations, which they had recorded as digital audio on their computer's disk. They used a completely separate speaker to play back analog audio from the movie, which was the sound track of the laser disc. Now, however, they want to record their trailer on a videotape. They ask how they can combine their narrations with the movie's sound track to produce the videotape.

Because Ms. Lee has an expensive stereo VCR, members of the production company can use a simple design. They use one cable (and an adapter) to connect the digital audio adapter card's OUT jack to the VCR's LEFT AUDIO INPUT jack. They use a second cable to connect the laser disc player's audio output jack to the VCR's RIGHT AUDIO INPUT jack. Of course, they use another cable to connect the laser disc player's VIDEO OUTPUT jack to the VCR's VIDEO INPUT jack. Then they put a tape in the VCR, start recording, and ask Ms. Lee's students to run their Trailers project.

When they play back the tape through a television set, they hear both the narration and the sound track. They check to make sure that the tape also plays both the narration and the sound track on a less expensive mono VCR. This works too, because a stereo VCR not only records the left signal and the right signal, but also records a third signal that is the sum of the left signal and the right signal. It is this third signal that a mono VCR plays back.

This simple design does not satisfy Ms. Lee's students. The students want to use the stereo VCR to record the movie's stereo sound track. They really want to mix their digital audio signal with both analog audio signals from the laser disc player. The members of the production company heave a collective sigh and dig out the stereo audio mixer box, which they have been trying to avoid learning how to hook up. All that we can say here is that this takes quite a few cables, quite a few adapters, and quite a few hours, but it produces the desired result.

Adding Background Music

Mr. Jackson tells the production company that he wants his music class to use a variation of the Critics' Circle project. He wants his students to make their spoken opinions more effective and forceful by using background music from an audio cassette recorder. A student who has experience with digital audio makes sure that she understands the **requirements**. She finds that Mr. Jackson wants a user's attention focused on a speaker's voice rather than on the background music. She explains that in this case a very simple **design** will suffice. Her design requires no additional equipment, so she needs no **production** sub-step. She **integrates** the available equipment by placing the recorder a couple of feet from the microphone and adjusting its playback volume.

She **tests** the design by asking a student to try speaking into the microphone, with the recorder's music playing in the background. When she plays the resulting digital audio, she finds that the music is too loud, so she repeats the integration sub-step with the audiocassette recorder's volume set lower. This leads to a successful test.

Her **final delivery** consists of emphasizing the limitations of her solution. She tells Mr. Jackson that putting the microphone in front of the recorder's speaker significantly degrades the quality of the music. She offers to select and set up an audio mixer box, in case Mr. Jackson finds that another project requires high-quality audio along with narration. In the **postmortem**, the production company makes sure they can locate an audio mixer quickly.

Summary

Several thousand students across the United States have had the experience of creating multimedia projects. The authors have visited some of their schools and homes. When we asked teachers and students what would be most helpful to their continuing multimedia progress, most said that they would like for us to provide new ideas for projects and new techniques for creating better projects, while maintaining the same priorities of achieving academic objectives. We dedicate this chapter and the preceding chapter to those students and teachers. We feel no requirement to help produce a generation of professional artists, musicians, or video producers. However, we believe that these two chapters contain suggestions that will help students to enhance their projects, achieve the projects' goals, and enhance their enjoyment and use of media in their future working and living.

We continue to urge you to introduce new techniques to your classes by means of examples. We recommend focusing on techniques that these two chapters discussed only after students have created several projects without worrying about whether they use each medium to its full advantage or whether they organize themselves as efficiently as possible.

References

Floyd, Steve. *The IBM Multimedia Handbook*. New York, New York: Brady, 1991.

Haykin, Randy, Senior Editor. *Demystifying Multimedia - A Guide for Multimedia Developers*. San Francisco: Vivid Publishing, 1993.

Murie, Michael. *Macintosh Multimedia Workshop*. Indianapolis, Indiana: Hayden, 1993.

For information on the Academy of Multimedia where high school students create computer-based multimedia training and other projects, contact Dr. Briant J. Farnsworth, Granite School District, Salt Lake City, Utah, Telephone (801) 268-8513.

Chapter 15

Variations

In this chapter, we explore:

- how to design your own variations of projects to achieve pedagogical objectives.

- how to extend and modify the projects already described in this text.

- reasons to do multiple versions of projects over the school year.

In this chapter, we address two related but distinct objectives. We seek to motivate you to devise your own variations of projects and give you a framework for doing so. We also provide brief descriptions of alternatives that we have devised to the projects described in earlier chapters. We strongly encourage teachers to engage in many multimedia student projects over the course of the year. A way to do this is to vary a base project to fit the needs of the curriculum and the growing skills and maturity of the students.

We begin by discussing why projects should be repeated and when project ideas may need to be modified for the classroom. Next, in the Theory section we offer a framework to help you in this process. In the Practice section, we offer practical suggestions for modifying some of the projects given in Chapters 7 through 12 using the concepts given in the Theory section. We summarize by describing some attributes to look for in evaluating projects for multimedia.

Background

Student-constructed multimedia projects encourage students to use a wide range of skills and knowledge to accomplish the job. If the class only does one project during the year, the students do not have a chance to build on their initial performance nor to apply their reflections to improve their performance. Teachers must also create an opportunity for the students to transfer the learning acquired in one subject area to application in another domain. Research indicates that transfer of cognitive skills from one domain to another is not automatic. If the transfer is not explicitly taught, supported, and practiced, it will not occur.

Doing multiple versions of a project is another way to indicate to the students and their parents that project work is an important component of the curriculum and not a marginal, almost recreational, activity. Raising the standards with each successive project reinforces this message. If you chose to repeat projects, you will often want to vary aspects of the project to enhance the learning experience.

You may also find that the original definition of a project does not quite match the particular circumstances of your classroom. The tasks may appear too difficult or they may appear too easy. A particular content area in the curriculum may require increased attention, perhaps in the form of a culminating project that builds on and integrates what has gone before. An issue may surface for the larger community, the school, the neighborhood or the town, that calls for rational and systematic treatment. Changes occur in the equipment and on-line resources making up the technical environment of the classroom, which force changes in the definition of projects.

Theory

To provide a framework for thinking about changing projects, we describe four dimensions on which projects may vary: the process, standards, subject matter, and tools.

Table 15-1 indicates generic ways to vary or enhance projects to make them more challenging. The need to "scale up" may arise when you encounter older students who are already experienced with student-constructed multimedia projects, or over the school year as your own students mature.

You may also find it necessary to scale down a project, making it easier, perhaps for younger grades, for remedial situations, or to fit a shorter time slot in the year. Table 15-2 indicates general methods for achieving this, using the same four dimensions.

We now provide more detail on these generic approaches, taking the dimensions one at a time. In the practice section, when we offer specific examples of variations of the projects described in the progression in the text, you will notice that changes in one dimension are often accompanied by changes in another.

Scaling Up

Table 15-1 outlines ways to make projects more challenging, based on the dimensions of process, standards, subject matter, and tools.

Table 15-1: Scaling up

Process: more responsibility
- Students design templates, programming, appearance of pages
- Students prepare template, programs, graphics
- Students set up equipment
- Students manage schedule
- Students from different grades have different roles

Raising the bar: increased standards
- Better writing
- Higher quality images, video and still camera work, drawing, audio recording
- Broader, deeper research
- More features
- More intricate interactions with users
- Wider audience: other classes & schools, parents, community

Subject area
- One academic discipline to another
- Entertaining topic to controversial topic

New tools
- Switch to professional tool, or any new tool
- Less automation, for example, VCR instead of laser disc player

Paying attention to the process of project creation requires you to move toward roles that have been described as coach, mentor, band leader, producer, or sponsor. None of these metaphors are totally accurate. Each teacher must define, in each circumstance, the responsibilities of the students and also allow opportunities for those responsibilities to grow.

When you turn over the job of managing the project to the students, the challenge grows significantly. Students must break down the whole task into subtasks. They must devise a reasonable schedule and they must monitor the schedule. However, this does not have to be an all-or-nothing situation. You can be the one initiating and facilitating a class discussion to generate a schedule. You can ask the class or individual teams to define at the start of the project an interim checkpoint to report back or to show progress.

A change in subject area, with an adjustment in the process to put more of the responsibility for project definition and management on the students, is an effective way to challenge students.

One aspect of the process is the time allocated for completion of the project. Giving more time does not necessarily make a project easier. Allocating more time while simultaneously raising the standard encourages students to go beyond their initial efforts and to refine their product.

Raising standards in a deliberate manner is an important strategy for teachers. This is especially true in times when "everyone is above average." If you introduce a new project as the next in a sequence of projects, you can use the students' own reflections, as well as the audience reaction, to define the new standards. Any change or broadening of audience raises the bar because new viewers have different expectations.

The decision to change the software tools or the platform may be forced by factors outside your control. However, if this situation does occur, you can take advantage of it by giving the students the challenge of investigating the new set of tools. Substantial learning and attractive student work can emerge from the use of a variety of tools. In their time at school and in their working careers, students will often need to confront new tools, new platforms and new procedures on a regular basis. Teachers and educational technologists, acting in a support role, can suggest to the students that the new tool will require some procedures like the old tool and some different and they, the students, should make note of what falls in each category.

Scaling Down

You can also consider these same dimensions in modifying a project for younger, less mature students (see Table 15-2). For example, you can design and implement templates and oversee their use quite closely. You can identify students who can manage some of the technical work and give them extra responsibilities. You may schedule showing projects to a wider audience at a slow and deliberate pace. This will allow each student to rework the material many times.

In Chapter 4, Roles of Existing Multimedia Content, we describe commercial products that combine the functions of authoring tool and content resource. Some of these even take the students through directed explorations. The material supplied in these packages is often rich in detail and exquisitely presented. However, the students do not face all the intellectual challenges of researching and organizing the subject area that they do when they start with an empty folder or stack.

Varying the type of subject area can make a project easier, more difficult, or merely different. Scaling down can be accomplished by narrowing the focus of the investigation and specifying the focus explicitly to the class. A tactic for younger students is to assign a second project on a new topic with the structure of the project exactly the same as in the first project so that the students are essentially identifying, creating and plugging in components. It is important, as we have indicated, to give students the chance to transfer general cognitive skills from one subject area to another to solidify their grasp of skills and to practice how it is done.

Table 15-2: Scaling down

Process
- Teachers and technical support prepare components of projects
- Schedule and monitor students' individual contributions
- Divide process into many subtasks
- Use older students as mentors at selective stages in process

Appropriate standards
- Be tolerant but be ready to encourage increased efforts
- Provide ample dress rehearsals before special performances

Subject area
- Explicitly indicate common factors when changing subject area
- Narrow focus within academic discipline,
- Introduce very familiar topic

Tools
- Prepare programs, templates, interfaces, and models for student use
- Use specialized, integrated packages for student multimedia construction
- Provide peer, older students, and other levels of support

Historical note: How Terms Change

Consider how the idioms connoting starting from nothing have reflected changes in technology:

- clean slate

- blank page

- empty folder

Be on the lookout for other idioms based on metaphorical references to older technologies.

Practice

In this section, we suggest specific ways to alter each of the projects described in the progression from Chapter 7 through Chapter 12 (see Table 15-3).

We use the dimensions of process, standards, subject area, and tools already discussed in the Theory section and indicate the circumstances under which you would try each alternative. The changes may affect more than one dimension. For example, a change in standards will generally require paying attention to the process and possibly making modifications.

Table 15-3: Variations and extensions

Project in Progression	Variations
Current Events	Subject Watch Glossary Continuing Story of X Then and Now Elementary School Pick a Headline
Critics' Circle	Voices from the Outside Major Presentation at Parents' Night
Trailers	For Outside Audiences Use Subtle Clues Mixed Grade Setting Compare with Actual Trailers Repurpose Laser Discs
Science Quiz	Production Model What Your Tax Dollars Buy Multimedia Yearbook Frog Dissection Quiz Geography Game Equipment Training
Memoirs	Production Company Visit to Senior Citizen Center
Research Magazine	Pen Pals to Payoff Trip Exchange Aftermath Technology Change

Current Events

Subject Watch

Elementary school teachers who wish to focus attention on a particular subject area—government, mathematics, or science, for example—as well as subject teachers in the higher grades can focus on their topics in what we have named Subject Watch, a version of Current Events. In each case, the teacher and class begin the process by planning and designing new main menus. These can be either in place of or in addition to the timeline and map pages.

For example, if your class is studying the topic of government, the students may begin by classifying stories according to which of the three branches of government they involve. Over time, these categories may evolve into something more complex (see Figure 15-1 and Figure 15-2).

If your class is studying mathematics, students can draw on the many feature stories based on polls, the census, or research studies, as well as the continual stream of sports statistics. Your students can position these stories in time and place in two distinct ways: where and when the news event took place and for what time period and over what geographical entity a point is being made. For example, a sports record may be "the best in 30 years" or "breaking a record that stood for 10 years." A report on infant mortality may contrast rates in regions of the United States with rates in countries around the world. You can encourage the students to make use of maps and other graphical aids in their story summaries.

Government Watch

Legislative
Executive
Judiciary

Figure 15-1: Menu screen for government watch: initial set of categories

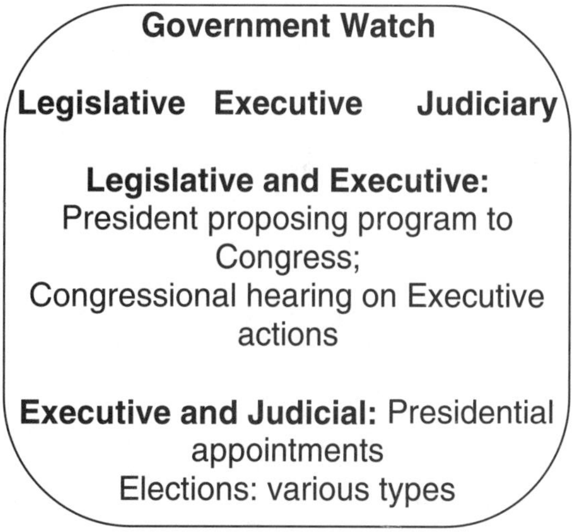

Government Watch

Legislative   Executive   Judiciary

Legislative and Executive:
President proposing program to Congress;
Congressional hearing on Executive actions

Executive and Judicial: Presidential appointments
Elections: various types

Figure 15-2: Menu screen for government watch, with added categories over time

Unfortunately, many news articles feature debatable interpretations of statistics. You can use this as an opportunity to engage your students in critical thinking. By requiring students to review and summarize a story and by providing graphical tools, you can encourage lively conversation on these issues. The on-line archive can ask the users to indicate whether they believe statistics were used appropriately and explain their reasons.

Science is also a subject area that is amenable to a Subject Watch activity. In some areas of the country this is almost too easy because newspapers have a scheduled day to publish a whole section on science. The class can start the archive with a simple listing of topics as indicated in Figure 15-3.

As indicated in the Current Events chapter, news events may relate to more than one category. You can make sure that the students are actually thinking about the news events by making sure that they link each entry appropriately.

Of course, you must balance this activity with your own science explorations in the classroom so that students do not retain the common impression that science is only the stuff that gets written about in newspapers. By calling attention to science news stories, you can disabuse students of the common notion that science has all been done and is only the content of a set of textbooks.

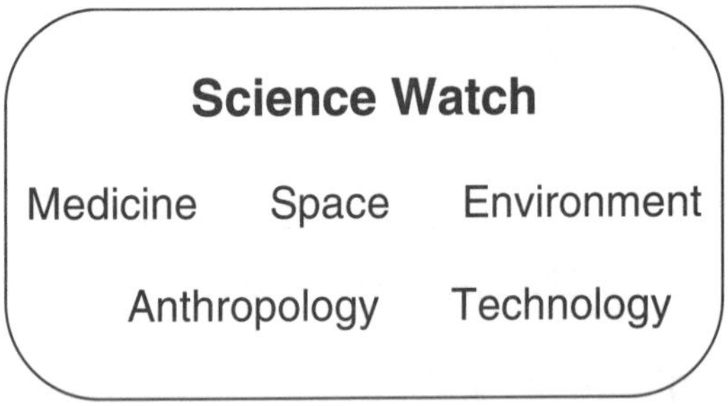

This focused approach to Current Events is appropriate when the curriculum area calls for specific topics. The multimedia archive provides hypertext and graphical tools to express relationships. It also provides efficient storage of the materials so you and your students can review, update, and reorganize the archive continuously over the course of the year.

Science Watch

Medicine   Space   Environment

Anthropology   Technology

Figure 15-3: Menu screen for science topics

Glossary

Current events type projects, as well as other ongoing activities, are enhanced by requiring students to contribute to an on-line glossary. Pop-up definitions and a cross-referenced, alphabetized glossary section add great value to students' projects. You can use the evolving glossary for vocabulary and spelling assignments.

Continuing Story of X

Teachers can modify an ongoing current events activity or they can initiate such an activity with the focus on a single evolving story. By definition, almost anything we say here will be dated, so we will not give examples from the current set of international crises, congressional initiatives, or local and national scandals. You can start the project by assigning some or all students to do research into the recent past. Public libraries and the school libraries may even have on-line references for finding articles on past events. This project and the multimedia product can be named the Continuing Story of X where X is replaced by something invented by the students. Fundamental questions arise: What is the name of the story? Whose story is it? Is the name changing?

You can encourage additional labels on the timeline beyond the dates. The nature and scale of the timeline may also be changed as the story unfolds. Students may choose to redraw the timeline as the story evolves.

Then and Now

You can make a simultaneous content and process change to the Current Events project by requiring students to relate their current article to something in the past. Not so long ago, several classes created multimedia essays focused on contrasting the Vietnam War with the Persian Gulf War. They recorded video from news broadcasts and they searched on-line encyclopedias for the historical material. Teachers and parents reported significantly increased depths of understanding. Unfortunately, it is likely that opportunities to compare current wars with past wars will continue to exist.

Elementary School

Current events is a common topic for the elementary school classroom. The project as described in Chapter 7 should be within the capabilities of young students. Here are some specific suggestions.

- Use the authoring system to develop an application that leads students through the process of making each link and constructing the pages for their stories.

- Suggest or require that students copy directly from the newspaper article and then restate the ideas in their own words. The fact that the original is on the screen forces the students to come up with "their own words." It also presents both versions to the other students.

- Be sure to spend class time and individual time on reflection. This project can produce opportunities to catch students doing something good.

Pick a Headline

The headline on a newspaper article reflects the style of the paper as well as the content of the article. The headlines for articles on the same event from different newspapers may exhibit more variety than the prose of the articles. People speak of "screaming headlines" and "second-coming type." Teachers can devise variations of the Current Events project based on student evaluation of the subtext and the appropriateness of the headline. Following is one such project.

Students produce an interactive Current Events-type project in which users read the article and then select what they think is the most accurate headline. Figure 15-4 schematically shows a page with a portion of the news story. Users read the story and then click to get a list of choices for the headline.

Figure 15-5 indicates the result of clicking on the choices button: a pop-up field appears with a numbered list.

Creators gather the choices from actual newspaper articles and add headlines of their own creations. They write a program to keep track of the choices selected and also maintain a list of candidate entries from the users. A variation to Critics' Circle described later in this chapter has a similar voting component.

Ongoing reflection on this project would include discussion of the nature of headlines and how they influence perception of the news. Article placement and use of photographs are other significant factors that can invoke thinking on content and communication issues.

PICK THE BEST HEADLINE

xxxxxxxxxxxxxxxxxxxxxxxxxxxxxxxx
xxxxxxxxxxxxxxxxxxxxxxxxxxxxxxxx
xxxxxxxxxxxxxxxxxxxxxxxxxxxxxxxx
xxxxxxxxxxxxxxxxxxxxxxxxxxxxxxxx
Click here to read choices

Figure 15-4: Sketch for initial screen for Pick a Headline

PICK THE BEST HEADLINE

xxx xxxxxx xxxxxx xxx xxxxxxx xxxxxx
xxxx xxxxxxxx xxxx xxxxx xx xxx xxxx

xxxxxxxxxxxxxxxxxxxxxxxxxxxxxxxx
xxxxxxxxxxxxxxxxxxxxxxxxxxxxxxxx

1)xxxxxxxxxxx
2)xxxxxxxxxxxxxxx
3)xxxxxxxxxxxxx
4)xxxxxxxxxxxxx
Choose one of the four given
OR
Click here to write your own

Figure 15-5: Sketch for screen for Pick a Headline with choices

Critics' Circle

Voices from the Outside

The Critics' Circle project as described in Chapter 8 uses as critics only the students in the classroom. Varying this project by using critics from outside the classroom or school increases the challenge to the students. As in Memoirs, student interviewers must perform in a public, professional manner. They must prepare the speakers by engaging them on the topic. They must perform the technical tasks of recording the audio comments and then digitizing them for inclusion in the multimedia product. They also must take photographs or prepare other images for a visual background to the audio remarks.

Students may have to choose which speakers to include in order to represent the spectrum of opinion on the topic. It may be appropriate and beneficial to select three or four representative voices and then have a mechanism for users to hear the other voices. After outside people appear as speakers in a multimedia production, they should be invited to see the completed product. This raises standards considerably, as these people will not want their words to be misrepresented. In addition, it is appropriate for students to collect written permission statements just as newspapers collect signed statements. The presentation should acknowledge all contributions.

The topic for a Voices from the Outside can be a popular movie or an issue of current interest for the community. Controversial topics can prove constructive to learning. It is, of course, important that teachers guide students to go beyond the obvious definition of sides of an issue and seek out varied and subtle viewpoints.

Technical Note: Tape Cassette to Digitized Audio

The multimedia equipment that enables recording of audio through a microphone usually also supports recording through a cable connection from an audio tape recorder. The connection may be labeled "line input."

Major Presentation at Parents' Night

The output of Critics' Circle projects reviewing popular movies or topics of local interest are excellent candidates for inclusion on a public program or a lobby kiosk at Parents' Night. You can target particular public events to give the students a goal. Alternatively, you may postpone the decision until the projects are complete and then decide if and when to present finished work.

Students can enhance their Critics' Circle-type projects by providing a mechanism for the users to vote on which speaker they agree with, or even provide a way for them to add their own commentary. Making the project interactive for users exercises the students' creativity, judgment and technical skills. One possibility is to add to the opening menu a suggestion to listen to all the opinions and then vote for the one with whom you are in greatest agreement (see Figure 15-6). This suggestion can be incorporated into the written text and the audio announcement. The enhancement we suggest is feasible using many different authoring systems. Below we describe an implementation using the commented pseudo-code that we have used previously.

The first page of the folder has an audio announcement. It is possible in most authoring systems to set this to play automatically when the page is entered. We suggest placing a page before that page, a new first page, with an automatic event that establishes variables for holding the counts for each speaker (see Figure 15-7). This event then links to the main menu that was the original first page. All other pages return to the new second page.

On each speaker page, Figure 15-6, there is a new button that invokes a program that

**Figure 15-6: Sample speaker page with digitized
image produced using the QuickCam camera
QuickPict software by Connectix**

increments the appropriate counter (see Figure 15-8). This button can be labeled AGREE. From any page, a TOTALS button will produce the current totals.

The students can also provide facilities to let the viewers of Critics' Circle provide feedback by entering their own, unrestricted text. Of course, more complex options are available for interaction and you can encourage students to devise and implement their own schemes.

```
var s1(4), s2(4), s3(4);
-- allocate variables
set s1 = 0; set s2 = 0; set s3 = 0;
-- initialize variables to zero
link seq+1; --  go to next page
```

Figure 15-7: Voting: pseudo-code for automatic initial action

```
set  s1 = s1 + 1; -- increment count by
                     one
```

Figure 15-8: Pseudo-code invoked by AGREE Button for speaker 1

Trailers

For Outside Audiences

As is the case with Critics' Circle, a Trailers project of artful selections of movie clips is highly appealing to a broader audience than the students in the classroom. Enhancements to make Trailers interactive include providing an opportunity for viewers to select one of the clips and see it again. A voting mechanism can also be implemented by creating YES and NO buttons using counters established at the start, in a manner similar to what we just described for Critics' Circle. Users click on YES if they want to see the movie and NO if they do not.

Using Subtle Clues

The Trailers design requires selecting and then putting together a sequence of clips to persuade a particular audience to see the film. The selection of clips can be based on more specific, and more subtle, principles. For example, you can assign the students the task of identifying a set of clips in which the music indicates increased tension. The use of visual clues to evoke reminders of the plot could also be the focus of the students' work. Teams of students could find and string together all sections that offered predictions on something happening in the story. Such assignments challenge the students' understanding of the action and their observation skills. We refer you also to Chapter 13 on advanced techniques.

Mixed Grade Setting

The Trailers project can bring together students from different grades for a cooperative effort. The older students can ask the younger students to choose from among a set of movies available on laser disc or CD-ROM. The older students can then lead and monitor a discussion among the younger students and learn what this audience liked about the movie. During the project process, the older students can go back to their young informants for confirmation and modification of their choices.

Compare with Actual Trailers

After making a trailer for a specific movie, students can view and report back on the actual trailers produced by professionals. Of course, movie theaters may not be showing the trailers after the main run of the movie is complete. However, many video tapes as well as laser discs include trailers and additional material not included in the original film. Examining professional trailers can serve to raise the standards and also to introduce topics of discussion of marketing, audience stereotyping, and film aesthetics.

Repurpose Laser Discs (or CD-ROMs)

You can assign teams of students to take educational laser discs and extract a sequence of clips with appropriate voice-overs for specific academic purposes. Some of the commercial discs have a feature supporting the use of bar codes to locate different topics. Students can use the bar code scanners and other mechanisms to determine the frame numbers for their project. The technical work would be very close to that done for Trailers.

Reminder

We discuss the requirements for obtaining permission to use commercial work in Chapter 4. Many commercial laser disc titles give explicit permission for repurposing for educational uses. However, each case must be examined individually.

Science Quiz

Production Model

The Science Quiz project, as indicated in Chapter 10, is a complex undertaking for a class. You may consider using the production model of organizing work (see Chapter 14) as opposed to individual groups. This is a change in process that can facilitate a change in the standards and expectations for the project.

What Your Tax Dollars Buy

Building on the technology introduced in Science Quiz, consider a variation that links scenes of school activities to text descriptions and indicates how school resources are used through graphs showing staffing requirements, space, and expenses. Teams of students can produce a kiosk presentation to inform and persuade the community to vote for the school budget. The project can begin with a piechart showing the top-level breakdown of the budget. Users click on sections of the pie to get increasingly detailed definitions. At the lowest level, video clips show actual school activities with text descriptions of what is taking place and why it is worthwhile.

This variation has an authentic audience, the voters in the community, and a very stringent, authentic schedule. Budget votes cannot be delayed because the project is not completed. This is an example of changing a base project by significantly raising the bar with respect to standards.

Multimedia Yearbook

The basic idea of matched sets of video clips, texts, and images can also be used for a multimedia yearbook. You need to organize early in the school year to collect materials. Each activity has three representations.

- Video clips can show activities such as club meetings and sports events.
- An image can be the standard shot of all the members.
- The text can describe the club or team and give the highlights of the year.

Many students, from classes throughout the school or even the district, can be involved in this project, which definitely requires the production company approach. An amusing device would be to incorporate a quiz in which users are presented with groups of video clips to be matched with descriptions or group photographs. "Can you recognize the computer club?" "What group of students is shown in this candid shot?" The multimedia yearbook could tell, in an audio recording, whether the viewer is correct or incorrect. The Yearbook project could make use of audio clips, particularly for introductory sections.

Technical Note: Archives

For a project such as a multimedia yearbook, teachers may consider the possibility of producing CD-ROMs as opposed to keeping the project on diskettes or on the internal disk of one computer. Critical factors here are the quantity of material, which quickly mounts up due to the storage requirements of video clips, images, and audio; the number of copies required; and the longevity required for the project. This is not a Science Quiz to be redone every year. The Class of '01 wants their yearbook to last.

Frog Dissection Quiz

In this project, groups of students prepare a multimedia quiz as a culminating activity following the frog dissection laboratory. The basic task of the quiz is to identify parts and functions on a labeled photograph of their frog and match it with the corresponding parts on a diagram or photograph from a reference book. The creators organize the questions in a hierarchy so that anyone failing a question can fall back to an easier question.

We suggest this particular topic because dissection is a very common activity in middle schools and high schools. However, there is an additional reason for this choice. Some people suggest that the increased realism supported by computer graphics makes it feasible to replace real dissections with simulated dissections. We would argue against that position. It is a fundamental fact that there is significant variability among life forms. The students' frogs differ from the perfect frog in the textbook. This project is designed to reinforce the anatomy facts and laboratory skills of the standard lab, but also make vivid this notion of variability.

The assignment for the project is to produce material for a multimedia quiz. Specifically, each group takes photographs using either a digital camera, a camcorder, or a regular camera. They then incorporate the images into the computer using the appropriate procedure.

Readers may think that this project is easy because it involves only still photography. However, it has its own rigorous requirements for high quality. To produce images that are clear enough to examine, students must devise schemes for lighting and maintaining sharp focus.

Once the photograph is in digitized form, the group imports it into their multimedia project. They also select and acquire appropriate photographs and diagrams from reference sources. Students devise and build sets of questions in several forms such as

- identifying parts of the frog by moving the mouse onto the appropriate areas of the image from their photograph,
- bringing in a commercial photograph from a reference source and making correspondences (that is, connecting lines) between similar parts, and
- writing commentary comparing and contrasting their frog and the reference frog.

The Frog Dissection project requires acquisition and manipulation of materials from commercial sources as well as student-created content. It produces an effective instrument for studying prior to school, state or, national examinations. Students in the class and other classes constitute an authentic audience for the project.

> **Note: But They Are All Alike**
>
> When discussing frog dissection with science teachers, we were informed that although the idea for a student-produced multimedia quiz has appeal and the notion of paying attention to real-life variability is certainly important, the frogs now used for dissection present very little variability since they are essentially bred from a single strain.

Geography Game

The format used in Science Quiz can be applied to subject areas other than science. Geography is an obvious choice for a variation along the subject dimension because it has both text and graphical aspects. Geography does require memorization. The standard practice of asking students to do their own rote learning of capitals and maps does not produce long-lasting results. When students create their own geography games and, as a consequence, spend time manipulating the maps and working with the facts, there is a greater likelihood that students will internalize the information.

Figure 15-9 shows one set of questions for a geography game.

We are assuming that the students have access to commercial maps and some support for the necessary scripting.

The game is designed like arcade games that get progressively more difficult. Students determine what feedback to give to players, including when and how to show the correct answers. You can use a variety of approaches for the actual creation of this game. One way of using the production company model is to include as many students as possible in the initial design phases. Then, when it is clear what the design is, teachers can assign a team of students to meet with the technical support people for the building or district and to study the authoring system manuals to put together the technical components of the project. After this is accomplished, the rest of the class can be brought back into action to put together the lists and tables that make up the content of the game. Different teams can have different regions of the world as their responsibilities.

> **Geography Game Events**
> 1. Show region such as Central America. Highlight a state or country. User must type in correct name.
> 2. Display state or country. User must click on correct location.
> 3. Display state or country name. User must list one other state, country, or body of water bordering on the first state or country.
> 4. Display state or country name. User must list all states or countries and bodies of water bordering on the first state or country.
> 5. Show map and highlight state or country and features such as mountains, rivers, lakes. User must name state or country and name features.

Figure 15-9: Geography game instructions

Figure 15-10 is an example of an accompanying map. Depending on the maturity of the students, you can

- build on the design given here,
- describe it as a suggestion but let the students modify it, or
- make it totally open for the students.

Because no one student or even group of students produces all the answers, the game will be a challenge for everyone. In any case, the students will spend considerable time-on-task. The class can also challenge other classes and parents to play the Geography Game.

We are not suggesting that you ignore the increasing volume of commercial multimedia products for geography. What we do suggest is that teachers and students use these materials to make their own projects. This more active use of the content increases the likelihood of long-lasting learning.

What is this country?

Figure 15-10: Sample map prepared for Geography Game

Equipment Training

Safety considerations make it necessary to instruct students on the use of the various types of equipment found in gyms. Teachers responsible for this training can work with older students to produce multimedia training materials for younger students. The project can combine video clips, text descriptions, and audio clips. There may also be diagrams and other images. The basic techniques of the Science Quiz can be used to produce the training system. This student-produced system could also be used in a self-tutoring capacity to prepare users to perform in front of the coaches to be certified as capable of using the equipment.

Making Do

What if a classroom doesn't have access to commercial maps or the teacher prefers that students spend time drawing their own maps? The students can use scanners to get the images into the system If the commercial maps are simply drawings without demarcations for states or countries, the students can use drawing programs to outline the borders that they want highlighted. The images on the screen will be composites of the commercial work and the student work.

Memoirs

Production Company

The Memoirs activity, as described in Chapter 11, involves every student in interviewing of members of the community. This certainly has benefits. However, as we indicated for Science Quiz, you may want to consider the production company approach. In this case, you send out fewer teams of students to gather the data on significant events by interviewing people. The number of different events to be analyzed will be smaller. However, you may expect and require a higher standard of performance for each task.

Visit to Senior Citizen Center

If students seek out older people, perhaps one or two generations beyond what students would find in their own homes, the content of the material will be different and the interpersonal skills required of the interviewers will probably be greater. The authors have direct experience doing video interviewing and compiling multimedia projects with senior citizens. We have also worked with classroom teachers and read about similar projects. We strongly recommend it for your students.

You and your class may choose to focus on interviewees over a certain age or include them within the larger sample of people. If you do choose to include a wide range of ages, it would be appropriate to include timelines in the presentation.

Research Magazine

Chapter 12, Research Magazine, lists several possible topics for varying the focus of this activity. The critical factors for you to consider are

- what subject matter includes information best represented by images, diagrams, audio, and video; and
- what topic benefits from involving classes from more than one school.

Here, we focus on two of the four dimensions for variation. We focus on this to show how you manage the process of the activity and changes in available tools.

Pen Pals to Payoff

A great deal of variety exists in how much you manage the process of creating the Research Magazine and how much you leave to the students. One approach is to initiate an arrangement by which two classes in different schools begin communicating simply as pen pals. They use E-mail for letters describing themselves, their community, and their school. They also use file transfer to send class work, including items of multimedia such as group photographs. No requirement is placed on what they send, but strong encouragement is given to keep in contact.

For younger students, the pen pal project may be all that you do. If you have older students and are ambitious, you can do more. After time passes, well into the semester or the year, you and the teacher at the other site can pose the question to your students of whether they want to do a major joint project with the other class. You can let the students define the process, although it is important that you ask about goals, audience, schedules, and resource constraints. If the students have had experiences with project work and with the technologies, this can stimulate and stretch their skills but will be within their capabilities.

Trip Exchange Aftermath

An initial step of a Research Magazine or a Pen Pals project is to identify the other school or schools. One tactic to use is to identify a group in your school that has contact with another school. A common example of this is music departments having exchange visits with other music departments. Because of the requirements of scheduling, it often occurs that many people in the band, orchestra, or chorus end up in the same history, English, science or mathematics class. It is not necessary that everyone in your class have met people from the other school, but some prior face-to-face contact is beneficial.

A variation of Research Magazine would be to make the content of the magazine a documentary on "what we saw when we visited X." Each class of students could respond to the observations of the visitors.

Technology Change

We can guarantee that the technologies with which you communicate with other schools, both the hardware and software, will change. We include in this prediction even the communications method. This means that students who communicated with groups around the globe or successfully produced a joint multimedia project will have to learn new tools. This is a benefit for learning rather than a burden. You can initiate the process of defining the new project by asking the class to compare the new technical environment with the old.

Summary

In this chapter we provided a framework of four dimensions for you to consider for varying projects and described specific variations of the projects in the text. We gave arguments for repeating projects and ways to vary the project when doing so. A framework for modifying projects was introduced and described in terms of making projects more difficult or easier. We referred to this as "scaling up" and "scaling down," but the effects are often much more subtle than those terms imply. We also gave examples of variations and extensions of projects and characterized the way we changed the project in terms of our basic framework.

Another way of varying projects is to begin from consideration of the subject matter. Take a school topic and see if any of the project ideas described in this text can apply. Here are useful questions to ask when considering applying multimedia to a topical area or activity.

- Does the subject matter intrinsically involve representations in multiple forms? Are students thinking about and manipulating important or tangential aspects of the subject matter?

- Would the project have a real audience? Are there users or viewers of the multimedia project to inspire substantial work? Will the exposure invoke deep thinking?

- Do the students need the repeated exposure to the materials or the repeated experiences with the skills?

- Does this take away from or reinforce other learning?

Chapter 16

The Idea Book

In this chapter, we explore:

- how to create and organize an on-line notebook of ideas for classroom activities.

- how to maintain the on-line notebook to help in project planning.

This chapter describes a productivity tool for teachers, curriculum specialists, and technology support staff that we call the Idea Book. Note that we cover substantive issues on project evaluation in the next chapter, Assessment. We begin by describing the concept of an on-line, multimedia notebook of ideas for classroom activities. In the Theory section, we indicate ways in which you can facilitate the achievement of educational benefits by suggesting organizations and features for this tool. The Practice section includes examples of how educators can use the Idea Book and how its benefits grow over time.

Background

The Idea Book is an on-line multimedia version of the card file or notebook kept by many educators to jot down ideas for lessons and classroom projects. Educators may also like to record their personal reactions to what goes on in their classroom and school, reflecting on positive and negative experiences. We propose here a multimedia version of these tools. Our focus is on educators, but students can make similar use of multimedia for their own journals.

You can use any multimedia authoring system to set up an on-line notebook. The entries for each idea can include all the media described in this book. The author can record an idea, along with subsequent reflections and annotations of the idea, using

- text,
- overlays of the text in the form of pop-up text,

- graphics sketched using any of the available draw programs,
- digitized images (for example, photographs of students at work),
- audio clips (particularly appealing for spontaneous reactions to events), and
- short video clips.

The record of an idea can also include an annotated listing of files and reference sources, both computer-based and not computer-based, that are connected with the idea. The hypertext facilities allow you, who may be the exclusive user, to establish multiple organizational frameworks for exploring the material. The multiple navigational themes can include grade level, time in year, time required by the project, grouping strategies, subject or topic within the discipline, educational goals, and so forth.

The projects described in this text and other multimedia projects can go into an Idea Book. However, the tool is not limited to multimedia or computer-based activities. Any classroom activity can be recorded in the Idea Book.

You can put ideas and reflections into the Idea Book when planning an activity or when making periodic assessments of what is happening in the classroom, school, or school district. Portions of the Idea Book can have a fixed structure with links to pages that are quite open-ended. Overall organizations can be retained, modified, or abandoned as you see fit over time and after use.

Technical support staff and curriculum specialists can keep their own Idea Book for use in helping classroom teachers. Classroom teachers can use it for lesson plans. In computer systems that are well integrated with modems and telephone connections, the Idea Book can include important telephone numbers so that, for example, teachers, while considering using a particular idea that involves some special need, can click on a number and call the building services as required. Even if such integration does not exist, the Idea Book can serve as a convenient repository for all the information or pointers to the information required for engaging in a particular classroom exercise.

The Idea Book is a living, growing document. You can always add annotations to the original material that represent later reflections. How did the project actually unfold? Was it a success? What are positive and negative lessons? What actually happened with respect to groupings? How did specific students participate and perform?

Although using authoring system facilities and including images and other media may make the Idea Book look like a polished and even glitzy presentation, its purpose is to serve your own personal and professional needs. You can choose what, when, and how much of the document to share with others. Facilities exist in most authoring systems to hide or insert password protection over selected portions. Alternatively, you can construct a separate document for public view by judicious "cut and paste" work.

How does technology, in this case the technologies of multimedia, serve the educator better than the old-fashioned tools? Here are some potential factors.

- The hypertext support of multiple organizations can improve access to the information. This means less flipping through the spiral notebook in search of the ideas that worked well for groups. Of course, the tool is only as good as its use and educators must use all the facilities to reap all the benefits. See also the side-bar on Arguments for an Old-fashioned File.

- The author can add and modify information right where it applies and not worry about filling up the note card in the card file or squeezing things into the margins. As we have indicated for the student projects, multimedia provides a robust form of storage for work, one that does not fray around the edges or get torn or stained.

- Teachers and other educators can include samples of actual work, in the form of material copied over onto pages or pointed to as files. You can also include photographs of work and digitized video clips of classroom activity as well as photos.

- For ideas involving the use of technology including multimedia, the Idea Book entry can include notes, story boards, and even working templates.

We close this section by noting that an underlying reason to use multimedia for personal productivity is that this will make you better skilled and more understanding when it comes to the subject-oriented student projects. People become better researchers, developers, and manufacturers of personal computer-based tools when they are users themselves.

The next section describes specific suggestions about format and organization for the Idea Book. There is no one correct form; one of the advantages of the multimedia approach is that the organization and format can evolve over time as the creator wishes.

Argument for an Old-fashioned File

You say, "I don't want to give up my old cookbook because even though some pages stick together, it always opens up to favorite recipes and I can remember how good a recipe was from the stains on the page." Perhaps it is not tomato sauce but paint from that day's activities or other debris from everyday life that adds information and grounding for your work. Consider the following: you can put in all sorts of annotations and make them colorful and audible. You need to do this to make the most effective use of this tool. You may put in links to tangential issues, pop-up overlays, links to pages describing common themes, and so on. This doesn't happen by itself, as it always seems to with the tomato sauce, but can be done.

Theory

In this section, we propose a structure for an idea entry and classification schemes that can serve as outlines for menus. We also indicate certain techniques that may prove beneficial as productivity aids for the individual educator and for a working team. As we have noted already, these are just suggestions. If adopted, these or any other structures will undoubtedly undergo modification when you put them into active use.

Individual Entry

The design concept driving this format for idea entry is to show on one page all the critical aspects of the project and to provide links to supporting information. The idea page includes

- one line description;
- grade level or setting, actual and potential;
- major higher-level educational goals;
- subject or discipline content areas;
- grouping or nature of group dynamics and group assignment plan;
- equipment needed and technical skills; and
- reference to project templates, programs, and sources.

The examples in Figure 16-1 and Figure 16-2 show how one teacher may categorize a two projects described in this book. Other sample activity ideas are in Figure 16-3, Figure

Current Events Archive
Students contribute news article summaries to class archive
Fifth grade class, all year   POTENTIAL: grades 1 to 12
Organization, Summarizing, Connections
Current events, geography
Individual contribution to whole class project—relate to other's work
EQUIPMENT: 1 computer, optional scanner
SEE CLASS94 file

Figure 16-1: Entry for Current Events

Science Quiz

Teams produce quiz relating recorded motion,
time verus position graphs, and text
Mixed grade middle school, 2 weeks
POTENTIAL: grades 5 to 12
Planning; insight to user; orchestration of
material
Physics & Math of Time versus Position,
Velocity, Acceleration
Significant team work
EQUIPMENT: micro-based lab, camcorder,
computer with frame grabber, disk space,
diskettes, space
SEE QUIZCODE file

Figure 16-2: Entry for Science Quiz

16-4, and Figure 16-5. Each of the entries, such as the activity's potential grade range, is one teacher's opinion. Your opinion may differ.

Figure 16-3 indicates a computer based activity that does not involve multimedia.

Gopher Burrowing

Students explore on-line Internet resources
using the Gopher facility
Homework assignment for juniors
POTENTIAL: grades 6 to 12
Follow directions, willingness to explore
Content suggested: college news stories
Teamwork feasible. Prepare report to class
EQUIPMENT: computer with modem and
necessary software
SEE GOPHER_LIST file

**Figure 16-3: Entry for exploration of Internet
using Gopher, a common access method**

The next two examples shown in Figure 16-4 and Figure 16-5 are not computer-based. The benefit of including descriptions of these activities is that they can be considered along with the others. If the Idea Book proves valuable, you will use it for noncomputer activities as often as computer-based activities.

The idea page for each activity also holds the links to more information, some on-line and some off-line. For example, you can use the mechanisms of pop-up scrollable text, links to other pages, and links to invoke audio clips in the following ways.

- One line description
- Pop-up scrolled text description
- Major higher-level educational goals
- Pop-up with reference to journal article
- Subject or discipline content areas
- Reference to school curriculum
- Grouping or nature of group dynamics and group assignment plan
- Record of actual grouping
- Equipment needed, technical skills
- Link to descriptions of school computer facilities and technical support staff
- Names of computer files

Shoe-tying

Teams develop program or lesson on how to tie shoes

Mixed grade middle school, short session on robots
POTENTIAL: anything

Planning; concept of program, concept of sensory feedback

Introduction to programming

Present to class, speaker
EQUIPMENT: paper and pencil, shoes with laces

AUDIO COMMENT

Figure 16-4: Entry for shoe tying description activity

Quiz Show

Class participates in a TV game show on curriculum area, working in teams
High school
POTENTIAL: anything

Limited higher level skills

Content area is subject of the quiz
Team work—any member of team can be called on for answer
EQUIPMENT: white board, token prizes

AUDIO COMMENTS

Figure 16-5: Entry for quiz show activity

The skeleton page shown Figure 16-6 would be linked to the idea entry through a linking button and would contain buttons to return to the idea entry or go to the next curriculum entry. Entries relating to the district curricula could be linked together so that it would be possible to review all the ideas in terms of District goals.

You can place critical information on equipment and technical support on a separate page. Alternatively, it is possible to link from each idea page to a standard page of information on resources such as names and telephone numbers. The link back to the last idea entry viewed may require more advanced use of the authoring system.

The sample resource list shown in Figure 16-7 indicates names, telephone extensions, and schedules for a hypothetical staff. The feature of linking to other pages can also be utilized in special ways, depending on the situation. In the example in Figure 16-5, the text that reads "limited higher level skills" could serve as an indication that a variation of the project exists, with the potential for something more in the way of higher order thinking, and that information on it is contained elsewhere.

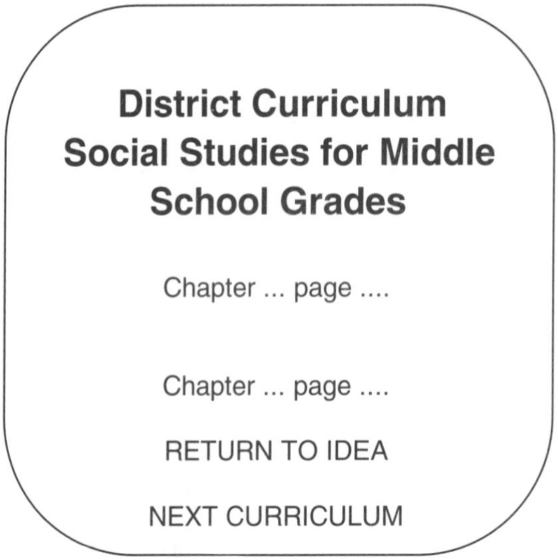

**District Curriculum
Social Studies for Middle
School Grades**

Chapter ... page ....

Chapter ... page ....

RETURN TO IDEA

NEXT CURRICULUM

**Figure 16-6: Sketch for description of middle
school social studies curriculum**

Technical Support Staff	Phone	Location
Ms. Ann Smith, coordinator	Extension 1111	
Mr. Bob Jones, technical staff	Extension 2222	Middle School. TTh
Mr. Jim Jackson, technical staff	Extension 3333	Pound Ridge MW
		West Patent TTh
Ms. Sally Stone, technical staff	Extension 4444	Bedford Hills MW
		Mt. Kisco TTh

Figure 16-7: Sample resource list

Figure 16-8 represents a brief but informative note on the activity described in Figure 16-5 on the Quiz Show.

Variation for Quiz Show

Sometimes I organize the Quiz Show, but I have had successes allowing teams of students to plan and run the whole thing. They prepare the questions; they categorize the questions into easy, moderate, and difficult categories; and they play hosts. The class responded very positively to their fellow students. For the host students, the activity invoked substantial learning experiences: reviewing the whole chapter, creating questions, and so on.

Figure 16-8: Additional entry on the quiz show idea

Using any of the means already discussed for producing digital images (e.g., a digital camera), teachers can have a file of snapshots of everyone in the class. This will make it easy to actually include with the project a record of who participated and, for activities involving groups, who worked together. This is useful as a quick reminder so that in subsequent activities the teacher can suggest changes in the grouping. Recording the grouping for each project is facilitated by establishing and maintaining an archive of students' photos starting early in the year. The students can participate in this. The individual photos are then copied into the archive by a "cut-and-paste" operation.

The individual idea entries may also have various buttons to link to the next idea following along different themes. We discuss this in the next section.

> **Making Do**
>
> As an alternative to using a digital camera, you can ask students to prepare a cartoon or graphic icon representing themselves. Of course, if the result is meaningful only for the child and not the teacher, it will have to be labeled with the child's name to be useful. This can be a powerful experience for students.

Classification

We now move from consideration of the entry for each idea to how the ideas are organized. In order to make the set of ideas accessible, you categorize the ideas and establish links from an initial set of menus. These classification menus represent the categories that are personally useful to you. Here are possibilities for the menus.

- subject area
- higher-level thinking
- grouping
- whole class or individual work
- whole class as a production company
- individuals
- technologies required

Note that these all correspond to the educational goals taxonomy used in this book. However, there are other possibilities. For example, there are several ways to view time for organization. The projects are classified according to when they occur relative to various calendars of the school year. Figure 16-9 shows a sample menu in which the first two lines indicate calendar year, the third line indicates timing within a term, and the last line indicates time of day.

A totally different approach is to use the sequential time in which an idea is put into the Idea Book. You may put in an activity suitable for Memorial Day or Black History Month earlier in the year. One benefit of the sequential organization is that we often remember things in terms of when we first thought of the ideas. The authoring system may provide a DATE and TIME mechanism for recording when an entry is made initially or when it has last been modified. Please be aware that this may be triggered even if you just look at the material without changing it.

The framework of educational goals used for all the projects featured in this book may be an effective way to organize activities. However, because some goals may pertain to all or most of the projects, you must be careful that you are not spending time linking everything to everything else.

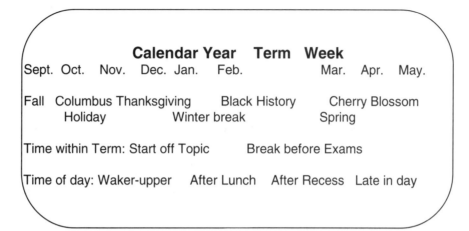

Calendar Year Term Week

Sept. Oct. Nov. Dec. Jan. Feb. Mar. Apr. May.

Fall Columbus Thanksgiving Black History Cherry Blossom
Holiday Winter break Spring

Time within Term: Start off Topic Break before Exams

Time of day: Waker-upper After Lunch After Recess Late in day

Figure 16-9: Scrollable menu for timing of activities, no ideas posted

The organizational structure established by these main menus can be carried out in a variety of ways. You can place an icon for each idea on a main menu. This is certainly the method of choice to begin your use of the Idea Book. Over time, the number of ideas will grow. In addition, you will develop your own concept of how you want to organize this information.

One mechanism you may choose to use when the number of ideas becomes unwieldy is constructing layers of menus. The initial menu points to menus for each of some set of categories. On the individual category menus, you can keep the feature that allows the user to see all the ideas. Alternatively, you can show only the first and the last idea and use linking buttons to connect the intermediate ideas. See the examples for each alternative. The examples show some made up and some familiar project titles.

In Figure 16-10, each idea title appears on the main Subjects menu. This is the situation at the start. We have included entries on the projects featured in this book plus a few others.

Over time, more and more ideas will go into the Idea

Subjects

Social Science
Current Events   Quiz Show   Trailers   Memoirs
English
Critics' Circle   Trailers
Science
Science Quiz   Pen Pals   Shoe Tying   Gopher
Math
School Store   Computer Music

Figure 16-10: Possible menu to ideas by subject area

Book so that there will be too many for a single menu. A two-level menu system is shown by Figure 16-11 and Figure 16-13.

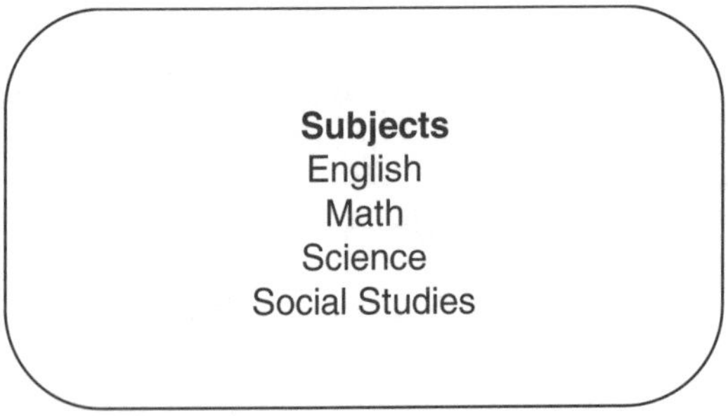

Figure 16-11: Menu to take you to detailed menus for each subject

Figure 16-13 is the menu for English, one of the subjects. There would be similar menus for mathematics, science and social studies as well. In the English menu shown in Figure 16-13, notice that the teacher has placed two buttons for links to ideas involving Critics' Circle projects and one button for a Trailers project. Utilizing subcategories is a way of making effective and efficient use of each page.

Another mechanism for handling the increasing number of idea entries is linking the entries in a chain. The user will not see all the ideas but only the first and the last, as shown in Figure 16-12, so the number of ideas can grow without overcrowding the Subjects' menu page.

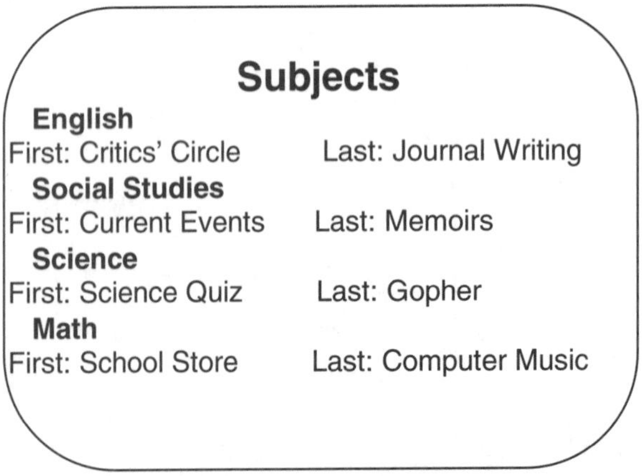

Figure 16-12: Menu by subjects, with links to oldest and most recent idea

Each individual idea will link to the next idea in the subject category. An advantage of this approach is that one's natural inclination when browsing is to examine either the first or the last or to systematically go through the whole list. If the menu has the first and the last idea on the list or thread, this facilitates making additions.

You can use these methods individually or in combination to build your own customized tool.

Other Techniques

The material in the Idea Book can link to off-line and other on-line material in three ways, depending on what you want and depending also on what is easily provided by the underlying technology

English

Critics' Circle:
 Romeo and Juliet   Animal Farm

Trailers:
 Schindler's List

Poetry Collection

Criticism:
Silas Marner   An Occasion for Loving

 Journal writing

Figure 16-13: Sample menu for English

and your local environment. The idea entry can contain a text reference. This is what is required if the material is not on-line and may also be the alternative to choose in other cases.

The idea entry can contain a button that causes the original material to appear on the screen. If necessary, the application in which that material resides, for example a word processing system, is invoked. (Systems that claim to be "object-oriented" have this feature, although we caution you that the terminology is not completely standardized.) A critical feature of this approach is that there is only one instance of the material and when it is modified, all other applications linking to it obtain the updated version. Alternatively, the creator of the idea entry can bring in a copy of the material as part of the Idea Book. This is referred to as "importing." With this alternative, there will be at least two copies of the given material in the system, which may or may not be what you want.

The material in the Idea Book can be shared with other educators. Depending on the features of the authoring system used, this does not have to be an all-or-nothing situation. For example, you can limit access to certain portions of the Idea Book and not others. Perhaps the informal, spontaneous remarks recorded as an audio file would not be shared whereas the other materials, including the project descriptions and the correlation with academic references and district curriculum guides, would be.

Practice

The Idea Book can be used at all stages of the process of project development as well as other times, such as preparing for presentations to colleagues and doing evaluations for report cards. Table 16-1 indicates some of the possible situations.

Table 16-1: Reading from and writing to the Idea Book

Teacher plans project or activity
- Search for ideas according to goals
- Review strategies for grouping and recall past groupings
- Assess technical requirements
- Determine strategy for start-up

Teacher assigns project
- Record actual groupings
- Record actual assignment detail (e.g., topics)
- Observe class
- Record observations
- Plan form of connection to Idea Book

Teacher reflects
- Record actual practice and reflections
- Acquire and insert in Idea Book photos, main menus, and so forth.
- Prepare grades
- Prepare presentation

Planning Time

When you are planning a new multimedia project is the time to review what the class or individuals in the class have created previously. It also can be valuable to review multimedia activities in order to assess if it would be appropriate to design a nonmultimedia-based activity to complement, test, or sustain skills and subject knowledge covered during the projects. It is at this point that the classification menus indicated in prior figures prove beneficial. General grouping strategies and specific assignments are another major part of the planning process. You can consult the Idea Book to determine the past assignments and try out potential groupings by moving photos or drawings of students on the screen.

For example, Ms. Jones wants the class to do one extended project for each of the historical periods in the curriculum. She also wants to vary the groupings, one time letting people choose their groups, another time keeping students with similar abilities together, and still another time mixing the groups. She uses the subject matter pages and the grouping history pages to see what she has done in the past and to record new possibilities. Mrs. Jones finds that manipulating and examining the plans graphically helps her. It has kept her from repeating too much or making too big a leap in expectation for the students. Seeing actual photographs of her students has inspired her to devise some groupings that proved amazingly successful.

The Idea Book also provides information on the equipment and resource requirements for past projects. (Recall Chapter 4 on the roles of existing multimedia content.) You can listen to your own comments and read the reflections on past experiences to prepare for the next project. If this project called for some special equipment, such as a camera or a library on CD-ROM, you can make the necessary arrangements or redesign the project to make do without the items. Frequently, new equipment, software, and commercial multimedia content matter are acquired. Teachers and computer coordinators can review the set of old projects to see if any can be improved by the use of the new resources.

Assignment and Creation Time

The principal uses of an Idea Book may occur during the planning and reflection phases of a project. However, to be efficient and not fall behind, you can use the assignment time to start recording the specifics of the project in the Idea Book. You can keep this up while the students are creating. The first step can be to record the project idea in the structured way you have designed and classify it by linking it to the appropriate menus.

For example, when Mr. Torres had his students choose their own groups, he decided to let them produce the record of grouping for what he called Mi Diario. Each group produced an authors' page with a digitized photograph of the group. Because he was using the school's digital camera software, these photographs had to be stored and carried on diskettes from the Media Center to his classroom where they were copied to the computers for the projects. After students did the transfer, they were to drop off the diskette on his desk. He then copied the photographs to his own system.

The first stages of the process of creation for the students may involve their choice of topics and resources. You may discover people and other resources that they want to record for later use. This information can be recorded in the Idea Book, either with the project or on a resource page as in Figure 16-7. This can be done at any time, but you may find it easier to devise the format for recording the project while the students are working on it. Should examples of student work be copied to the teacher's workstation or can you rely on accessing material on a network? You must include in your considerations the trade-offs between the advantages of being able to link quickly to the samples and the costs either in space or in tying the Idea Book too closely to a particular workstation or environment. Many educators want something they can put in their pocket, so to speak, and take home. In this situation, you can learn to accept clicking on a button and seeing some message saying that a file is missing. You may also choose to make audio or video recordings of classroom activity even when the project itself did not involve these media. Teachers or students from other classes trained on the equipment, or support staff, for those lucky enough to have such resources, can make the recordings.

Reflection Time

When the project activity draws to a close, you can record some of your reflections for your own use. Now is the time to use the facilities for making audio clips and for copying students' work and annotating it with audio buttons, pop-up text, and links to more extensive remarks. It is also the time to review the classification of the project with respect to its coverage of educational goals and subject matter. Did the project achieve the goals you had anticipated? Did it achieve other goals that you may want to emphasize next time?

Grading and Presentation Time

You can browse through your Idea Book at report card time, in preparation for parent conferences, and on other occasions when it is critical to recall details of students' school achievement. The record provided by the multiple media, cross-referenced by project experiences, adds to the cursory data of the standard gradebook.

For example, Ms. Lee is preparing for spring parent conferences. In the fall, parents saw the Current Events Class Archive as it was progressing. In the winter, they saw Trailers, which was a great hit. However, at the close of school, Ms. Lee wants to demonstrate, in a systematic way, that the students have acquired technical and higher-order skills as well as content area knowledge. She uses the classification menus to do this. She also identifies one important achievement or area of improvement for each child and gathers evidence to show the parents. She uses features of the authoring system governing user access rights to disable buttons, block pages and hide fields, as appropriate to protect the privacy of her students and not reveal her own confidential thoughts.

Summary

The Idea Book is conceived as a productivity tool for educators, a private tool but also a way to practice multimedia authoring. However, it may have public uses. The Idea Book can be a source for presentations to colleagues. Similar applications can serve to hold student portfolios.

In this chapter, we have provided approaches to the Idea Book, including suggestions for structure. The Idea Book can also be treated, in whole or in part, as a multimedia journal, with facility for capturing experiences in text, graphics, images, audio, and video clips. You must weigh the benefits and the limitations of an Idea Book against the benefits and limitations of traditional methods.

Chapter 17

Assessment

In this chapter, we explore:

- the reasons for and objectives of assessment.

- the meaning of authentic assessment and mastery learning.

- forms of authentic assessment.

- specific assessment activities for the projects in this book.

This chapter begins with a background on the necessity and objectives of assessment, as applied to project-oriented work. The Theory section reviews the framework of educational goals we previously established and describes the process for underlying authentic assessment and mastery learning. In the Practice section, we describe assessment activities for specific projects using both projects in Chapters 7 through 12 and additional activities.

Background

Assessment is the judging, analysis, and evaluation of student work. Assessment of student multimedia projects is no more difficult or mysterious than good, conscientious assessment of any substantial student effort. The public nature of the work actually encourages constructive feedback and reflection. Because multimedia projects may be new for the school and therefore subject to close scrutiny from parents and administrators, the assessment process may need a high level of justification and rigor. In this chapter, we put forth several frameworks to satisfy this need.

Assessment can take a variety of forms. When we say assessment is important for student-constructed multimedia projects, we mean all forms of assessment. For clarity of discussion, however, we distinguish three types of assessment:

- informal remarks made in passing by teachers to students. Informal assessments are communicated to students but do not get recorded.

- formal grades for individual students, reported and recorded in files that remain in existence for a long period of time.
- project evaluation, often a private assessment performed by teachers to answer the questions "should we do this activity again, and if so, should it be modified in any way?" Project evaluations may also be done by or for school administrators.

Informal Assessment

Informal assessment, which often takes the form of "catching the student doing something good," is valuable for all activities. One of the most positive aspects of student-constructed multimedia is that it produces many opportunities for this and is seldom a problem with teachers. Multimedia projects are public. It is common and socially accepted for teachers and other students to look at what is appearing on the screen while a student is working and to make comments and ask questions. These assessments are spontaneous reactions to what is being displayed and will be positive, negative, or openly questioning.

- "What a great drawing!" "How did you do that?"
- "That diagram is incorrect." "Check your spelling."
- "Can I find out more about this?" "Because you spend time on [A], where do you explain [B]?"

These opportunities for feedback and refinement may not exist, or may not take place as frequently, for most other work.

Hearing comments from the students' peers helps change the nature of the task from doing an assignment only for the teacher to serving a larger purpose or a larger audience. Actually, we have even heard students say that they examine and reexamine their multimedia work, whereas they seldom reread their own text essays.

It is often highly productive to schedule a session in the middle of project development in which students exchange comments on each others' work. Consider this scheduled reflection as being somewhere between informal and formal assessment.

These two factors together, making incremental improvements based on informal assessments and viewing the project as something generated for a larger audience, produce a strong positive effect on the quality of the work.

Formal Grades

It is the formal grading of something as open-ended and seemly subjective as multimedia that causes the most apprehension for teachers new to multimedia project work. Although it may indeed not be reasonable to assign numerical scores from 0 to 100 to multimedia projects, a range or set of marks such as "poor, fair, good, excellent" or "incomplete, fine, outstanding" is feasible. If students and parents want to consider these equivalent to D, C, B, A and I for incomplete, A, and A+ respectively, they may do so. Limiting the options to "incomplete" and "fine" is called "teaching to mastery" and is particularly suitable for student-constructed multimedia projects. We will discuss this more in the Theory section.

If the rules and practices of your teaching situation allow you to enter free-form comments as part of the student record, then you do not need to determine grades for projects. However, as we indicate below, if all other work receives letter grades or their equivalent, and the multimedia projects do not, you are conveying a negative message about this work.

There are many distinct though interrelated reasons both for doing an assessment and for reporting the assessment in formal grades. Exploring the reasons will serve as a guide for what to do in your classroom.

- Assessment lets the students know how they are doing. The public nature of multimedia furnishes feedback to students. However, by its nature, it is irregular and incomplete. Students deserve constructive feedback and they deserve closure.

- If other work receives grades and project work does not, many students and most parents will assume that the project work is not important. The project may have an authentic audience, that is, a group of people genuinely interested in, and perhaps even needing, the presentation. This factor may help to maintain motivation on the part of the students. However, the dichotomy between what gets graded and what does not get graded will eventually affect performance.

- Similarly, if project work is not assessed by teachers, it will be difficult to train the students to evaluate their work themselves. Students should have help, both formal and informal, to determine how they can improve and then be give a chance to do so. Teachers model this process by evaluating both students' work and their own work.

- The process of evaluating project work is a learning experience for the students themselves. It can call attention to critical issues of the underlying content as well as issues of organization, aesthetics, and reasoning. The evaluation process addresses all four categories of educational goals.

- If class time and school resources are devoted to project work, then parents and administrators will, sooner or later, require some form of assessment.

The objectives of assessment include the following:

- inform or confirm for students what they have accomplished, what could be their next set of goals, and what requires attention;

- demonstrate the importance of open-ended project work in the curriculum, that is, work in which students must determine for themselves if they have included sufficient sources, produced an effective product, and completed the job;
- provide opportunities for self-reflection;
- continue the learning experiences with respect to the educational goals: higher-order skills, interpersonal skills, content area, and technical issues; and
- inform parents and administrators of student progress.

The questions then become (1) how to perform assessment in a way that does not take away from the excitement of the activity and (2) how to conduct assessment fairly. Indeed, some advocates of multimedia argue against giving grades to project work such as student-constructed multimedia. They say that grades would detract from the spontaneous, creative flow of energy that occurs when students do projects. They also argue that grading would be too difficult to make fair because of both the scope of work and the variety of skill levels.

Our response to these arguments is that they are good arguments against bad assessment practices. Assessing student-constructed projects is not as easy as checking true-false questions, but it is not unlike grading essays. The public nature of multimedia facilitates the process of assessment and reflection. In the long run, it hurts students to devote significant amounts of their time to something that is not part of their official assessment. It also hurts students when people make private or implicit evaluations that are never shared and discussed.

Private versus Public

A natural and beneficial aspect of student constructed multimedia is the public nature of the work. However, it is certainly possible for students to want to work in private and show the final project only to the teacher. You must decide whether this is something you want to permit because of a student's individual needs and inclinations. The projects in Chapters 7 through 12 were all designed to be public.

You may also record assessments in prose or in annotations made directly on the students' work using pop-up text fields, links to teacher produced pages, or audio recordings. Using the various modes of multimedia to communicate and document is more than a gimmick. It allows you to place the comments at a precise position in the work and to use variety of formats and media to express yourself. In addition, the experience of navigating teachers' comments in hypertext may prove stimulating to students and encourage them to reexamine their work.

Project Evaluation

Last, we turn from assessment of students' work to assessment of the activity itself. What worked and what did not work? Did it achieve the educational goals for the students or for a reasonable subset of students? Was it worth the time and resources consumed?

Project evaluation is not a unique requirement for multimedia projects, but because such projects may be new in the school, and because they do require significant resources, they are subject to increased scrutiny. Teachers, therefore, should be prepared to present an evaluation of the results.

In most cases, well-planned projects are worthwhile, but improvements can almost always be made. Also, once a project has been completed and you, the teacher, have student work to exhibit, you can make a stronger case for resources than could be made beforehand. Chapter 16, The Idea Book, provided possible options for describing ideas for projects and recording reflections on what actually occurred.

Project evaluation can also involve the students. You can ask students:

- What did you learn from doing this project?
- What would you like to do again?
- How should we plan for next time?

When called upon in this way, students can rise to great heights of both eloquence and practicality. This can itself be a learning experience. It also produces evidence of what really went on in the classroom.

The most important assessment is what the students retain after they have left the classroom. Long-term assessment done six months, a year, or even many years later is generally not feasible, but it is important for evaluating project work. A research study in which an assessment was made of students' knowledge a year after the classroom activity found that students who had constructed multimedia on a topic (in this case the Civil War) significantly out-performed the students in the control group with respect to depth of understanding. The two groups performed roughly the same on retention of facts such as the dates of the war. We note that if simple facts were the only type of material covered by the testing, no differences would have been detected. This study is consistent with anecdotal evidence.

Theory

In this section, we review what is being assessed and also ways to assess work. This will provide an opportunity to relate terms and concepts such as "authentic assessment," "mastery learning," "rubrics," and "portfolio assessment" to what you can do with your students. Figure 17-4 gives a summary of the who, what, why of assessment.

The "what" involves the educational goals determined by the teacher in the planning phase of the project. This includes student understanding of subject matter as well as the other areas described throughout this book, starting with Chapter 1. For any particular project, you can choose to focus on narrower or broader sets of goals, while keeping in mind that producing the multimedia project generally does require a broad combination of skills and knowledge.

The "who" of assessment includes, of course, the classroom teacher but also the students themselves, assessing their own and their peers' work. Assessments, themselves, have audiences. Certain projects have very specific, very defined audiences. For example, the Science Quiz project produces an on-line quiz to be taken by other students. The Trailers project produces an advertisement for a movie. The people who view or use multimedia projects provide what is termed an "authentic assessment" of their worth. Their experience and reactions indicate the success of the project.

Types of Assessment

This leads to consideration of the "how" of assessment. At the risk of being simplistic, we suggest four approaches, indicated in Table 17-1, and then give suggestions on reporting strategies. Later, in the Practice section of the chapter, we offer specific examples of each of these types of assessment.

Table 17-1: Approaches to assessment

Holistic:	react to total effect
Analytic:	construct and apply itemized rubric
Portfolio:	consider work in context of student's development
Indirect:	test learning of content and skills another way

Holistic Assessment

The assessment of the multimedia project can be in terms of its absolute, total effect. This is a holistic evaluation. If the project addresses some tangible need with a defined audience, the audience performs the authentic assessment described above. The questions to be addressed are:

- Does it work? Does it make me want to go to the movie? Does it teach the interpretation of graphs? Does it answer the research questions concerning a population of students?

- Does it do the job? Does it capture the significant, opposing views on a topic? Does it correctly organize the news events of the last few months? Does it portray the stories of a generation? Did it present correctly representations of the same event in different media?

- Do I like it? Does it move me?

When holistic evaluation works, it is easy and well-accepted by students. It cannot be used for fine distinctions, but that in itself may be an appropriate message to students. Many assessments in the work place and everyday life are holistic.

Analytic Assessment

You may make assessments in terms of an itemized analysis of the project's components. This should be based on the educational goals originally specified for the project. You may organize questions into the four categories of educational goals that we have used in this book. Here are the categories with sample questions.

- Higher-order thinking skills: Is the organization correct? Is it appropriate? Does the organization reveal a deep understanding of the interrelationships of the topic or is it only a linear presentation of isolated facts?

- Group and interpersonal skills: Did the group work together smoothly and effectively? Did they develop their own process or did they need to be guided at each step?

- Content material learning: What has the student learned about the topic? Does the artifact include correct text and diagrams and images on items A, B, and so on? Is the output a simple restatement or paraphrasing of the research material or does it indicate student understanding?

- Technical skills: Does the project include the technical features required for the assignment, for example, link button, audio recording, and programmed response to user input?

An individual teacher or a group of teachers can develop a checklist of items and a scoring system to cover the skills and understandings incorporated in the project. This is termed a *rubric*. It is often possible to reduce the assessment to a series of yes or no decisions. This can be effective but can also become too mechanical.

If scoring a particular project with the rubric yields a grade that is different from your immediate "gut feel" reaction, it may be time to change the rubric. Of course, if you have shown the scoring system to the class, it is too late and you must make plans for next time. The questions in the next two paragraphs can guide the design of a rubric.

Do you want it to be possible for high achievement in one category to make up for deficits in another? For example, does great aesthetic value or clever scripting make up for lack of content coverage? If you do not want to allow this trade-off, then your rubric would include a point scale for each aspect being assessed. For example, on a 100 point scale with 5 categories, each category could earn at most 20 points. You then could assign a letter grade to the sum of the five scales. If you do want high achievement in one category to supplement weak performance in others, you could use the same ranges for letter grades, but allow some or all of the categories to receive more than 20 points in the exceptional cases.

Do you have some requirements that are absolute? If projects do not meet these conditions, they are rejected entirely, or automatic grade deductions are given. Many teachers take this approach for one or more of the following:

- project not meeting final deadline;
- work exceeding resource limits, for example, taking up too much disk space;
- factual errors in subject matter; or
- failure to apply the basic concepts of the discipline to appropriate situations, for example, omitting a bibliography.

The choice is yours. No matter how you design the rubric, it is still your decision on what to make a passing, that is, acceptable mark. You can still demand mastery.

Portfolio Assessment

Your task of assessment may become easier and more informative if performed in the context of prior work and in preparation for future work. Multimedia projects, perhaps because of their novelty, can all appear equally wonderful. However, when compared with other work, particularly with work created over time by a group of students, it becomes feasible to examine the work for improvement. For example, students may start with organizations in which an initial menu links to every item or with merely linear organization. Later, with experience, each subject may have its own organization, including novel ways for the user to proceed through the material. Chapter 5 described many examples of organization.

The students' own assessments of what the multimedia project taught them about the subject content would also be a candidate for a portfolio. This could be part of a student journal and could contain reflections on other activities.

Reform efforts based on portfolio assessment argue that the only accurate portrayal of a student is a collection of different types of work gathered over time. Those who argue strongly for practicing portfolio assessment also emphasize the student's role in selecting items for inclusion in the portfolio. The student does the initial assessment. This makes the student aware of and responsible for his fate.

> **Classroom Experience**
>
> Rick Corinotis and Anthony Tamalonis work in a middle school in Brooklyn with 7th and 8th graders. They have an ongoing relationship with each other that allows for consultation on issues. When students move into Rick's 8th grade classroom, he knows that they have done project work in Anthony's class. The two teachers can reflect and improve what they do based on the long-term effect.

Indirect Assessment

Assessment of student-based multimedia projects can also be achieved indirectly. Instead of or in addition to examining what the students have produced, teachers can use independent means to assess the skills students learned. This can include standard before-and-after testing. Using the four categories of educational goals, possible forms of indirect assessment include the following:

- Higher-order skills: Observe and examine students' text essays and their oral performance during class participation. Are they well or better organized? Do they examine things from multiple viewpoints? Can they discuss subject matter from an abstract point of view? Do they think about their audience? Can they argue persuasively? Do they plan and schedule their work effectively?

- Group and interpersonal skills: Observe students in class and in other group situations. Do the students listen to and respect each other? Do they work together effectively? Do they organize themselves to work together effectively?

- Content material learning: Give written tests and assign oral presentations. Do the students have a grasp of the complexity of the subject matter? Do they distinguish major from minor matters? Do they understand and utilize different representations, or do they parrot back the text from the book or from lectures?

- Technical skills: Examine subsequent uses of technology. Do students transfer skills from one tool to another? Do they more readily anticipate the uses of a new technology? Are they more comfortable with the initial difficulties of learning to use a new tool?

Indirect assessment also provides an opportunity to reinforce skills and concepts. Through discussions with the class as a whole or with individuals, you can remind your students of what they did in the multimedia project and what may be useful ideas for the current task. This so-called "teaching for transfer" is applicable to matters of content, general skills such as organization, and working in groups.

Reporting Strategies

Your reporting of assessments in various forms depends on the intended audience, that is, the student, the work group, the parents, and so on. The mechanisms of multimedia help you make sure that students notice and think through substantive comments instead of simply looking at the bottom-line grade. You can navigate around the multimedia document and annotate it with text and audio remarks, adding to the document pages directly or indicating these comments by graphical annotations and hot buttons. Your comments can relate to either the subject matter or the presentation. Figure 17-1 and Figure 17-2 give some examples of this. Note that Figure 17-1 is intended to be difficult to read.

A strategy used by teachers for traditional work such as essays is to hand back the assignment with comments, asking the students to look them over and return for an appointment the next day. It is during this appointment that the letter grade is given out. You may apply this same scheme for multimedia projects. Alternatively, following the working towards mastery approach, the student could be given an opportunity to improve the work and then return for a final grade. You may choose not to accept anything that is not at the "mastery" level.

The comment in Figure 17-1 concerning the combination of background and letters given in the comment by Ms. Jones represents an important principle. The student creators may really like what they have produced, but they need to be offered the feedback that at least one member of the audience found it less than satisfactory.

The comments shown in Figure 17-2 are a critique of the organization of a portion of a student document. We do not have the full example here, but hopefully you get a sense of the issues. You may enter assessments in your record book in the standard way. However, this technology also allows multimedia documents or selected portions of them to be incorporated in student portfolios. You may show these portfolios to parents at conference time. They represent substantial student work.

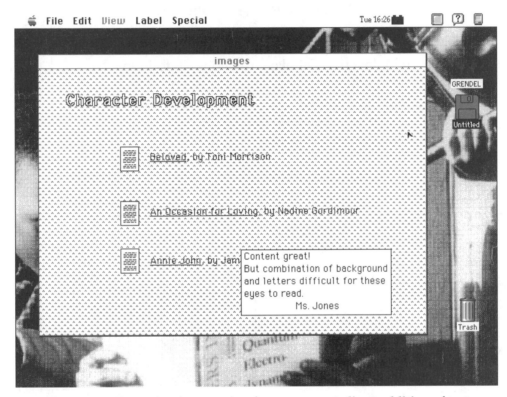

Figure 17-1: Example of annotation for assessment, direct addition of text

The implementation of portfolios requires systematic management of files. Because students work in groups made up of different groups, it may be necessary to have a database containing pointers to multimedia documents. Movement from the student record to a particular multimedia work may or may not be automatic. Figure 17-3 indicates schematically what an individual student record would be. Three projects are included. The Grade/Status column indicates the grade and also the status. The Location/Name column holds information on where the student's work can be found. Notice that Current Events is ongoing but the teacher has recorded that Aviva's participation is "good." This project resides on the permanent classroom computer file. The other projects are on diskettes in the file cabinet. The Trailers project for Aviva and the rest of her group requires the laser disc of the movie *A League of Their Own*.

Othello
Setting   Marriage   Fight   End

I don't know from looking at this menu page where you describe Othello's relationship to Iago.
 Also, after what you have written on Desdemona and looking at your beautiful picture, I want the option to get back to this page.
 Perhaps you need to put in some more links.

Figure 17-2: Example of annotation for assessment: pop-up field

Student Record	Aviva Meyer		
Project	**Grade / Status**	**Group**	**Location / Name**
Current Events	Good participation On-going	Whole class	Classroom computer #3 hard file
Critics' Circle	Great Complete	with Marianna, Stephanie, Keith	CC Diskettes in file cabinet AMSK
Trailers	Great Complete	with Ada B, Ada, Aimee	TR Diskettes in file cabinet A_TEAM League of Their Own laser disk

Figure 17-3: Student record of multimedia project work

To be complete, we mention the issue of the "when" of assessment, which has been addressed in many of the other sections. Assessment can occur during the activity, informally at the time of the official presentation of work, after it is completed, and some time after completion in the context of later work.

> **History: Continuous Quality Improvement**
>
> One of the latest trends in business, called "continuous quality improvement," refers to practices in which people continually reflect on what they are doing. They seek to cut down on any deviation from the ideal and not be content with work "coming in on spec," that is, fitting a fixed minimal definition of acceptability.

The attributes of assessment are summarized in Figure 17-4. You may use it as a prop to stimulate discussion at staff meetings.

Assessment

What is being assessed?
- higher level thinking
- interpersonal skills
- content
- technical skills

When does assessment occur?
- during the activity
- during presentation or use
- over time to evaluate progress

Who is doing it?
- students
- teachers
- peer students
- others

To whom is assessment reported?
- students
- parents
- the record book

Why is assessment performed?
- confirm seriousness of work
- establish basis for improvement
- part of student's work

How is it done?
- holistic reaction
- itemized analysis
- portfolio
- indirect assessment

Figure 17-4: Attributes of assessment

> **An Example from a Senior High School**
>
> Norman Leveille oversees student multimedia project work both in computer applications courses and subject matter courses. He partitions his assessment into the categories of planning, process and results. Planning covers the research on the content area of the project. Process concerns how the students worked together, what help he needed to give and so on. Results covers the final project: how does it look, does it work, are the facts correct.

Practice

In this section, we apply the terms discussed earlier to some of the projects from the Chapters 7 through 12 as well as one additional, generic project. For the specific projects, we will focus on the one or two of the approaches to assessment indicated in the Theory section that we believe can be most appropriate.

Current Events: Itemized Analysis and Portfolio

The educational goals for the Current Events project are summarized in Table 17-2. For the Current Events project, assessment of students' progress can be in the context of the project itself because contributions are made each week. In one sense, it is its own portfolio and allows an individual student's work to be seen within the context of their own progress as well as in comparison to her peers. The class archive does not have the feature that each student selects what is to be included, so you should consider including this factor in other activities.

We suggest a simple rubric for an individual entry, given in Figure 17-5, and then a set of questions for evaluating progress. You can allocate points corresponding to your priorities. One tactic would be to give one point for each factor indicated in Figure 17-5. This facilities scoring. However, you may want to emphasize the importance of, for example, writing, which you could do by weighting that item heavier than the other items.

Current Events Check-List	
Evaluation Factors:	**Points:**
Article page	
• Summary given in appropriate language, student's words	
• Proper citation	
Links	
• Map to article correct	
• Timeline to article correct	
• Other: (prior story)	

Figure 17-5: Individual entry rubric

Table 17-2: Goals for Current Events

Higher Order Thinking Skills
- Summarizing
- Relating distinct events to each other
- Selecting and naming important events
- Recognizing and analyzing distinct coverage of the same event
- Organization

Group and Interpersonal Skills
- Participating in a large group project
- Sharing tools

Content Material Learning
- Awareness of current events and how they evolve
- Expository writing
- Locating events on a map
- Bibliographic citations

Technical Skills
- Writing and entering text into a multimedia folder
- Scanning photographs
- Building buttons
- Following cookbook instructions

> **Classroom Tip**
>
> If getting students to put something "in their own words" is a problem, teachers can request that students actually copy the original text, properly punctuated with quotation marks, and then follow it on the screen with a restatement in their own words. This approach is successful for many teachers, perhaps because it reframes the task as explaining something to an audience of one's peers.

You should put yourself on a schedule for reviewing the class archive to assess progress, as well as making notes of what happens during class sessions or when people from outside the class read the archive. Consider the following questions.

- Looking at each student, has his or her writing improved in terms of level of vocabulary, use of language, and depth of understanding? The writing portion of the project is a summary, so improvement in writing might mean either shorter or longer entries. Do other students appear to read this student's articles? Is the choice of topic and newspaper changing, either in response to guidance from the teacher or spontaneously?

- Looking at the archive as a whole, has it grown in sophistication and depth, in response to stimulation by the teacher, as a result of news events happening in the world, and as a result of engaging in the activity itself?

- Do the students use the archive outside of the official assignment? What is the response of outsiders to the archive? Is the writing better or worse than they expect?

The class Current Events Archive is a natural candidate to be featured at parent conferences and at staff meetings. Showing students' work in the context of their own development, together with development of their peers, provides credibility for any evaluations.

Critics' Circle: Itemized Assessment and Indirect Assessment

For the Critics' Circle project, we describe assessment of a very specific technical skill and then evaluate the learning through assessment of other activities. Table 17-3 shows a subset of educational goals for Critics' Circle.

Table 17-3: Subset of educational goals for Critics' Circle

Higher-order Thinking Skills
Recognizing a spectrum of different opinions on the same subject

Group and Interpersonal Skills
Working successfully in a group, including accepting distinct roles

Content Material Learning
Exposition (spoken comments and written summaries)

Technical Skills
Using draw program or clip art to create an icon

One of the requirements for this project is to create graphical icons to represent the opinions to be used as buttons on the main menu page. The user of the project should have some prior inkling of what each critic will say when he clicks on each button. In addition, these icons should not be unrelated graphics but relate to one another stylistically and conceptually. This leads to the rubric in Figure 17-6, in which we suggest two approaches to scoring.

Icon rubric	younger	older
• Working button	5	2
• Button with drawn icon	2	2
• Icon communicates who critic is or what viewpoint is	2	0
• Icon communicates nature of critic's opinion	0	3
• Icons follow consistent style	1	3

Figure 17-6: Weighting of points for constructing an icon, younger and older students

In each of these two scoring systems, 10 points are possible. For younger students, we emphasize the basic linking. Students will receive 5 points simply for producing a working button. Many students will be moved to draw a cartoon of themselves; the content of the viewpoint is secondary. For older students, mastering the basic linking is not sufficient; we want them to go beyond drawing self-portraits and to concentrate on communicating issues. Because we expect at least some students to think in terms of overall design, we want the grading of the icons to reflect this. Thus, for the older student, a working button with a smiling face will not produce as high a grade as a set of buttons that convey ideas.

Critics' Circle is a project designed to invoke higher-order mental skills. For this we may want to pursue indirect means of assessment to confirm that skills were developed to the point where they could transfer to another domain. At some point shortly after the Critics' Circle project is completed, you can assign a standard written essay on a topic for which there are a variety of views. This could be a short assignment or one involving research. You should discuss the new assignment in terms of the previous one regarding subject matter, organization, process, and exposition. The questions, however, become, "How does one determine what the different viewpoints are?" and "What are minor differences and what are major differences?" You can now use the multimedia project as a source of terms and metaphors for issues that arise in written exposition:

- How do you convey, in writing, the menu of views?
- What is a succinct description, a textual icon, for each view?
- How do you make the transition from describing individual views to summing up and reconciling different views?
- How do you convey the fact that there is a person behind each viewpoint?
- Is background or context required to make sense of any of the opinions and where would it best go in (linear) text?

The multimedia example can also serve as a counter example when appropriate. In multimedia projects such as Critics' Circle, distinctions appear absolute and organization is explicit. Major points are presented separately from background and details. Generally speaking, these are also the goals for students' written essays in grade school through high school. However, more sophisticated writing may contain some surprises for the reader as the creator carries them along in the linear exposition. Teachers can point out these different approaches.

You can assess and grade the essays the way you always have done it. However, your expectations and feedback to the students can include outcomes from the multimedia project.

Trailers: Holistic Response

Trailers invokes all the educational goals indicated in Chapter 9, and you could do a systematic analysis of a student's performance with respect to each and every one of them. However, we recommend the holistic assessment approach. Because students are familiar with trailers, that is, coming attractions, they can judge what they like. If the total effect of the trailer is positive, it makes sense to assign the work a positive evaluation. If the total effect is negative, if it does not move its audience, then it really does not matter if the creators went through the process and did the mechanics.

Letting audience reaction determine the assessment is especially appropriate if the specified audience for the trailer is represented in the room, for example, teenage boys. As we indicated in the Chapter 9, the audience reaction, in addition to being an authentic assessment, can also initiate a discussion of stereotypes. The presence of the multimedia project serves to diffuse the focus on specific individuals.

A scheme for incorporating the results of class voting into marks for the record book is shown in Figure 17-7. If grades A through F are required, you can translate the "Satisfactory" into B or C depending on your usual practice.

Incomplete	Unfinished work
Satisfactory	Working trailer
Good	Moves audience according to (majority) vote of class
Great	Voted best trailer in the class

Figure 17-7: Grading for Trailers

One variation of this approach is a method inspired by the Olympics for figure skating and gymnastics. Appoint a panel of six to nine judges from students in the class or recruited from other classes. Judges vote on technical merit and artistic merit. Scores are totaled or averaged. One additional nuance is to drop the highest and lowest marks.

Science Quiz: Holistic Response and Indirect Assessment

Science Quiz is another candidate for a holistic evaluation. However, we recommend that teachers at least spot check the correlation of video clips, narratives, and graphs, just to make sure that nothing got jumbled. For this project, the quiz-takers are the authentic evaluators, particularly for the advanced version of the project with hints and adaptive responses. Extensive use by quiz-takers should reveal errors. Narratives that are misleading will also become evident.

The students' acquisition of the data for Science Quiz is assessed by requiring students to take each other's quizzes. This is an indirect self-assessment of their work on their own quiz. Students can also be asked to write narratives describing movements videotaped by the teacher and to sketch the associated graphs as part of a standard, written examination. Finally, if the students are required to give public demonstrations of the use of micro-based laboratories, this will certainly reveal their understanding of the underlying concepts.

Generic Research Project: All Types

Let us now turn to a multimedia project in a general research area other than any in Chapters 7 through 12 such as the world economy or Shakespeare. Assessment starts with the planning step, specifically with the definition of educational goals. For an itemized assessment, you can devise a rubric for "unsatisfactory," "satisfactory," and "great" performances for each item on the list of goals. You can then make students keep working until they reach the "satisfactory" or the " great" levels, ensuring mastery learning.

An important caveat is to give credit where credit is due, and only when credit is due. If you have defined the overall design and promulgated it through definition of base or background pages using features of the authoring system, the professional look of the finished work is not the achievement of the students. Similarly, use of clip art is a skill to be mastered, but it is not creative drawing.

All or portions of the students' work can be collected and saved in portfolios. English and social studies are especially conducive to a portfolio approach. Typically, classes study a set of literary works and a set of countries, regions, or time periods over the course of the year.

You can apply indirect assessment by giving standard tests. Test students on the economic concepts covered, and assign standard written essays on the literature. Of course, all activities consume class time, so you will have to weigh the benefits of the indirect assessment against the costs.

If the project has an authentic audience, you must decide if and how to incorporate the audience's response into the formal assessment. Students can contribute ideas about how and when the project is to be presented. The ideal situation would be a request from an outside source to produce an educational kiosk on a topic. Possible examples are

- a report on activities in the schools for consideration prior to community voting on the school budget;
- an instructional kiosk to handle the most common questions from visitors or customers to a library or other similar facility; and
- a registration system to collect information or process transactions from clients.

For each of these projects, the holistic response corresponds to these statements which amount to "did it work."

- Did the budget pass? To probe more deeply, did many people use the kiosk and emerge with a positive view of the schools?
- Do visitors have their questions answered or do they require the assistance of the staff?
- Do people use the system or avoid it, and is the collected information consistent and complete?

As your projects become more ambitious, answering the question of success may become more complex. You can provide significant learning opportunities for your students by involving them in the assessment process.

Summary

Assessment for student multimedia projects may appear to be a complex process because these projects produce many opportunities for learning and therefore many factors to assess. However, educators need not view it as particularly difficult, subjective, or even fundamentally different from other grading. You can choose the breadth and depth of your assessment.

It is our experience that students work very hard at multimedia, creating and achieving high levels of quality in the projects because of this increased time on-task. You may have to face the fact that students want to keep working on projects past the time allocated and past the time for assessment. This is both a positive and negative feature of multimedia projects. It is good that students want to be engaged in constructive work and want to perfect what they have created. It is a problem when they miss clearly stated deadlines or mis-apportion their time. In any case, this problem is not inherent to the assessment process.

Assessment of the overall worth of multimedia projects is an ongoing activity. Certain experiences reveal situations that need to be changed, such as students wasting time working with broken equipment or scheduling snafus. Spending time reflecting on and recording what worked and what did not work, what counted and what did not count, is invaluable for the future.

References

Adams, Marilyn Jager. "Thinking Skills Curricula: Their Promise and Progress." *Educational Psychologist*. Volume 24, no. 1, p. 25-77, 1989.

Bloom, B. S. "The Hands and Feet of Genius: Automaticity." *Educational Leadership*. Volume 43, no. 5, p. 70-77, 1986.

Brooks, Jacqueline and Brooks. Martin. *In Search of Understanding: The Case for Constructivist Classrooms*. ASCD, 1993.

Cohen, Philip. "Challenging History: The Past Remains a Battleground for Schools." *ASCD Curriculum Update*, Winter 1995.

Herman, Joan L.; Aschbacher, Pamela R.; and Winters, Lynn. *Practical Guide to Alternative Assessment*. ASCD Association for Supervision and Curriculum Development, Regents of the University of California. 1993.

Langer, Ellen J. "A Mindful Education." *Educational Psychologist*. Volume 28, no. 1, p. 43-50, 1993.

Lehrer, Richard. "Authors of Knowledge: Patterns of Hypermedia Design." *Computers as Cognitive Tools*. S. Lajoie and S Derry, editors. Lawrence Erlbaum Associates. Hillsdale, NJ, 1992.

Nickerson, Raymond. "On Improving Thinking Through Instruction." *Review of Research in Education*. AERA. 15, p. 3-57, 1989.

Prawat, Richard S. "The Value of Ideas: Problems Versus Possibilities in Learning." *Educational Researcher*. p. 5-16, August-September, 1993.

Willis, Scott. "Refocusing the Curriculum: Making Interdisciplinary Efforts Work." *ASCD Education Update*. Volume 27, Number 1, January, 1995.

Wilson, Linda. "What Gets Graded Is What Gets Valued." *Mathematics Teacher*. September, 1994.

Wittrock, M.C. "A Constructive Review of Research on Learning Strategies," *Learning and Study Strategies: Issues in Assessment, Instruction, and Evaluation*, edited by C. E. Weinstein, E. T. Goetz, and P. A. Alexander. San Diego, Calif: Academic Press, 1988.

Chapter 18

Moving Forward and Providing for the Future

In this chapter, we explore:

- how you get started by helping a few students create a few multimedia projects, using information in the preceding 17 chapters.

- how you move forward to benefit more students by integrating more projects into more curricula.

- a practical example in which you can provide for your school's future by preparing an addendum to the five-year strategic plan.

The Background section introduces three phases of using student-created multimedia projects. In the Theory section, we first discuss the major challenges that you will face as you move forward. Then we list major trends that we think will be important in the next five years, as you provide for the future. Finally, we present four scenarios that illustrate what we expect to be typical uses of multimedia near the end of the 1990s. In the Practice section, we suggest that you consider writing a detailed road map that will guide a school's use of student-created multimedia projects for the next five years.

Background

This final chapter encourages you to consider extending creation of multimedia projects to appropriate additional grades and subjects. The process of preparing, assigning, creating, and reflecting on a project, which we described in Chapter 6, is the same whether students in your school are creating one project or fifty projects. However, the context in which you and your students perform these four steps depends strongly on whether you are pilot testing this new pedagogical tool on a small scale or are well into a subsequent phase of disseminating the tool throughout your school's curriculum.

Different activities characterize three phases of using student-created multimedia projects in a school or district. In the first phase, you get started by using the previous chapters' information to benefit a few students who are studying a single subject. In the second phase, you move forward by involving significantly more people and integrating creation of multimedia projects into significantly more curricula. In the third phase, you provide for a future that includes expanding use of such projects and raising expectations by preparing an addendum on multimedia projects for a five-year strategic plan. Figure 18-1 illustrates typical activities that take place in the three phases.

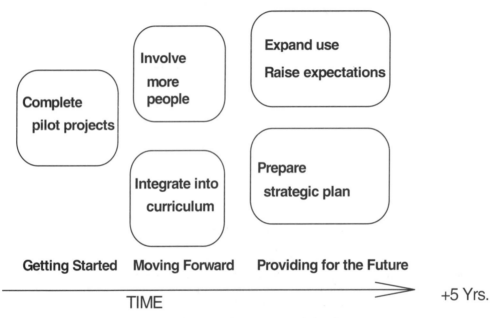

Figure 18-1: Road map toward the future

In previous chapters, we discussed many aspects of student-created multimedia projects with a strong emphasis on using them as integral parts of mainline academic activities. We discussed practical considerations not only for getting started but also for continuing without losing momentum. Previous chapters contained many suggestions that you can use while getting started more or less alone and also use in cooperation with many other educators.

We now continue by discussing changes that you can expect to see as you participate in a pilot test and then move forward to wider use. We concentrate on activities that are more or less unique to introducing student-created multimedia projects. However, for context, we mention some activities that apply to introducing essentially any new educational technology.

Getting Started

In the first phase, you and your students get started with multimedia projects by performing some or all of the following activities.

- A few selected educators become knowledgeable about multimedia projects, perhaps by reading about and participating in this book's suggested activities.
- These educators participate in helping a few K-12 students or one class create one or more multimedia projects, using the process that we introduced in Chapter 6.
- Those educators and others decide that the projects were effective in helping students achieve academic goals, despite normal ups and downs. They record recommendations for making the downs less prominent.
- The same people feel that, although using multimedia projects may not have used resources particularly efficiently on a small scale at the outset, there is promise that expanded use will make this educational technology efficient enough to justify further use.
- Participants and supporters draft a set of recommendations for support and logistics that can facilitate moving forward to involve significantly more teachers.

On the one hand, you may reasonably decide that your situation, environment, and goals justify moving forward out of the first phase after successfully completing just one of this book's projects, at one grade level, and in one subject. On the other hand, you may decide that the first phase should include completing all six of the book's projects and a few variations of your own design, in several classes, including at least one interdisciplinary project.

Moving Forward

As you move forward from the pilot test phase, you and your colleagues are likely to proceed as follows.

- Evangelists from the pilot test, bearing messages of concrete success, encourage other teachers to go forth and do likewise.
- School administrators and community members support extending the efforts, based on improved student outcomes and perhaps on positive community responses to attractive demonstrations.
- Several additional teachers become excited about the pilot results and volunteer (or are elected) to use additional projects in additional subjects and grades.
- These teachers receive some time off from their regular teaching schedule for preparation. They succeed in scheduling some common planning time with teachers who participated in the pilot test.

- Plans are well underway to implement the pilot test's recommendations for common logistics for equipment and supplies.

- Plans include designating a teacher or educational technologist to act as a support consultant. This augments one-on-one customized assistance from evangelists with a more nearly business-as-usual operating environment.

- Discussions indicate the possibility of occasionally expanding the standard short class period or combining two successive classes, perhaps as part of an interdisciplinary effort.

- Educators' famous ability to make do with less than ideal resources promises to apply to the case of student multimedia projects.

- Student creation of multimedia projects gradually changes from the status of miracles-on-demand to the status of business-as-usual.

Success in moving forward through the second step depends on meeting the challenges, and taking advantages of the trends, that we discuss in the next section. Success in providing for the future, which we discuss in the Practice section, also depends on understanding these challenges and trends.

Theory

We begin the theory that underlies progressing from a pilot test of student-created multimedia projects, to wider dissemination, and then to preparing part of a five-year strategic plan, by discussing some challenges. You may need to overcome many of these challenges in order to give this pedagogical tool's benefits to more students in more grades and more subjects. Subsequent parts of this Theory section describe some trends that we expect you to see in the late 1990s and then relate some scenarios on which you may want to base some of your planning.

Challenges

We have seen outstanding student-created multimedia projects demonstrated at more than one school as dusty museum exhibits. When we asked how the projects originated, we heard that the one teacher who made the projects successful got a corresponding promotion and split. This is one reason to involve several teachers, even in the first phase, and to expand teacher involvement rapidly. Students missed out on the benefits of this pedagogical technology because their schools failed to overcome the challenges that we discuss next.

Staff Development

In many cases, the most difficult part of expanding use of multimedia is providing staff development for additional teachers and support personnel. Most staff development is on-the-job, with relatively little use of workshops and courses. Some of the people who can provide the most effective staff development are teachers who are already achieving good outcomes. Incremental, iterative staff development produces a chain reaction that starts slowly and grows remarkably rapidly as each new adept can help several additional teachers. Mathematically speaking, when a population's rate of growth is proportional to the population's size, the population grows exponentially, so leave plenty of room. (Agnew, 1960)

The goal of staff development is to help most teachers to become capable of making their own hardware and software work most of the time. When teachers can not solve their problems alone, they need help from a human support network. Staff development includes making sure that everyone knows whom to ask for help in particular areas. It is also important to ensure that nearly everyone becomes the expert whom others ask about some area, because trades work better than donations. People in the network share experiences, both good and bad, and share their students' projects. Involving some students as sources of knowledge in this human network benefits both teachers and students. Participating in such a network is one of several suitable roles for students in a multimedia production company, as we discussed in Chapter 14. The human support network is vital. Augmenting the human network with a computer network is merely highly desirable.

Experience indicates that it extremely useful to have at least one support person who selects equipment, solves the hardest problems, and is available for consultation. Several experienced teachers have told us that a support person who is a teacher finds it especially easy to understand other teachers' objectives and problems. However, the support person needs relief from a full time teaching load, partly to make other teachers comfortable with asking for help.

Summer workshops in a wide variety of formats greatly increase the effectiveness of on-the-job staff development. Some workshops offer credit and can be quite demanding academically. Some offer teachers the opportunity to bring in students as partners. Some provide for counseling and sharing throughout the following school year. Many include actual work on projects the attendees can use in their classes.

Schools that do not offer any formal staff development can loan reading materials, hardware, and software during the summer and provide suitable telephone numbers that borrowers can call for help.

Colleges and universities have an important role to play in staff development as well as in teaching new educators how to use student-created multimedia projects. Colleges and universities can teach multimedia most effectively by integrating multimedia not only into educational technology courses but also into other courses. For example, when inservice and preservice teachers take a social studies methods course, they should learn about specific student-created multimedia projects, as some of the many tools they can use to help their students achieve desired outcomes. Several institutions of higher learning are taking this approach and more are likely to do so in the next five years.

Several research universities are investigating how best to facilitate active learning for all students by means of closely related techniques.

Obtaining Multimedia Computers

Many schools can begin creating multimedia projects using computer configurations that students already have available in classrooms. Typical schools have computers with sufficient processing power, memory capacity, disk space, and display capabilities to create at least the Current Events project. We have noted that Current Events concentrates on using an authoring system to create hypertext, which is arguably multimedia's most important single concept. Thus getting started with hypertext is not only perfectly reasonable but highly worthwhile. Students can add a few commercial clip images from diskettes to get an essentially complete feeling for multimedia. A school may decide to defer obtaining multimedia equipment that suffices for creating the rest of this book's projects until students have used existing equipment to achieve initial successes with hypertext.

A school's first step toward obtaining multimedia equipment can be a small one. In fact, students can create essentially any project with only a single multimedia computer, which one group of students uses at a time. Equally importantly, one new computer that is capable of scanning images or capturing video can support dozens of groups of students who spend most of their project time using existing computers. The existing computers need only display at least 256 colors.

A school's second step can be somewhat larger, because that step involves supplying many groups of students with computers that include digital audio adapters, along with speakers, microphones, and perhaps CD-ROM drives. If a school has excellent technical support and reasonably recent computers, adding multimedia upgrade kits is a good choice. However, upgrading existing computers that are too slow to display reasonable digital video may be poor economy.

If you or your school decide to take the big step of obtaining many multimedia computers for many groups to use, you face a major dilemma. On the one hand, whatever you purchase in a given year will be available the following year at significantly lower cost. Thus, to save money, you should avoid purchasing much more performance or capacity than you need in any one year. On the other hand, whatever you purchase will become functionally obsolete as more powerful computers become commonplace and as applications change to take advantage of the greater power. Thus, to avoid throwing away equipment that will not run the latest applications, you should purchase computers that will remain close to the state of the art for as many years as possible.

We advise buying the fastest computers with the largest amounts of memory and storage that you can afford. However, we suggest that you not get the very fastest computer that is available in any one year, unless you are sure that you need the speed, because there is a law of diminishing returns. The fastest computer tends to cost about twice as much as a typical computer, but tends to be only about half again as fast as a typical computer, so you do not quite get your money's worth. We also advise buying a system that you can expand. For example, you may well want to add a CD-ROM writer, so that your students can write their own CD-ROMs.

Selecting optimal hardware is not easy. It may not even be part of your job. However, we all need to keep up with what is available. During a long blink, you may miss a price reduction that converts a useful function from being exorbitant to being worth considering. Many computer magazines and multimedia magazines available on newsstands can help you keep sufficiently up to date to at least know the right questions to ask.

Using Networks

With or without multimedia projects, a school benefits from having a local area network. Students, support personnel, and budgets benefit from having a classroom's student computers networked to one another, to computers in other classrooms, to school-wide server computers, and to networks that reach outside the school. Some of the benefits are that a network can

- save money on disk storage,
- facilitate sharing files among students,
- widen access to and on-line archives, and
- allow many students and educators to share a few high-speed modems.

Although designing a local area network requires considerable skill and experience, understanding what such a configuration can do for your school is easy. A school's budget can benefit from a network's ability to centralize disk storage and modems on a server. Many students access the server from their respective computers and thereby share access to files on the server's disks and share use of a few modems. Storing application programs and other large files on a server's disk obviates storing identical information redundantly on dozens of individual student computers' disks. This not only saves the initial cost of purchasing unnecessary disk space, it also the reduces the continuing expense of support resource that would otherwise be required to install and maintain the same applications and files on many groups' student computers. Sharing a few fast modems obviates attaching a slow modem directly to each student computer and each faculty computer. This not only can reduce cost, it can give students a higher data rate for exchanging electronic mail and files with the world beyond the school walls.

Creating increasingly demanding multimedia projects significantly increases a local area network's benefits. None of the projects described in this book requires a local area network. However, Critics' Circle, which Chapter 8 describes, involves several digital audio files, each of which may be sufficiently large to occupy several diskettes. A network allows students to share this project without worrying about the number of diskettes that the project will occupy. Similarly, Science Quiz and Memoirs, which

Chapters 10 and 11 describe, involve digital video files, which may occupy literally scores of diskettes. Moreover, whereas students are likely to capture audio on the same computers that play back audio, students are likely to share one computer that is capable of capturing digital video. In this case students routinely move captured video files to the computers on which the students run the authoring system and create projects. A local area network makes moving large digital video files especially easy and convenient. On any network, however, you may need to consider whether transferring large files will interfere with other users.

Moving large files, without moving tall stacks of diskettes, is handy for other reasons as well. For example, many groups of students may share a single computer that grabs images or operates a scanner. The same consideration applies to libraries of resources that all students share, such as clip art libraries and sound effects. An additional consideration is that some such resources have licenses that restrict purchasers to installing the resources on only a single computer but allow accessing the resources over a network.

Finally, Research Magazine, which Chapter 12 discusses, involves exchanging large files with distant schools over a wide area network. Without a local area network, the natural way to send files over a wide area network is to attach economical modems directly to the student computers that contain the files. Economical modems are slow, so sending a large file may require several hours. With a local area network, however, the natural way to access a wide area network is to attach a fast modem to a server that many student computers share. Having many groups of students share the same modem, one after another, helps a school afford the fast modem. Many multimedia applications on a network such as Internet's Mosaic browser for the World Wide Web merely limp along at 14.4 Kbps and require 28.8 Kbps for acceptable performance. If a large school can use a single modem, the school is likely to be able to afford a 28.8 Kbps modem and may be able to afford a leased telephone line running at 56 Kbps or even 1.544 Mbps. In the late 1990s, many schools will have an opportunity to connect to Internet at high data rates, such as by using a cable television system. High speed links would be out of the question if each student computer needed a separate link.

Distributing Equipment and Supplies

All teachers involved in multimedia projects need access to multimedia equipment and supplies, not only computers but also video cameras, VCRs, lights, television monitors, projection televisions, and LCD panels that go on existing overhead projectors. Students also require supplies that range from index cards for story boards, to public domain music for digitizing, to blank audiotape and videotape.

Your school may want to make supplies available in a resource room, media preparation room, or library, along with computers that many groups use to capture images and video. The more that a school can provide for teachers in a manner consistent with other school practices, the better. If it is feasible to use some resources of a local college, industry, or business, having one person arrange the logistics is more effective than having each teacher forage separately.

Ordering multimedia supplies or reserving time on the computer in the resource room should be as easy as ordering more mundane equipment. Figure 18-2 illustrates the sort of sheet that every teacher could have, telling how to get what is available. Note that the same sheet could tell how to get help with particular sorts of problems.

- To reserve resource and media preparation room facilities, call 754-3098 or E-mail Patricia@lake.edu.
- To arrange for authoring computers in classrooms networked to servers with Internet gateways, call Mr. Bryan or E-mail bryan@lake.edu.
- To arrange for the year's presentation projection facilities such as LCD panels, scan converters, and television monitors, call 754-4888 or E-mail Davie@lake.edu.
- To discuss using Sullivan College's set of Adobe tools call 777-3489 or E-mail media@Sullivan.edu.
- To discuss the procedure for checking out equipment and supplies such as camcorders and laptop computers for students and teachers to take home, call 754-3459 or E-mail nancy@lake.edu.
- To get consultation on using the scanner from Mr. Bryan, call or E-mail bryan@lake.edu for an appointment.
- For a list of past student multimedia projects and how to access them, see the top left shelf in the media room.
- For a list of community resources such as a business that might allow students to use an expensive software tool or video editing facilities, see the middle of the left shelf in the media room.
- For a list of CD-ROMs and helpful on-line references about how to access them, see the top right shelf in the media room.
- For reference materials useful for student media projects, including copies of the school's assessment criteria, see the second top shelf in the media room.

Figure 18-2: Hypothetical list of sources of equipment and supplies

Integrating Projects into Curricula

Integrating student-created multimedia projects into the general curriculum is simultaneously one of the most challenging and one of the most important parts of improving and expanding students' use of such projects. Using projects to structure a new interdisciplinary program is an approach that is worth considering. For example, creating a series of multimedia projects could well be the concrete and authentic outcome of an interdisciplinary effort among such groups of disciplines as English, art, and history.

Rigid and short class periods can pose problems for all sorts of authentic learning. Whereas 40 minutes of a traditional lecture may be all that students or teachers can tolerate, 40 minutes may be insufficient for a group of students to wrap their minds around any creative activity such as student multimedia projects. Students appreciate time to be creative, think about what they have done, decide what they will do next, reach a suitable interim stopping point, and then clean up to allow another group to use the same equipment. Many teachers have temporarily solved this time problem by obtaining permission to combine adjacent periods in related subjects.

Students who create multimedia projects may benefit from different classrooms, as well as different class periods. Students need convenient and reasonably private spaces in which small groups can plan, brainstorm, and work together on their creations. Students also need spaces for their groups' computers. Computers that groups use to record and play back audio need more separation than other computers. Whereas earphones work well for individual use, such as in a language lab, group use requires loudspeakers. Loudspeakers interfere with neighboring groups, especially when students are speaking into microphones. Everyone benefits from equipment that can remain set up, so that the students and teachers need not install or set up equipment again to continue projects that last longer than one day.

Dealing with Popularity

One sure sign that student-created multimedia projects are progressing is that every day or two you get a request to demonstrate some projects. Although satisfying such requests represents an opportunity for students to present their creations, it can also become sufficiently time consuming and distracting to make further progress impossible. Some ways that schools deal with this problem are as follows.

- Designate an afternoon each month as open house and limit visits to that afternoon.

- Set aside a computer in the library as a kiosk on which visitors can actually use recent projects. Such a computer requires enough disk space to hold several projects. Consider tying the projects together with a main menu that helps a visitor select one of the projects.

- Place student projects on a local university's server and use the school's publications to make the community aware of the opportunity that these projects represent. Consider using a World Wide Web (WWW) server, as we discuss in the Appendix.

- Offer to send teachers and students to carefully selected meetings to give talks and demonstrations.

- Sponsor a multimedia project fair, perhaps with special outside funding.

- Keep educational objectives for today's students in proper balance with evangelizing and promotions that will benefit future students.

- Keep students focused on creating future projects rather then resting on their laurels by demonstrating previous projects.

Dealing with Student Influx

Bringing new students into a school poses a constant challenge to any multiyear program. You may devise an excellent progression of projects that starts with learning to create basic projects in early grades and builds on students' knowledge to help them create complex projects efficiently in higher grades. But how do you handle a student who transfers into a higher grade from a school that did not lay the same foundation? Your challenge is to help a new student meet your high-priority academic goals from the outset, while interacting with a group to pick up necessary multimedia skills gradually. You may decide to bypass less important multimedia skills to which you assign lower priority. Alternatively, you may attempt to interest one or more such students in creating an earlier grade's project, altering the subject matter to fit the higher grade.

Deciding How Far to Go

Another significant challenge is determining the extent to which helping students create multimedia projects is more effective and efficient than alternative pedagogical techniques. In order to answer this question, you must have alternatives in mind. Making any such comparison is difficult and somewhat subjective. Although we believe that creating student multimedia projects is appropriate to some extent for essentially all students, excessive use is clearly ineffective and inefficient.

Raising Expectations

As you become more adept at facilitating student creation of multimedia projects, as your support network improves, and as your school acquires hardware and software that allow students do more with less effort, you should increase what you expect students to achieve. For example, you should expect students who create the Science Quiz project next year to do better than this year's students did. We suggest that you take advantage of having more than one year of projects by reflecting on each project in this wider context. As you execute the process that we discussed in Chapter 6 and feed back improvements, your own part of the projects will become better and better. You should expect correspondingly more from your students.

In the first phase, it is wonderful to see students increase their attendance, improve their motivation, and complete a project. As you move forward from this pilot test phase, you might ask yourself whether you have allowed attendance, motivation, and glitz to distract you from ensuring that your students achieve the academic goals for which you selected the project. By raising what you expect from students, you help them improve their understanding of content, logical abilities, insight into organization of information, scores on traditional academic examinations, and communication skills.

The next part of this Theory section describes trends that will, among other effects, allow students to improve their projects without necessarily spending more time. The last part of this Theory section presents scenarios that emphasize ways in which students will use improved communications skills.

Trends for the Five-year Horizon

As you move forward from pilot testing student-created multimedia projects to involving significantly more people, and as you provide strategies for the future, you will find that many of the following trends will help significantly.

Computers

- The price for a computer that has a given performance, capacity, and function will continue to decline. If a particular price buys a computer that will meet your students' needs this year, a cheaper one will meet the same needs next year.

- The performance, capacity, and function of a typical computer will continue to increase as new versions of programs provide new functions and make increasing demands on hardware.

- The last two trends will work in opposite directions to leave the price of a typical computer approximately constant.

- The fastest available personal computers will become significantly faster. For example, in the early 1990s only a high-end engineering workstation had a sufficiently powerful main processor to play back full-motion, full-screen, true-color video. By the late 1990s, high-end personal computers will have the same capability.

- Larger and cheaper disks will encourage students to create and save large audio and video files.

- Most base model computers will be able to display natural images, rather than being limited to low resolution or few colors.

- High-quality video compression and decompression hardware will become affordable. Whereas MPEG and other hardware-assisted compression and decompression methods are out of reach of most educational budgets in the mid-1990s, a school will be able to afford one MPEG compression adapter and several decompression adapters in the late 1990s. MPEG titles on CD-ROMs will become common.

- Many base model computers will come with built-in multimedia hardware, not only for playing CD-ROMs and digitizing and playing back audio, but also for medium quality video. Including audio and video in personal and business communications will become commonplace. Creators will expect that recipients will be able to play back these advanced media.

- Different types of computer hardware and operating systems will remain common. However, it will become much easier to move content from one such platform to another and to communicate among different platforms.

- Multimedia computers will appear in many disguises such as those embedded in furniture for use as kiosks and those embedded in game machines, telephones, and television sets.

- Lap top multimedia computers will become smaller, lighter, more affordable, and more prevalent. Most of us will want one and many of us will feel that we can afford one and acquire one.

- Set-top boxes (also known as cable converter boxes) on home television sets will become almost indistinguishable from personal computers, thus bringing interactive functions to a television. The primary difference from a computer will be that a set-top box's remote control device substitutes for a computer's keyboard. Although we do not think that interactive television will be pervasive within five years, you might want to keep an eye on this technology. Many students will read about interactive television and some students will use it as an additional source of information.

Computer Peripherals

- CD-ROM drive prices will drop below $100.00. Almost all new personal computers will include such drives. Quadruple-speed and faster drives will be the norm. New and perhaps incompatible standards may provide capacity greater than 650 MB.

- CD-ROM writer drives will become cheap enough to connect to many computers. Your students will be able to put their own information on a CD-ROM disc and either mail the disk to another school or take the disc home to show their friends and family. Such a disc is ideal both for accumulating a student's multimedia portfolio and for backing up a computer's files.

- Prices of camcorders and VCRs will continue to drop.

- Larger and higher resolution computer displays will become more affordable, making it somewhat more pleasant to read large amounts of text on a computer screen.

- A typically configured multimedia computer may look like the one that Figure 18-3 shows.

Applications

- Large numbers of professionally created multimedia titles will appear on CD-ROMs, including many targeted for combinations of education and entertainment in the home.

- Student-created multimedia will become common in college applications, reports, and some job resumes. Including media in addition to text as part of letters and reports will become second nature.

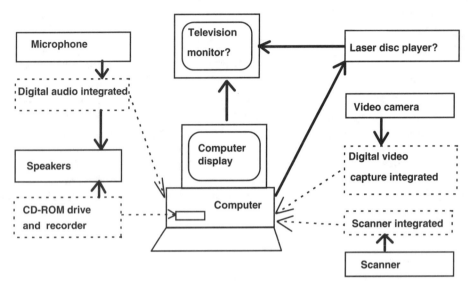

Figure 18-3: Late 1990s hardware

Multimedia Software Tools

- Many specialized authoring systems and multimedia tools will appear, requiring increasingly careful selection of a few products that meet students' needs.

- New authoring systems will allow nonprofessionals to create multimedia content that others can access remotely over the Internet. In the mid-1990s, mostly professionals use the standard authoring tool, HTML, to create such content.

- User-friendly tools, such as Mosaic and Netscape browsers on Internet's *WWW*, will help many more people access useful and interesting information by way of on-line network services.

- More sophisticated software, along with more powerful hardware, will make it possible for students to create larger and more elaborate projects. You will need to decide whether to encourage or discourage this trend, depending on whether creating such projects contributes to your students' achieving goals that you set.

- Many multimedia tools will be available for use at home by preschool children, grandparents, and everyone in between. Less expensive tools will produce fancier special effects. Your students will need more coaching to take advantage of this wealth of opportunity, in and out of school.

Information and On-line Services

- You and your classes will have access to more on-line services. Promises to provide a significant fraction of the country's schools with Internet access may actually come to pass by the turn of the century.

- Connecting to on-line services at higher date rates will make it increasingly reasonable to send and receive large quantities of multimedia, both media for use in projects and completed projects. More schools will connect using high-speed telephone lines or television cables.

- More students will rely on remote on-line information sources as their primary sources of references. Asking the right questions to get useful answers will become increasingly challenging and important.

- You and your students may access interactive information over televisions as well as personal computers.

School Environment

- Communities will continue to scrutinize school budgets and achievements. In addition to improving students' scores on traditional examinations, creating multimedia projects can yield demonstrable evidence of what students are learning and doing.

- Increasingly diverse student populations will benefit more from teaching methods that take advantage of other media, in addition to text.

- Schools will need to make efficient use of increasingly many generations of old computers.

- Interest in and expectations for educational technology will continue to increase.

Projects

- More students will take projects home on CD-ROMs to show friends and family.

- Remote collaboration on projects by way of Internet or other networks will become more common and fruitful.

- Typical projects will become larger, particularly including more audio and video.

- Typical students will acquire extensive multimedia skills earlier in their school careers.

to the all patients who have this patient's condition. She then records a personal introduction and adds several existing video clips that apply to the particular patient. Debbie organizes this information so that a patient first sees her introduction and then sees her telling the patient how to navigate through the hypermedia in order to find answers to common questions. If the patient asks no specific question, the patient sees a linear presentation that starts with the major points and proceeds to play all the material, with occasional repetitions of the offer to answer a question. Finally, after assembling and checking her creation on her computer's disk, Debbie produces a writable CD-ROM disc.

Debbie spends a great deal of time thinking about the particular information that a patient will need. She misses the sorts of brainstorming sessions that contributed so much creativity in school; she wishes more nurses were involved in the pilot test. However, because she no longer needs to record all the video separately for each patient, she can actually prepare the disc in about 15 minutes and can give a patient a total of three hours of video information. She finds, as in school, that having to focus on important points and having to organize patient care information well helps her to learn a great deal in the process.

Debbie has found that patients to whom she gave CD-ROMs telephone her much less frequently. Patients telephone her occasionally with questions that she either has not answered on their CD-ROMs or has not answered well. She writes down such questions and occasionally records new answers for inclusion in future discs. Because she receives fewer calls, she can now handle more patients. She makes it a practice to telephone discharged patients from time to time. She and her supervisor are pleased to find that the expatients use their discs regularly to refresh their memories and to answer their questions, rather than doing without vital information.

Three People Involved in Education

Dan Meyer is a graduate education student who is practice teaching a tenth grade class in a large city school. The day before yesterday he had an especially rewarding experience. He brought his multimedia laptop computer to class and helped his students log on to several databases and retrieve information about defense industry plant closings. Word got around. Attendance was higher yesterday than it had been all semester. Dan felt challenged to come up with a similarly interesting activity for today. At the last moment he thought of some anchoring questions and corresponding on-line information repositories that would interest the students. He is now worried about tomorrow. He expects many excited students to show up for class, but he does not know what to do for an encore. He is also unsure how logging on fits with what his students expect to learn this year.

Joe Minkin, an experienced environmental engineer, is running late. He promised his wife that he would bring home an adventure movie staring one of her favorite heroes, select and order a new video camcorder for their vacation, and finish booking their vacation to the Caribbean. Joe uses his on-line service's access, retrieval, and ordering capabilities to find his wife a movie that perfectly suits her tastes, find the best buy on a video camera, and find the optimal Caribbean vacation including visits to a fitness spa. He sometimes wonders why only he logs on and why he, rather than his wife, selects the electronic equipment they buy. He has to be at the school board meeting at eight o'clock to discuss how the district can maximize the benefits from their proposed expenditures on technology. The advantages that on-line access makes to his life convince him that all students, not just male engineering-oriented or science-oriented students, need such skills. His recommendations and votes reflect his insight.

Mrs. Smith, an earth science teacher, runs a curriculum coverage computer program that determines in which required topics individual members of her class have achieved competency. The program tells her that several students have not yet covered a required topic on severe weather patterns. Mrs. Smith uses another program to help her select a curriculum block that meets the following criteria:

- It covers the missing topic.
- It has no prerequisites that these particular students have not covered.
- It uses resources that are available in Mrs. Smith's district.
- It fits reasonably well into one of the themes the class has been pursuing.
- It coordinates with a history subject that the students are studying in Mr. Jones' history class.

The program suggests a curriculum block in which students create a multimedia kiosk describing hurricanes in Charleston, South Carolina. Mrs. Smith hopes that the project will interest the girls in the group who seem to be reluctant to participate fully in class discussions.

Mrs. Smith notes that the selected curriculum block uses specific library references, an outline for discussion, five links to related topics that the students have recently studied, a 15-minute digitized audio recording of an expert discussing this topic, and five minutes of related digital video with synchronized digital audio. The media come with documentation indicating that they are in public domain and may be repurposed. Mr. Brown's physics class has used the video recently. Mrs. Smith sends Mr. Brown a note asking how his class responded to the video. Mr. Brown indicates that one of his students' projects might be appropriate as a demonstration for Mrs. Smith's class and that he would appreciate the opportunity for his students to get some practice presenting their project's concepts clearly and effectively to a class of younger students. Mrs. Smith is a little concerned about losing the focus on her primary goal of teaching about the science of severe weather patterns, so they agree to discuss the projects over lunch.

Mrs. Smith uses the curriculum block's resources to prepare for the class. She devises a way to work around the one resource that turns out to be unavailable in her district. She assigns the library references and uses the audio and video during class. She decides to ask Mr. Brown's students to send their project for her students to work with, but not to come present the project to her class. Mrs. Smith videotapes the class activity. After class, she accesses the school's database to record that these three students have successfully covered the missing topic, so that the next run of the curriculum check program will no longer flag an unsatisfied requirement. She also records a more detailed assessment of one student's performance. She then uploads her new videotape to the district's database for use by other teachers who also must do without the unavailable resource. Mrs. Brown's hopes for the girls are borne out by the fact that the girls warmed up to producing the kiosk's tangible result.

Life of a Student

With the encouragement of her parents and high school academic advisory committee, Mary Ann Lee, a student in California, has decided to spend the first semester of her senior year in Sitka, Alaska. She plans to work as a tour guide on a Glacier Bay cruise ship. She has studied Alaska using her library's resources, communicated with some Alaskan students over the Internet, and used an interactive travelogue on a CD-ROM. However, she knows that actual travel remains a more stimulating and educational experience.

Mary Ann needs to keep up with her studies. She has decided to apply to a college that requires two years of calculus. Math is not her best subject. This college also has a foreign language requirement, which she has not yet begun to satisfy. Alaska's new fiber-optic link will allow her to meet both requirements using interactive multimedia correspondence, including two-way video, along with rapid worldwide database access. She finds that Alaska and California are two of the minority of states that have such capability.

Mary Ann's head mentor and coach, Dr. Judkovics, felt that Alaska's newly developed apprenticeship program has much to offer her in these two subjects. Also it promises to help her develop some needed independence. Dr. Judkovics, Mary Ann, and her parents have worked together to customize an academic program with which she and her parents are comfortable and in which she can excel. They have had two-way contact with the school that offers the two courses as distance-learning modules, as well as with people in Alaska, at least once a week. Dr. Judkovics plans to monitor her progress and revise her interactive lessons, carefully adding Russian language modules that are keyed to Sitka's history.

Mary Ann is looking forward to being away from home for the first time, yet being able to see and talk to her family every day. The fiber-optic video network lets her open a window into her home while she works on her courses. She is confident that her stay in Alaska will help her make the transition to college, both academically and emotionally.

Lives of Three Other Students

Richie comes from a home that has no personal computers, camcorders, or CD-ROM players. His home has almost no books but does have television and radio. Richie has felt jealous and resentful of students from homes that have more equipment. However, his school's educators were instrumental in providing public multimedia computers, including connections to on-line services, for Richie and other students in similar situations to use when not in school. These computers are in a local Boys' Club and in the city library. Two days a week, the school facility is open after school hours and provides later transportation for students who normally would take school busses. Richie has heard that his school just received donations of multimedia laptops for loan to students over weekends. He wonders what it would be like to take one home. Would he be able to keep it safe from his brothers and people in his neighborhood?

Ruben is a first year college freshman. He is overwhelmed by being away from home. He wants to succeed and wants to become independent of his family. He hails from a middle-of-the-road, middle-class high school that gave him some experience in using Macintosh computers. His college uses only Intel-based computers. His first English assignment is to write an essay about a student's life in the Middle Ages and include several digital images. Although the assignment does not require audio, he is surprised to find several students in the public lab recording background music to impress the instructor. He finds that these students, too, used Macintosh computers but that they appeared to know enough about multimedia computers in general to make the transition very easily. After determining that the computers had digital audio adapters, they were able to bring in their own microphones and audio cassette recorders and connect up systems that worked. One student even converted some images he brought from high school from Macintosh's PICT format to a format suitable for the Intel-based computers in the public lab. Ruben benefits from his school's having instructed him to keep things simple, understand the assignment, and focus on the content objectives. He trades this expertise for having one of the other students show him how to prepare audio for next time.

Ashley, at age three, is enamored of Broderbund's *Grandma and Me.*. She will enter first grade with three years of computer experience and with high expectations.

Practice

Suppose that your principal or superintendent has asked you to draft an addendum concerning multimedia projects for your school district's strategic five-year educational technology plan. People will use your addendum to put in place a detailed plan to achieve the district's strategy. Assume that one of the district's goals is to include student-created multimedia projects among many pedagogical approaches to achieving general academic objectives. Assume that another of the district's goals is to empower students with multimedia skills. Key people in the district know that today's students, as adults, will routinely create interactive multimedia as a major means of communication

If you are not yet affiliated with a district, consider a district that would interest you. It could be a school in a large urban area such as New York City or a rural midwest district. It could be in a school with large numbers of Hispanic or Asian students. It could be one of the following possibilities.

- Olean is well endowed with multimedia computers. Some are already quite old. Educators in Olean have had experience and success using student multimedia projects as part of their main line curriculum, both in high school biology and in fifth and sixth grade social studies. Teachers want improved compression and decompression so that their students can create full-motion, full-screen video and play the video back on their school's computers. They also want to purchase at least one CD-ROM writer. There is tremendous enthusiasm for using computers in this district, based on its long history of successful pilot tests. There is also an active community of volunteer parents and retirees. The district's largest employer, a high-tech company in the defense industry, has incurred some recent downsizings and plant closings. As a result, the community is scrutinizing school budgets as never before.

- Ralston County has an uneven distribution of multimedia computers that they have used in pilot tests. They think some are still useful for multimedia. They know that some pilot tests were successful and have questions about the others. The dynamic teacher who was involved in the projects left last year.

- Louiston District is struggling to meet the challenges of large classes, high student turnover, and children with a wide variety of abilities. They have a policy of no tracking. They have had some measurable academic successes with multimedia projects. They know that they need a plan for recognizing what works, particularly how successful teachers managed their classes under trying circumstances. They need to plan for replicating their successes.

- Mt. Dennis is reaping the benefits of recent heavy investment in technology. Their community is highly affluent with highly demanding parents and highly regarded children. Mt. Dennis's parents want to move faster than educators are prepared to move or feel that it is responsible to move. Some educators would like to see students spending more time on sports or play rather than being glued to their computers day and night.

- Deming has largely avoided computers. Their unified school has one computer that is connected to a laser disc player, and they have one laser disc. They use this system to comply with state mandates on one subject. Their state has just mandated additional student competencies, including creating multimedia projects. However, they believe that they have five years to meet the computer-related competencies. They need a plan for time tables and staff development. They are geographically isolated from other districts that have experience in these areas.

Unless you select Deming or a similar district, you may assume that your district has already had significant successes in getting started with student-created multimedia projects and is now moving forward into the second phase.

Your first step might be to find and analyze the district's overall plan for educational objectives and for using technology to achieve those objectives. If you are using a hypothetical district, make reasonable assumptions about the rest of the strategic plan.

If you have already had some experience introducing new educational technologies to colleagues, you might think about how your experience relates to introducing student-created multimedia projects and think about what techniques that you used before are likely to be effective or ineffective in this new situation. You might consider whether there is anything different about introducing student-created multimedia projects that makes this effort different from introducing word processors or a school band.

Much of your addendum might consist of saying how you would plan to meet the challenges, take advantages of the trends, and prepare students to partake of the scenarios that make up the preceding Theory section. You might also consider the following as you construct your addendum.

- While the district's plan probably includes goals, you want to add more detailed and specific goals that relate to your addendum.
- What part of your district's overall technology plan does your addendum cover?
- Who do you think would be the most beneficial people to use your addendum? Should these be the same people as participated in writing the strategic plan itself?
- Whom should you consult before writing your addendum? Should you involve members of the community? Should you involve commercial vendors' sales people?
- What is the current environment for educational technology in your school? What are the most important problems, and which problems might student multimedia projects solve?
- What sort of planning process is most appropriate for developing this addendum?
- Should your district upgrade existing computers to support multimedia or buy new multimedia computers? What related equipment is available and what should your district obtain?
- How will computers that students use to create multimedia relate to computers that students use for word processing or for playing professionally created titles?
- How does your plan provide for the students whose homes do not include multimedia personal computers? Will you provide access to multimedia computers and related equipment outside of school hours and off the school site? Will you loan out equipment?
- What competencies will your plan recommend for faculty as facilitators? How do you plan to obtain these competencies? Should you plan for stand-alone,

specialized courses and seminars or for on-the-job staff development? Should you plan to hire educators who bring this experience from colleges or from other districts? What additional support staff does your plan require? Do you have a realistic way to obtain this support staff?

- Do you plan any special multimedia courses for students, as opposed to teaching multimedia skills as part of existing courses that use multimedia projects to meet their own objectives?

- Although each teacher will initiate individual projects throughout the year, should your plan recommend additional interdisciplinary projects such as creating kiosks for the school lobby or publishing a widely circulated magazine?

- How does your plan provide for students who transfer into your district from districts that have higher or lower competency requirements and different hardware and software?

- What is your plan to integrate multimedia projects into the curriculum and to develop common objective assessment criteria?

- How do you recommend that teachers share projects, information, and teaching materials?

- What professional resources and people should your plan recommend?

- Should your plan aim your district at the stars, as in the following example?

Q: What does a really advanced site look like?

A: Francisco Bravo Medical Magnet High School in Los Angeles, California, runs cooperative programs with several nearby medical institutions. Bravo has three well equipped computer labs and two computer resource centers. Each classroom contains a computer that is networked with others throughout the school. Network access to the library gives students quick access to resource materials. The school has its own video and multimedia studios.

Bravo considers itself one of the most technologically advanced high schools in the nation. Its main goal is academic preparation, specializing in the medical area. It attracts a diverse group of students who are not only highly academically inclined but also interested in biomedical areas. Electives include radio and television production and multimedia production. Available medical electives prepare students to enter medical jobs immediately after high school, although almost all students indicate that they will go on to further study before taking jobs. The school transmits its own multimedia newspaper over the network to all teachers and students. The school administration tries to run a paperless operation. Distributing important bulletins on-line, but not on paper, helps motivate all members of the school community to learn to log onto the network and then to do so frequently.

Summary

In this chapter, we discussed a three-phase, multiyear view of student-created multimedia projects. We divided introducing this educational technology into getting started on a small scale, moving forward to benefit significantly more students who are studying more subjects, and providing for a future that integrates such projects into all curricula that can benefit thereby. We noted challenges that may face you during each phase, trends that are likely to help you meet these challenges, and scenarios that indicate some of the value of learning multimedia technology skills themselves. We suggested that you practice planning for your school, or a particular hypothetical school, to use student-created multimedia projects to the optimal extent over a five-year time frame.

References

Agnew, Ralph Palmer. *Differential Equations*. New York, New York: McGraw-Hill, 1960, p. 1.

Goolrick, Ray. *Funding Classroom Technology - Teacher's Handbook*. Atlanta: IBM EduQuest. This handbook contains several good references. Call (800) 426-4338 for further information.

IBM EduQuest. *Education Technology Planning Guide for Grades K-12*. Atlanta, GA: IBM Corporation, 1992. For further information write to EduQuest, Zip H06A1, 4111 Northside Parkway, Atlanta, GA 30327.

Institute for Academic Technology Publications. Telephone (919) 405-1942 or E-mail to LIBRARY.IAT@mhs.unc.edu. They have several files of lists of books on specific topics. In particular, they have a list on computer laboratory design compiled by Carolyn M. Kotlas, MSLS.

MultiMedia Schools. Veccia, Susan Ed. ISSN 1075-0479, Wilton, Connecticut: Online Inc., (203) 761-1466, bimonthly.

Appendix : Multimedia Publishing on the Internet's WWW

It is now possible to publish multimedia on the Internet's World Wide Web (Web or WWW). The Web refers to computers, called servers, which are located throughout the world and interconnected by way of the Internet, that respond to information encoded in the hypertext transfer protocol (HTTP). These servers hold multimedia documents, called Web pages, created using the hypertext markup language (HTML) rather than using the sorts of standalone authoring systems that we discuss in Chapter 3. You may be able to display Web pages if you have a computer connected to the Internet with Web access, have an application called a browser, and know the Universal Resource Locators (URLs) for some Web documents. Netscape and Mosaic are two well-known browsers. CompuServe, Prodigy, and America Online have other browsers that you can use as part of their services. You can obtain browsers and several other sorts of tools free from some Internet server sites. Using a typical URL (http://www.binghamton.edu) shows you the home page for Binghamton University.

For example, you might create a WWW home page that describes several Research Magazines, which we discuss in Chapter 12. In addition to a contact from whom users can order the magazine on diskettes, your home page could contain links to several samples of the magazines' contents, located on servers throughout the country.

Because of large files and some functional limitations, we do not now recommend publishing all of a Research Magazine on the Web. As we discuss in Chapters 2 and 12, many multimedia projects include large files. On the Internet, large files may require a user to wait a long time before seeing an HTML document. HTML authors spend a great deal of time figuring out how to reduce sizes of media files. For example, they often reduce the number of colors in an image, as we mention in Chapter 13. As the Internet's speed increases, distributing large files will become more practical. People, companies, and organizations are proposing extensions and alternatives to HTML. Some extensions and alternatives approach the functions of standalone authoring systems, although it is not yet clear what functions will become standard or how soon improvements will occur. The Internet is undergoing rapid development. This book's foundations in technology and pedagogy prepare you to explore new multimedia network developments as they becomes available over the next several years.

You can use a text processor to produce an HTML document by including tags, which are special symbols that indicate formatting and other instructions that a browser obeys. The result is an HTML source file, such as the one that Figure A-1 shows. When you look at such a source file, only your imagination tells you that the resulting Web page will look like Figure A-2, which a browser might show to a user. The names and references in both figures are fictitious. Several special HTML editors attempt to provide WYSIWYG (what you see is what you get) formatting for Web pages, to enable you to work directly with the form that Figure A-2 shows. A local university might let you put your HTML document on their Web server, so that your Web pages will be available to people who have Web access. Many books, workshops, or seminars are available to help you learn specifics about the HTML language and the Web.

```
<HTML>
<HEAD>
<TITLE>This is the title </TITLE>
</HEAD>
<BODY>
<H1>Research Magazine Available from Owego High School</H1>
<HR>
Chapter 12's Research Magazine's Advisor invites you to browse some highlights and to
request a copy of the Research Magazine by sending him an E-mail at
David@owego.edu.
<img align=right src="file://boys/david.gif">
<p>
Click on the following line to access the Research Magazine highlights.
<UL>
<LI><A HREF="http://www.school1/research.htm">Owego High Research
Magazine</A>
</UL>
</BODY>
</HTML>
```

Figure A-1: Sample source document using a version of HTML

Document Title: This is the title

Document URL: file:///AI/DAVID1.HTM

Research Magazine Available from Owego High School

Chapter 12's Research Magazine's Advisor invites you to browse some highlights and to request a copy

of the Research Magazine by sending him an E-mail at David@owego.edu.

Click on the following line to access the Research Magazine highlights

○ Owego High Research Magazine

Figure A-2: Web page that the source document could produce

Index

—Numbers—

1 KB, 47
1 MB, 47
150 KBps, 43
16 million colors, 30, 38
30 frames per second, 30
340 resolution lines, 355
525 scan lines, 354
550 MB of data, 43
65,536 colors, 54

—A—

access time, 43
adapter, 26. *See* Chapter 2
Adobe PhotoShop, 67, 321
Adobe Premiere, 321
Agnew, iii, 253, 427
America Online, 98, 116
analog, 27, 28, 30, 31, 42
analog video, 43, 353
anchoring task, 147, 148
animation, 10, 65, 67, 68, 102, 307, 316
annotating documents, 114
antenna input, 357
Apple Macintosh, 18
archive, 177
ASCII, 35
assessment, 16, 191, 211, 228, 269, 301. *See*
    Chapter 17. *See reflection*
assignment, 120
assignment sheet, 156
assistance, 189, 423. *See* Chapter 18. *See*
    Preface
    community, 444
    help, 145
Asymetrix Multimedia ToolBook, 52, 53. *See*
    Chapter 3
audience, 163, 403, 406
audio, 9, 27, 40, 41, 42, 313, 315, 330, 359
    feedback, 210
audio card
    digital audio adapter, 54
audio mixer box, 363
authentic, 119, 159, 379, 380, 418
authentic assessment, 401, 406
authentic learning, 18

authentic task, 213, 220
authentic use, 241
authoring system, 7, 52, 58, 62, 326. *See*
    Chapter 3
AVI, 303

—B—

background, 64, 313
binary file, 36
bit, 35
Boolean searches, 100
Bps, 35
brainstorming, 160, 185, 340
bulletin boards, 281
bullet-proof, 325
button, 3. *See* links
Byte, 34, 35

—C—

camcorder, 316. *See* video camera
capture, 10, 28, 37, 38, 41, 46, 316, 317, 333
capturing video, 39
catalogs, 23
categories of existing multimedia content, 94
categorize projects, 166
CAV, 349
    constant angular velocity, 349
    standard play, 349
CD-DA, 41, 43
CD-R
    compact disc-recordable, 49
CD-ROM, 27, 35, 43
chat mode, 282
check for numeric input, 326
Cinepak, 46, 66
citation, 99, 176, 177, 254
class snapshots, 393
clip, 12, 99, 213, 216
clip art, 37. *See* Chapter 4
clip media, 106
CLV, 349
    constant linear velocity, 349
    extended play, 349
coach, 159
colearners, 329
color, 26, 27, 30, 77, 312
    reduce number of colors, 321

About the Authors

Palmer Agnew and Anne Kellerman teach, consult, and run workshops on educational technologies with educators, teachers colleges and universities, small businesses, parents, and K-12 students. Sites of their workshops have included New York City, Sitka, Alaska, and Shenyang, China. They teach several graduate-level courses at Binghamton University (part of the State University of New York) and in the New School's distance learning program. Their courses cover many aspects of multimedia including multimedia networking and multimedia and society. Their last assignments prior to retiring from IBM were in the headquarters of the Multimedia and Education Division.

Palmer Agnew also works with educators on educational multimedia content relating to geology, which is one of his favorite subjects. During his 34 years at IBM he traveled widely, learning about and consulting on multimedia and other educational technologies. His travels included a wonderful country-wide tour of many K-12 schools in which students were creating multimedia projects. He represented IBM in several elementary and secondary school areas. He holds six patents. He has taught undergraduate physics. He earned an MS in Applied Mathematics from Cornell University.

Anne Kellerman has a special interest in constructing educational multimedia content relating to documenting the histories of people. She has several years of experience as a senior manager at IBM, where she originated and managed large, complex, state-of-the-art projects involving major partnerships with educational institutions. She has worked with several teachers colleges and universities on incorporating technology in course offerings for in-service and pre-service educators. She holds several patents. She has taught high school physics and earth science. She has an M.S. in Engineering Physics from Georgia Institute of Technology and has taken many courses and seminars in education, technology, and business.

Jeanine Meyer is a visiting professor at Pace University. She directs the core computer information systems course, which all Pace students take, and works on multimedia projects with faculty. Prior to Pace, Dr. Meyer worked at IBM as a researcher and research manager, and later in several positions, focusing on grants and partnerships involving K-12 schools, universities, and industry. She has been involved in many workshops for teachers and technical staff on topics that included multimedia, computer music, micro-based laboratories, and robotics. She has served on panels for the National Science Foundation and also reviewed many proposals that relate to educational technology for the New York City Board of Education Division of Instructional Technology and the Westchester Education Coalition. Dr. Meyer is a contributor to *ACM Computing Reviews* and is an elected member of the board of trustees of the Mount Kisco Public Library. She holds a Ph.D. in computer science from New York University, an M.A. in mathematics from Columbia University, and a S.B. from the University of Chicago.

Anne Kellerman and Jeanine Meyer share more than their work in technology and education. They are sisters.

More Information

We are interested in how we might help you make better use of multimedia in your classrooms. If you would like to tell us, please either tear out this page, fill it in, and fold, stamp, tape, and mail it or send the information over E-mail to Internet address 71621.1506@compuserve.com

Name _____

Affiliation _____

Street Address _____

City _____ State _____ Zip _____ Country _____

Phone _____ E-mail _____ Fax _____

What academic levels do you teach (grade, undergraduate, graduate)?

If you teach teachers, what levels do they teach or will they teach?

How many years have you worked with multimedia?

In what academic subjects do you use multimedia projects?

For what primary educational goals do you use multimedia projects?

Would ideas for additional projects help you?

Would templates for projects help you? If so, specify:

   What types of computers do you use?

   What operating systems?

   What authoring systems and version numbers?

   Would you use templates on diskettes, CD-ROM discs, or Internet?

Do you have ideas for projects that you would like to share with others?

Would you like to share projects that others could use as templates?

Would a live workshop help you?

Would you like to participate in on-line discussions or on-line workshops?

Would you like to add comments or suggest topics for workshops or discussions?

Return address:

Place
stamp
here

Palmer W. Agnew
5   Oakland Road
Owego, New York 13827-1113

468